P9-DXO-512

Contents

THE WISDOM OF THE OVERSELF

The Wisdom of
the Overself

Paul Brunton

RIDER
London Melbourne Sydney Auckland Johannesburg

Rider & Company

An imprint of the Hutchinson Publishing Group

17–21 Conway Street, London W1P 6JD

Hutchinson Group (Australia) Pty Ltd
30–32 Cremorne Street, Richmond South, Victoria 3121
PO Box 151, Broadway, New South Wales 2007

Hutchinson Group (NZ) Ltd
32–34 View Road, PO Box 40-086, Glenfield, Auckland 10

Hutchinson Group (SA) Pty Ltd
PO Box 337, Bergvlei 2012, South Africa

First published 1943
Second edition 1969
Reissued as a Rider Pocket Edition 1983

Printed and bound in Great Britain
by The Guernsey Press Co. Ltd, Guernsey Channel Islands

British Library Cataloguing in Publication Data

ISBN 0 09 152311 7

*Fraternally dedicated to
those sincere pioneers of a nobler
epoch whose deep need and silent
thoughts called forth this work*

1
Prefatory

THIS book was written in fulfilment of the promise made in *The Hidden Teaching Beyond Yoga* which, indeed, was really an attempt to clear an intellectual pathway for its abstruse and abstract tenets.

The Indian villager who has hoarded his money, coins, gold or jewels (for he has not yet acquired the banking or investment habit) proceeds to bury his most valuable treasure in the deepest ground, to be dug up only by the hardest labour. I, too, have placed my best-regarded truths deep in the work which has been offered last to an audience drawn from the four corners of the civilized world. Consequently some plain hints were scattered here and there in the first volume that until the reader had the whole teaching put into his hands, he could not judge it aright and was indeed liable to form misconceptions.

It was as natural that hasty criticisms should arise upon the appearance of *The Hidden Teaching Beyond Yoga,* as it was natural that it should offend readers who looked for pleasing pages rather than truthful ones. Nevertheless if I gave offence it was only because I sought to save mysticism from its worst foes, who are not only outside its frontiers but also within them.

Narrow, small and intolerant minds can never comprehend the double interpretative and creative nature of the task here undertaken. Therefore I can extend to my critics—and especially to those who have been so prolific in ill-informed snap judgement—an intellectual sympathy and humble good will. We shall understand each other well enough one day. But it will not be in this world where everything—as well as everyone—is judged by appearances. I am quite content to wait.

The two volumes now lay before readers a teaching which constitutes an endeavour to acquaint this epoch with the fundamental meaning of existence and which, in such explicit fullness, is for the first time written down in a Western language. An exposition in such an ultra-modern form was until now quite non-existent. Readers who bore patiently with the first volume until they could receive the total impression, the integral statement of the hidden teaching instead of complaining that they were confused because they could not see to what end it was all leading, who refused to detect contradictions where none really exist, may now find that they have not gone unrewarded.

They may begin to understand better why the earlier volume had to clear up the intellectual foreground and leave hidden in the background the real goal of all this effort, the Overself. They may perceive why it had first to prepare their minds for the teaching which is here specifically set forth and why it had to provide the aspirant with mental glasses to help him see through the ideological mist that so often surrounds him, so that he need no longer sway like a pendulum of pitiful credulity between conflicting doctrines and contending beliefs. They may also begin to appreciate why the serum of mentalism had to be heavily injected to counteract the poison of materialism, which generally infects not only most rational thinking but also, if more subtly, much religious and some mystical thinking. What mentalism seeks to get home to people is the difference between mind and brain, between an untouchable essence and a touchable thing, between an invisible principle and a visible lump of bone-covered flesh. If they grudge the amount of space given to this subject, we must plead the grave necessity not only of proving such a little-known and hard-to-believe truth in a manner acceptable to educated modern minds, but also of impressing the seeker after the Overself with the overwhelming importance of comprehending this bold tenet.

All this work was not only preliminary but in a different sense primary. For whilst it cleared a path for the still subtler revelations of the present volume it also established a view of the universe which may be radically new for most readers. And even those who had neither the time nor taste for the intellectual strenuousness of metaphysical matters could at least profit by noting the findings of someone who had both.

It may well be that these pages will appeal only to those who have the perseverance to get over their first fright at unfamiliar forms of thought and who are prepared to force their way, however slowly, through a subtle metaphysic to the subtler truth about this God-dreamed universe which it seeks to express. For the intellectual study of the way to what transcends intellectual experience cannot be an easy activity. But if any cannot comprehend this teaching in all its completeness, let not this fact depress them. Its profundities and difficulties exist and are admitted but its surfaces and simplicities also exist and are within their grasp. Let them take the latter therefore and leave the rest unworriedly for future personal growth, whether it be within the present incarnation or a later one. Even their faith and interest will alone suffice to bear good fruit. And even those who feel they have neither the external conditions nor the internal inclination to undertake such a quest may feel heartened merely to know that the Overself *is*, that life is significant, that the world makes a rational whole and that righteous conduct is worthwhile.

It is now needful to explain that I went to great pains to explore the most recondite sources in quest of the material which has partly gone into the making of this book, and that in the course of this exploration the hidden teaching was discovered not in a perfectly unified system but in scores of broken fragments which have been scattered in different hands amongst Asia's present-day cultural inheritors—not a few of them being non-Indian. And although the first volume mentions that the texts were Sanskrit—because this also was at one time the sacred language of Eastern Turkestan, Tibet and China—it must not be thought that they all were necessarily Indian. Moreover not every text has survived to this day in its original language but quite a number of the most important now exist only in Tokhari, Chinese and Tibetan translations for example. Their disappearance from India would alone, were this the sole reason, suffice to explain why uninitiated Indian critics find certain features of this teaching unfamiliar and unorthodox.

Hundreds of texts were examined in the effort to trace and collate basic ideas. The conflict of venerable and respected authorities over many momentous points shrouded them in grey shadow but opened my eyes to the inescapable need of disentangling myself from all authority whatsoever. This was a course contrary to Asiatic traditions and notions but it could not be avoided if I were to remain faithful to the ideal which had been glimpsed.

If therefore I began these studies with Indian texts I was compelled to abandon my original premise that the full and pure teaching could be found in them alone and had to widen my research until it again became an all-Asiatic one. The Ariadne's thread which finally led me through this metaphysical maze was indeed placed in my hands whilst visiting Cambodian China, where I encountered amid the deserted shrines of majestic Angkor another visitor in the person of an Asiatic philosopher. From him I received an unforgettable personal esoteric instruction whose final vindication unfortunately had to wait a little longer and whose inspiring demonstration of the value of a human guide to make a clearing through this thick jungle of obscurity and mystery, was memorable.

All this is but a preamble to the statement that with these volumes a doctrine is presented which in all essential principles is not a local Indian tradition but an all-Asiatic one. According to the testimony of this philosopher who personally initiated me into the Yaka-kulgan (Mongolian) metaphysical school, which studies a particular phase of this doctrine, so far as India is concerned the teaching spread there from its original home in Central Asia. But dead history does not lie in my domain and this point need not detain us.

It would have been much easier to emulate a portentous academic parrot and merely write down what other men had written or said as it would have been more self-flattering to parade the breadth of my learning by peppering both volumes with a thousand Sanskrit, Tibetan and Chinese quotations, names or words. But life today points a challenging sword at us. I was too sensitive to the iconoclastic spirit of our age, too enamoured of the austere figure of truth rather than of her discarded robes, too troubled by what I had physically seen and personally experienced in this world-shaking epoch to be satisfied with anything less than a fresh living reconstruction.

For these reasons there was no hesitation in making use of sources unknown to antiquity just as there was none in recasting everything learned into a form shaped by the scientific experience and metaphysical knowledge of the West. Not that I—who claim no higher status than that of a blundering student—arrogantly sought to improve on the ancient teaching, for its basic essentials are indeed impregnable and will remain untouched for all time, but that I sought both to improve on its contemporary presentation and to make a human application of what often seems to Western view an inhuman metaphysics. Despite our incursions into celestial realms, we still want—and want rightly—to remain incorrigibly human. Hence although this book has been written in an intellectualistic form to meet the requirements of our time, whoever believes it to be inspired by purely logical concepts alone or to be merely a modernized re-interpretation of mildewed ancient documents and ant-eaten palm-leaf texts, will be greatly in error. For the encouragement of aspirants let it be categorically noted that several of its statements are the outcome not only of such re-interpretation but also of present-day living experience. Were these the sole reasons they would nevertheless alone have justified heretical innovations, for that which actuates these pages is the simple desire to help others over life's stiles to the fulfilment of its higher purpose. And to implement this more effectively I have sought, creatively instead of imitatively, to help a widely-scattered group born in this epoch work out its own inner understanding of existence and display its own cultural vitality. The need today is not old dogmas but new dynamisms. Our century must speak for itself. We must let the past instruct us, not enslave us. In such a way alone can these difficult doctrines be made as clear to modern man's mind as the water of a Swiss lake is to his eye. Therefore this teaching will henceforth be offered on its own merits, not on the value of any tradition which may lie behind it, and offered to free minds, not to shackled ones.

Let it finally suffice therefore to say that in the effort to provide these ideas with a systematic form and scientific presentation, in the desire to help students by progressively deducing one truth from another in an orderly and consistent manner, in the aspiration to couch these doctrines in a medium understandable by living contemporaries and in the need to ground the whole on verifiable facts rather than on dictated dogmas, I have had veritably to reconstruct this aged pyramid of external revelation along modern lines from base to apex. That which is here presented is a fresh reincarnation and not a revivified corpse.

In any case, culture is becoming cosmopolitan. No idea can nowadays hope to remain a merely national possession. Whatever is worthwhile tends to spread its wings over all frontiers. And after all, the best reply to Eastern critics is that the inner light is present in all men, Western no less than Eastern; that the flash of insight into Truth may come to them anywhere; and that the discovery of the Real is not conditioned by geographical limits but by personal ones. Philosophy, in my integral sense of the term, is no longer a living force in the present-day East although metaphysics still continues a somewhat precarious existence and mysticism a somewhat anaemic one. To picture the Asia of today through these two to seven-thousand-year-old Sanskrit texts which are the available remnants of this teaching—as enthusiasts who say the Orient is spritual and the West is materialist often do and as I in the inexperience of youth once said—is as romantically erroneous as to picture present-day Europe through the Latin books of medieval scholastics. Such enthusiasts are dazzled in the present by what the East was in the perished past.

Today I walk in utter independence of thought and, like Emerson, "without school or master". My life has been a constant seeking after truth and if I have passed at any time from one standpoint to another, the goddess who has lured me on must also share the blame, if blame there be. I have for years been engaged in examining and testing within my own experience—no less than in the observed experience of numerous other men—a host of ideas and exotic exercises which were alleged to offer theoretical or practical paths to various promised mystical yogic occult and sacred lands. It is not my fault if the results have not always been conducive to consistency.

I have said it before and must make it plain once again that I do not write as one wearing the mantle of a teacher—much less as one wielding his ferrule—but only as one sharing the struggles of a student. I know well the difficulties and darknesses, the errors and falls which measure every mile of this quest. But I know also unearthly visitations and heavenly communions and something that brooks no denial bids me leave a record before I pass from this earth. Any higher rank than that of a student among students is hereby disclaimed, but this need not minimize the importance of what is here communicated.

The letter of the present attempt is admittedly a bold one but the spirit behind it is only a humble one. The temerity of printing these thoughts may be great but the timidity of withholding them at such a time as the present will surely be greater. Amid the confusions and despairs of a desolate epoch wherein the structure of civilization has tumbled over our heads like a house built of thin cards, it is the inescapable duty of whoever knows that a high Hope exists for mankind to speak the lost word for the sake of those who will listen. Therefore those of us who do care for humanity's true welfare must put forward such ideas, must burn reverent tapers before them not for ourselves alone but for others also, for men live by their dominant ideas however false or however true these may be.

I write for the few who, awakened by the world war into seeing that neither dead materialism nor blind mysticism can alone suffice, have had many a question brought to their lips and who therefore seek a higher truth which includes what is of worth in both views and yet transcends their defects. Men must come and knock at the doors of such a school out of their own interior prompting, out of their own hard reflections upon the meaning of the afflictions and elations of life, out of their own awakened desire to suffer blindly no longer. They must come to the condition written of by Virgil: "Weary of everything except to understand". And the awful experiences of this war-mangled era, with its living horrors and buried hopes, will have brought not a few amongst mankind nearer to such a condition.

If these thoughts were really too far out of the world to reach the people who are haplessly inside it, then they would have no right to lift a pen and stir ink. But because mind is the unacknowledged basis of all living, knowledge of the truth about mind cannot do other than provide a better support to such living. And that this is so, that the hoariest truths about reality and its shadows can be brought into touch with the practical concerns of personal and national life, should become abundantly clear to anyone patient enough to study the teaching in its fullness.

These leaves are sent out across the window without adolescent illusions about their reception and if a few of them shall flutter down to rest awhile beside a friend or two and remind him of his divine origin and destiny, it shall surely be enough.

2

The Meaning of Mentalism

WE must begin to philosophize with the hard facts of experience, not with the unchecked pre-suppositions of fancy. Knowledge that does not begin with experience can never attain certainty but only dwell in the realm of conjecture.

But, alas! the first fact is an extremely awkward one. Experience itself is not really what it seems to be. The suggestive studies of the earlier volume in the relativity of time and space, the startling glimpses of the magical spell which illusions can cast upon us, the revelatory discoveries of the mentalistic nature of all things no less than the semantic analyses of meanings and the words in which they are clothed, have combined to put us on our guard against the deceptions of these senses and the tricks of consciousness; in short, to make us somewhat wary of this thing that is called experience.

Man fits every experience into the pattern of his existing ideas. It seldom occurs to him that his pattern is so faulty and so limited that only by going outside it can he find out what his experience really means. Kant in his speculative way and Einstein in his scientific way have told and taught us that ordinary human perception is confined to mere appearances; that, indeed, it never gets at what is ultimate in this world and is condemned to view the God of Reality under graven images. We know only what the senses tell us. Our experience is purely relative to them. Therefore we never get at the absolute truth about things but only at the way they affect our senses.

Let us look at a simple example. It is well known that our eyes are constructed like little cameras. Now if Nature had constructed them instead, as she easily could have done, like little microscopes we should all see every day a world astonishingly different from the one which we actually do see, whilst if she had constructed them like little telescopes we should all see an amazingly different sky every night. She could have altered the vibration-range of our ears so that they would catch numerous clear sounds where at present we catch only dead silence. Nay, she could have gone still further. We have five kinds of sense experience but Nature could just as easily have given us five extra senses, an addition which would have magically transformed us into superhuman beings. Who knows that these things may not yet happen, albeit with evolutionary slowness, that Nature may not take it into her head one day to alter her handiwork in this fashion?

Again, the eye sees a smooth surface when it sees a polished table-top whereas through a powerful microscope it sees the same table-top as an extremely rough surface composed of miniature hills and valleys. Are we to believe the naked eye or the microscope? This analogy is a just one. For the unphilosophical majority are also surface seers. They do not suspect that relativity governs all existence, including their own. Thus everything has a double character or aspect and this is why we need a double standpoint. Are we to take only the practical view or also the philosophic one?

We perceive only partially and incompletely when we perceive anything through the senses. When we set up the presentations of the eyes, ears, hands, tongue and nose, that is when we set up human experience as really being what it purports to be, we are merely surace seers. The things of our experience really bear to the things as they are in themselves a relation resembling that of the hat, coat, shirt, trousers and shoes which a man wears, to the man himself. The senses help us to know certain things only by shutting out many more things from our range of experience. Hence to know the world as it really is, we should have to expand our field of awareness to a higher dimension.

When two railway trains are moving in the same direction at the same speed, a passenger seated at a carriage window in one train will not witness any movement on the part of a traveller seated in the other train. Each would, in fact, regard the other as stationary if he had only the evidence of sight to inform him. This is a familiar everyday experience both of the meaning of relativity and the meaning of illusion. We cannot trust all we experience as being accurate nor can we trust all accurate experience as being more than merely relative. To be aware of anything is to be aware of its relations, both to other things and to oneself. Therefore knowledge can exist only by being based on relations, that is to say, it is always relative. The philosopher must split knowledge into two forms: (*a*) the state of things as they are presented to our five senses, (*b*) the state of things as they really are in their essential nature. The first yields a view based on appearances whereas the second yields a truer one. Taken merely by and for itself the practical standpoint must necessarily confess that truth is unattainable, but taken as a pointer to the need of an absolute standard of reference, it plays its part in the quest of truth. The appeal to practical criterions may silence our doubts about the reality of what is given to us in material experience but it will not solve them. For to understand reality we must first understand the unreal.

It is not so easy to tell what a "thing" is as the man who has never stopped to reflect upon the point may believe. For, guided by the unquestioned impressions which he gets through the eyes and fingers, he takes it for granted that it is obviously at rest and remains constantly the same, when in fact there is such a continual circulation of its secret elements, such a shifting play of its electrons, for example, that the thing in itself slips through intellectual fingers as ungraspable. This seems strange and sounds absurd, yet, scientifically viewed, things in their ultimate character are indeed fields of electronic and protonic energies moving at prodigious speeds. Nowhere in this vast universe is there, strictly speaking, such a state as absolute rest. Whenever we believe that something has been found in such a state, we merely entertain an illusion. For its rest is only relative. It is, as Einstein has pointed out, only an *appearance* of rest. Actually even the particles of a stone lying seemingly inert by the roadside are swarming in incessant motion.

If we penetrate into the hidden structure of the microsmic world of atoms, what do we find? Its electrons are constantly rotating, its protons ceaselessly vibrating. If we look into the human consciousness we find it in motion with a constant whirl of thought and sensations. Is there any thought which has more than a momentary existence? When we analyse our consciousness we find that thoughts too numerous to count stream through it. They succeed one another incessantly. They are born in an instant but die the next moment.

Mentalism demonstrates that our experience of the whole world is nothing but our thoughts of it. These thoughts, as will be explained in detail, have no continuous existence and vanish only to be succeeded by others which are similar (but not identical) and thus give the illusion of smooth continuity. Hence the world we know is in a state of ever-becoming rather than of settled being. Thus a law of movement rules everything material and mental. Now motion implies unsettlement, the dropping of an old position, thing or thought for a new one, that is it implies change. But this makes the universe not so much a structure as a flow. The reality of the world lies in its restlessness. The vaunted stability and solidity which the senses place before us are mere appearances—this is the verdict of reason. Such therefore is the inescapable illusoriness of the *form* which human experience takes.

A mechanism which is used for night advertising signs nicely illustrates this point. If two small adjacent boxes are fitted with electric bulbs which are made by a suitable mechanism to light up alternately, at any single moment either one of the bulbs will be illuminated or none. Yet whoever looks at them will see a continuous light flickering back and forth from left to right and back again. Even at the moment when no burning bulb is registered on the retina of the eyes, when no glowing light is actually in existence, the eyes report the contrary! Here we must remember our earlier studies, which demonstrated that the mental process involved in seeing sense-illusions and the mental process involved in seeing so-called material things are similar.

Provided sufficient heat is brought to bear upon it, there is no substance, not even the hardest of metals, which cannot be melted and then transformed into gaseous vapour. And provided sufficiently powerful microscopic investigation is brought to bear upon a gas, it reveals itself as made up of scintillating points of *light* which are in perpetual movement. And yet ordinarily the senses tell us nothing of light as being, from the scientific standpoint, the ultimate stuff of the universe or of restlessness as being the ultimate state of the universe!

There is never a moment when the perpetual world-vibration pauses, never a fraction of a moment when the oscillation of any atomic energy comes to rest. Nothing abides. Because it wants to be more truthful, science has recently come to speak in its descriptions, of Nature as consisting not of things but rather of a tissue of events, a continuous series of happenings, that is a process.

We cannot trust our eyes and ears and hands in this matter for their range is too limited to show us the true state of Nature. Only the untutored and unscientific now hold the naive belief that the world is solid stable and stationary otherwise than in appearance. For they set up the familiar experiences of everyday as their standard of explanation. Theirs is the "finger-philosophy" which makes what is felt by the fingers into a criterion of ultimate reality! This common conception of the world is, of course, essential for practical life because it has a limited truth of its own, but when we rise to the philosophic standpoint we discover that it does not resist scrutiny. Perfectly right though it be in its own place, such a view becomes wrong here. For it does not exhaust all the possibilities of the universe. Thus reason reverses the judgement of the senses and philosophy silences the voice of opinion. "Culture inverts the vulgar views of Nature. . . . Children, it is true, believe in the external world. The belief that it appears only is an afterthought," was Emerson's wise comment in his *Essay on Nature*.

What science has discovered with the help of cunning instruments ancient sages discovered more than two thousand years ago with the help of concentrated thought alone. "No man can twice enter the same river," asserted Greek Heracleitus. "Whoever perceives in truth and wisdom how things pass away in this world, in his eyes there is not 'It is' in this world," declared Indian Buddha, who also pointed out that nothing remains the same for two consecutive moments.

But still farther back in time than these two men was this doctrine taught by ancient sages from Asia in the East to America in the West. They taught, exactly like modern scientists, that the entire universe is in incessant motion and that this motion takes a rotatory, wheel-like circular form. And they went still further by pointing out that as the point where a circle originally begins or ends cannot be indicated, so the points in space or in time where the cosmos originally begins or ends cannot be indicated too. It is indeed quite immeasurable. Hence they represented both the way in which the world is made and the immeasurable flow of things within it under the illustrative symbol of the Swastika, which is another form of the wheel. Its crossed spokes stand for the polar axis crossed by the equatorial line whilst its rotating activity stands for the fact that the earth is dynamic and not dead "matter".

Science has turned solid matter inside-out and found it practically empty. The emptiness of material substance is disproportionately and fantastically immense when compared with the tininess of the electrons incessantly moving within it. This means that the very ground we walk on is almost wholly empty space. But our sense of touch makes it feel firm, compact, motionless and impenetrable. This particular sense furnishes us indeed with an illusory experience, due of course to the limited range within which it can work. It is not surprising therefore that, as even more important facts have unfolded themselves, some prominent scientists have already begun to affix their reluctant sanction to the belated discovery that materialism, the doctrine that everything which is present in physical sense experience is the final reality, the belief that the concept called "matter" does represent something which is the ultimate existent thing within such experience, the view that the universe consists only of this matter in motion, is an untenable theory.

The old science said that the physical world is merely a shifting mass of rigid lumps of cold dead matter, of indivisible particles called atoms. But when asked what was this substance which it named matter, it became somewhat incoherent. It could not explain without admitting that vast unsolved mysteries were involved in the answer. And finally the new twentieth-century facts, which were first discovered out of the apparent emptiness of a vacuum-tube and later developed out of experimental research into sub-atomic working, forced the old science to liquidate itself. With it went the belief in an ultimate matter which exists in space, changes in time and affords a foundation for the universe.

The new science now openly declares that atoms are not the last word nor matter the last substance. Atoms have been divided and found to be "waves". Waves of what? we ask. Certainly not of matter but of energy, it replies. A sum of dynamic processes has replaced the old-time storehouse of inert substances. But beyond the discoveries made by radioactive research was the revolution begun by relativity theory and carried further by quantum mechanics. For this has replaced the old-time world-structure of inert substance by a series of dynamic events. The world's stuff is not a stable one but a process of happenings. The universe is a "becoming"—not a thing, and certainly not a material thing. The world's stuff is not an inert mass but a series of changeful happenings. We live, in short, in a world where the first and final reality is not an immobile thing but an ever-active force which, astonishing but true, appears as though it were a thing.

Thus the scientists who have discarded belief in matter still believe in energy. The latter has become their ultimate "stuff". But the energy out of which they would derive the world is as uncertain as matter. For when we ask for its production we get only its supposed "transformations", that is, sound, heat, light, etc. We do not find a pure energy-in-itself. Why? Because it is a conceptual creation useful only for practical purposes. Scientists have never perceived it. All that they have perceived of it are its *appearances* of sound, light, heat, etc., but never the isolated energy itself. As a detectable reality, it is still as uncatchable as matter. As a mathematical theory for practical purposes and as a calculator's symbol for technological purposes it takes a useful place, but it is still a supposition. It is supposed to work behind the universal movement, but it has never yet been exposed to view.

In the end, the final justification of the materialist is not reason, as he so fondly thinks, but mere belief. For it is only by an act of simple faith that he accepts the testimony of sense-experience. The science of the nineteenth century boasted that it alone dealt with the real world. The relativistic science of the twentieth century has begun ruefully to admit that it can deal only with a world of abstractions. For it has found that it is handling only some particular characteristics of a thing—nothing more—and certainly not the thing in itself. It is steadily moving in a particular direction which will compel it—and this prediction will be fulfilled during our own century—in the end to see, through its own facts and its own reasoning, that the world-stuff is of the same tissue as that out of which our own ideas are made. It will then be seen that energy is not the prime root of the universe, that ultimate reality being mental in character cannot be limited to it and that it is but one of the chief aspects of this reality and not an independent power in itself. Mind is itself the source of the energy to which science would reduce the universe. Energy will be found, in short, to be an attribute of mind, something possessed by mind in the same way that the power to speak is possessed by man. This is not of course that feeble thing which all we humans usually know of mind and which is but a shadow, but the reality which casts the shadow, the universal Mind behind all our little minds.

Modern science began by studying and describing the properties of things; it can end only by discovering their ultimate substance. But in order to attain this end it is slowly being forced, by the revolutionary significance of its own discoveries, to turn a somersault which will land it in metaphysics. In the end its final conclusions must merge themselves into those of metaphysics, which has found out that matter is nothing more than a mere verbal invention and that energy is nothing more than the activity of mind.

Scientists may well tell us after deep research that all physical substance is in incessant motion and that its atoms are congeries of whirling energies, but all the same we really do see solid and stable things. No argument can do away with the plain fact of this everyday experience. We stand in the presence of a startling paradox. How shall it be resolved? Can we take two conceptions which stand so far apart, so widely opposite, and bring them together? The answer is yes. Sunlight, when passed through a clear glass prism, turns out to be not what it seems for it breaks up into seven colours. A diamond scintillates in the light yet it has the same chemical constitution as a piece of black charcoal. First sight is therefore not necessarily true sight. The senses can tell us something about things as they appear to be but little about things as they really are. And if we turn back to the first volume of this work we can learn through the investigation of illusions that it is perfectly possible to see different forms and shapes which have no other existence than mental existence.

If we see a thing at perfect rest and science tells us it is really in a state of perpetual restlessness, then we are entitled to conclude that the anomaly is caused by the limitations of our own perceptions which in the end are only our own consciousness. The stability which we see cannot be anything else than a mentally constructed one. We are entitled to relegate the thing's actuality to the realm where it must have always been, namely, of the mind. This is the fundamental meaning of all changes of form as it is the fundamental explanation of all relativity. The paradox becomes rationally explicable and thus disappears if we realize that when our experience of the time-space-matter world is traced to its hidden origin, it reveals itself as mentally made.

Thinking and feeling make up the world we know, for every sensation is thought or felt as such. In what, apart from the entire congerie of ideas and emotions, does this world consist? There is nothing else. There is no physical world in the sense in which the unenlightened man assumes there is one. There is only a continuous series of thoughts which manifest themselves from moment to moment except in dreamless sleep. Perception and thought are but phases of the mind's action with the first depending on the last. We think and the world appears. We lapse into thoughtlessness, and the world disappears. The conclusion that the mind and the world are inextricably intertwined is inescapable. When we make a final analysis of the whole world, it is found to be of very different stuff from that which it appears to be. For every individual material object, from solid rock to fleecy cloud, resolves itself into a fragment of mind, i.e. an idea. The immense multitude of such fragments whose totality forms the universe are nothing else than varying modifications of a single original element—Mind. We must glimpse this great truth that Mind, as a non-material essence, is the ultimate being out of which both energy and matter have been born.

The World's Relativity.

Mentalism derives its name from its fundamental principle that Mind is the only reality, the only substance, the only existence; things being our ideas and ideas finding their support in our mind. Mentalism in short is the doctrine that in the last analysis there is nothing but Mind.

Experience certainly seems to place things outside it but the mentalist analysis reveals that they are mental products and hence we cannot really step outside them—because we cannot step outside our mind. It was shown in the first volume, when considering the enigmatic existence of the world and when turning the searchlight of scientific examination upon the working of our five senses, that the objects of which they become aware have their place only in the mind and that the whole world is a mentally constructed one. It was not possible however in such an introductory book to provide adequate explanation and final proof of this doctrine of mentalism—so startling and so unbelievable as it seems when first heard of—or to clear up some inevitable difficulties and explore fully into its profounder significance. The present work may help to fill this gap.

When we look more deeply into the physical world, whether it be in the form of common experience or in the form of scientific revaluation of that experience, we find that it is really the world of what our senses tell us. Our senses can only tell us about the colour, size, bulk, weight, form, hardness, temperature and other properties of a thing; they cannot tell us that there is also a separate stuff or "matter" which exhibits these properties. When we say that there is such a stuff we are merely stating an opinion, not a piece of knowledge. For when we look more deeply into what the senses tell us we find that it is what our own minds tell us.

Everyone grants that we are aware of things in the world only in the way in which our senses are aware of the properties they exhibit. But the mere physical contact of the senses and their environment does not suffice to produce such awareness. Something more is needed. Only as we are mentally conscious of what the senses tell us are we conscious of the world at all. Strive as we may, do what we like, it will always be impossible to get over this "mentalness" of the only world about which we have any right to talk. Not even the materialists can get over it. Not even they can show us a world entirely free from such "mentalness".

The term "mentalism" as used here does not mean the half-baked form which, under the name of "objective idealism", some of its elementary tenets have assumed in the doctrines of a number of Western and Indian metaphysicians who have only half overcome the materialistic tendencies of their outlook. They distinguish between mental things and material things and say that although we can know only the former, the co-existence of their material external counterparts must still be admitted. By mentalism we mean more precisely this: that *all* things in human experience without any exception are wholly and entirely mental things and are not merely mental copies of material things; that this entire panorama of universal existence is nothing but a mental experience and not merely a mental representation of a separate material existence; that we can arrive at such conclusions not only by a straight-line sequence of reasoned thinking but also by a re-orientation of consciousness during advanced mystical meditation.

But the materialist in his turn may now put in a pertinent nose to allege that mentalism would theoretically blot out the entire existence of the universe before it could appear in a perceiving mind, for whilst the planet was uninhabited during tremendous periods of geologic time there would exist no human being to think of it, no idea to represent it. Therefore it could not be accounted for? Here too the orthodox religious critic may object that no human observer could ever have observed either the event of divine creation or the period of planetary preparation which followed it—for human beings had yet to be created by God—and consequently no human mind could have personally known anything about it at the time; thus no idea of it could have come into existence.

Some preface is necessary before this criticism can be answered. Now whether we view the present-day world which is perceived by the senses as consisting of so many separate ideas in consciousness or as so many separate appearances to an observer, we cannot bring it to stand utterly alone and isolated in a self-dependent existence. Something unifies all these shifting items of experience, tethers all these varied external events together. When we work out their significance we find that this thread on which they are strung is the mind which knows them. Some perceiving mind must always be present at the same time along with them for they are in it and of it. The sequence of experiences gets its continuity from the experiencing mind's own continuity. There is no self-sustained reality, no independent existence in the *known* world—which is the only one we can intelligently consider—apart from mind. Whatever is thought, felt or observed is somehow related to a mind which thinks, feels or observes.

To believe that ideas can exist separately without a thinking being to hold or generate them is to believe an absurdity. We get the knowledge of the world's existence through the five senses only because we also get the knowledge that we ourselves exist. Ideas cannot hang in the empty air. They must have a ground upon which to rest. That ground is there always, whether it supports thoughts or not. It is this mental principle which enables us to doubt the face-value of material appearances because their own existence refers to it. To think of the world at all pre-supposes the simultaneous existence of a thinking mind.

Now the thinking self is surrounded by the not-self, that is, by everything external to its body. Whatever is included within this external sphere is called the world. The two cannot be separated. The very idea of a self implies its being distinguished from what is not the self, that is, what is external to it. Therefore both presuppose each other's existence. The self exists through its world and its world exists through it: both are inter-locked. For although *felt* in experience as separate and opposed, they are *known* in analysis as joined and united. They always appear together, always exist together and always vanish together. Actuality does not yet permit us to separate this relation between the two. They are always present together in ordinary consciousness, never in our common experience is the mere self alone.

Much of the materialism which professes itself unable to understand mentalism because it is blinded by what it feels to be the striking contrast of outside things to inside thoughts, is due to the neglect of noticing that they are only distinguishable but not separable from the knowing self. These two elements in any kind of experience—the knowing self and the known not-self—always stand as contraries, but this does not prevent them from being in indissoluble union in every act of awareness of such experience. They may seem apart in space but they are not apart in the awareness itself. A thing cannot be disconnected from some knowing consciousness and our studies in illusion have shown that this "mentalness" need not prevent it from being experienced as external to the body.

Thus whatever we experience is always coupled along with the experiencing self, or in the more technical language of Einstein, the observer enters into every observation. Hence the two are inseparably coupled in each indivisible moment of individual consciousness. The belief that the world-idea can exist without being present to some such consciousness is absurd.

With this preamble it is time to take up our critics' objections again. The nebula which cooled down into the solar system, deposited its strata and upheaved its mountain ranges, no less than the gigantic dinosaurs and myriad herds of vanished animals, are said to have preceded us in time. The sciences of geology, astronomy and biology have painted a fascinating picture of the prehistoric past for us. But it is still only a picture. And what else than consciousness now renders it existent to us? We forget that after all these are only our mental reconstructions, that is our imaginations. All that we know of the Stone Age in Europe, for example, is something constructed by our imagination. We imaginatively depict it as being abruptly seen by someone. The fact of an imagination existing points beyond itself to the existence of a mind. The fact of an appearance points to a living observer of this appearance. Neither an imagination nor an appearance can be accounted for unless it is traced to some such consciousness.

If the principle of relativity when thoroughly understood has revealed each thing as an appearance, the latter implies the existence of some thinking being to whom it appears. What is said about the world's earlier life by the physical and biological sciences, for instance, cannot be said save as implying the presence of an unconsciously supposed living observer who is able to think it. For how can the brown rocks and blue seas be thought of at all unless they are thought of as being seen? And how can anything be seen at all unless it is seen in someone's consciousness? The two things—scene and sight, the existent and the known—exist in an almost mystical union. Whom Nature hath joined together let no man put asunder! Has not the teaching of relativity revealed that, consciously or unconsciously, the observer is always there in every act of perception as in every act of description?

It should now be clear that in the objections raised by both the materialist and religious critics there is present an unreckoned observer, for even when they think of a time when the planet was uninhabited they are only thinking of it in terms of some mind's perception of it; nor is it possible for them to do otherwise. A planet apart from such perception simply does not and cannot exist. By sheer necessity, they unconsciously place themselves or else some imagined living observer in a perceptive relation with the uninhabited planet and then only proceed to talk about it! They can think of no existence which is not known existence. The world-scene from which they believe they have conveniently eliminated an observer, pre-supposes by its very existence the co-existence of such an observer! Whoever sets out to mention or describe an uninhabited world or an unvisited scene is forced to assume as the basis of his reference the presence of someone who experiences either world or scene.

It is quite a misconception of the position of mentalism to make it assert that the world does not exist when we are not thinking of it or that a mountain disappears when there is no man to behold it but revives again when somebody is present! This is only the critic's assertion of what he wrongly believes mentalism to be. What mentalism really asserts is that the world's existence in itself without a knowing mind alongside it *can never be established.* Every materialist *unconsciously* assumes the presence of such a mind when he assumes that the world can exist independently. A world which is not an object of consciousness has yet to be found. Even when he thinks the world away from himself and foolishly believes that it is still present independently of a percipient mind, he is quite unaware of the fact that he is setting up an invisible spectator to whom it must appear as the world. Let him try to talk of a bygone planetary scene or an unvisited polar region without talking of it in terms of some being's perception of it; the feat cannot be done.

If finally it be objected that the world does not actually disappear from existence when we cease to think of it, as during deep sleep for example, the answer is that if by this the critic means that it does not disappear from the sleeping man then the objection is utterly inadmissible, but if he means it continues to exist for those who are awake the mentalist must agree with him completely in this. What he overlooks in the former case is that the thesis still remains, for he has again unconsciously thought an imaginary spectator into being and made him the unsleeping observer of the world, which now exists in the mind of this imagined percipient.

Finally let us not forget what is an irreversible law of all world-experience: full suspension of the mind's activity results in sleep or coma, full resumption of it in wakefulness. The deduction must therefore be made that the mind's activity, namely, thinking, is indissolubly connected with the experience of the world that comes with wakeful state. Indeed, it is this very activity that gives rise to such experience. For mind and nothing else contributes all the elements of its own experience. And this is all that mentalism claims, that the known and the existent coincide and defy the efforts of the keenest intelligence to sunder them.

If we really try to think of a mindless world, we find the feat to be an impossible one. For existence pre-supposes life of some sort and life pre-supposes intelligence of some sort, too. And intelligence indicates of course the presence of mind. Consequently, if we take mind out of the world, we are forced to take away the world itself. There is then only an utter blankness. If we understand this, then the question what happens to the world during the inter-perceptual intervals between the periods of actual awareness of its presence and the kindred question of how a pre-historic un-inhabited planet could have been observed become impossible and consequently unaskable ones. The questions are wrongly put: they pre-suppose what cannot be admitted and no answer is therefore possible. An unobserved landscape itself certainly ceases to exist for us the moment we turn away and cease to see it, but a similar idea may continue to have an independent existence in other observing minds. But the problem involved can be reshaped and re-expressed in other terms: What mind is involved in these cases?

After all, this world in which we live, move and have our being every moment and every hour, comes to our notice only because our body is sensitive to it in five different ways, because we feel, see, hear, smell and taste it. Its colours, shapes and distances, for example, exist for us only because they exist for our eyes. They are experiences of the eyes; they are sense-impressions. But sense-impressions are themselves meaningless if they are not supported by or given to an individual mind which has them. If the reality of the known world lies in sense-impressions, then the reality of such impressions lies in a living mind. The individual, therefore, stands behind the world although, paradoxically, he is also included in the world.

This paradox must be cleared. For if we make the mind of an individual the *sole* source of his experience, then we fall into the piquant situation of making him the *sole* creator and governor of this vast and varied cosmos of shooting stars and circling planets. But this is an absurdity. His mind may issue a decree but a tree will refuse to turn into a river at his bidding. It stubbornly remains a tree. Therefore it is clear that there must be another factor somehow present underneath the individual experience of the world, a creative and contributive factor which is as beyond his control as it is beyond his consciousness. It is to the united activity of these two elements—the individual and the unknown super-individual—that we must look for an intelligible explanation of the existence and structure of the experienced world. Thus although we started with sense-impressions as our first view of what is real in the experienced world, we are compelled to conclude with a super-individual mental factor as our final view of what is real in it.

In the first volume it was no more than hinted that the uninhabited early world must have been as much an object of consciousness to some mind as is the inhabited world of today. The moment has come to step across this gap in explanation. The statement in the eleventh chapter of that volume must be expanded to lead the reader up to the higher position which will now be unveiled.

It has been found that our sense-impressions do not arise from a separate and external material world. They must therefore arise from a creative power of our own minds which functions independently of our intentions and above our conscious self. But although we know that our own minds do play a subconscious part in the making of experience as in their drawing upon the capital of previous experience, we cannot squeeze the birth of things *solely* into our limited finite minds, do what we may; no human being is personally and voluntarily responsible for the world around him. And yet we are faced by the proven fact that these things and this world are nothing other than thought-structures and their beginnings must be the product of some mind. There must be an unknown cause for the constant succession of thought-forms which are presented to us for experience. This cause exists and must be accounted for. The thought-forms which enter individual consciousness must therefore be the mental correlate of a super-individual mind, which possesses the power both to form them and to impose them on the individual mind.

Why then should they not arise in a mind more unlimited than ours and to which even now we unwittingly belong? Why should we limit mental possibility to the little circle of one man's experience? Why should we not conceive of the whole of things, selves and the world as being originally thought into being by a super-human mind which exists in intimate relation with our own? For we have no right to insist on making the world an object of consciousness only to a being possessed of the five senses, that is to say, only to a human or animal being. This would be an anthropomorphism of experience, an illegitimate setting up of a limited experience as being the highest possible form of all experience.

Existence cannot be limited merely to what is given in human sensations, to pictures of what is presented to the five sense-organs only. It is an error to limit existence to being a mere content of the limited human consciousness. Even a little investigation shows how absurdly limited this consciousness is for it cannot even see the millions of beings inferior to man in the form of microbes which fill the air. That a being superior to man may have a place in this varied universe must be granted by the intelligent. He cannot be the last word in Nature.

The universe is in a sorry state indeed if it has nothing better than the present form of human consciousness to show for all its endless travail, all its sharp pains. It is unreasonable to believe that when there are a myriad different forms of life in the universe below man in the scale of evolution, there cannot also be some other forms above him, nay, that there cannot also be some ultimate form of supreme intelligence which takes a cosmic view of things. It would then be impertinent indeed to foist on such a superior intelligence only the senses developed by man's partial experience, when it could become world-conscious in its own larger way.

It must be a universally diffused mind or it could not carry the consciousness of the myriad things and beings in the world. It must be a primal, permanent and self-subsistent one or it could not take in all the changes and vicissitudes incessantly occurring within the continuous duration of the world. It must be always linked with the universe or it could not be an observer of the universe. It is such a boundless mind which would be the necessary observer of an uninhabited world or an unvisited scene. And not merely on the basis of right reasoning alone but on the basis of ultra-mystic insight also, the hidden teaching affirms the existence of such a supreme Mind.

We are not merely the self-absorbed witnesses of our own impressions but also the co-sharers of a common experience. Despite the relativity of detail in all observations made in time or space, a hill is not a hill to one person and a river to another. Its *general* identity as a hill is a fact for all observers. The sensations of millions of men are connected and at least superficially alike for the same physical universe presents itself to all. This connection indicates that they have a common ground. The fact that similar perceptions of the external world exist for others as for ourselves shows that we are all bedded in one and the same constantly perceiving permanent Super-Mind.

A landscape present during wakefulness and also during dream will in both cases appear externally in space. But whereas the first one will be seen at the same time by all other creatures possessed of eyes who happen to be there the second one will be seen by ourself alone. For the first scene originates independently of our personal thinking whereas the second arises out of our personal thinking alone. This difference is as important as is the similarity that both landscapes are purely mental. It exists because we all live in a universe of ideas and because the first landscape does not cease to exist for its original thinker, the all-inclusive cosmic mind.

The same answer will fit the further objection that the world's existence does not depend on our voluntary thinking, is not the personally willed product of each isolated and individual mind, but is forced upon the individual's senses, whether it please him or not. Even those who can understand that mind is both actor and spectator in this universal drama of lights, colours, sounds, smells and feels; who can comprehend that the very act of thinking is a creative one inasmuch as it manufactures its own time and space; who can appreciate that the cosmos in its entirety is but a thought-form and that nothing can come into human experience which does not come as thought, cannot understand how when they have no deliberate intention of creating a world, their thinking can do so and yet remain wholly unaware of the inner workings of the process when it is taking place. The world-image does not come into existence at their arbitrary will; it is something *given* to them. They experience it within themselves all right but they know they do not originate it.

The doctrine of a cosmic thinker, working subconsciously behind the individual mind in a manner shortly to be explained, will fill this gap in their understanding. They must here recognize the working of another Mind upon their own. If the individual and his space-time world are indissolubly joined; if it is the individual's consciousness which by its very nature includes the world; and if therefore consciousness is the reality of both; this is because both are but manifestations of a third thing which itself transcends them and which must therefore be a higher form of consciousness. If the similarity of sensations has to be accounted for, this arises because the higher consciousness which stimulates all individual minds into the activity of sense-perception is one and the same thing—a common universal Mind.

The world which spreads itself out before our gaze is thus an intimation of the presence of an omnipresent Mind which imprints it on our senses from *within*. Every object is therefore not only an idea in an individual mind but also in the universal one. For the latter is not an arbitrary creator nor something separate from and independent of the individual. Both contribute to the making of the individual's world. *How* all this happens and the psychological process whereby the individual mind receives these ideas is described in the following chapter.

How is it that the world continues to exist during the many intervals, such as sleep, when it has become non-existent in the sensations of many individuals? How does the furniture in a closed room continue to exist when there is no perceiving person inside the room itself? How indeed did the whole cosmos exist before it existed in all the sensations of living creatures and how will such sentience continue after all these creatures have perished? The only possible answer to all these questions is that we must recognize a relation not only between the world and the individual but also between the world and a universal mind. Further, we must recognize that the mental operations of all men are in the end related to each other and this is why they all see the same world in the same space-time order.

What is this relation? It is nothing less than their own multiple existence in a single larger Mind as thousands of cells exist in a single larger body. That which determines one man's world-experience from *within* himself also determines another man's. There is indeed a hidden unity enclosing all human minds as a larger circle encloses many smaller concentric ones. Hence if an unvisited Polar region is unknown and unthought by anyone else, it is at least known and thought by the universal Mind. Its primal existence is not conferred by human but by divine thought. A thing is not *solely* an idea in an individual consciousness even though it is this consciousness' own idea. Therefore the mentalist need not deny the existence of all these things which have not at any particular moment entered his field of experience.

What shall we call this supreme Mind? Such a nebulous term as God must first be defined before it can properly be used. But it has already acquired so many different meanings in so many different intellects that a definition which will be satisfactory to all is difficult, perhaps impossible to find. Therefore we are justified in using a self-explanatory term. And such a term—the *World-Mind*—will henceforth be used throughout this book to indicate this universal Intelligence. Put into poetical language, the World-Mind is the Soul of Nature.

Can Things be Thoughts?

But experience takes a twofold form. There are not only the things which are presented to our attention by surrounding environment but also the thoughts which we present to ourselves introspectively. How can the external world, which is so obviously the same for all of us, be placed on a level with the internal world of our personal and arbitrary fancies? How can its rigid and unyielding form, which is relatively at rest and stable, be equated with the plastic inward world of thinking, which is pulsating in flux? Things are in a state of fixity but the thoughts about them constantly change. The images and ideas appear or vanish more or less according to our will and yield themselves to our desires, whereas the sense-impressions are more or less unaffected by our will or wish. Moreover the physical world forces itself upon us independently of our control whereas the imaginations about it are subject to our control. How is it possible to bring into one and the same category an idea like that of a memory of a tree, which represents the inner process of knowing about a tree, and the actual tree itself? Nobody finds that both the images of individual fancy and the objects of bodily experience are the same in his experience but everybody does feel a strongly-marked difference between them.

This is perhaps one of the bulkiest stumbling-blocks in the path of most students of this doctrine. It is indeed this striking contrast which forces mankind to assume that the surrounding objects which make up its earthly environment are substantial and real whereas it assumes that thoughts, ideas, memories, fancies and mental pictures are comparatively unsubstantial and unreal. How then can they be one and the same in substance?

The answer is that this distinction is certainly a genuine one but it is only of degree and not of kind; it is a distinction without a difference; it does not destroy the essentially mental character of the world outside. What is usually called a thing is a creation, as will be shown later, primarily of the cosmic mind. What is usually called a thought is the creation solely of the human mind. But ideas differ in the force, the intensity and the vividness with which they arise in consciousness. Nevertheless they remain ideas. Although only mentalists accept the objects of physical experience as mental states, everybody without demur accepts the thoughts about them as such. Now thoughts arise solely for the invidual who has them whereas things exist for all alike. This is the second important distinction between them.

Why is there such obvious difference between the two categories of experience if both are really mental in character? Why do we seem to be so certain and definite about our experience of things? The answer is that we experience the one under a different set of conditions from the other, although both sets are purely mental. The difference between material things and thoughts like recollected memories is exactly like the difference between the experiences of wakefulness and those of dream, that is the former are common to all but the latter are quite private. The strength with which a sense-impression forces itself upon us lies in its cosmic origin, the weakness with which a fancy arises within us lies in its human origin. Thus, anyone can reconstruct physical sensations by using memory images, but the reconstructed sensations lack the sharpness, strength and actuality of the original ones.

Ordinarily we do not grasp the fact that we are here dealing with a difference only in *the quality of our awareness* but make the mistake of believing it to be a complete difference in kind. It arises not only because of the cosmic origin of our environment but also because the mind is sharply and continuously focussed when outward-turned but only vaguely and fitfully focussed when inward-turned. The consequence of the first activity is external physical experience and of the second, internal imaginative experience, but they are both of the same ultimate mental tissue. Hence at certain moments of heightened intensity even the thought-forms of the second group take on all the compelling actuality of the first one. Such moments are experienced by a lover separated from his beloved, by the poet, painter and novelist at the high points of their creative moods and by the advanced mystic sunk in deep devoted contemplation on his ideal saint. We need not deny that external things *seem* quite different from internal thoughts but we must emphatically deny that—however heavy, however solid they may be—they can possibly exist outside the mind's own experience. The comparative weakness of private fancies, the comparative strength of sense-impressions, and the undeniable difference in sharpness, actuality and immediacy between these two classes of thought, deceive us into non-recognition of their concealed sameness, of the fundamental oneness of stuff out of which they are wrought. This will also explain why the mind should split its activity in such a manner that one type of experience is public whereas the other is private and peculiar to personal outlook, character and feeling. The World-Mind possesses the power to send forth its imaginations, to project its thought-constructions and to fill its own seeming void with countless thoughts of things in such a way that they are apprehended by all mankind. Each individual spontaneously receives these ideas through his *own* mental operations. The stubborn persistence of the world-idea, the similarity of the total impression which it makes on countless minds, the sense-felt vividness and concreteness of it, are really powerfully and mesmerically imposed upon us. Our thoughts and fancies about it are relatively feebler and fainter efforts. It is held to our gaze and experience by the World-Mind's thinking as though it were stable and fixed and reflected accordingly into our individual minds. We write "as though" advisedly because even this stability and fixity of the external world exist only according to our own present time standards. What is fixed for a million years by the reckoning of our finite mind can easily be equated in World-Mind's thinking to a single second! For time is a purely relative affair.

All such questions will however answer themselves as the present exposition unfolds. They arise in the minds of people who have consciously or unconsciously begun by setting up the existence of matter as an entity by itself. They have in very fact *imagined* the materiality of the world through taking it for granted, and are consequently the victims of what they have themselves created. For life has planted them in a universe of thoughts whereas they have taken it to be a universe of matter!

What then is the *essential* difference between the idea of a remembered episode which arises voluntarily in the mind and soon vanishes and the idea of a lofty mountain which arises involuntarily in the mind and persists throughout many human lifetimes? Both ideas are inevitably and ultimately ephemeral, although the first may endure for a few moments and the second for a few hundred thousand years. The *felt* distinction between both blinds us to the fact that not only is the act by which an object is known mental, but the object itself is mental too. Whatever we perceive outside us is certainly outside the body and in the place where we perceive it. But as the body, the thing seen and the space in which both exist are themselves proven fabrications of the mind, the ultimate view can only be that the whole thing is an appearance in consciousness.

We only know our mental states although *some* of them appear as "things". We see only our mental images although *some* of them appear to be outside. The man of the world receives a shock, which produces laughter in most cases but terror in a few, when he is told that if he stands aside in detachment from his experience, then all the pageant of moving creatures, all the long lines of streets and houses which environ him, become only forms taken by his mind. For he believes this to contradict every moment of his experience and to conflict with his most cherished notions. Hence he refuses to turn an intellectual somersault but immediately scorns such obvious nonsense. The doctrine of the "mentalness" of everything seems indeed at first sight to involve such a reversal of his natural ways of thought as to be assuredly an absurd one.

He has indeed to undo the work of vast periods of time, of prolonged evolutionary epochs covering countless rebirths, when the need of coping with *external* environment reigned imperiously above the need of inward reflection about that environment and about himself. Thus arose the habit of looking outward through the five senses alone, of taking matter to be a real entity instead of taking it to be a thought, of misunderstanding his own experience and being finally incredulous of the fact that it is only a form of consciousness.

But why should the common-sense criterion of absurdity be regarded as the final and conclusive one? It is the irony of human ignorance that those who loudly assert the mentalist to be deluded are themselves steeped in delusion! For the essence of their error consists in believing that when the mentalist denies the existence of matter he also denies the existence of things and people or else turns them into mere spectral ghosts of their former selves. On the contrary, he says that they are certainly there. And he admits that they are present not within our heads but outside them. Only, he points out, they are mentally made. He does not deny the existence of solids, liquids and gases. Only, he remarks, they are mental existences. He accepts the feeling of resistance and the touch of pressure as indicating the presence of a solid body but declares that these feelings are really sensations of the mind itself.

Just as a single seed may, as it grows and matures, show itself in a variety of ways as stem, leaf, flower and fruit, all of which are so different in our experience, so the mind shows itself too in a variety of ways as substantial, fanciful, earthy, watery and gaseous, which are admittedly different, but our experiences of them are still no less mental in origin. Just as the senses of sight, touch and taste tell us that fluid milk, soft butter, congealed cheese and solid bakelite seem wholly different from each other whereas reason tells us that they are only four successive forms of one and the same essential substance, so the senses yield us many different kinds of experience but reason tells us that they are only experiences of one consciousness, not of different kinds of matter. Mind is like the one soil out of which all the different grasses, plants, trees, vegetables, fruits and cereals grow. Everything we see is generated by mind, however varied its appearances may be.

Thus we may firmly grasp this great fact that the world is externalised *in* and *by* the mind. All the differences between the various elements such as water, earth and air do not invalidate it because they are really differences in mental experience. Mind may wear a thousand disguises as widely different as stone and gas but we must pierce through them all to the hidden actor itself. Both stone and gas exist only through and for our mind.

Nor does the mentalist deny the existence of all those things like electrons and protons which science uses to explain the world-stuff, but he says that they too are ultimately ideas. His typewriter does not change its nature as an item in his experience merely because he has come to apprehend that *in the end* it is a thought-form. It remains what it always has been and he continues to tap its keys as before. He knows that his experience of the world, which include his experiences of its tangibility, even though they are not the direct products of his own consciousness, are nevertheless the variations of it. He knows too that the events which occur within that experience do not happen *to* him from outside but rather from within his field of awareness.

It would be a gross error therefore to mistake mentalism as committing itself to the doctrine of the world's non-existence. The mere affirmation that the world is a form of thought definitely implies that as thought—but not as an independent material entity—it must certainly exist. The student must fully and clearly understand that when it is said that matter as such is meaningless and non-existent, we do not also say that the form of experience which passes itself off as external is meaningless and non-existent.

He who can appreciate the truth of these statements will also appreciate their astonishing consequences. Anybody who believes that the innumerable forms of the material world and the countless phases of existence are ultimately more than mental ones, believes in materialism, even if he has read the *New Testament,* the *Bhagavad Gita* and all the ancient and modern mystics. The well-known Indian doctrine of "maya", when stripped of the thick growth of exuberant mystification which entwines it, simply means that matter is an illusion of the mind.

In what, finally, has the mentalist's progress consisted? Not in moving from a lower reality to a higher one, but in moving from a lower concept of reality to a higher one; that is, from matter to consciousness itself. Yet the critic would foolishly tear out of existence this one thing which alone makes that existence seem real, this one principle which experience, rightly understood, pre-supposes!

We may deal with the admittedly hard problem of world-existence in two ways; we may either shelve it or solve it. The materialistic theory pushes it behind an unknown and unknowable "matter" and thus merely shelves it, whereas the mentalistic theory actually solves it. Remove thought and you remove things; annihilate mind and you annihilate matter.

When a man first hears of mentalism he is opposed to it partly because of its paradoxical unfamiliarity and partly because of his own deep-rooted prejudice in favour of materialism. He does not like this doctrine of mentalism because it rocks his sense of reality like an earthquake. When however he has studied it a little this prejudice begins to wither away and he becomes reconciled to the idea as a possibility. When he has studied it thoroughly and experienced the mentalness of the world in yoga contemplation or in moments of heavy bereavement, the incontestable grandeur of this liberating doctrine takes entire possession of his heart and mind. Even he who holds or puts forward materialism, who says: "This is the universe as I define and observe it," thereby interprets the universe and merely holds or puts forward his *idea* of it. Could he but comprehend what he is doing, he would comprehend that he is giving his assent to mentalism. He is indeed, however much the fact be disguised from his own self, a mentalist who has not yet risen to the level of reflective self-awareness!

The outstanding consideration for all mentalists today is that science has taken the first step towards the discovery of this truth. Distinguished men like Jeans and Eddington have given a mentalist momentum to scientific thinking and consequently deserve our high praise. This is so and must be so because the human mind cannot rest in materialism. It will be led by its own necessary evolution through successive stages to the truth of mentalism and thence to the majestic finality of what is ultimately real. Whatever science has been in the past, whatever it is in the present, the affirmation may be unhesitatingly made that it will be nothing less than mentalistic in the end. It will be driven to endorse out of its own practical wisdom what an Asiatic sage wrote thousands of years ago out of his immediate insight in the *Maitri Upanishad:* "The world is just one's thought."

3

The Birth of the Universe

CERTAIN thoughts will come naturally to the student's mind at this stage. If we take an historic view of the universe we are confronted by three connected questions which have framed themselves on the lips and troubled themselves into the heads of every cultured race of antiquity, of the medieval period and of modern times. They are: When did the world begin? Whence did it come? How did it arise?

The cosmology of the hidden teaching begins its answer to these questions by explaining that the universe is an endless affair. There is no moment at which it has not existed, either latently or actively, and consequently there will be no moment when it will not continue to exist, either latently or actively. This is so because the world does not arise by a sudden act of creation but by a gradual process of manifestation. For being a vast thought and not a vast thing, it is brought into being by the World-Mind out of *itself*, out of its own mental "substance", and not out of any extraneous stuff such as matter is supposed to be by materialists—whether they be scientific, religious or metaphysical materialists. The World-Mind does not have to put out metaphorical hands at some specific moment and begin to mould matter, like a potter moulding his clay into the shape of a cosmos.

The cosmos, being a thought-formation, can never really disappear any more than a human idea can really disappear when it is put aside from attention. We may understand this point better by considering how thoughts exist in a man's mind. What happens to them when they vanish? Where do they come from when they appear? At any time he can call them up again even though during the interval they have seemingly been non-existent. His ideas are manifestations of his own mind, not creations out of some external stuff. In the same way the World-Mind manifests something of its own self in the cosmos. And its own self, as will be shown later, being uniquely eternal and undying, it is inevitable that the world-ideas which have arisen within it are eternal and undying too.

Thus there is no particular moment in the universe's long history when it could be said to have been first created. It has never had a beginning and consequently will never have an end. It has never been started so it can never be finished. It is eternal because the stuff to which we can ultimately trace it is nothing else than Mind, to which there is no conceivable beginning and no conceivable end. Mind is what it has been since the beginningless incalculable past; as Buddha said: "unborn, uncreate, unoriginated". There is no first or last moment for it.

This tenet is usually illustrated in the hidden teaching by asking the student to draw a circle. The point whence he commenced to draw it marks its beginning and the point where he stopped marks its end. He must think of this circle as a *type*, standing for all the circles which ever existed. It will then be impossible for him to assign any particular point as its actual beginning or end. The points previously marked were merely temporary. The circle is then understood to be really an endless and beginningless figure. Even if it be said that the universe was specially created on a particular historic day, as the founders of religions are compelled to say when they address the masses who, being ignorant of the true mentalistic character of time, take it to be something absolute and fixed, this day can be but a temporary mark at best. It is like the temporary mark on the student's circle, for there is no moment when Mind was not. The manifestations of Mind have therefore always been in either abstract or concrete existence. The Swastika-wheel of the universe gyrates without end.

It is a scientifically-ascertained fact that the planets and stars and nebulae which light up the firmament are of different ages. Some are young and others are old; some are almost new-born but others are dying. Therefore the belief that once upon a time God suddenly created the world—which would make all these astronomical bodies of equal age today—is not an acceptable one. It is more reasonable to believe, with the hidden teaching, that the universe never had a beginning and will never have an ending, that it is eternal and self-sustaining because it is the body of God—if we like to use this much-misused term—who is eternal and self-sustaining, and that a perpetual evolution of the entire universe and its creatures is constantly proceeding.

Whoever can perceive this will then be able to perceive its corollary: that causality is only a temporary truth, a mere mark like the one which is used tentatively to begin the tracing out of a circle, and that ultimately there is no real first cause and no real final effect anywhere in this series of things without a stop. Nothing exists by itself and all things exist today as an indirect consequence of innumerable causes stretching like an endless chain through the beginningless past. Whoever can comprehend that every event is somehow connected with innumerable other events, that a web of inter-dependence is thrown across all things without exception, can also comprehend that no single manifested thing can be self-sufficient or self-existent in the full meaning of the term nor even as having a single cause or a single effect.

We naturally forget that what we ordinarily consider to be the obvious cause of an event is only an outstanding and final moment in a host of untraceable earlier changes which converged and met in it. We also overlook that what we ordinarily consider the creation of a new thing is only the latest fruit of the indirect co-operation of innumerable older things. Under such conditions of an infinite regress of causes which are only pseudo-causes and effects which are only pseudo-effects, the question when the world was created is not a proper one because the problem has initially been mis-stated. There are certain erroneous pre-suppositions implied in these interrogative words. Such a question cannot therefore be answered, not because philosophy is ignorant, but because the question itself is not rightly put.

The universe is therefore as old or as eternal as the World-Mind itself. It is an idea, but nevertheless it is an everlasting idea. Creation begins and ends nowhere and nowhen. There is no place or moment of which the first cause or final effect can be stated with certitude. How then can the starting point of the entire creative process be defined? How then can we make any selection which shall be other than arbitrary at all from this endless series of inter-connected events? Whichever one is chosen will be the beginning of creation only from a most superficial view. How nebulous is the conception of the universe which presumes to assign a "date" to creation! Every such date will vary with the mere caprice of the "dater"; he will hatch out a creation theory to suit himself. It will depend on human temperament or taste.

The world is a complex of countless numbers of connected events. Consequently no absolute single cause can be strictly assigned to any single event. From the fact that however far we attempt to trace back to a first cause of the universe, we find every so-called cause itself to have its origin in a preceding cause, and that the latter is in its turn the effect produced by a previous cause, it is right and reasonable to infer that there is no beginning in the universe and consequently there can be no end. This means that the process of everbecoming is an eternal one and is the very law of the universe's own being. For no particular thing is a cause alone or an effect alone but must always be both at the same time.

Such a situation demolishes the metaphysical truth of the old notion of causality, although it leaves it quite untouched for practical purposes. It cancels the *ultimate* truth of the law of cause and effect which governs all world phenomena, although it leaves its *immediate* truth untouched. When we recognize that the chain of reciprocally-dependent links which constitutes a cause is beginningless and endless we have to drop causality as a metaphysical principle. This must not be misunderstood. We are not here speaking from the practical and scientific standpoint but from the philosophic one. We are saying only that an *adequate* cause cannot be found by finite human intelligence but only some of the factors contributing to such a cause. Beyond this it is impossible to go. There will always be other factors which have not been ascertained. In theological words, God alone knows all.

If, philosophically, the notion of a sudden first creation is an untenable assumption, the related notion of the possibility of creating something out of nothing is equally untenable. But the believers in a Deity made in Man's magnified image ascribe the genesis of the universe to just such an act.

Looked at from the outside, the universe comes forth out of nothingness and passes away into nothingness. But looked at from inside, there has always been an eternal hidden reality in its background. This reality is Mind. The world is only its manifestation. For if every effect is previously contained in its cause and that again is confined in what preceded it, the chain goes back and back and stops only when it stops with the source of all ideas—Mind. Thus Mind embraces all things but is itself embraced by none. Hence mentalism teaches that the universe has the same origin as any idea, that is, in and for a mind; therefore the correct way to regard the relation between the universe and its originator is to see it as being similar to the relation between any human idea and the mind in which it is begotten. The World-Mind does not need to "create" the universe out of nothing when it can bring it to birth out of its own self. And as a mental principle it does this by projecting the world as its idea. The world is its self-projection.

How did the universe come to assume the character which it possesses? This is answered by the doctrine of mentalism. Mind or rather World-Mind is immanent throughout the universe. The universe has arisen out of its constructive meditation but it has arisen in orderly self-determination fashion shaped by its own memorized mental impressions of a former state of active existence. The ceaseless procession of images, picturing forth suns and stars, lands and seas and all things visible emanate from the World-Mind under a divine immutable mysterious karmic law like water trickling from an inexhaustible fountain.

Karma is a twofold law, one being general and the other special. The first is ultimate, and applicable to everything in the universe for it is simply the law of every individual entity's own continuity. Whether it be a planet or a protoplasm it has to inherit the characteristics of its own previous existence and thus adjust effect to cause. The second is immediate, and applicable only to individuals who have attained self-consciousness, thus limiting the start of its operations to human entities. This makes the individual accountable for thoughts and for the deeds born of his thoughts.

It is through mutually-acting karmic processes that this universe becomes possible. The World-Mind brings forth its general world-images not by any arbitrary fiat but by their natural continuity as the consequences of all those that have previously existed. They are a continuation of all the remembered world-images which have appeared before, but modified and developed by their own mutual inter-action and evolution, not by the capricious decree of a humanized God. The World-Mind makes the universe by constructively thinking it. But it does not think arbitrarily. The thoughts arise of their own accord under a strict karmic and evolutionary law. It must be emphasized that on this view the universe constitutes a self-actuating system, although it must equally be understood that the system itself depends on World-Mind for its own continued existence and continuous activity. All the karmic forces and thought-forms carry on their mutual activities, intertwine, inter-act and evolve of their own accord in the presence of the World-Mind just as plants grow of their own accord in the presence of sunlight. But it is to that very presence that they owe their own sustenance and existence.

All this pre-supposes a prior existence of the universe wherein its present general karma was made. We have already seen that the cosmos itself is continuous, and that its past is beginningless. But intervals of non-existence periodically interrupt its history. These are only temporary, however. There are no real breaks in its existence but there are apparent ones when it lapses into latency. For it rotates through changing phases. Each successive appearance of the remanifested universe follows inevitably after the one which had previously gone into a latent state. When the collective karmas of all individual and planetary centres exhaust themselves a cycle of world history closes. The manifested universe then retreats and the World-Mind rests from its labours. But dawn follows night and the cosmic dawn witnesses the re-imagining of all things once again. When the same karmas begin once more to germinate and to reproduce themselves a new cycle opens and the visible world comes into being once more as the heritage of all the existences which were to be found in the previous one. The characteristics of a previous cosmos determine the nature of the one which succeeds it.

This antithesis of work and rest, of Becoming and Being, of a rhythm curiously like that of the in-breathing and out-breathing of living creatures, immediately confronts us when we try to understand the World-Mind's relation to the universe. The present universe is not the first which has manifested nor will it be the last. Each separate world-system—such as the present one—is merely a unit in a beginningless and endless series. In this sense only is the universe indestructible. Each is a heritage from one that existed before, a precipitation of karmas which have succeeded in bringing about their own realization.

The history of universal existence is therefore the history of an endless chain of alterations between potential being and actual becoming. Thus the universe is undergoing an evolution which is being worked out according to strict karmic law and not by mere chance, as materialists think, nor by arbitrary commands of a personal creator, as religionists think. The modern scientific notion of evolution is only a half-truth. The real process is a rhythm of growth and decay, evolution and dissolution, following each other with inevitable sequence. It is the combination of these two phases which makes up a universal movement that knows no finality. If cosmic nebulae develop into solar systems, these in turn dissolve eventually into cosmic nebulae again. The universe of forms ever returns to its starting point: it is without beginning and will be without end; this is why it is subject to birth and death, degeneration and renewal, that is to *change*. It is like an ever-rolling wheel moving onward through these alternating aeons of activity and rest. Hence the ancient teachers represented it under the figure of a revolving Swastika-wheel.

The Karmic Impressions.

The mysterious working of karma, this force which moulds the conditions of every centre of being from protoplasmic cell to vast cosmos, must next be uncovered. If the world were nothing but a collection of material objects karma could never come into play. But because it is, as mentalism shows, a collection of thought-formations and because there is a World-Mind as the unitary ground connecting all these formations, the possibility of karma as an operative force exists. For karma would be meaningless if there were not some kind of orderly continuity between the past, the present and the future of all those things and creatures which make up the universal existence. But this implies that Nature must keep and conserve some sort of memory in her secret recesses.

If every individual preserves a record of his own history, why should it seem fantastic for the World-Mind to preserve a record of its own history? And because its existence is inseparable from the manifested cosmos, in doing this it preserves an all-comprehensive record of the universe's own history too. No thought, no event, no object, no scene and no figure has ever been wholly lost. This implies that the memories of globes and stars and nebulae utterly remote in space and time are still preserved. But human imagination must stagger away from the boundless consequences of this truth, its finite limitations here defeating its own activity. And because memory is not an object which the senses can grasp but something entirely immaterial, this in turn involves the existence of something mental. A mental principle which shall be cosmic in its spatial sweep and permanent in its embrace of time, is and can be none other than the World-Mind itself. Thus the foundation of all karmic working can be traced to the World-Mind. The rise, abiding and dissolution of karma is indeed a twin-function to that of its ideation.

We have learnt that in the end everything must return to its divine source, if not before by its own evolution then certainly at the end of a cosmic cycle by the universal rhythmic dissolving movement which then attains its climax. If we turn backward in thought to such a time when the universe was not in visible tangible existence, to one of those cosmic periods when the World-Mind had taken in its breath as it were, we find a mysterious state of nothingness that is yet not a nothingness. Mind alone is, a great

Void alone reigns, it is as if there were no existence at all. There is not a thing, not a thought and not a creature. Nevertheless the *possibilities* of the birth of all things, all thoughts and creatures do somehow exist. Just as different soundforms are latently stored in the tracks which have been made on the surface of a gramophone record, so different thought-forms are latently stored by karma during a period of universal rest within the World-Mind. And everything in the universe without exception being such a form or collection of forms, it follows that everything will then still have a potential existence. Just as a massive oak tree once had an invisible and intangible existence in the acorn or the gentle fragrance of a white flower once had an unsmelt existence in the tiny seed, so the earth and stars and sun which we see around us today once had an immaterial existence in the germinal form which their own karma had stored within the memory of the World-Mind. Every starry body in the firmament with its particular distinguishing characteristics and every creature which dwelt upon it with its own desires, tendencies and capacities were memorized by the wonderful faculties of World-Mind. From this it will be seen that memory played a potent part in creating the world of which we are conscious. During these periods of its own suppression, therefore, the universe still existed as a seed-like possibility.

The World-Mind is all-containing. Since the beginningless past it has gathered these cosmic memories. The patterns of all that goes to constitute a universe previously existed in it in this potential form. The archetype of everything found in Nature first existed in this illimitable storehouse. Just as the silent registrations on a gramophone record are converted under suitable conditions into vividly heard words, so the invisible registrations in World-Mind were converted at the ripe karmic time into vividly experienced things. Just as shouts uttered in a narrow mountain ravine call forth echoing sounds, so the karmic impressions stored during a cosmic night repeated themselves in the space-time world as they passed into actuality and thus appeared again in tangible visible form.

We must not make the materialist mistake of regarding this universal mind as though it were a kind of box in which the myriad thought-forms which totalize into a universe, are piled up. The thoughts originally pre-exist in it not concretely but in the abstract sense that ideas of an intended effect pre-exist in a musician's mind. Such pre-existence of the world-ideas is possible only through the agency of karma. If our finite human mind can latently hold so many and so different ideas at one and the same time, why should not the infinite World-Mind find it possible to hold the innumerable units which sum up as the whole world-idea?

This karmic seed-form must not be misunderstood. Because everything is really mental, because everything is a thought-formation the memorization of it held by the World-Mind is not a second and separate substance but is the very essence or soul of the thing itself. If we compare the World-Mind to a piece of wax then the impression made on the latter by a metal seal represents the memorized unmanifested world and the force or pressure applied to the seal represents karma. And just as the moulded picture is not distinct from the wax itself so the innumerable karmic impressions which compose the memory-image of the whole universe, which is but a great thought, are not distinct from the World-Mind too.

A man forgets his own life and the external world during deep sleep but remembers them completely again the following morning. If all his ideas are latently and mysteriously preserved during the sleep state despite apparent annihilation, then we have a hint from Nature to help us understand how it is possible for all the ideas of the World-Mind to be latently and mysteriously preserved even when they are no longer actualized during the cosmic night. Just as not a single thought-form is really lost by the individual mind during sleep so not a single thought-form is lost by the World-Mind when a cosmic period closes and everything vanishes into apparent nothingness, but really returns to the original unity whence it earlier proceeded.

The karmic impressions are so subtle and so abstract from the human standpoint that a further analogy may help to clarify their meaning. A poet, by which we do not mean a mere versifier, who sits down to write an imaginative poem will not in the beginning know the precise sentences and exact words which his poem will contain nor the full course and final shape which it will take. He will most likely feel some vague intuitions and uncalculated inspirations pressing within him for expression and only as he goes on to create definite word-forms for them does he begin to see his way more clearly. What is happening? The actual and spontaneous composition and progressive development of the poem has brought down into this space-time world of visible forms some-thing which previously had existed in his so-called unconscious mind only as a mental possibility. In the same way the universe in its potential state is a mental possibility existing in the World-Mind, a possibility which has no graspable existence until it appears in actuality as a visible form. Every thought-formation—which means every thing—that exists in this world is born of its corresponding impression in the formless world. The volume and variety of world-appearances arise from the impres-sions which have resided since the beginningless past in an unbroken chain of continuous transformations in the World-Mind. Every activity, every existence leaves its impress in the World-Mind and the cumulative result of all these combined impressions displays itself eventually as the universe.

Thus the general karmic memories of the unmanifested world, like invisible pictures upon a sensitive photographic film which wait for the time when they shall be developed into visibility, rest in the World-Mind and wait for the time when they become activated. Then their energies are released and cause the springing to life of a fresh cosmic manifestation. When the necessary cyclic hour strikes, the potential planetary and cosmic thought-forms amassed within the World-Mind since the incalculable past become self-active, just as when the necessary wind or lunar influence is ready the ocean manifests its potential waves. The sum-total of all the impressions which thus become actualized, the heritage of all the forms and lives constitutes a cosmos.

To make the next point clearer let us return to our early and elementary study of the way we receive knowledge of external things. The vibration which travels from the surface-sense along a nerve path to cells in the brain-cortex, is concerned only with separate sensations. When these are associated, co-ordinated and brought into consciousness as seeing, hearing and so on, the sense-experience becomes a percept. When such a percept is stored in the mind and later recalled or reproduced, then the faculty of memory comes into play. A little reflection will show that this faculty is merely a particular form taken by the image-making power of the mind. If the human mind memorizes through the use of its imagination, then the World-Mind must in its larger way use the same faculty too. If this point is understood then it will be easier to grasp the next point, that karma, being the kinetic memory of Nature, is necessarily coupled with the imaginative power of Nature.

It is thus out of these stored memories, that is imaginations of innumerable forms, that the World-Mind recalls, constructs and evolves everything. The seed-memories of the world-idea, retained and transmitted since an earlier cycle, revive, reappear and develop through the mysterious memorizing and imaginative powers of World-Mind. But it does not activate them in a chaotic or an arbitrary manner. On the contrary there is an orderly sequence in the process, for each of the myriad thought-forms contained in the world-idea is at every stage of its history an inheritance from that which preceded it.

All the potential thought-forms are not brought into activity simultaneously. Out of the innumerable host available, a selective process inherent in the intelligence of the World-Mind and working always with the immutable law of karma, accepts, associates and gathers together those only which make for a gradual unfoldment in time and an orderly unfoldment in space. They do not emerge altogether but successively. Hence the universe never appears as ready-made, but as a gradual evolution.

Through its power of constructive imagination, *which is its first characteristic,* the World-Mind brings the cosmos into being. It can emanate anything because imagination, the most plastic of all elements, is its central activity. There is no limit to the metamorphoses of forms which imagination can take. Consequently, there is no limit to the evolution of forms which we behold around us in the universe. The fecundity of images which the World-Mind has put forth is thus easily explicable. If it is possible for the finite imagination of man to produce a wonderful variety of forms and patterns in his arts and crafts why should it not be still more possible for the infinite imagination of World-Mind to produce, under karma of course, the innumerable host of forms and patterns which crowd the universe? Hence there are countless other solar systems in the cosmos besides our own, containing every type of living creature in a diversity far beyond the most fantastic imagination of man.

The history of the progressive unfoldment of the universal picture is thus but a history of the protean transformations of the multiplied images which subsist in the World-Mind. Creation on this view is simply Mind's protean power to assume any and every form which it chooses; it is essentially a process of imagination. But in the end it does not matter whether we say that World-Mind is imagining or willing or thinking or constructing or dreaming the universe for all these activities must necessarily be one and the same to it. We may better understand this point by asking ourself: Is there any psychological difference between the states of the novelist so absorbed in the highest pitch of creativeness as to be carried away by the adventures of his hero, the religious mystic rapt in perfect contemplation of the sufferings on the Cross to the point of producing stigmata, and the dreamer so caught in an intensely vivid nightmare as to awaken trembling with fear? All these states necessarily include and synthesize will, thought, imagination, creativeness and dreaming.

Under an infinite diversity of forms World-Mind is for ever manifesting itself. Just as under the very multitudinousness of a dreamer's dream-creation there lies buried the fact of the singleness and unity of the dreaming mind, so under the very multitudinousness of things in the waking realm there lies buried the fact that they are all manifestations of one and the same Mind. And just as the separateness of the dreamer's world exists only on the surface and is secretly connected with him, so the separateness of the waking world exists only as a surface impression. In the end there is really a unity.

The Birth of Individuals.

Just as innumerable stored-up thoughts co-exist in the depths of the individual mind although they emerge into consciousness one at a time, so innumerable stored-up individual minds from previous universes co-exist in the depths of the World-Mind and emerge after the dawn of cosmic manifestation into different kinds of consciousnesses. One and the same light refracts itself into a million photographs, each different from all others. One and the same World-Mind refracts itself into a million entities, each different from all others. And just as the objects in the universe come into existence by the power of karma, so do the individuals too. The new creature emerges into the universal existence in much the same way as the new thing, that is through an actualization of the train of its old karmic impressions which are themselves the resultant of a still earlier existence. The individual and the world rise together at the same moment out of the past which trails behind both. Its karmas are associated with those of the universal existence and do not appear separately or subsequently. The one starts into activity synchronously with the stirring of the other. When the World-Mind's energy manifests itself it takes a twofold character and both the universe and the individuals are born at the same time. The universe is not manifested first nor the individuals either but both together. To put it in another way, as the ripples of karma flow across the lake of World-Mind they move through both the universe and the individual at the same instant and, operationally, in the same way.

To understand the arisal of living beings out of an apparent void, we must understand that the break in the continuity of individual life which occurs during deep sleep and more crucially between the re-incarnations, occurs only on the surface and not in the depths. The World-Mind acts as a receptacle in which are deposited all the missing links of memory and all the missing mental energies. Hence no creature is really lost, whatever the appearances are. The activities of thought, emotion and willed act strung on an "I"-thread which constitute it, fall in the World-Mind's memory like seeds falling in the furrowed earth. The World-Mind's memorization makes individual activity possible, subtly supports and sustains it. Hence when a world-period is ripe for external manifestation, all the germinal impressions of innumerable individuals which were mysteriously but latently preserved and waited for this hour are recalled to find their birth in an appropriate environment. Every individual existence is thus the summary of innumerable earlier existences.

The world and the individuals dwelling in it are not only re-incarnations of previously existent forces but they also go on developing themselves and mutually inter-act. Such interaction occurs in the following manner. Out of the experiences of accumulated existences certain impressions tend to repeat themselves so strongly that they assume a structural character, that is, they become energy complexes. Just as a stream of water naturally takes the path of least resistance and flows downhill, so these impressions tend to unite first because of habitual repetition and later because of associations and affinities thus established. Thus the impressions are not indiscriminately combined but according to a natural process of growth. These complexes may take the most varied forms. Even the five senses of seeing, hearing, etc., are such complexes operating in a functional manner. For sight and hearing are primarily activities of the consciousness. We have seen that Nature is simply another name for the handiwork of the World-Mind, a handiwork to which we involuntarily and unconsciously contribute, too, because every object in Nature is known only as a phase of our own consciousness. The excitation of karmic impressions within the World-Mind is reflected in the individual mind as a general picture of the world. The individual has to take it into the very centre of his own consciousness, which he can do only by his own act. That is to say, the world-picture must be so assimilated as to be made his own through experience.

Although the World-Mind manifests both the individual and world together at the same moment, the individual is the centre around which the world revolves. This is partly because it is only when the world-image is felt to be his own conscious experience that it can assume any reality for him and partly because he is able to call himself "I" and exist as a separated self only through the setting up of an objective environment.

It will be shown, when these studies are sufficiently advanced, that the hidden meeting-point of the World-Mind with each conscious being has a special existence of its own and must therefore be given a special name of its own. The name which will henceforth be here used is the "Overself". It is consequently from its own Overself that every individual receives the world-picture. We have pointed out in earlier books that the Overself has its human habitat within the heart. Although associated of course with the whole body it has its most intimate association with the heart. Just as a king's rule may extend over a whole country and yet it may also be said to be definitely centred in the palace where he resides, so the Overself permeates the entire body and yet is also definitely centred in the heart. Hence the heart is the focal point where the World-Mind through its intermediary the Overself affects the personality. The karmic forces become active within the heart therefore and there break into space-time existence. Like light-photographs on a sensitive film, they develop into a tiny seed-like thought-form. This is the matrix of the world-to-be. Were this to remain there, then the individual would experience it only in the form of a dream. Indeed, in an earlier period of cosmic evolution such was the strange way in which the immature human race did pass its existence.

In order to provide the conditions for a more fully externalized and awakened experience the co-operation of the brain and the senses is required. These act partly in the same way as a transformer which increases the voltage of an electrical current, and partly as a microscope which enlarges the appearance of an object. Unless the world-image is caught by the brain, consciousness will remain at the dream level and physical experience becomes impossible. Hence the thought-form is transmitted to an image-magnifying centre in the outer layer of the brain by processes analogically like those used in the wireless transmission of a newspaper photograph (which reduce the photograph into numerous points of electrical energy and then build it up again from the transmitted electrical impulses), and to the special sensitive centres for seeing, hearing, touching, tasting and smelling. Here the brain reconverts the received vibrations into a highly magnified picture of which the individual becomes conscious, just as a radio set converts electrical waves into a series of sounds and at the same time highly amplifies them. When all this has been accomplished the individual becomes fully aware of the transformed and magnified world-picture, which the mind now projects *as if* it were something outside.

It should be noted that the functions of the brain, nerves and five senses, although correctly described by physiologists, still take place as much within the mental sphere as is the world-image with which they deal. But the latter's "outsideness" gives rise to the wrong notion of its being formed out of material substance. Science is honest when it says that thought is the concomitant of molecular movements in the brain, but it is merely indulging in imagination when it says that thought is the product of molecular movements in the brain. Its knowledge of the world's face is tremendous but its knowledge of the world's soul is rudimentary. Only deeper enquiry will show it that the external world is not reflected in the mind like an object in a mirror. Mentalism shows that the power which creatively builds up the sense-perceptions of an external world is the mind itself.

Just as the heart acts as the transmitter of blood to the entire body, so the Overself-centre in the heart acts as the transmitter of consciousness to the brain. So long as there is a transmission of the seed-picture from heart to head so long does waking consciousness of the world remain. Ordinarily this means therefore that both its transmission and magnification by the brain-plus-senses "transformer" are continuous and incessant throughout the day. The alternation of sleep and wakefulness is externally regulated through another centre situated underneath the cerebral cortex. This centre comes into activity with wakefulness and when, with the internal withdrawal of the Overself-current into the heart, wakefulness can no longer be maintained it remains passive during sleep.

This inner transmission is constantly going on and the brain is constantly magnifying the original karmic impressions into physical sense-impressions. Hence the individual's sensations actually arise from within himself. The materialists who discover that all sensory activities are correlated with certain brain centres and who would therefore make the brain the source of our sense-pictures are not wrong as far as they go, only they have not gone far enough. They have not mapped out all the functions of the brain. The sense-pictures are indeed manufactured in and by the brain of each individual himself. But it manufactures them out of material supplied from within, from a source unknown to and unsuspected by those who would make the feeling in the tips of their fingers the sole test of reality. The creative activity which brings the world-experience into being for every individual proceeds ultimately from his own Overself.

The reader must attend carefully to what follows. It is hard to follow at first but easy after it has once been grasped. It is only surface thought which makes us believe that we experience a thing which is here and now before us without contributing anything to its nature. But deeper thought shows us that there is something within our minds which builds up order among our sensations of the thing and which makes them cohere together as the unified perception of it. When we look at a particular thing it produces a complex group of certain sensations of colour and form within us, but we do not get our conscious experience of the thing in little pieces, only in one unified whole. That is to say, we do not consciously get it in the shape of separate sensations with each one standing alone like a separate star in space. Although the metaphysical need of analysing the different elements which enter into experience earlier compelled us to abstract them intellectually from such experience, we must not forget that in actual fact these elements do not stand alone. They are always combined. The constituents of consciousness cannot be isolated from each other. When we see a thing we do not see it in bits and pieces. We see the whole picture or not at all. The mind's unknown activity binds all the sensations of sight, sound, taste, touch and smell. The different sensations which are built up to compose a perception are like the different chemical elements which go to compose a compound. We do not see the sodium and chlorine as separate entities in a lump of table salt. Similarly we do not see the red colour, hard surface and round form of a fountain-pen as separate entities. The mental zone wherein sensations are gathered and bound together into a whole perception is altogether out of the individual's consciousness. It is only the percept, the final and finished image which is presented before his attention.

Moreover the sense-impressions of a thing do not of themselves give us the recognition of that thing. For this certain powers of the individual mind must come into play. First, memory must tell us what it knows about the thing and thus classify it; second, reason must consider and judge it. But primarily it is the image-making faculty which handles the sensations, completes the work and presents us with a finished external thing and which supplies continuous and independent existence to that thing. It is this imaginative activity of the mind which is the basis of all our sense experience, not a separate material substance as is commonly supposed. Nevertheless the entire operation wherein all this occurs must not be thought of as proceeding by successive stages in time, although we have so to split it up for intellectual analysis, but as one where all is achieved at the same instant. The perceiving act has no independent material correspondence which is different from it.

But before this experience is possible, before the sensations can be turned into a recognizable object, certain relations have to be set up both among the sensations themselves and between them and ourself. A man, for example, may travel in a train from the eastern to the western coast of an entire continent but if he is asleep during the journey he will have no knowledge of the event. This means, metaphysically, that the man's ignorance can disappear only when he becomes conscious of the distance of his journey and its duration in time. In other words through the very act of observing a thing the observer unconsciously externalizes it and at the same time imposes his space-time conditions upon it. The surface self must know things as being separate from each other, which means that it must put them in space. It must know events as happening before or after each other, which means it must put them in time. No object could appear at all if it did not appear in space, as no event could happen if it did not happen in time. For objects stand near or far from each other as events occur before or after each other. Hence every time we observe an external thing or event we are compelled to observe it as existing in a particular kind of space-time. This is *not* because the thing or the event is itself in such an order but because our human observing process itself works in that particular way. And unless we can observe the world in this way we shall not observe it at all, which means we shall have no experience of it.

Our mind is so constituted that we are unavoidably obliged to experience the world in the way we do. Without our conscious knowledge and in an instantaneous process, the mind thinks over its sensations, interprets them in terms of this particular space-time order, and then pushes into our conscious field the resulting thought-form which it constructs and it is this that passes for our own personal experience.

Before we can have the idea of a thing as such it must be thought of as something apart from us. This in turn means that we must have the foundational power to think of it as being distant from our body. Hence mind must necessarily be able to spatialize its creations, *which include the senses themselves*. Its ideas must appear to be extended in space if they are to be perceived at all. The same considerations apply to events happening in time; our mind must also be able beforehand to set out its creations in the form of a successive series.

To bring the karmic impression of a thing into actualized being, the mind has to provide it with relations of extension, size, distance and direction, and thus make space along with it. Thought-forms of every thing projected by the World-Mind so appear as to be outside the thought-form of the body and therefore they all co-exist in space as the whole system which we call Nature. The body itself is a special thought-formation which rests apart from all others and yet still remains mental, just as a fishing-net in a river is apart from and yet wholly immersed in the water.

It is only after we enquire deeply that we can at all discover that the world which is presented to our senses is really presented to our mind, because the senses themselves are forms of consciousness. The thing *is* there outside us, but it is only the idea we have formed of it in our mind. The one seems outside us and the other inside us but ultimately the essence of both is mental. Mind actually creates what it experiences and actually experiences what it creates. The experiencing mind creates the experience out of itself in such a way that the illusion of receiving it from an external source holds sway.

An artist sketches a mountain-range and a valley. Through proper shading and perspective he makes us see the landscape in full relief although he makes no actual elevation or depression on the paper. In the same way the revived karmic impressions, when associated together, picture an external world for us but do not place it actually outside mind, although we feel that it is so placed. The so-called material world is simply what seems external to thoughts. Consciousness is simply what seems internal to thoughts. But the material world is really the form which consciousness takes when it projects itself through the five senses and holds its ideas as something other than itself. The world which *seems* presented from outside to the senses is *actually* projected from within by the mind. Thus the doctrine of mentalism finds its justification.

The space-time order prescribes the limits of our existence, draws the outlines of our universe of experience. The limits set to our perceptions by space and time are unavoidable ones, being the price paid for being able to perceive a world around us at all. The karmic pre-existence of world-ideas is, as we have said before, like the abstract existence of the ideas of an intended musical effect in a composer's mind. The karmic potentials are out of space-time whereas the actualized things are of course in the space-time imposed upon them by their observers. Their actualization is necessary only for actualized space-time beings like our finite human selves and not for the World-Mind itself. Hence their existence is necessarily a relative one. Hence too the inescapable relativity of human experience.

In the earlier volume it was explained that all the constructive and unifying work which transformed the sensations into a conscious percept was the work of the mind itself. It was not advisable to enter more deeply into this tenet at the time as there is no surface consciousness of this work. All these processes occur beneath the threshold of our consciousness, so we do not realize that it is not all one mind which manipulates them. Now it is possible to see that the World-Mind as the Overself also is active in us. To call the latter "subconscious" is really to degrade it. More correctly should we say it is "co-conscious" and much more correctly still, "overconscious". However from the angle of current scientific understanding we are compelled to continue the use of this inadequate term of human experience.

It was also pointed out in the same volume that science, following the materialist view which makes the external object prior to the conscious idea of it, cannot connect them together but is forced to leave a gap in explanation. Mentalism however makes the connection by making the idea prior, in one sense, to the object. It is now possible to understand why such priority arises. For the process of personal experience consists in constructing an idea of the World-Mind's idea and at the same time perceiving it as an objective thing. The fact that World-Mind knows the idea of itself confers prior existence upon it. Thus World-Mind's master thought is certainly prior to our humanly constructed and humanly perceived thing. But both being in the end ideas it is likewise correct to say that a material object, apart from the idea of it, never exists at any time.

Thus we build up our own space-time image of environment from this subconsciously supplied seed-like thought-form. The space-time *form* which moulds the perception is contributed by the individual mind whereas the *material* which assumes that form is contributed by the World-Mind. The individual's own mind subconsciously anticipates *how* his experience shall come, that is extended in a particular space-order and changing in a particular time-series, whilst the World-Mind provides *what* he shall experience.

The relation between the experiences of each conscious being and the World-Mind is illustrated by the relation between the pictures which appear on a photograpic film and the light which makes those pictures possible. This is the mystery; that which *we* understand as consciousness itself becomes possible only through the finite mind's magnified projection into time and space of its own percepts. It appears to be continuous (despite the daily testimony of experience which shows how it may be irregularly interrupted by injury, disease or drugs and regularly by sleep), but this is not really so; the sense impressions follow each other so rapidly as to give the illusion of manifold experience, in the same way that a whirled torch gives the illusion of a fixed circle of glowing light. It is a constant movement of momentary gleams, a prolonged string of momentary awarenesses. Actually as soon as a thought-moment arises, passes and vanishes, another takes its place at once, not haphazardly of course but necessarily originating out of the one which went before. The conventional conception makes thoughts move across a background of world-consciousness but this is not correct. It is the thought itself that provides us with the particular kind of spaced and timed consciousness with which we are all familiar. Beneath two successive thought-moments there is Mind, the occult link which makes them orderly and makes their consciousness possible.

This is in line with mentalism's declaration that the physical world instead of being a stable thing as it seems to sight and touch, is really passing through a process of never-stopping change from moment to moment. For our world-ideas have no continuous existence but only a disjointed one. They arise only to vanish again immediately. The illusion of smoothly continuous existence which we experience is explained by the fact that each disappearing idea is succeeded by another which is similar to it but not *actually* identical with it. Thus a regular ever-running succession of thoughts marks each conscious being, a perpetual combustion-process of mental stuff goes on. Therefore every thought is really a new one: no two thoughts could ever possibly be identical, although they are usually similar.

Thoughts, whether they be abstract ones or pictorial images, are emitted from the deeper layer of mind not like a flowing stream of continuous water from a tap but like a steady series of separate bullets from a machine gun. Consciousness of outside things comes with the coming of thoughts about them and the latter emerge with the regularity of the to-and-fro movements of a steam-engine piston or with the rhythmic chug-chug of an electric locomotive. It is merely a ceaseless flow of such staccato movements of ideation, a succession of moments like lightning-flashes across the night, which makes up our world-knowledge. The process is far too swift for us to note it, however.

All ideas are thus momentary members in an uninterrupted series. Each appears, only to be displaced by another one. Our present physical form of consciousness is but a rapid succession of changing thought-moments, each member of the series being individually conscious and the whole producing the illusion of a single stream of integral awareness. The rapidity with which these conscious moments succeed one another need not seem impossible when we remember the scientifically-ascertained rapidity with which the oscillations of moving electricity succeed one another, that is many billions of oscillations per second. The ancient Asiatic psychologists even claimed to have measured the duration of this thought-moment to the tremendously minute fraction of a fragment of a second involved. It does not really matter whether or not we accept their figure—a billionth part of the time taken to snap one's fingers—because our finite human intellect cannot cope with such infinitesimals anyway. The essential point is that our particular form of spaced and timed conscious sense-experience lives as long as a thought lives and ceases as soon as a thought ceases. But as the next thought follows practically instantaneously its intermittency is never noticed.

The world in its ever-fleeting, ever-changing yet ever-continuous character is really like a moving cinema picture whose scenes flash so vividly before our eyes and whose figures talk so convincingly to our ears. But if we remove the celluloid film from the cinematographic projector, we discover that it is made up of countless thousands of separate "still" pictures. A sense of reality is imparted to us only when they are made to move swiftly and continuously. Similarly, the smoothly continuous multiplication of countless thousands of mental pictures of the world, similar to each other but never identically the same, fuse together and create the impression of a stable world. The totality of all these successive mental constructions, of this ever-flowing series of conscious perceptions, constitutes our world experience. Nevertheless we allow ourselves to be deluded by its appearance of smooth stability. We do not understand that it is really a mental flux and thus become literally obsessed by our belief in a static matter.

The foregoing has been a scientific view of the situation. It explains why all things are really momentary and why the entire universe is really a Becoming. Philosophically speaking, however, this momentariness of consciousness applies only to the personal self, not to the Overself. Here, as our later studies shall reveal, there is unbroken continuity of awareness. Here nothing is really outside us and all events are really in an everlasting Now. This incessant movement from one conscious moment to the next supplies us with the materials of world-experience but it also breaks our integral awareness and gives rise to a sense of passage from past to present and anticipation of the future and thus to our sense of time. Instead of realizing with the Overself that life always "is" continuously present in an eternal Now we feel that it "was" or "will be". Incidentally, could we but grasp the implication of our experiences in time and space we would grasp the idea that something in us, something which must be immeasurably sacred, is out of time and transcends space. These however are points which must be studied later.

The World As Our Idea.

But our mind does not create the thing for anyone else: it only creates it for our self. Our sensations may resemble another man's but that does not make them identical with his. There are two sets of sensations here, not a single set. Hence our sensations cannot be *identical* with his even though we both listen to the same music, because they are our very own, produced by our own mind, whereas his are produced by his mind. Our sensations of these sounds vanish the moment we stuff our ears with cottonwool but his sensations continue because they are a different set. What we can correctly say about them is that they are *similar* to his, that the sounds we hear are *like* the sounds which he hears.

Thus the experience of the world really becomes each individual's own, quite independent of although quite similar to the experience of other individuals. An illustration of this point may be useful. Each eye in the human body sees the same scene from a different angle and consequently formulates a different picture. Yet the two pictures coalesce into a single one which alone actually enters consciousness. The World-Mind's idea may analogically be regarded as that supplied by the right eye, and the individual's own subconsciously-made image as that supplied by the left eye; but the one of which the individual actually becomes aware is the final picture resulting from a fusion of both. Each centre of conscious life really has its own version of its environment, which it does not merely register but also interprets.

Just as a thousand different lakes reflect the hues and tints of one and the same sun, so a thousand different conscious beings reflect one and the same world-idea as an experience common to all of them. It is because each set of sensations is roughly similar that we become aware of what is roughly one and the same universe. Yet just as each wave on the surface of each lake catches and reflects the same sunbeams separately in its own individual way according to its size, strength and shape, so each creature catches and reflects the world-image according to its own modifications. Just as two different cameras cannot both at once occupy precisely and exactly the same point in space and time and consequently cannot simultaneously photograph a scene in precisely the same way, so one conscious being cannot perceive the world in precisely the same way as another. Each experiences the world-idea in its own unique way and adjusts it to the form of its own intellect. It supplies its own space-time characteristics and consequently conceives its own experienced world.

But our mind does not stand isolate and alone. Beneath it is the World-Mind. Beneath our thought-form of the thing there is its base—the World-Mind's stimulus which provokes it into being. Hence the character of our creative power is only a semi-independent one. World-Mind thinks its ideas *into* our mind. It is the thinking of the World-Mind that is *primarily* responsible for the world. We share the ideas, participate in the sense-images thus evoked, it is true, but we do not project their original stimulus. There is a cosmic activity within ourselves. The world is originally the product of World-Mind, and only secondarily by reflection the product of our mind. And such reflection is perfectly possible because each little circle of a single individual mind lies within the larger all-containing circle of World-Mind. The individual re-creates in its own consciousness the idea reflected into it by the former. We assimilate in our individual minds the fruits of the World-Mind's planting.

Consequently we can neither say that man is confined to his own creations nor admit that he is merely the passive recipient of another mind's pre-existent creations. The truth includes both views but is not exhausted by them. The human mind is not entirely passive to the reception of ideas from World-Mind but it is both active in one way and passive in another. The cause of its ideas lies partly in itself and partly in World-Mind. The World-Mind is the hidden cause which stirs our world-image into being but actualization it belongs to us. We are co-conscious with the cosmic mind of the world spread around us; it is not our exclusive personal possession. The World-Mind's master perceptions are shared and shareable by the single finite minds only within the limits of their capacity. Each looks through his little window on the universal scene in his own limited way whereas the World-Mind, working through us, perceives its idea of the universe in an unlimited way.

Were there not this element of World-Mind present in our own individual minds, we could not respond to its stimulus and perceive the things lying about in space and moving about in time at all. It is this kinship which makes possible our awareness of the external world. Without the constructive activity of the individual the world could not take the form under which we know it. Without the co-presence of the World-Mind there could be nothing continuous and significant to enter that form. All the experiences which we gather through the five senses, all our sensations of an external world are derived ultimately from this mysterious radio-like communication of being, consciousness and activity from World-Mind. It is we who think the external world into a particular space-time form of existence but it is the World-Mind which obliges us to do so. Without this close relation the whole universe would vanish from the ken of all conscious beings and they themselves along with it. Were this supreme mind to cease its ideative activity for a moment, then they would all be stripped of the source of their sensations. Just as a man's thoughts can be said to exist only so long as the man keeps thinking them, so does the world-thought have its own existence only so long as the World-Mind keeps thinking it. Were the latter to cease its imaginative labour for an instant, the world would, in Shakespeare's words, "dissolve and leave not a wrack behind".

And so somebody has said: "Things are because God *sees* them."

Here we may perceive a further significance of our earlier studies in illusion and hallucination. The world we experience is an actualization in the individual mind of the master ideas which exist in the World-Mind, a conceptual construction imposed on it as an illusive brigand is imposed by a frightened traveller upon a shadowed bush. Again, an hallucination has no separate and independent ground other than a certain innate tendency or unconscious presupposition in the character of the sufferer. If this tendency be taken as symbolically equivalent to the cosmic impression, then it stands in a similar relation to the hallucinatory vision itself as does this impression to the actualized idea.

The universe is indeed an enchantment placed upon us by the World-Mind. We are all enclosed within the scene set up by it but the scene itself is a thought-created one, the power which makes us feel its reality is a mental one and even the senses so bewitched are forms of consciousness. Hence the operation of the cosmic upon the individual mind is nothing short of magic! Those who scout the possibility of cosmic mind being able to present to the gaze and hold in the experience of its immense progeny of individual minds this great panoply of the universe should consider all the annals of proven cases of thought-transference, telepathic action, mystic visions, yogic magic and mesmeric phenomena. If such things are possible among finite individual minds themselves how much more must it be possible for the cosmic mind to transfer its own great world-idea to us? Thus if we examine our own narrow human life we may find there a revelation of the wider universal life.

The scientifically ascertained and verified facts of hypnotism constitute an important group of confirmations of certain aspects of mentalism. For when the operator makes his subject see a coloured playing-card when there is only a blank piece of paper before him he is making him see what obviously exists only as a mental picture, a thought. And when the subject is told that he is standing beside a furnace and then breaks out into actual perspiration, he is demonstrating that it is perfectly possible for a thought to register on the nerve system, on the senses and in the brain in a way that the untutored believe to be possible only to physical experiences. And when he is made by suggestion to see a wall confronting him, what is this but a vivid demonstration of the fact that mental constructions can be seen outside the body, spatially? Hypnotic phenomena therefore, like the phenomena of illusions, reveal mentalistic truth and raise vast questions for the thoughtful enquirer. In so far as they show that suggestions, i.e. thoughts, can cause objects to appear tangibly within a man's experience, they show that mentalism is true. The annals of hypnotism amply prove this possibility of making an external world exist before our eyes even though it is a form of consciousness and nothing more. In other words the universe is produced from within and not from without man's mind. The power that produces it is subconscious to him but it is there. It is in part the World-Mind and in part his own hidden past. And the strength of its production is the strength of the mesmerism he undergoes. The World-Mind, being present at all times and in all places, can perpetually sustain the existence of the universe in the perceptions of all the innumerable creatures within it.

But whatever be the origin of our experience, the fact remains that we are conscious only of our own ideas, and that our perceptions of things must necessarily be but pictures in the mind. We see our own constructions in everything which we see. Nature is our own idea. Whether a thing exists outside us which corresponds to these pictures or not, it also could never be known to us if at all as anything other than an idea. Do what we will we cannot introduce the external existence of matter at any point of our experience. These ideas are not only the *only* things which we really experience, not only are our notions of separate material objects utterly deceptive ones, but they have no actualized existence apart from our own minds. This is why and this is the true sense in which the ancient Asiatic seers called the universe, "maya", a term usually but inadequately and imperfectly translated as illusion.

The World-Mind does not work like an architect, does not have first to project an idea of the world and then set to work constructing it in matter. The universe is not the handiwork of a humanized Creator shaping a lot of amorphous material stuff nor is it the result of the play of blind unconscious and unguided forces. For we must think of the world-ideas as forces lying latent within the World-Mind and inseparable from it. And because they are inherent in its nature they constitute a *self-actuating* system. Every such impression is simultaneously actualized by the mere fact of its being thought of in space-time terms: it *is* then the so-called material object. It is impossible to separate the World-Mind's recollected idea from the re-created thing: the idea appears at once as a thing because of the mere fact that it is re-thought and re-sustained in World-Mind's consciousness.

When we understand the true part played by the mind in every sensation, we shall understand that all our knowledge is but the transmutation of consciousness into the world. All our experience is summed up in the statement that we think it. What materialist even can go beyond this position—except in imagination or belief which again is mental experience! Mind can start no activity which is not akin to its own nature, mental. He who grasps this and draws its corollary, that the vast array of things which make his environing world are necessarily mental things, has unearthed the Rosetta Stone which can henceforth enable him to decipher the hieroglyphic of both his own and that world's existence. Even the materialist admits that we form an idea of every object, only he maintains that this object is material, independent and apart from the idea of it. The mentalist too accepts the existence of an object but denies that it is material, independent or apart from his idea of it. For he says that this object is only the idea of it. Were the external thing really one and the thought of it really another, then we would sometimes know the thing alone and sometimes the thought alone. But this never happens. Therefore the thing and the thought are one and indivisible.

If we wish to understand aright, then we must rise from the corporeal flesh to the celestial Idea, from the crude and exploded notion of matter to the refined and sure notion of Mind, from guidance by inferior feelings to guidance by superior intelligence. The innumerable stars that powder the Milky Way exist mentally alone, so far as we know or can ever know. The impressive pageant of worlds upon worlds which stretch themselves out in space are but ideas garnered within our mind.

Mind is its own seer and seen, self and not-self, experiencer and the thing experienced. It is one but it has many functions through which it is able to present innumerable different manifestations of itself to innumerable different "selves". The latter in their ignorance take the presented world because of its "outsideness" to be non-mental in its nature and fail to see that their separation from it is only a surface one. It is certainly outside the body but not outside the mind. Thus what is essentially a mental activity is taken to be a material substance.

This is insight, that there is nothing in the world but Mind. This is the meaning of mentalism.

The hour will certainly arrive when science will be bold enough to declare its conclusion that matter is but a myth arising out of a misunderstanding of the place of the five senses, that all sensation is entirely mental, and that therefore we never know of a material world but only a mental one. Matter, in short, is not something which we seem to experience in Nature but is really a characteristic of the way we think of Nature. The laws of material Nature can ultimately be but the laws governing the appearances and changes of the World-Mind's forms. This long-played drama of the cosmos is entirely enacted within the mind and nowhere else.

4

Studies in Dreams

"WE have heard many an argument in favour of mentalism," say some sceptical readers, "but still we remain unconvinced. For both our innate feelings and our inherited thinking are strongly offended by so far-fetched and startling a doctrine. It is impossible that it could ever prove to be true."

This objection is quite excusable. Nature has indeed anticipated it. She has provided a means of helping mankind to prove within their own experience that instead of being absurd, the fact of mentalism is really almost an everyday experience. For in the dream which so often comes with the night there is both a clear illustration of mentalism's meaning and a pregnant hint of its possibility.

It was within the experience of the generation which is now passing through middle age and certainly within the present writer's experience, that students were told by the purveyors of learning at whose wise feet they had to sit in their ignorant youth, that only primitive peoples and infantile mentalities paid any attention to dream life. It was said to be, in short, a subject fit only for the superstitious, the uneducated and the barbarian. So science turned a scornful nose away.

Since those days something of a change has come over the educational scene. Psychology, having put on a respectable morning suit, took a seat amongst the accepted guests. Under the long tail of its frock-coat there crept in a junior offspring of more dubious character and less certain credentials. But once in the scene he planted himself with such firm feet and such vigorous hand-waving that he was finally permitted to stay. And his name is Psycho-analysis.

Freud's teaching that dreams are mostly unconscious wish-fulfilment, suppressed desires seeking vicarious satisfaction, and his view that the unconscious mentality of mankind is principally occupied with sexual craving could, even on the unwarranted assumption of their complete correctness, be true only of particular cases and become absurd when applied to all cases. But if Freud has been severely denounced and as staunchly defended for his sexual obsession, he has undeniably rendered useful service by compelling medical thought to ventilate an awkward but important subject which had hitherto been conveniently side-stepped. He also asserts that the influence and events surrounding early childhood provide the chief forces in the adult life. We are inclined to quote many striking cases, where the character which emerged in adult life was strikingly antagonistic to the patterns engraved upon the mind in early life. The truth is that the habits and tendencies are not only inherited from parental attitudes, childhood surroundings and racial influences, as Freud rightly says, but much more essentially from less obvious sources still, that is from former existences on this earth. His theories will need substantial pruning before they can survive the test of time. But his best service has been to focus scientific attention upon enquiry into the unconscious regions of mind and upon the tantalizing problem of dreams.

For dream is an entry into the first hinterland of the mind.

Sleep in general is something more than a mere physiological and psychological fact; when its profound significance is fully grasped it is a password into a higher comprehension of truth. A condition whose continuous loss would ordinarily cause insanity or death and one in which we spend roughly one-third of our lives cannot in any case be deemed an unimportant one. A sixty-year-old man will probably have spent nearly twenty years in dream and deep sleep. Those fantasies of the night which we call dreams and those blanknesses of the mind which we call slumber must surely have an important place in Nature's scheme. Human experience is not limited to the waking state alone but extends itself through these two other states also. Consequently a thoroughly scientific and philosophic view of human existence must bring all three states into its consideration, otherwise it will be incomplete and imperfect.

These three states embrace all the varied aspects and all the possible facts of such existence and when it is said that metaphysics seeks to base its reflections upon *all* available data and not merely upon some limited group of facts, which is what individual sciences, arts and cultures usually do, it is meant that both sleeping and mystical experience, not only waking and physical experience, must also be sympathetically accounted for and critically appreciated at their proper worth.

This partiality for the waking state which we all feel is a justifiable one, both on practical and as we shall see later philosophic grounds, but this ought not to blind us altogether to the value and significance of the other two states. Science and metaphysics must enlarge the field of their analysis, must make dream and sleep facts as much a part of it as they have so thoroughly done with waking facts.

Wakeful life represents only the peak of an iceberg which thrusts itself above the surface. We must study the iceberg as a whole if we would understand its meaning adequately. We may by watching the workings of our own mind in its three phases of sleep, dream and wakefulness, and not by limiting our investigation to the last phase alone, arrive at better understanding of its profounder problems.

There are large changes of bodily condition which separate

dreaming and waking life into two different classes. When a man lies stretched upon his bed and sleep settles on his body its pulse falls, its blood-flood is slackened and all the organic functions slacken down. The energies and movements of the waking state do not come to a dead end, however. The heart beats, the lungs breathe and repair work starts on the tissues. Ordinarily as the sensations which describe environment fade away, attention begins to wander and he begins to relax the control by will and the critical intelligence which operates during fully conscious life. The number of thoughts grows less and less as sleep approaches. Finally the room melts away and vanishes into nothing as his consciousness is mysteriously and entirely isolated from the physical world; it sees nothing, hears nothing, smells nothing, feels nothing and tastes nothing; and then a dream enters it.

The process of dreaming fascinates savage and savant alike. It possesses a mystery and magic of its own. How do they originate, these strange night-plays which are often performed by many actors but never witnessed by an audience of more than one? The dream has been a happy-hunting ground for the intellectual fanatic, the superstitious primitive and the medical doctrinaire. There is no theory of the origin of dreaming that is universally applicable. Only a broad comprehensive view will avail here. This is because there is no single mechanism which may start a dream working but on the contrary one or more of several different mechanisms may be responsible for it. The subject is a complicated one and can only be simplified at the cost of scientific truth. It is easier to explain deep sleep although it is a profounder state than it is to explain the dreaming condition. For if some dreams are symbolic and will bear interpretation, many others are not and mean nothing more than what their surface shows; if some reveal repressed sex wishes most of the others are blamelessly innocent; and if some are reconstructed out of the materials supplied by wakeful experience others are entirely new constructions. Hence those who, like the doctrinaire psycho-analysts or the uncritical soothsayers, would gravely interpret every dream without exception according to a particular rule, are merely wasting both their wits and their time. Moreover, the dramatizing power of the dream consciousness is so amazingly flexible and expansive, that it is useless to interpret dreams by rule-of-thumb methods, stereotyped books or psycho-analytic theories alone.

When dreams become grossly and grotesquely exaggerated they provide a useful insight into the mechanism of normal dreams, just as illusions provide a useful insight into the mechanism of normal sensation. Close and careful observation will show that this occurs chiefly when an external physical experience is the real starting point of the dream. They pertain to the instinctive side of man and, indeed, we humans share this particular kind of dream with the higher animals. A stimulus received from the surface of the body when lying recumbent on the bed, a functional disturbance in the body itself, a slight pressure on the skin from some unwonted source—these are quickly incorporated by the dream fancy and moulded into tremendously disproportionate events. Who has not awakened after experiencing a nightmare wherein he was being suffocated by some grim monster, only to find that the weight of unduly heavy bed-clothes was the cause? Who has not undergone a series of startling fights with a wild animal, only to find that an undigested supper was at fault? A knock at the door of a bedroom may be turned by the dreamer into a clap of thunder just as the striking of clock chimes may be magnified into pictures of a regiment moving on parade to the tune of a military march. This tendency to magnify things far beyond reasonable limits and events far beyond reasonable relation to their original cause also exists in many drug addicts who, when actually under the influence of a drug, will see a little puddle of water, for instance, under the illusion that it is an immense sea.

Why have these sense impressions become quite abnormal when reflected into the dreamer's mind? It was earlier explained that the seed-like karmic energies of the world-image are transmitted from the habitat of the Overself in the heart and received within the head. Here in a sensitive centre within the brain's outer layer it undergoes tremendous magnification and through the other specialized brain-centres breaks into the individual consciousness as his sense-impressions of external world experience. The situation which develops in the dreamer's or drug-addict's mind is that the original physical impression or bodily disturbance becomes queerly dramatized into something fantastically remote from it which floats for a far longer time through the dream consciousness than it would actually require in the wakeful one before it vanishes. Thus the weight of unusually heavy bedclothes is turned by fancy into the terrifying episode of an adventure with a wild bear which is hugging the dreamer's life out of him. The dream mind in such a situation indeed constructs pictures and creates events which are nothing else than a highly imaginative reconstruction of the first physical excitation. This is because the dramatizing and symbolizing tendencies form a natural part of the imagining faculty in the freer unrestrained states of dream reverie and mystical vision.

Now we have earlier seen that imagination is the first characteristic of the World-Mind. Consequently it is also the first characteristic of the conscious beings who are its progeny. This wonderful image-making faculty is a natural possession of the mind. The faculty of forming pictures is as innate in the individual as in the cosmic mind. It is perfectly natural for the restraint-freed mind to go on evolving pictures. This is the very same faculty with which he unconsciously "creates" the form of his world during waking hours, but it works then under the stimulus of the world-image provided by the World-Mind's karmic potentials. In the situation now described, however, the dreamer does not receive the full image but only that tiny fragment of it represented by the particular physical disturbance which started his dream. Consequently the image-making faculty is largely free to run wild on its own and does accordingly begin to enjoy such freedom, as the highly dramatized results themselves show. It cannot run completely wild because it has to develop its images on the foundational basis of the original bodily disturbance, with which it must remain in relation however remote, hazy or distorted the latter be.

In addition to this, memory also will often contribute its share by reproducing fragments of past experiences which then get incorporated in the same dream; whilst the magnifying process developed in the outer layer of the brain runs wild too and through purely mechanical action evolves the transmitted impressions, whether memory or sense-derived, far beyond their normal warrant, like an erratic automobile running away at a higher speed than intended by the driver. The brain-centre has started into automatic activity on its own account because its function has been partially dislocated. Hence a tap on the door evolves into a thunderous noise. Another queer and chaotic consequence of these relaxations is that a mixture of fragmentary experiences follow each other without sequence and finally constitute the tissue of such dreams.

When we consider next the wide class of ordinary dreams which have no physical disturbance as their origin, we may first note that the mind does not pass directly into the deep sleep condition because the mechanical action of the brain-centre still continues if somewhat erratically. Its sentient principle of imagination flickers into intermittent life.

Why is it that rational order and natural unity seem to disappear so often in these motley dreams? Figures and events appear and disappear haphazardly without logical connections. This disorder and confusion are explicable when we remember again that the brain-reception has been partially and temporarily set free from the heart-transmission so that the image-making faculty works mechanically to a large extent on its own.

Where the magnifying centre remains in order whilst only the image-making faculty runs wild, the dream is then disorderly but not exaggerated. It draws its material partly from the contributions of memory and partly from mere exuberance of fancy. The inclusion of the first gives a weak connectedness and intermittent rationality to some parts but the inclusion of the second makes the other parts seem wildly disjointed and grotesquely senseless.

The force of suggestions drawn from the memory of waking experiences motivates many of these dreams. The episodes are fed either by previous thoughts, emotions, passions and actions, when both scene and circumstance can be easily traced to something said, thought, felt or done during the previous twenty-four hours, or else the creative fancy draws upon forgotten but stored-up previous impressions of the past for constructing its dream edifices. They may re-appear wildly and fantastically distorted, however, because the restraining influence of the higher intellectual faculties of reason, critical reflection and judgment are outbalanced by the wild running of the image-making faculty. There is then a partial failure in discriminating and classifying the images. But although the higher intellectual faculties of rational judgment, adequate discrimination and proper classification are retarded or reduced during dream they are not suspended altogether. They exert a certain degree of control which is not always uniform, being generally feeble.

Generally the dreamer's hours are given over to the free and unrestricted play of a picturesque imagination. The brake of reason and will is loosened, the dramatizing and symbolizing tendencies come into more unfettered activity. Similar ideas or contrasting images are mechanically associated together although often feebly recognized and badly sorted. The final result is a dream whose tangled and broken threads contrast with the tidy orderliness and rational continuity of wakeful experience.

Generally the greatest binding force between two ideas is their essential resemblance and so the imagination easily joins ideas together even where they have only faint similarity. Dreams obtain a pseudo-rationality in broken scraps through this association of ideas which follows after the original stimulus. Nevertheless we must never forget that this analysis is made from a waking state standpoint, for these dissociated bits of revived memory and these colourful sparks of dream imagination are related together in a manner which seems to the dreamer at the same time plausible enough, however absurd and illogical it seems to him after awaking. The most incongruous people and the most disconnected happenings are presented together in a long series which, when critically remembered after awaking, seems ridiculous but which when actually perceived while asleep, seems structurally harmonious and natural. For however grotesque they be dreams still follow the general pattern of wakeful experience in so far as they follow the inescapable necessity of presenting their images in space, their events in time-sequence and their human figures with understandable attitudes.

It is a just plaint that most dreams are idle and profitless. But if such are rightly regarded as unimportant it is equally true that there is a curious class of uncommon dreams which possess special significance. Discrimination is therefore required in our examination. A purely materialist explanation of dreams will not account for all of them. Nor is it right to assert, as some ancient Indian and modern Western psycho-analytic schools assert, that our dreams draw their material solely from waking experience, past or present, forgotten or remembered. For the mind is not only reproductive but also productive; it can not only reproduce figures and things already known in our waking life but also produce figures and things never known in our waking life; it can not only recall accumulated impressions of the past but also foresee or even create impressions of the future. Many dreams may represent the mere continuance of waking thought, physical experience or mechanical bodily responses but sometimes dreams have no connection with previous waking life or present bodily disturbance.

Where a dream is really sensible and significant, this is because the consciousness has completely retreated into the heart-centre, has dispensed with the contribution of the brain, and is once again working in complete accord with the master world-image which it finds within the heart. Such a dream then has at least as much status as a definite experience as ordinary waking life but it is a different kind of experience. And its higher worth and significance will be intuitively felt after awakening.

How absurd and superstitious, in the light of all the foregoing, is the lore of the soothsayer which professes to provide a prophetic interpretation for *all* dreams! Nevertheless we know, if not from personal experience then from recorded statements which are too authentic to be disputed, that this lore is not without some valid basis in so far as it applies to a single class of dreams only. A dream may be an accurate perception of some event happening at a distance in space or time; that is to say, it may be a genuine clairvoyant vision in the better sense of this much-misused term. How is it then that some dreams can thus take shape as forecasts of future happenings?

We talk of instants in the time-series occurring before and after each other, so that those which were the future become the past. But it is only the compulsory intensity of attention which enables us to build a barrier between the two "times", an intensity which makes the present seem real and the others illusory. Without it we would have to deal with a time that would be all one stretch. Just as mentalism, when understood, refutes the materialism which would set the boundary of the five physical senses, with their concomitants of clock and calendar time, to human experience and knowledge, so does it actually refute the parallel belief that past time is dead time, future time is non-existent and present time is living time. The consequence of this erroneous belief is that past and future seem illusory and the present alone seems real.

This teaching points out that even on such a superficial view time must be all of one piece; it is either all real or all illusory but cannot be both in patches. However, the deeper view is that such an attempt to label the elusive stuff of time can only deceive the one who tries it; for time, as was shown in *The Hidden Teaching Beyond Yoga*, is no more real and no less illusory than are ideas for it is mental. It will be seen therefore that the problem of prediction cannot be adequately solved until we have solved the higher mysteries of mind. This endeavour will be made later. Meanwhile we should note well that the fact that sight, smell, taste, touch and hearing operate in both the waking and dream states should of itself suffice to show that those senses are really mental structures within the larger mental structure of the body itself. Now because the time-feeling is itself nothing less than an idea, because the same time-series which rules waking life does not rule dream life, and because bodily sense-experience is mental in essence, it is possible under certain conditions which are more easily provided for most people by dream than by waking, for the mind to perceive in advance of their physical occurrence events in which the body is involved, and to project itself sometimes into the future with fair accuracy. This is the rationale of most prophetic dreaming.

It may happen that we dream things and thoughts, persons and events, which cannot be ascribed to earlier waking perceptions by any stretch of theory. Such dreams leave extremely vivid after-images and their memory is hard to shake off, even after several years have passed. They may indeed exert an unsuspected yet profound influence in shaping some attitude of our wakeful life. The sense of familiarity with new places or persons may, on rare occasions, be due to this cause. These dreams arise out of our karma and are either actual transcripts or vague reminiscences of former happenings. Their roots are deep down in earlier incarnations and they revive events which happened then.

Then there are rare dreams which are most important because they originate from an altogether loftier level of mind than the animal part of our being. The man who will not listen to the sublime whisper of his Overself during his waking hours will respond more easily during his dreaming ones, when the veil is thinner, partly because his egoistic will is more relaxed and partly because he is actually nearer the source of consciousness. It is dreams of this superior and spiritual character which bear good fruit after the man awakes.

Akin to them but also rare are those half-remembered dreams wherein one who has learnt to live in the Overself appears to friend, student or follower to exalt, warn, guide or encourage at a critical time and invariably in a clear connected vision at the moments preceding death.

He who has brought the sense-impressions of his waking state under complete and *informed* control will thereby have also brought the sense-impressions of his dreaming state under equal control. Consequently his dream life will become a willed, orderly, coherent and rational existence and hence quite different from that of ordinary dreamers.

How Dream Compares with Wakefulness.

It is now necessary, if we are to advance from the stage of psychological understanding to the higher stage of metaphysical significance of dream, to bring out in what ways it differs from wakefulness and what characteristics they both share in common.

The first point to be noted is that dream experiences are not normally vivid enough to bring them up to the level of waking ones. The images and ideas which fill the dreamer's mind are vivid indeed but it cannot be said that they ordinarily rise to the degree of sharpness which attends the same images and ideas when he is awake. The difference is there and disappears only in the case of most exceptional dreams, whether of the lower order such as terrifying nightmares or whether of the higher one such as aesthetic or spiritual experiences. The difference in force and clearness between the two states is primarily due to the fact that wakeful life brings the mind to a narrower focus, a more centralized attention and a sharper intensity of experience. Dream life, on the other hand, has a broader focus, a more diffused attentiveness and a weaker intensity of experience. Consequently we suffer more strongly when awake than when a'dream, just as we enjoy more deeply during the same condition too. Waking consciousness is more crystallized and hence more concentrated than dreaming consciousness. This explains the comparative faintness of dream impressions and their somewhat blurred outlines.

Nevertheless there have been men of developed mentality who have persisted in decrying this difference. Thus Descartes confessed: "The visions of a dream and the experiences of my waking state are so much alike that I am completely puzzled and I do not really know that I am not dreaming at this moment." And it was Chuang Tzu, the Chinese mystic, who complained after a night spent in a curious dream wherein he flew about as a butterfly that he did not know if he was a butterfly now imagining itself to be a man or a man who had dreamt himself to be a butterfly! These attitudes obviously represent a slight exaggeration on the part of these distinguished men for certain differences do ordinarily exist between the two states. The dream state must be judged by its universal manifestations and not by such exceptions.

Both Frenchman and Chinaman fell into the error of a class of metaphysicians and mystics, not uncommon in India, who go to the extreme length of arguing that if we complacently denounce the dream state as being an illusory one when judged by the light of the wakeful state, there is just as much right to let the latter have its own turn and be judged by the dream state. They believe, in short, that the dream life is on a footing of perfect equality with the wakeful life in every detail. They aver that there is absolutely no distinction between the two states.

That they have arrived at such a conclusion by the constant

dwelling on a single topic to the exclusion of all others which leads to its unsuspected exaggeration, as it leads the mind to an unbalanced condition, will be obvious to psychiatrists. Such metaphysicians and mystics point out correctly that while a dream lasts we consider it as the wakeful state. But dreaming is stultified by the mere act of waking whereas the wakeful life is uniformly continuous from day to day. We find continuity from one waking day to another, we do not find it from one dream to another; physical things continuously present themselves for a lifetime within our field of awareness but the dream imaginations about them or the memories of them flit through us far too briefly and too disjointedly to seem at all comparable with them; and finally, although we return to a wakeful environment every time we awake, we do not ordinarily return to the same dream world every time we fall asleep. Experientially, today's wakeful world is the same as yesterday's, but tonight's dream world is not the same as the previous night's. The scientific reason for such an important difference will shortly be explained.

Again, it is only during genuine waking that we are aware of the possibility of these two states whereas during dreaming we do not know that the existence of the first one is even possible. It is only when awake that we know a dream state can exist but when we are dreaming we do not know that a waking world can exist. This is because consciousness has half-withdrawn inwards during dream and does not know what now lies outside its own proper sphere, whereas during wakefulness it attains the crest of its own evolution. The larger state then naturally includes the lesser one, just as a larger concentric circle includes a smaller one. Self-awareness, for example, is then markedly less fully developed than when awake.

When we study our own consciousness we are able to distinguish three modes of its existence. In waking, the first, it has fully expanded itself; in sleep, the third, it has completely contracted itself; in dream, the second, it is midway between the other two, that is half-expanded. Hence the waking self possesses a peculiar strength which is usually ignored by those critics who, recalling the provocative question of Descartes and the quaint dilemma of Chuang Tzu, would equate it with the dream self. But this is an important difference for it points to the fact that dream marks the first stage of a return to mind of the individual consciousness projected from it, as sleep marks the second stage. It will be made clear in the next chapter why the term "mind" should not, as these studies advance, be equated with the term "consciousness". If we compare the mind to a lamp and the latter's light to consciousness then the illumination of the dream world is dimmer than that of the wakeful one. Wakefulness, dream and sleep are merely the mind disclosing itself in three progressive degrees. On the mentalist view, mind is *more* than consciousness and is given primacy over it.

Consciousness itself is but an aspect of mind. It expands or contracts by stages. Thus it is in a night-like state during deep sleep, in a twilight state during dream and in a bright noonday state during waking. The waking state of consciousness is thus the state in which it opens its eyes widest, the dreaming state is that in which they are but half-opened, whilst in the sleeping state they are quite shut. This fact of the graded opening of the aperture of consciousness explains why in the waking state we know that the other two states also exist whereas in the dreaming state we are ignorant of the existence of the waking one. For a longer range of vibration includes a shorter but the shorter cannot include the longer.

We have already noted that imagining is the basic activity of the universe, and that therefore it is the first characteristic of man himself. From an evolutionary standpoint, he has retreated in the dream condition halfway back into his original self, when his image-making faculty worked in a freer, fuller and less restrained manner. Hence the profuse outpouring of imaginations is natural during dream.

When we are in the midst of a dream we do not consider that the things seen in it are imaginations but regard them as genuinely real. Why then do we alter our view of them after we awake? Why do we not experience the contrary and pass similar judgment during dream upon waking things? The answer is first, that both experiences rest upon different levels in several respects although not in others. The wakeful world, in fact, does possess a higher value than the dream world. For permit its mind to come into clearer and fuller conscious activity. This is the basic difference between the two states, although they are identical in this that they are both nothing else than mental constructions.

The waking state is for us the most conscious of all, the most important of all. These are undeniable factors which thoroughly justify the supreme emphasis which practical life, science and metaphysics have traditionally bestowed upon them, but they do not justify the supreme neglect of the dream and sleep states which has been the consequence of this emphasis.

Dream is a different state from wakefulness and could only be equated with it by an unscientific distortion of the facts. Those Orientals who say that both states are precisely alike are indulging in poetic licence, not science. Were the two states really identical we would be entitled to ask why Nature went to the trouble of making them possible when a single state would have amply sufficed for her purpose. Nature had a still deeper purpose in differentiating the two states than those heretofore mentioned. Were human existence to be always a prolonged and unbroken waking one; were human consciousness to be always confined within the circle of what came to it through ever-open eyes; then it would be like an existence in the world of a single colour where every object would be white and where knowledge of the existence of red, yellow and green could never arise. Nature has consequently provided us with five senses which have to limit, in order to concentrate, our awareness. Unfortunately in our ignorance of this situation we set up these perceptual limitations, which are obtained by a *shutting-out* of all other impressions, as being the fullness of possible experience!

Dreams however come as tutors to tell us wherein we have erred. Nature further breaks up human modes of mental life into the triple degrees of unconsciousness, semi-consciousness and consciousness (corresponding to deep sleep, dream and wakefulness) and thus renders it possible for man to grasp certain tremendous truths. He is so powerfully mesmerized into the belief in world-materiality, so strongly chained during his wakeful condition to self-identification with his body alone, that Nature has to enable him to detach himself periodically from his bondage by periodically breaking up both his wakeful state and his earthly life. This she does by interrupting the one with sleep and the other with death. The subconscious absorption of the lessons of these experiences bring him after great lapse of time to three intuitions which manifest themselves as innate beliefs of a religious, mystical or philosophical character. They take different shape according to the contemporary context of his race, country, century and personal culture but their essence is, in popular language, that God exists, that man is immortal and that he can enter into communion with God.

At first he comprehends these cardinal truths quite dimly but still enough to make him feel that there is a higher Power to which he must look upward. This is the stage of the *religious* devotee. As he gradually evolves he develops clearer intuitions which cause him either to look inwards and sense something of the stable peace which is inseparably linked with this Power (the stage of the *mystic*), or to ask certain questions which come to agitate his reason but finally find a rational answer (the stage of the *metaphysician*). But no religion is knave-proof and no mysticism is fool-proof. So the passage of further time brings an effort on the part of Nature both to balance his inward growth by outward results and to unfold that assured and abundant insight which transcends reason and intuition. Thus he enters the stage of the *philosopher*. Thus too the obscure instinct which first arose within him now attains clarity and distinction.

From this it may now be understood why mystics, following the course of their ecstatic feelings, often declare the world to be but a dream, whereas philosophers, following the course of their serener insight, declare that it is only *like* a dream. By this is meant that both possess mentalist characteristics. And the philosophers would add that it would be truer to say that the world is a dream grown to maturity.

It was Sir Henry Holland, a distinguished English medical man of the last century, who pointed out, on the basis of experience amongst elderly patients, that persons who have lived to a ripe old age begin to feel that all their life has taken on the texture of a dream. This is a definite advance on the common and conventional standpoint. It brings them closer to the mystical standpoint. But it is not the ultimate truth. For from the philosophic standpoint both states are expressions of one and the same reality, which is indeed the hidden base of all human experience. Let us not make the mistake of saying that earthly life is a dream, for it is not. All that we may correctly say is that it has certain points of likeness to and certain points of difference from a dream.

Therefore the philosopher finds no excuse for inaction in his understanding of the world's existence. It is here in this physical world, which the ascetic despises, which the materialist over-valuates and the mystic under-valuates, that man has to fulfil his spiritual destiny and realize his higher individuality, and nowhere else. For it is only through the maturity of wakefulness and by means of its paramount contribution that man is able gradually to become conscious of his Overself.

The second point to be noted about the two states is that the wakeful world is a common one, being shared with other men, whereas the dream world is an individual one. The theatre in which the wakeful drama is enacted is public, but the theatre of each dream drama is private. Each conscious being wondrously fabricates its own imaginings. Each drama is aristocratically exclusive to the dreamer. No one else than himself has any part in its making. He may indeed perceive other persons in his dreams but it is certain that ordinarily those persons do not simultaneously see him in their own dreams, whereas in the wakeful state each does perceive the other.

The still face of a dreamer reveals nothing of the stirring adventures, the joyous raptures or the bitter experiences through which his consciousness may be passing at the time. The world into which he enters is a dreamer's own secret: even someone in an adjoining bed, whether awake or asleep, cannot also enter it. Each particular nocturnal imposture of dream is imposed by mind upon one man alone and none else.

The scientific explanation of the continuity of the waking world as contrasted with the discontinuity of the dreaming world is, of course, the fact that the first draws its existence primarily from the World-Mind's permanent master-image whereas the second draws it solely from the individual mind's ephemeral visions.

It is possible to garner a profound significance from this fact that each dreamer's world belongs to him alone whereas the waking world is common to all mankind. Here Nature gives every man, in his own personal experience, a key to the mystery of world creation. In the fact that the individual is able to create his own image of his dream environment, he may comprehend how he can receive and reproduce his own image of the waking world emanated from the World-Mind.

Most people do not know that this larger being exists within them; even those who do know it do not know what an important element it really is in making their world experience; whilst those who realize its importance know very little about its operations anyway. Here, in the image-making power of the finite self, they are provided with a suggestive glimpse of the image-making power of the infinite self.

There are few limitations upon the imagination of the dreamer and none upon that of World-Mind. He freely makes his own dream world which may be most unlike that of another dreamer. He finds in himself a sample, as it were, of its boundless freedom and magical power. The powerful and original working of imagination during dream, even among those who are the most seemingly unimaginative people when awake, reveals it to be one of the most wonderful and deeply inherent properties of mind.

What is the genius doing but dreaming his dreams? Wrapped up in his creative work, he rises during his most absorbed and rapturous moments into a superior kind of dream condition. Every genuine artist who is not a mere hack will testify to the truth of this statement. The imaginative faculty can create entire romances during wakefulness, as it does for a novelist; how much more is it able to create them during dream with even greater ease because it can then express itself directly in thought and not indirectly through the limitations of an artistic medium? This is one reason why the most commonplace person is able to show an imaginative creativeness when a'dream which he is unable to show when awake.

Whatever be the parentage of a particular dream, all dreams are necessarily born of this image-making power of mind. The revelation of dream is thus a revelation of this innate power. Nature teaches every man through his dreams that he has in miniature the same creative capacities as the World-Mind. When he asks how it is possible for the World-Mind to super-impose the world-image on individual minds, Nature assists him to find an answer by giving him the dream experience wherein, it is plain, the dreamer brooding over his fancies is able to super-impose a private world-image upon himself. After all, he is watching only what his own mind throws up, although he does not know it at the time.

Higher Dimensions of Time and Space.

The third striking point about the two states concerns their timing.

We recall our dreams in disjointed fragments and sudden revealments. They are rarely remembered as perfect wholes. The process moreover is usually as swift as it is unexpected. They are quickly lost on awakening, save for blurred broken memories of the last scenes. We often reproach dream for this swift transiency which makes us remember it only in meagre scraps.

Most of our remembrances of dream experience are gathered during the moments before awakening and in that twilight-state of consciousness which is between both; they are only half-waking impressions of what we dreamt. Dream does not appear in wakefulness at all—save for these scraps of confused remembrance which mark the pre-waking borderland. Such memories are glimpses which are caught when the door of dream is momentarily ajar. It quickly shuts tight, however, and we are left in a slower vibration of consciousness altogether. And even those glimpses, being from a half-awakened standpoint where one state slurs over into the other, are necessarily not pure remembrances but a mixture of observations, distortions and interpretations resulting from the difference in standpoint between that of the dream self and that of the waking one.

The trouble is that the kind of time which is valid during dream is of such extreme rapidity that the attempt to bring dream experience into waking consciousness is exactly like the attempt to gear two toothed revolving wheels into each other when one is revolving at an extremely high speed and the other at a relatively slow one. The feat is impossible for the first cog cannot be brought into harmonious working with the second one.

In the same way dream experience is too rapid to fit into the movement of wakeful consciousness. The mind cannot ordinarily function simultaneously in two worlds so utterly at variance with one another.

If five minutes of dream time are sufficient to string together a series of episodes and incidents which require five days of wakeful time, it is quite clear that the dreaming mind works with an extreme swiftness which is utterly incredible to the waking mind. Somebody has even recorded the dream of a journey round the world which occurred after a candle at the bedside had been extinguished but before it had stopped smouldering! We must accept this fact that all dreams belong to an entirely different time-order from that of wakeful life.

It is difficult to discover this because we can examine and study our waking experience as something occurring in present time but we can only examine and study our dream experience as something which has occurred in past time. However, it is discoverable by taking such a case, for example, where it is only a bodily disturbance or environmental change which causes the dream. It can then often be verified that the dream has taken no longer than the second or two which marks the duration of the stimulus itself, because such dreams are usually followed by an actual awakening from sleep. It is common knowledge that in such a case a fraction of a second may suffice for quite a long dream of events which would need several hours of waking time for their complete fulfilment. We can fly in an aeroplane from London to Calcutta in less dreaming time than it takes to walk the length of London's principal street in waking time.

A sudden knock at the bedroom door once startled a sleeper and set going a series of vivid dream pictures concerning a thunderstorm of which he found himself the victim. The storm lasted for a half-hour in his experience but the entire event really took no longer than the start and finish of the knock at the door. A Frenchman was half-awakened by a rod which fell on his neck whilst he was in bed and during the actual moment or two which the process of full awakening required, he dreamt of a long series of different historical episodes wherein he was tried and guillotined during the French Revolution.

If we take the trouble to think beneath the surface of these two incidents, we shall discover that the mechanical measurement of time by a clock is not the same as the conscious measurement of time by experience. The speed with which perceptions succeed each other in the mind really marks time for us, not the speed with which two hands move round a clock dial. What, owing to the large number of images successively involved, would require a great length of time to experience during the waking state, will ordinarily require a mere segment of the same period to experience during the dreaming state. Time is really measured by the rate of movement of the sequence of images and ideas in the mind, not by wheels running round inside a clock. The whirling rounds of this earth on its axis and around the sun indicate time but do not create it. And even then they measure only one of its possible forms for us. We cannot measure dream-time by waking-state clocks. A dream that lasts an hour in experience may last but a minute on such a clock. The reverse is also possible. Drug addicts are familiar with the experience of feeling that a simple act like lifting a foot will seem to take a whole hour of their temporarily altered time-sense. This shows not only how unstable time is, but also how *mental* it is. If no other proof were available that time was completely mental and completely variable, then the dream would provide it.

We experience time as the measure of the mind's running movement in ourself but imagine it to be something outside us. Its character, speed and reality are only its character, speed and reality *for us*. It is simply a way in which the mind works, and because mental action can occur at any point between the lowest and highest rates of vibration, it can correspondingly be timed accordingly. When we are bored minutes are converted into hours. When we are fascinated hours are converted into minutes. What does this mean? It means that we do not move in time but time moves *in us*. "Man, know'st thou that morning, noon and eve are all within thee?" asked Muhammadan Sufi mystic Baba Fareed.

Although the value of waking time for all everyday life continues undiminished, nevertheless time as a thing is a human invention, useful for mathematical and practical purposes but not for philosophical ones. It is a form of consciousness, not a fixed thing, for it can neither be perceived nor conceived by anyone. It can vary indefinitely for it is relative to the individual. That which a man, walking on well-extended limbs may regard as one hour might be regarded as five hours by an ant, crawling on its tiny feet. Therefore we need not be an x-chasing mathematician to discover its relativity.

The moment after we have returned to the wakeful state we can confidently declare the dream to be but a mental construction. If we extend this backward glance a little further we have also to declare that all that happened to us in the wakeful life of yesterday is now nothing but memories, that is mentally reconstructed events and scenes. The philosopher does not stop here but extends a forward glance also. He converts the present experience also into idea for it likewise is a mentally constructed thing. When we remember that earlier studies showed the present instant to be wholly unseizable because of its immediate lapse into the past, that the attempt to grasp even a single point in time is for ever doomed to failure and that the present moment must therefore be a mentally-constructed one, we begin to understand that it is the continuous repetition of this ever-moving *idea* of a real present moment that we experience as time.

We unconsciously take it for granted during the course of a dream that the dream itself is without a beginning and will be without an end, but on awakening we discover that this apparent eternity of dream-time was after all only our imagination. Time, in short, is only a changeable idea but an idea which the conscious being, whether flung into a fleshly body or a dream one, cannot help having.

The fourth noteworthy point about wakefulness and dream concerns their spacing. The tremendous rapidity of dream time is matched by the almost simultaneous here-there of dream space. The common-sense and conventional waking viewpoint quite naturally holds that because things stand in relations of position, size and distance to one another and to our body, they are lying extended outside us. This opinion is arrived at because the common-sense viewpoint places the mind somewhere inside the head and consequently identifies it with the body itself. Its belief is that space is constructed of points which, being added together, yield extension. The total of all such points constitutes space, which is therefore regarded as a kind of box into which everything is put because it has to be put somewhere. Space, in short, is presumed to lie all around and all outside the mind.

Consider the same subject from the dreaming viewpoint. A dreamer finds himself walking the wide streets of a metropolitan

city like Buenos Aires. He walks a dozen miles along its
magnificent boulevards. Then he awakens and asks himself:
Where are this large city and those long distances? Can he locate
them? Obviously the Buenos Aires of his dream can be placed only
in his mind, from which it has emerged like a fruity plant from a
seed. Yet it had length, height and breadth. It existed in space.
Therefore it follows that space itself must be placed in the mind,
not the mind in space as is usually and incorrectly done.
Dimensions in space are therefore but the co-existence of ideas
within the mind, not of things outside it. This point can only be
understood, however, if the previously-mentioned distinction
between mind and consciousness be remembered. Mind is the
hidden root of consciousness. Such a distinction will be fully
explained in the subsequent chapter.

The space-time scale whereby we measure wakeful things and
events is quite different from that used in dream. We do not lose
time and space perceptions in dream, but form new *ideas* of them.
The place-order changes, the rate of succession alters. That is to
say space and time are still there but they are different from the
familiar experience of them.

It is not hard to grasp that the dream world does not exist for us
except as a series of ideas upon which our attention is fixed, and
therefore it is not a place but a state of attention. Its spatiality is
symbolical and lies in being attended to. Can we not move on a step
farther and grasp the harder point that even the wakeful world
belongs to the same spatial symbolism and possesses its extension
and distance through being attended to? How can we rightly take
two contradictory attitudes towards one and the same mind's own
experience? If we analyse closely we shall find that our knowledge
of the world's existence is *always* coupled with our attention to it,
that attention to things is the essential pre-requisite for awareness
of things and that the degree of attention given is exactly
proportionate to the intensity of consciousness shown. Space, in
short, lies within the mind and not, as is commonly believed,
outside it. Those who deem the mentalistic doctrine fantastic may
learn from this undeniable but usually underrated if not unnoticed
fact of dream-spacing how in accord with Nature this teaching
really is. "Before we are awake we do not understand that what we
see in dream does not exist externally," says the *Wei Shihershih
Lun*, an old Chinese summary of mentalism, which then points the
moral that we also do not understand that what we see in
wakefulness does not exist externally but only as a mental image.
Nevertheless the truth that each man's world is really his own
imagination externalized is as hard for him to believe whilst he is
awake as it is for a dreamer to believe that his dream world is
likewise his own imagination externalized.

Consciousness possesses the mysterious capacity to assume
any form of any size. We can construct a mental image of an

aeroplane, a cat, a pin-head, a mountain or a man with equal ease. Not only is this true but it can extend in every direction without being compelled to suffer the limitations of distance. We can think of the room wherein we are seated as easily as of Australia, which may be fifteen thousand miles distant. Distance does not prevent any object from existing as an idea, either during wakefulness or during dream. We become aware of the sun, which is millions of miles distant, as easily as we become aware of our finger, which is but a single foot away. Our consciousness can contain as much indeed as the vast, varied and extensive universe contains on the same space-time level. If the world were really outside the mind that knows it, only a miracle could ever have brought it inside.

The fifth point about the two states concerns the similarity of their sense-experiences. The five senses operate during dream just as they operate during wakefulness. We have eyes, ears, nose, tongue and skin in the dream world. We can smell the attractive fragrance of dream flowers, hear the musical tolling of dream bells, feel the painful sharpness of a dream sword, speak endearing words to a dream friend and taste the appetizing sweetness of a dream drink. And all these objects are experienced through the senses although we discover after we awake that both the sense-objects and the senses themselves were only thoughts.

When we consider that the golden sun and the silver stars shine in the dream sky overhead as they shine in the wakeful sky, that the dream ocean heaves its blue waters in billowing waves and that the dream forests are as cool and dark as the wakeful ones too, that we weep with dream pain and laugh with dream joy; we have to admit that the two worlds share our sensations to a startling extent. There is a dream-duplicate of everything that can be seen in space or experienced in time when awake, even though the resemblance is rarely perfect.

When the mind looks inward and hunts after novel fancies for its night life, it finds every desire vivid with actuality, every image palpable, touchable and visible, every sound hearable and every odour smellable; it discovers thoughts that can be handled verily as though they were solid things. And how awesome is the spectacle of dream-senses held captive by their own pageant of images of horror and fear in a nightmare.

The correctness of the analysis of sensation and perception which was made in the first volume of this work, an analysis whose conclusions placed the thought of the thing as prior to and substitutive of any material thing itself, can now be confirmed by a reference to dream. For in wakefulness we have the privilege of standing outside the dream situation and therefore of comprehending its inner working from a superior vantage-point. During dream we receive sensations from external objects and become aware of them as perceptions. *Yet these perceptions arise without the presence of any material thing.* The thought then appears to us as though it were the experienced material thing. But upon awakening we find that the thing was only a thought.

Thus the assertion which seemed so incredible when it was first heard becomes quite plausible when we see its working illustrated by dream sensations. The wakeful and dream experiences are two different standpoints wherefrom one and the same mind views its projected images as if they were external to itself. Only—in the first case they are its own refashioned echoes of the World-Mind thinking in it whereas in the second case they are entirely its own original productions.

The sixth point in our survey concerns the stuff of which both worlds are made. In dream we can carve solid marble into a statue. We firmly believe at the time in the existence of a dream-created statue as we firmly believe in a wakefully-made one. But our dream substance is purely mental. The matter of our dream statue exists only in our faith in it. The moral is that what imagination dynamized by intense faith impresses upon our consciousness we accept for the time being as completely substantial.

Nature thus provides in dream a valuable lesson to instruct us how objects can exist only as ideas and yet seem to be made of matter. She warns us that just as the dreaming man never questions the materiality of his dream images, never realizes that they have no external physical counterpart, never doubts that the heat he feels and the cold he shivers with are nothing less than thoughts, so we too are liable to fall into the same error of never questioning the materiality of our waking images. We naturally find quite incredible the mentalist statement that the chair on which we sit down is essentially and ultimately of the same stuff as our own minds, even though the science of physics has emphatically instructed us how illusory is the common belief in the substantiality of matter. Metaphysics may come along and successfully argue us out of this belief but still we remain uncomfortably uncertain about the point in the background of our feelings, however much our reason may yield its reluctant assent. Hence Nature is benevolently ready to help us by providing a practical illustration in every dream to show how such an apparent impossibility does actually and frequently happen within every man's personal experience.

We have here an important lesson for the materialistic critics who would make wooden sticks and heavy stones the criterion of reality. The materialist can never offer as invulnerable an explanation as the mentalist of such psychological situations as dreams where things are actually felt and seen as substantial although not physically present. Dream matter is indeed precisely like waking matter in this specific point, only the latter is longer lived. But we can never see or experience any matter at any time. We see or experience particular objects only. We think they are made of matter because it seems to be extended in space and to offer resistance to touch. But that spatiality and resistance can be nothing more than manufactured ideas is shown by dream experience.

If you believe in the reality of matter, you have consequently to believe in the absolutely fixed character of space and time, for matter is extended in the one and changes in the other. But many occurrences in dream experience reveal that space and time are found to possess no fixed existence of their own and to be entirely mental; it follows that matter, which can appear only under the conditions provided by space and time, must also have no fixed existence and be entirely mental. Materialism, however, makes matter an absolutely fixed entity. If it is really not, then it is no longer matter. But mind answers perfectly to this description. Therefore matter is really mind.

We know beyond a shadow of doubt that it is the mind itself which operates in this way during dream. We cannot say of the dreamer that two entities are really present; his mind and some substances outside it. Hence although this twofoldness apparently exists it must be properly understood which means it must be understood as being nothing more than an idea. If it is possible for mind to be bifurcated in this way during dream then it is surely possible for it to be bifurcated during wakefulness. This is what actually happens; man's field of experience is then also bifurcated into outside things and inside imaginations, the chief difference being that the contrast between external and internal ideas is so much more forceful during wakefulness.

Why does such a difference occur? It has already been explained that the process of falling asleep is a centripetal process of drawing inwards, when our mind naturally drops its externalizing, spatializing and form-making tendency a process which culminates at its farthest end in deep slumber. When however we begin to awake, our mind goes into reverse gear and again begins to externalize its world-pictures as if they were really outside. Dreaming is a middle stage where the mental pictures are not so sharply-focussed by the mind, not so vivid and real-seeming as in waking. With the wider opening of the aperture of consciousness in wakefulness, consciousness then attains its fullest point of projection and its utmost degree of intensity. From this enlightening comparison we may gather that the clear compelling substantiality of our world depends upon the sharpness and the concentrativeness with which we focus it. Therefore this substantiality is in the mind, not in the world. Matter is only a concept.

Nevertheless this difference between the two states is powerful enough to mesmerize man into the belief that it is one of kind and not of degree and that the twofoldness pertains to substance and not to appearance. Consequently he deludes himself that the wakeful world is factually material and only the dream world is mental. The dreamer believes his consciousness to be extroverted but after he breaks through the charmed circle of his private world and awakes, he learns that his belief was a misunderstanding and that his consciousness was actually operating in the very reverse direction for it was introverted. But if the dream scene is discovered to be an internal imagination of the dreamer after he awakens and yet it was an external actuality to him at the time, does this not show how easy it is for consciousness to misunderstand its own experience?

Now quite clearly there is an occult power at work during the dream state which magically turns thoughts into things and ideas into forms for the perceiving mind. But if the mind can create its own dream world of cities or farms, and also people them with its own living, moving and talking creatures, why should it not be able to create its own wakeful world too? When we remember all the variegated experiences which mind invents for us during dream, we should ask ourself why it should not be possible for it to invent the universal wakeful experience for us also.

Were we franker with ourselves we might honestly call this kind of dream experience, this instantaneous creation of several living and moving people out of a single person, this unexpected overhearing of long conversations in the silent void, a revelation of the magical power of the mind. But if to perceive our own images is to perceive them as external things; if we can evoke a whole new world and people it too; if we can be so mesmerized by our own thoughts as to live entirely within them during dream; if, in short, an entire world-experience can be imposed on himself by a man's own mind, how much more should it be possible for an entire world-experience to be imposed upon him by this same wizard-like mind working in collaboration with the immensely more powerful cosmic mind during wakefulness? The World-Mind does indeed present a universe of external forms and visible figures during the wakeful state of its progeny, just as the latter present to themselves their own private universes of external forms and visible figures during dream. But whereas the World-Mind remains fully aware of the mentalistic character of its construction its human participants deceive themselves into assigning a materialistic character to their experience, just as their senses trick them into seeing the sun move right across the sky. The second error can only be rectified by reason whilst the first can only be rectified by a combination of reason and mystic experience.

To the reflective mind, dream is a phenomenon which would be *inexplicably* miraculous were the miserable doctrine of materialism the final truth. To recognize what the universe really is is to recognize what we ourselves are; and that is to attain true being. Such recognition can come only in stages however and the first stage is to get rid of our anti-mentalist bias and free ourselves from our obsession with the materialist explanation of visible and touchable things.

When we understand through our acceptance of the doctrine of mentalism that the power which magically evokes this mysterious dream world for us is part of the same power as that which evokes the familiar wakeful world, we begin to comprehend something of the extraordinary possibilities of mind. In the exposition of karma in *The Hidden Teaching Beyond Yoga*, the creative influence of thought upon environment was briefly mentioned. Here it may be added that whereas the mental creations of the dreaming self are immediately objectified before it, those of the waking self operate under a different time-series and necessarily take longer—oftentimes unto a new reincarnation—before they can be objectified in its experience. But that we partially build our surroundings and circumstances by our thoughts remains a practical working truth.

Let it not be believed, however, that the reduction of world phenomena to the status of mental phenomena turns them into mere illusions, thin ghosts or even non-existent things, as some logic-entrapped metaphysicians, many Indian mystics and most Western uninstructed critics of mentalism believe. The Indian mind has always been particularly prone to belief in such an exaggeration, which has been well-voiced in English literature by George Borrow* an author who was famous a century ago, in these words: " 'Would I had never been born!' I said to myself; and a thought would occasionally intrude. But was I ever born? Is not all that I see a lie—a deceitful phantom? Is there a world, and earth, and sky? . . ."

The question here involved is essentially one concerning the meaning of reality. The critic who enters an objection that mentalism makes the world seem icily unreal enters what is absurd to anyone like the mentalist who knows that it enjoys at least as much reality as the act of thinking which produces it. We have to find a better term than "unreal". The world's real nature is as though covered by a veil and ordinarily hidden from us. But that does not render it non-existent, null, void and a sham, which is one of the unfortunate suggestions that the word "unreal" brings to those who have not analysed it—which means ninety-nine persons out of a hundred. We must ask them to think what they mean when they assert that the world is real whereas dreams are unreal. To attend to the meaning of this word is to take a first step toward

---

* Borrow, as is well known, was admitted by the Gipsies into their warmest friendship, was even treated as one of themselves and shared their traditional secrets. The sentence quoted is particularly interesting because the present writer's researches convinced him that the Gipsies originated in the Garhwal section of the Himalayan foothills. The Gipsies are ethnologically and culturally of Indian origin. The chief of a European Gipsy tribe once privately revealed to the writer that a predecessor, when lying on a death-bed, initiated him into a secret invocation of the "All-Mind" and then into its corollary, the doctrine of mentalism as expressed in the usual Indian form which asserts earthly life to be but a dream. This tribal chief was also taught at the same death-bed initiation that because mind was creative, a thorough realization and unremitting application of this doctrine in a particular way was the secret of successfully developing occult powers.

profounder thought about what is ultimate in life. For although it has been admitted that wakefulness has superior claims upon us in various ways, nevertheless neither the world of waking nor that of dreaming experience can claim to be the ultimately real world since each is relative to the particular space-timed way in which the mind functions at that particular level. Each is but a *state* of the mind. Each reveals the conscious being as being held captive by its creations. No dreamer ever believes himself to be deceived in his perception of things or people during sleep, whatever opinion he forms of them after he has awakened.

Here indeed is something to think about, that the life which he always accepts as real at one time should be rejected by a man as illusory as soon as he can alter his standpoint. The sense of reality is admittedly at its strongest during wakefulness but nevertheless it is strong enough during dream to make us frightened when we suddenly meet a wild beast and joyous when we meet a beloved person. Neither in the waking world nor the dream world does it desert us. This feeling must evidently come in both cases from the same source. What is this source? We may answer this question by asking ourselves another. What is present in both waking and dream as their essential "stuff"? We know now that this is mind. Consequently the feeling which makes all experience seem real arises from the fact that something real is certainly present within it and that presence is none other than mind. And such is its paradoxical working that although it presents only its own thoughts during dream these assume at the time the appearance of real objects and real persons remaining outside of and apparently different from itself, whereas those it has known during the waking state are supposed no longer real when they re-appear in dreams for they are then imagined ones, that is, thoughts!

The hidden teaching says however that what gives both dreaming and waking experiences their validity is one and the same thing. One and the same mind must be working through both these phases and because they are transient and relative to each other this mind-in-itself is by comparison permanent and absolute and consequently the real essence of these states. Such an essence constitutes their hidden reality.

If we look upon the world as real in its own right, as being a self-sufficient material construction and nothing more, then we have fallen into a pit of illusion. If however we perceive that the world as a mental construction is real only because the principle of mind manifests in it, we perceive aright.

Thus the experience of dream unfolds for us a piquant illustration of one of the higher tenets of advanced mentalism. It provides us with mentally-constructed shows whose scenes are but Appearance and whose background as mind is Reality. If we can purge ourselves of materialistic preconceptions and look at wakeful experience from the same detached impersonal standpoint we must realize that it too offers us mentally-made shows whose scenes are also Appearance and whose background is also Reality.

The seventh and last point in these studies is a simple one. Whilst the course of a dream runs smoothly and concerns pleasant things only we usually remain asleep but when it carries us into something dreadful like a nightmare the shock or fear thus evoked awakens us more quickly. It is so with wakeful life, too. During times of peace, pleasure and plenty we are content to drift enjoyably along the surface of events and to let others worry their heads over life's meaning. But the melancholy loss of a beloved one, the painful parting from possessions, the personal sight or experience of brutal violence or the agonizing tragedy of war's unforgettable horrors shocks us into an abrupt awakening. Then only does the question of life's significance receive any adequate attention. When the pressure of sorrow is flaccid, we are bewitched by the mere appearances of things but when it becomes sharp we seek some relief in religion, mysticism or philosophy.

When we awaken from dream life we awaken into what is at best but a continuation of the same self-centred tale of ephemeral joys and passing sorrows. Both kinds of experience in this sense exist in the same dimension. But if we could engage ourself in the adventure of awakening out of wakeful life itself, we would if successful pass from Appearance to Reality and thus enter an entirely new, immeasurably higher and gloriously superior dimension. It is the business of philosophy to tell us about the possibilities of such an adventure and to guide our stumbling feet towards its sublime goal.

5

The Metaphysics of Sleep

WE have not yet exhausted the full metaphysical significance of sleep as a mental state. For ordinary human existence is a threefold affair and its consciousness an intermittent thing. A man may be stunned into unconsciousness by a sudden blow or an accidental fall. Psychologically he then enters the same state as that which he enters through the working of Nature in sleep or swoon. Not only does mind express itself through the waking and dreaming states, but also in a third state wherein sleep attains its profoundest intensity and when consciousness completely vanishes. This condition is what we must study next.

Let us for the sake of literary convenience henceforth call this state of deep dreamless slumber by the simple term "sleep". Let this differentiate it in the reader's mind from the other two aspects of life: dream and wakefulness.

It is commonly believed that the profound torpor of mind, the utter inactivity of muscles and the complete stillness of the five senses which characterize sleep have no other meaning than that of a halt called by Nature to the day's activities for the rebuilding of wasted tissues, no higher meaning than the recuperation of spent energy and the felicitous rest of tired mental faculties. That the study of this state, no less than dream, could be a gateway to the increase of worth-while knowledge, is seldom known. That the most characteristic feature of deep sleep—which is the complete lethargy into which consciousness falls—proffers a golden seam to questing minds will be a strange and an unfamiliar notion to us.

But metaphysics, we have elsewhere said, must be based on the facts of experience. There are three main phases of human experience—the waking, dreaming and sleeping phases. Experience may change its character with these changing states but it remains mental experience throughout. A man plunged in sound slumber is as much an expression of human existence as a man plunged in waking activities; therefore his experience is only to be neglected at the peril of losing the fullness of truth.

It may seem strange to describe as a sphere of experience this vacuum-like state of the mind, this utter void of consciousness. But is it really so? We seem to lose consciousness during sleep yet we remember the fact of having slept. It is not possible to remember anything unless we have previously known it. Therefore something in us must have known that we were asleep. This however is consciousness in another form. Sleep is something which enters and leaves human existence. How could we even remember that we had slept at all unless some subterranean awareness of the fact existed at the time? If we declare that we were aware of nothing during sleep, something in us must have paradoxically been aware of this negative awareness or we could never have connected sleep with waking and thus could never have known that we had slept at all!

Were sleep really an absence of all kinds of consciousness how could we afterwards remember its refreshing pleasantness and speak of it with satisfaction? Some kind of consciousness must have been present to provide us later with the idea of this pleasantness. Again, how could we recollect every morning the events of yesterday and link them in orderly sequence with those of today unless the mind were still somehow present during the sleeping break?

That the sleeping state does not really annihilate everything in the mind is revealed by the fact that the sense of individual identity, the entire cocoon of thoughts, desires and characteristics which makes up the personality, emerges afresh with each morning resurrection of self-awareness from sleep. Were there not some kind of continuity of selfhood within the mind, we might fall asleep thinking we were one man and wake up thinking we were another man. We cannot therefore rightly set up the waking and dream consciousness as exhausting the continuity of the mind's existence. It is clear that unconsciousness is really a mis-description of its most mysterious phase.

What is it that really ceases to function during sleep? It is not the mind itself but only a particular *form* of its functioning. Those who doubt or deny this possibility should study the curious medical annals reporting cases of somnambulism. Here the sleep-walker actually sees without using his eyes. This has been definitely proved because the pupils of his eyes have been found quite insensitive to light. He may move safely through dangerous places or pit-falls, walk in a perfectly straight line alongside the parapet of a roof whence he might easily fall to the ground floor of a house but doesn't, or work at some task intelligently and accurately without being awake. Somnambulists indeed show a higher degree of mental faculty when asleep than they ordinarily possess when awake; their reasoning power, imaginativeness, memory, will and bodily control are markedly heightened.

Now it is noteworthy that whereas both the dreaming and the waking man can recollect previous experiences, the somnambulist can remember nothing of what has passed during the night. At whatever point in his sleep he may be awakened, he will never remember what occurred to him a minute earlier. Whereas in wakefulness and even in dream a man is aware of his actions and the five senses function consciously, the sleep-walker does not know what he is doing and has no sense-reports. This is indeed the unique characteristic of somnambulism. Unaware himself of what is happening, some intelligence is nevertheless directing perfectly the movements of his body and keeping it under proper control. Without personal knowledge of his whereabouts and without taking the slightest thought for his own well-being, he yet returns safely to bed from his oft-times dangerous adventures.

Is this not sufficiently startling? What is its significance for us? If it means anything at all, it means first, that mind can operate in two phases, the one conscious and apparently normal, the other unconscious and seemingly abnormal; second, that we would be more accurate to designate the mind as uncommunicative rather than as unconscious during sleep; third, that mind does not exhaust its possibilities with the single phase of consciousness which we know as a continuous and laborious activity of thinking; and fourth, that the innermost layer of the mind does not depend on the five physical senses for its awareness. It means, in short, that as yet we have hardly begun to understand the tremendous mystery that hides in our own mind. Quite certainly we have here a condition wherein some kind of consciousness must exist. Yet it is not the kind we know of during wakefulness or dream.

History even records that scientific, mathematical, literary, personal and philosophical problems have all yielded to the wizardry of the dreaming or sleeping mind. There is no limit to the type of problem which may be solved in this way. The most profound inspirations, the most sparkling solutions and the sagest intuitions about a course of conduct to be adopted in a difficult or perplexing situation, have emerged from sleep.

How often have those who belong to the scribbling brotherhood woken up one morning with strange thoughts running exultantly through their heads and got out of bed to reproduce their ideas hastily on paper? When we remember that numerous lines of a whole poem, *Abou Ben Adhem,* worked themselves out in the sleeping mind of the poet Coleridge; that problems which agitated many a man before falling asleep were solved immediately and spontaneously on waking again the following morning, although they had been dismissed as insoluble; and that names which were forgotten and not findable were recovered after sleep, the only and obvious conclusion is that in some mysterious manner the mind carries on a subterranean activity during the night which enables it to present a finished result to consciousness on the following day. It is this deeper layer of mind beneath the threshold of conscious thinking which is the secret source of all those glorious artistic inspirations, all those recaptured missing links of knowledge and all those intuitive decisions which triumph over perplexing situations. "God giveth truth to his beloved in sleep," sang the Biblical psalmist. To say, therefore, in the face of proven mental activity during the sleep state that it is a lapse into total unconsciousness, is to take only the surface value of experience and to ignore all that lies beneath it.

What we have now to grasp is that there exists a part of the mind which seems unconscious to us but which really has an extraordinary and marvellous consciousness of its own. There is indeed a secondary consciousness which underlies our ordinary and familiar consciousness. A sound metaphysic therefore cannot limit the use of the term "mind" only to its particular thinking phase of "consciousness" alone. Mind is more than consciousness, as we know it. We have to recognize and admit that two types of awareness are possible; one is the everyday kind with which we are all familiar but the other is recondite, mysterious and utterly unfamiliar. This unfamiliarity ought not to be allowed to let us fall into the superficial and materialistic error of setting up the first kind as being the only kind that exists—which is what the unphilosophical majority does.

A horse which is racing along at a speed for which a camera shutter has not been prepared to cope with cannot be successfully photographed. The resultant picture will be either a featureless blur or a foggy blank. The inability of our familiar ordinary consciousness to take in the mind's state during deep sleep is like the inability of the camera to take a picture of the galloping horse.

It is well known that the vibrations of light, for instance, extend into wide ranges where the phenomena they produce entirely elude our sight. Quite evidently, consciousness too is active in ways which elude the limited range of our *thinking* intellect. The feats of open-eyed somnambulists, the inspirations and intuitions of shut-eyed slumberers reveal that there is a level where mental vibration is so rapid that the ordinary thinking faculties cease to function altogether. Here the mind works spontaneously in a quite incomprehensible way, *but it works*. Thinking would indeed be a prisoning limitation upon it. It does not need to think in the discursive and logical sense in which we understand the term.

On this analogy of different ranges of light-vibration we may also understand why sleep-born intuitions can instantaneously bridge the broad gap between data and conclusion, whereas the thinking faculty has to plod the laborious road of a long series of reasonings to arrive at the same conclusion. For such an intuition is the product of mind when it is working within a vibration-range beyond what is ordinarily experienced during dream or wakefulness. In short, the mind during sleep has a kind of consciousness of its own, although because it does not move from one idea to another it is not intellectual consciousness. Therefore we must try next to learn something more about consciousness. Moreover, if, as mentalism has told us, the world is an appearance in consciousness, it is quite necessary to ask: What is consciousness?

From the Conscious to the Unconscious.

What is it in us that is conscious of seeing, of hearing and of thinking? Is it the brain? Pah!—a lump of mere flesh not much different from what we can buy in any butcher's shop. The notion that consciousness is an emanation kindled in the cells of the cerebral cortex in the brain is a mistaken one. Out of this superficial notion are born most of our metaphysical illusions. Unfortunately men annex their own conflicting ideas to these terms, so a pathway must first be cleared by defining the use which will be made of them here.

By *brain* is meant that touchable and seeable portion of the human body canopied by the bony skull and filled with winding convolutions of grey and white substance, which anatomists handle in the dissecting room. By *consciousness* is meant the sum total of the changing series of sense-impressions, perceptions, thoughts, feelings, images, intuitions, ideas and memories which we know directly as our own and which cannot be got at by any dissection with surgical knife. Strictly speaking, however, all attempts to define consciousness travel in a circle because it is itself presupposed in every definition. What we can most effectively say is that it is "a knowing".

The brain quite clearly is to some extent a mechanism. Consciousness equally clearly is in no sense a mechanism. Those who equate the two perform a veritable miracle unheard of in the annals of Nature. For no machine can operate in the wonderful way that the higher mental processes, such as reasoning, remembering, inferring, imagining, judging and choosing, operate.

The fantastic and comfortless guess of materialism that consciousness is only a secretion of the brain does not and cannot explain how consciousness is at all possible. Only the surface-thinker can ever believe that matter produces it, for only he fails to see that it is already present among the very facts upon which he starts to build a plausible argument in which it shall presently issue forth as the supposed creation of matter. But when his clouded wits are clarified, he will realize that he can no more start without the presence of consciousness amongst his initial facts than he can start to walk without using his legs.

Nobody can observe consciousness in the same way that he can observe anything else. For all his observations of everything else will themselves require the presence of consciousness. He who, like the "behaviourist" psychologist and the materialist scientist, dwells in metaphysical twilight and spends his time observing certain contents of consciousness only and then triumphantly exclaims that he cannot find consciousness anywhere and that therefore as an independent thing it is non-existent, is as foolish as the woman who searches everywhere for a necklace which she is already wearing on her own body. His observations are comical rather than convincing.

The rational doctrine of mentalism alone answers in a satisfactory manner the question: How is consciousness possible? For it explains that consciousness is itself only a phase of an immaterial principle, mind; that we begin at the wrong end when we believe that it is a function of the brain; and that we begin at the right end when we discover that it is the light of the brain. Mind is analogically like light, for both are unique and have a privileged position in the scheme of things. Light makes everything else visible but itself remains paradoxically invisible. What we take to be a beam of light, for instance, is an illusion of the senses. It is really a beam of dust particles. Light reveals the presence of a high mountain but not its own presence. It enables us to see a roomful of different forms but is itself quite unseeable because it has no form at all. So, too, mind makes us conscious of everything else but not of itself. We do not detect it beneath our changing experiences because it is itself without change.

We behold all things in mind as in a mirror. But being beyond the reach of our senses, we observe the images and fail to observe the mirror which reflects them. Consequently we mistakenly assign reality only to the things and unreality to the mind itself. Nobody who has sufficient subtlety of intelligence to understand what mind really is, how ideas are formed and how we become aware of the external world can ever become a materialist. For he will comprehend that his experience of the world is, when traced to its ultimate origin, rooted as an idea in consciousness, and that the prior existence of mind alone makes consciousness of the body-idea possible.

To believe consciousness to be nothing apart from the bodily brain merely because it is not within the limited range of physical sense-detection, and to make it the parochial inhabitant of a little place in a little head, is to fail to perceive that by the very law of its being it must fall outside such a range. This mistake sets up problems which need never exist and also binds men to a naive materialism from which they cannot depart until sufficient discrimination, attained by metaphysical reflection, mystical experience or divine grace, enables them to climb the steps leading upwards to truth. A wiser age, whose area of intellectual awareness will be less self-limited, will cease trying the impossible, cease trying to account for the existence of a unique principle like mind, of which ordinary consciousness is but a phase, in terms of anything except itself.

Consciousness being what it is only those can doubt its immaterial existence who cannot reflect deeply enough within themselves. For both that which doubts it and that which affirms it is the immaterial principle itself. Even before the sceptic, who is supposed to respect the primacy of reason but doesn't, can utter a word or think a thought in opposition to its existence, it must be there to make these acts possible! Mentalism, of course, carries these ideas even farther. For when the sceptic sees, hears, tastes, touches or smells a thing, then and then only does he pronounce it to exist. But these acts of his sensing, when traced both to their first and farthest points, are discovered to be mental acts. His acceptance of the thing's existence rests entirely on the appeal to his own mental existence, for no one can get outside it. Let him try to jump outside his consciousness and no matter where he lands he will nevertheless always still be in it! It is the one thing he cannot call into question.

Nobody can ever form a notion of anything that lies beyond it. Nobody can arrive at the slightest comprehension of any object unless and until it enters his thinking, that is unless it is known as an idea. Yet when we reduce things to their final terms as mental constructions, the result seems so alien to our sense of what Nature is that few will grant it! Nothing is so self-evident as the primacy and reality of consciousness, yet unfortunately nothing carries less conviction when first propounded! But we cannot legitimately doubt its existence whatever else we may doubt. We may fall into illusions about it but even illusions depend upon our being aware of them. Hence, when we rise to the full stature of our reason, we must finally admit that consciousness is the one thing of whose reality we are most certain and of whose existence we are least doubtful.

Such is the quaint and melancholy paradox of man's existence! That which he declares to be wholly beyond his understanding is itself the whole foundation of that understanding. For it is solely by means of immaterial consciousness that he professes to be unable to understand consciousness! Could he but attend properly to the point, he would see that because of the experience of awareness itself, because of the experience of memory, because of the capacity for abstract metaphysical reflection, because of his own artistic creativeness and because of the ability to discover universal laws, he stands really in the presence of a super-physical principle.

The scientist of today has successfully investigated a myriad of things from the nature of vaporous clouds to the origin of granite mountains, but he has not successfully investigated the mystery of *the beginnings* of his own consciousness. This is because he can start his study of its origin only *after* his own consciousness has already originated and not before. It is then too late to solve the problem of such origin. Whatever he may think or do about it already carries the inescapable pre-supposition of consciousness within it and has to be thought or done by its light. He cannot even directly examine his consciousness because he cannot make it an object of his own awareness, just as no man can make his own face an object of direct awareness but has to see it indirectly in a mirror. The scientist too can look in the mirror of thoughts, because it is their accumulation that makes up his wakeful consciousness, but this is only an indirect process for the consciousness of *thoughts* is not the consciousness of *pure thought* itself. He cannot detect the latter's existence apart from and without the ideas and images which it generates. And it is this which is here called "mind".

Nobody can say what shape consciousness has, nor what colour it possesses nor what odour it gives forth nor what sound it yields. An image does not exist in consciousness as a blue carpet exists in a large room, for instance. For the carpet is in definite space-relations of size and position to the room, whereas the principle of consciousness itself cannot be seen and hence cannot enter into any such relation. In short, it is something which the senses cannot grasp and which is therefore quite non-material. Yet we know by our experience that it *is*.

The great error of all materialism, whether it be that of the naive populace, of unmetaphysical science or of unmystical religion, is to confuse mind with consciousness. For the consequence of treating them as convertible terms and failing to make a careful distinction between them is that they have then to make mind a result of material activities and not prior to them. Thus mentalism not only explains the arisal of all materialistic doctrines but also absorbs them.

Consciousness of course would be a meaningless term for ordinary humans unless there were thoughts and images of which to be conscious. Not for a single moment does consciousness remain unoccupied. It must ordinarily feed on something. But we need not make the common mistake of believing that mental life completely exhausts itself in a particular form of conscious life, completely vanishes when there are no thoughts and no images. For this kind of consciousness is only a *state* of mind and like all states necessarily contains the possibility of evanescence. A break in consciousness such as sleep is a significant hint of the existence of some deeper principle that underlies it. It must therefore not be confused with this principle, which is pure mind itself.

A useful analogy to help us understand this situation—but like most analogies one which must not be driven too far—is that of the cinema picture. In a theatre the white screen is itself unseen when wholly covered by the contrasting lights and shadows of the picture, for the latter holds our entire attention. Similarly the mental world-picture holds our entire attention during the wakeful state and here its consciousness corresponds to the cinema picture. What does the invisible screen itself represent? It is that which is present in us during deep dreamless slumber, that out of which both dreaming and waking consciousness itself arises, that which is the essence or stuff of all conscious thoughts, images and ideas; it is the underlying principle of mind. The materialists however always mistake the waking consciousness itself for the screen. Mental processes are closely connected with physical processes in the brain and it is out of this connection that this materialistic illusion arises.

Mind is the general raw material of all our particular thoughts. All thoughts are virtual in mind but actual in consciousness. All conscious thinking makes a tacit reference to what is beyond consciousness. We know the ever-present mind only through the thoughts which are its products and through the consciousness which it thrusts across its own seeming dark void.

When we stand on the threshold of mind it seems, because it hides behind its partially parallel working with the brain, as unknown and as impenetrable as a black abysmal fog. Are we therefore to think that we stand before a virtual void? The answer is that we may know it is present by the effect it produces, by its manifested result and by its undeniable activity. The first effect is self-consciousness, the first result is world-awareness and the first activity is thinking. These three alone suffice to show it cannot be an utter nothingness. How can that through which we are able to know the existence of ourselves, of others and of the world not exist itself? Indeed, in Fichte's phrase, "It is everything and it is nothing." It is because mind is prior to the space-timed personal consciousness that it remains unknown.

We are not aware of the mechanically-produced radio-transmitted electrical waves which may exist at the moment in a room wherein we happen to be. A twirl on a radio set will catch and convert these waves into sounds of melodious music. The waves are there, however, even when the room is silent, and being there they are real. The fact that our eyes, ears and fingers cannot register them, that their existence is not apparent to us, does not diminish their reality. In the same way, mind as the essence of consciousness truly exists, truly possesses reality, but eludes the grasp of both thinking and sense-perception. If we like to talk in degrees of reality, then it must even be more real than our particular form of space-time consciousness because the latter itself rises and sets in it. Mind is therefore unique and there is nothing else that we know to compare with it in all existence.

Consider next the generally unnoticed and lazily unappreciated significances of memory. Blinded by familiarity as we are, we do not understand its immense metaphysical importance, its sublime anti-materialistic import. When we reflect deeply on this wonderful faculty we may begin to understand that it tells us of our immortality. For it can exist only because the mind's own existence is continuous and unbroken.

What are memories? They are mental images of the past, recovered thought-forms, pictures which repeat themselves in consciousness. Whence do they come? They can come only out of ourself. Obviously there must be something within us which serves as a medium for the joining together of past ideas to present ones. There must be a subtle element linking them all together, holding them and keeping them for us as in a kind of storehouse. Otherwise they would be so cut off from each other that we could never recall the vanished thoughts at all. The mere fact that we can remember events of the past, the very act of recognizing something that we have seen before indicates the presence of a connecting link between present conscious states and those of the past.

Now what else could that link be but the mind itself? And as the past states may have been lost to consciousness for several years, there must exist a layer of this complex mind which is hidden deep beneath common consciousness. The mere fact that images and ideas can be revived out of apparent annihilation shows that they are somehow preserved in this layer. It shows also that the mysterious blankness of the mind is not the same as its non-being. It reveals that we do not lose contact with the past because there is this permanent element in us. And it has already been noted that the remembrance of our own personal identity after awakening from deep sleep and the subsequent recognition of familiar people and places cannot be possible unless the mind exists even beyond the sphere of what, *viewed from our side*, seem to be its conscious states. Such an existence must necessarily be a secret one.

We may begin to understand the mind therefore only when we begin to set up a psychological division within it. Its roots are hidden beyond our consciousness but its fruits are visible in consciousness. It would be the greatest error as the greatest ignorance to ascribe impotence here merely because *we* are not conscious of its workings.

The subterranean consciousness has paradoxically and misleadingly been called the unconscious. Every modern young undergraduate now knows that we possess an "unconscious mind"—thanks partly to the efforts of our Freudian friends. Actually it is that wider consciousness of which ordinary consciousness is only a part. We can hardly call that unconscious which contains in itself all the potentialities of consciousness. The fact is that the consciousness which mind possesses actually surpasses both the lower and higher limits of cerebral consciousness. For it is the inscrutable complex mind that projects this limited consciousness into wakefulness and withdraws it into sleep. Nevertheless let it not be thought that there are a pair of minds, the one conscious and the other unconscious. There exists but a single mind in us but viewed from our side it is conscious in a finite human way only. Our kind of consciousness is a *state*, not a separate and different kind of mind. Mind therefore is present even before the work of conscious thinking has begun. It is the inner unknown consciousness.

We are compelled to posit the presence of this deeper mind even when we are unable to enter into its mysterious processes. All explanations of man which omit it from their reckoning are not actual but merely verbal ones.

Thus the conclusion is that we may not rightly say that mind must only operate in the full glare of daylight. We may not rightly deny that it is active even when our consciousness does not accompany its activity. All world-experience must first pass through certain limited forms of space and time before it can reach the individual awareness of human beings at their present stage of evolution. Outside of those special forms they can necessarily know nothing. Why then should we lay down the rule that our particular space-time consciousness must necessarily and inevitably walk with all the operations of the mind? For in taking away such consciousness from the mind we do not take away its own existence.

It becomes obvious therefore that we must bifurcate the life of man. But we are not to deceive ourselves into thinking that the hidden one is any less real or less conscious than the manifested one. It is beyond the reach of human thinking but the fact of its existence is not beyond the conclusions of human thinking. And this is the best service which metaphysical thinking can render, to convince us that it *is*, to enable us to conceive that it must be, and to understand that it is the secret source of our surface life.

The Source of Intuition and Inspiration.

When anyone speaks of unconscious mind it should now be clear that the two terms contradict each other and that he really means uncommunicative mind! But is the subliminal region really so silent as never to enter into communication with us? Henri Poincare, famous French mathematician, neatly solved many a hard problem of his science by dropping and forgetting it altogether after he had consciously concentrated on it for a while. Later, when pre-occupied with other matters, the correct solution would suddenly flash into his mind. Who has not had a similar experience of being unable to remember a certain fact, then dropping the search after it until, during later moments of repose or reverie, of lazy listlessness or changed attention, the wanted fact unexpectedly emerged above the threshold of consciousness? What conscious effort could not do was successfully performed by the mysterious movements of the deeper layer of mind, the final result of its workings being then delivered to his knowledge.

Although the waking self is so ignorant of the workings of the deeper mind and the latter is not normally accessible to it, it does nevertheless often receive similar results in the form of a sudden intuition or a spontaneous inspiration.

Locke gave high but justified testimony when he declared that "the thoughts that come often unsought, and, as it were, drop into the mind, are commonly the most valuable of any we have". The intuition offers in a single emphatic flash that which the intellect may arrive at only as the last result of many long continued reflections and many different physical experiences. Where reason cannot think out the right solution of a perplexity, intuition can step triumphantly forward with an immediate presentation of it. Reasoning is self-conscious, active and inquisitive whereas intuition is spontaneous, receptive and passive. An intuition need have no logical connection with former thinking. Hence it may open up an entirely new horizon on that particular subject. This we may now easily understand because we have already granted the mind a power to be active in its own mysterious way, which enables it to dispense with thinking and yet send up its results to the surface consciousness.

It is interesting and instructive to note that intuition is at its soundest when it takes a negative rather than a positive direction. It speaks to us chiefly to forbid a certain course of proposed action, not to recommend one. Its voice is usually a warning one. This has been attested by two reliable witnesses who, with more than two thousand years between their lives, have made their highly important attestations in strikingly similar terms. These men were the Greek Socrates and the American Emerson.

We may begin to get a correct intuition about a certain matter but our emotions, prejudices or desires in connection with it may be so strong that they push themselves aggressively forward, over-whelm the nascent intuition and thus it quickly sinks into the background, ignored and forgotten. Only after the lapse of time can it reappear and show its wisdom to us again or only after we have followed the course indicated by personal feeling and suffered in consequence of our mistake do we remember remorse-fully the right leading which once came to us as quietly as a star at night. But with Socrates such a lesson was not needful. He possessed complete faith in the guidance of intuition, his daimon or divine monitor as he quite correctly called it. Consequently he never failed to obey it.

Most Athenian citizens who reached middle life customarily played a hand in the game of politics; indeed the game nearly obsessed them. Nevertheless, in obedience to his intuition, Socrates stood out almost alone in abstaining from a political career. How wise this guidance was, how much trouble it saved him from, was evidenced by the fate which overtook him later. For if as a philosopher or prophet his ideas were so obnoxious to his countrymen that they finally sentenced him to death, how much more obnoxious would they not have been in the far more tumultuous atmosphere of politics? The outspoken way in which he would have flayed the skin off hypocritical platitudes and high-sounding humbug would have quickly made a host of enemies for him. Had he disobeyed his intuition and entered politics, the consequence would surely have been a much earlier conflict with the authorities and probably a much earlier death.

Socrates' own description of the way in which his intuition worked, as given at the trial where he was condemned to death, possesses both a pathetic and a philosophic value. His memorable words are well worth repeating: "You have often heard me speak of an oracle or sign which comes to me. This sign I have had ever since I was a child. The sign is a voice which comes to me and always forbids me to do something which I am going to do. Hitherto the familiar oracle within me has constantly been in the habit of opposing me even about trifles, if I was going to make a slip or error about anything; and now, as you see, there has come upon me that which may be thought, and is generally believed to be, the last and worst evil. But the oracle made no sign of opposition, either as I was leaving my house and going out in the morning, or when I was going up into the court, or while I was speaking at anything which I was going to say; and yet I have often been stopped in the middle of a speech, but now in nothing I either said or did touching this matter has the oracle opposed me. What do I take to be the explanation of this? I will tell you. I regard this as a proof to me of what I am saying, for the customary sign would surely have opposed me had I been going to evil and not to good.''

Let us skip the centuries and match against this remarkable statement the equally lucid one of Emerson: "I do not pretend to any commandment or large revelation. But if at any time I form a plan, propose a journey or a course of conduct, I find, perhaps, a silent obstacle in my mind I cannot account for. Very well: I let it lie, thinking it may pass away; if it does not pass away I yield to it, obey it.''

An important point about intuition is that it does not arise deliberately but spontaneously, not voluntarily but involuntarily. It is an unexpected voice and usually comes just at the precise moment when it is really needed, not merely when it is asked for. Sometimes it comes to guide, sometimes to bid us renounce, sometimes to bid us take cheer, sometimes it brings a sudden alteration of outlook, opinion, judgment or decision.

There exists a type of intuition which is universally possessed by mankind. Only, it does not manifest itself in any extraordinary manner and it does not have to be sought after by any unusual method. It is the genuine faculty although it seldom occurs in a pure form but almost always in association with desires, emotions and egoisms which blur its outline. This is what is commonly called conscience, the inner voice. It is a distillation of many accumulated life-experiences and takes the form not only of moral conscience but also of critical judgment and artistic taste. All these are the effects of experience gained not only from the present earthly incarnation but also from many a former one. The experiences themselves are buried in the deeper layers of memory but they leave such intuitions as their legacies.

What is the mystery of poetic intuition or artistic inspiration but the mystery of the hidden activity of this deeper mind? All those themes and variations on themes which shape themselves by slow degrees or sudden flashes whilst a work proceeds, may be and often are purely intuitional. Some signs of inspiration are the heightened imaginativeness which comes into play, or the natural ease with which the work flows, or the abundant energy the artist brings to it, or the creative heat which burns within him, or the innate certitude which hovers around him at the time—if they are beyond the normal level of their possession. The artist, the poet or the inventor can bring such a work into imaginative being by a single lucid perception into which, it is most important to note, reasoning need not enter until afterwards and then only to elaborate, criticize or discipline it.

How genuine a thing is this inner guidance is shown by the way in which it alters the plan of an artistic production from the lines originally designed by conscious thinking and develops it into something contrary to the first intention, as well as by the way in which it often takes over the work and leads the artist himself along a road whose end he may be quite unable to foresee. It is also shown by the phenomenon of a production being shaped by fitful spurts out of many little fragments, which exist at first without order and without coherence. Here there is manifested a light and power which are not ordinarily the artist's own. Only when the work has attained a certain volume will the manner in which these anarchic fragments ought to be arranged, elaborated and connected, then appear. Until such a moment the effort will be like the manufacture of different pieces for an elusive mosaic pattern. Some poets, indeed, have confessed to receiving the last lines of their verses first!

All artists worthy of the name can use their technique only as a net, which they must raise and throw over the intuitions which fly suddenly out of the mysterious consciousness of the deeper mind into the familiar consciousness of everyday for a few divine moments and are gone.

The Fourth State of Consciousness.

We have travelled so far in these considerations that we may have forgotten that they arose originally out of our considerations of the sleep state. The forcible or even voluntary prolongation of wakefulness over several days without an interruption by sleep, would ordinarily lead to wild hallucinations and eerie visions in the untrained unprepared man but might lead to something illuminative in the advanced one. The failure of a subcortical brain-centre signals a return to the condition of sleep. It is not that the centre itself becomes fatigued. Its continuous activity merely measures the continuation of wakefulness and does not create it. Sleep arises when the Overself gathers all the forces of its projected personality together and brings them to rest in the heart-centre so that the individual image-making faculty also ceases to operate and sensations cease to be born. The world-image with all its variety consequently vanishes from its ken.

Incidentally could we but detach ourselves from a body-based standpoint which makes us the unconscious victims of materialist illusions, we would understand that here in sleep is an additional proof that world is mentally constructed. For when thinking arises, when consciousness functions, both the wakeful and dream worlds exist for us. Our thoughts take birth with the onset of wakefulness and die with the onset of sleep. For us the world's existence begins and ends with our thoughts too. If we see the world in dreams it is because the world being but a thought, our thoughts are still active. If we do not see the world in deep slumber it is because our thoughts are no longer active and the world, being but a thought, is consequently unable to exist for us. Thus the mind's activity in world-making is here displayed. The individual being thinks its five different kinds of sensations into existence and thus experiences an external waking or internal dreaming world; but when it ceases to generate thoughts it passes into the unconscious state of sleep, when there are no sensations and consequently no world for it.

And we need to be able to forget the world. There are hours when all sensations are a torment. Sleep is a natural want in all creatures. We well know the rest and refreshment, the strength and invigoration, which we derive from those nightly hours of retreat. Even the dumb animals hide in a corner when they are ill and then settle down to all-restorative sleep. When physical suffering reaches its worst climax, a wounded man will become quite unconscious, that is he will involuntarily enter the sleep condition as his last refuge.

Sleep also proffers man the chance of forgetting not only his bodily pains but also his mental hurts. Do we sufficiently realize the priceless quality of this strange gift from Nature's benevolent hands? The troubles of the daytime may be almost unbearable but we may be sure that the moment we fall into benign slumber they will vanish as though they never were. Are those sceptics right then who complain that Nature is *always* merciless, always "red in tooth and claw"?

There are many who regard their sleeping hours as enforced breaks in their busy waking ones and begrudge them accordingly. It is not too much to say that they regard natural sleep as being as much a loss of time as if they had been stunned by an accidental blow or anaesthetized by an administered drug. Such persons may hear, first with an intellectual shock and then with a sceptical sneer, the statement that sleep, through its recuperative effects, does not exist merely for the sake of making their wakeful life possible, but exists just as much for its own sake. Yet this is what the hidden teaching affirms and what it will now make clear. Sleep is primarily the consequence of the personality being temporarily reclaimed by its divine parent. Its first value lies in the spiritual restoration which is thus effected.

We always arise from its depths feeling refreshed and peaceful.

Its after-glow is a diffused well-being, a tranquil satisfaction. We receive a hint of the intense felicity of this state when we awaken out of it for then we feel a delightful world-released serenity. It is noteworthy that the discursive movement of the mind from thought to thought is always suspended during slumber. We must conclude therefore that these qualities belong to the very nature of the thought-free mind. So far as it leads to a benign refreshment, an immense soothing and a serene laying-aside of all carking cares, the condition of sleep is also given us by Nature to provide an object-lesson in the worth of release from the tyranny of our restless thoughts.

What happens when we enter into sleep is that we enter also into this mind which is the real origin of our consciousness. Both the thought of the body and the thought of the world which held our consciousness in such an iron grip are now removed.

Consider next the strange fact that when we bestow attention entirely on the book we are reading, we simultaneously withhold attention from the chair in which we are sitting. The consequence is that if our reading is perfectly concentrated, the chair ceases to exist for us. The unnoticed is in fact the unknown. This is a simple fact of everyday experience but it is ordinarily overlooked. Our earlier study of illusions has shown its great importance. We may now go still further. Throughout the day we focus attention upon the outside world and we are simultaneously aware of it, whereas during sleep we make no such effort at all and then the world disappears for us. There is something which confers reality—however temporarily—upon the world by the mere act of making us perceive it. That something is mind.

If the world is mentally-constructed and if it draws its reality from the mind itself, then because slumber is a state where all mental constructions vanish, where all objective experience dissolves and where all ideas drop out, it follows that the mind has here withdrawn more into its own natural self, its own pristine state.

We have already learnt that the mind is the principle in us which really sees, hears, tastes, touches and thinks; that these activities are only ways in which it reveals itself in wakeful and dream consciousness but nevertheless they are ways which do not exhaust its fullness. What we must endeavour to grasp is that this same mind is still present during sleep even though the other kinds of consciousness are not. The waking, dreaming and sleeping selves are not really three individual beings, separate by nature. When a particular one of them is expressed it hides the other two from us but this does not alter the fact that it is only one and the same mind expressing itself under three different sets of conditions. And only because it is always present, because there is no break in the continuity of the mind itself, do we naturally experience a sense of reality when awake or dreaming. How important and how precious therefore should it be to us!

We have indeed actually dipped deeper, as it were, into the basis of its being when we have slipped into slumber. We have returned nearer to its innermost reality. Thus, from this metaphysical standpoint, the third state of mind is the most valuable of all but from the practical prosaic standpoint, the least valuable of all. For alas! what is the use of being a millionaire if one is ignorant of the fact at the time? Sleep frees us from all the fears and pains which shadow life but it also frees us from all the hopes and joys which brighten it. This is because man then ceases to limit himself solely to the consciousness of the flesh. But he also ceases to possess the consciousness of anything at all. Quite clearly such consciousness cannot be an ultimately satisfying condition. Millions of men plunge into such slumber nightly but, philosophically, are no wiser next day, when moreover they lose the peace thus gained and have perforce to pick up their anxieties anew.

Is sleep really the ultimate state open to humanity? For its transitory character makes us look elsewhere. Here the higher teaching steps in and explains that Nature has indeed given man this move-up closer to the reality of mind, but because he has not earned the right to it by his own effort, she soon takes it away from him again. For he has entered sleep carrying with him the deep mental seed-impressions of earthly desires, the strong emotional tendencies which bind him to physical life and the powerful egoistic chains which cannot co-exist with the freedom and integrity of the mind's own pure nature. Because he has not earned the right to a release from this bondage by his own personal effort, Nature does not allow him to enjoy the consciousness of his thought-free liberation during his sleep but only as a soothing afterglow during the few moments after his awakening. In a sense it might be said that she mocks him by making it always a past experience and silently telling him that if he wants to make it a present one he must go forth and earn it.

Is this not a hint to man that were his thinking to be *deliberately* brought down to its lowest ebb, thus making his mental state during wakefulness as similar as possible to what it is during sleep, *and were this to be achieved with complete intellectual understanding of all that his enterprise involves,* he would *consciously* experience this same happy calm condition? Such indeed is the rationale underlying some of the higher yoga exercises given at the end of this book. It is an indisputable fact exhibited by experience and proved by mentalism that many of the troubles and most of the illusions which a man has are brought to him by his thoughts. He can free himself from the tyranny of those troubles and these illusions therefore to the degree that he can free himself from the tyranny of his thoughts, provided again he does this with adequate and intelligent understanding. In such mental quiet lies peace, healing and freedom.

Such a superior mental quiet must not be confused with the ordinary kind—so popular among the neophytes in yoga—which can be obtained by the ordinary methods. These methods do indeed give a man mental stillness but they also leave the idiot in full possession of his idiocy, the self-deceived in undisturbed proprietorship of his illusions. The state which is sought and obtained by the philosophic student, who not only knows its inside and outside but knows that he knows and how, is immeasurably better. It is mystical experience grown up and come to an understanding both of itself and the world. It is related, as will be demonstrated towards the end of this work, to the common mental quiet achieved in meditation as a mature adult man is related to his own self when an ignorant child. This indeed is the mysterious fourth state beyond waking, dreaming and sleeping which the hidden teaching holds up before the gaze of aspiring men as a goal worth working for. What they now experience unconsciously during sleep they could experience consciously during wakeful life. All men may attain it although, merely because few ever seek it, few actually do attain it. It is free from all the interruptions and alternations of the other three states; it is tenable at all times and in all places and whether we are awake, a'dream or asleep; and because it transcends the unconsciousness of sleep it may be called the transcendental state. Such a state is a paradoxical one and beyond ordinary comprehension because it is a union of deep sleep and full consciousness.

The three states are not enough. Mankind have the possibility to advance beyond them, to win from Nature's tight grasp a fourth state which shall transcend them all. Its inexpressible felicity is there, waiting as it has always waited for the few adventurers who will act as pioneers for the whole race. It is through meditating upon the inner significance of these three states that we arrive eventually at the significance of the mysterious fourth state. It is always there deep down within us and we never really leave it at any time, not even when we become active in wakefulness or fall unconscious in sleep. And now we may grasp why it is that we do lose consciousness during sleep. For the mind's native state to which we then return possesses a vibrational range vastly beyond that possessed by the wakeful intellect. The latter is periodically drawn inwards by a powerful magnetic force to this innermost part of its being but finds itself quite unable to expand its own range to catch the wider consciousness of the fourth state. Consequently it swoons and passes into sleep. As its own limited life is snuffed out during the sleep it naturally denies later that any kind of consciousness existed then.

We set up our finite consciousness as the crux of mind when it is really but a bubble from the latter's depths, a whispered and remote revelation of its pure being.

"The conscious cannot be derived from the unconscious. Man is divine," wrote that astute statesman Lord Beaconsfield. Here alone does mind return to its primal selfhood, to the genuine unbroken unity against which sleep's pseudo-unity seems but a transient and suggestive hint. Here it *is*, but it is not anything in particular, not this or that. The fourth state is the undisturbed and unbroken awareness of mind-essence.

It may perhaps now be a little clearer why the hint was given in the previous chapter that humanity can attain its fullest spiritual self-realization only when clearly conscious of this physical world, that is to say only in the wakeful state. The more attention is concentrated the more vivid are the mental images which result. Such concentration achieves its intensest degree during wakefulness and this is one reason why earthly life seems more real to us than any other. Such is the immense importance of this earthly life, which some mystics foolishly deny as an illusion and many ascetics foolishly despise as an evil, that here the achievement of our highest destiny becomes possible. For here the intellectual thinking consciousness can work at its widest stretch whereas it cannot even come into play during deep sleep. Our intimate relaxation with the hidden reality of mind, our knowledge of its constant presence, can here be brought into full daylight as it were. The physical world is the crux. We must realize truth about life whilst yet in the flesh, if it is to be truth and not a substitute for it: this is why neither dream nor sleep will suffice to provide the conditions adequate for such realization. The Spirit of Heaven must descend to earth and enter through the door of the body and be a welcomed guest whilst we are fully awake, not whilst we are a'dream or asleep.

Thus the transcendental fourth view takes all the other three states within its wide scope and therefore embraces the whole of life. He alone who can attain it may rightly call himself a philosopher and none else. But such a view must not be mistaken for a merely intellectualist one; on the contrary, it is a profoundly mystical insight.

6

The Secret of the "I"

DESPITE what has been written already about them, the metaphysical significance of both the dream and sleep states has not yet been exhausted. It is easy, even after we have begun to believe in the truth of mentalism, to make the mistake of taking the world as being a form of consciousness—and even to take all other men as such—but to forget to take our own personality in the same way. A little further reflection about dreams can help us to correct this subtle error. Consider the case of a man who dreams that a terrible tragedy has overtaken his family and who weeps in inconsolable despair at their heartrending sufferings. But in the morning he awakens and the entire episode vanishes. The brick-built house which seemed so solid, the wife and children who writhed in pain so convincingly, now become shadowy phantoms. He finds that the events were nothing more than mental creations.

We have here to ask ourself the question: Who was the weeping man of this dream? He could not have been quite the same as the waking individual if only because his mental faculties and facilities were altered and because he did not possess the physical body which lay unmoving upon the bed. Not only were the incidents a series of thoughts, not only were the different members of his family a series of thoughts too, but even the sufferer who wept along with them must have been a mental creation for he also vanished with the dream.

Dream also demonstrates how a ragged beggar may think himself to be a bejewelled king and how a king may think himself to be a beggar. But the arrival of wakefulness shows that the dream-self was at the time but an idea, and is now but a memory, that is also an idea. If we can apply this lesson we can also convert the whole of our past wakeful-self experience into a memory. But a wakeful memory is not less a thought-structure than a dream one, however much more vivid it may be. Therefore the wakeful self must be such a thought-structure too. For if we take a retrospective glance at the stretched-out span of our own life, at the years of infancy, childhood, adolescence and maturity which relentless time has buried in the past, at all those years whose motley episodes are recoverable only as memories, everything that has happened to us now seems like the happenings of a prolonged and vivid dream. It seems such an appalling thing to believe that those events which were so solid, so substantial and so real when they were actual are only *like* dream-stuff. Yet does such a belief really strain probability too far? Those years when we lived so ardently and intensely, when we experienced the loftiest exaltations and the most poignant emotions, when we felt the strongest passions and endured the bitterest sufferings—where are they now? Where have they gone? They are now only recollections of the past and they have gone into the deeps of memory! What are such remembrances? They are simply a series of mental pictures, that is, they are no more than thoughts in and for the mind.

If all our past personal experiences through the years—no matter whether they are as few as five or as many as sixty—turn out in the end to be a series of transient ideas, what are we to say of our coming life which extends into the future? Nay, what of the vivid present in which we are living with such immediacy? Will they not turn out to be the same when we investigate them, because the present will inescapably become the past and the future will inescapably become the present? They will then appear to possess neither the same reality nor the same value which they possess now. Yet this day, this minute, this very moment through which we are now passing must actually possess precisely the same characteristics which they have before or after. This is a curious situation but reflection will show that its consequences are still more curious. Because past, present and future constitute the whole of our human existence what else is demonstrated by it than that our own wakeful existence is itself only a thought-series and that our personal experience is a mentally constructed affair?

If only a man will pause to reflect he will perceive how his own life fully verifies this truth. Let him take a highly emotional attachment which happened several years ago which made some woman seem to him like an adorable twin soul for whose love and for love of whom he had been born, but an attachment which eventually ended in estrangement and final parting. What is the feeling which this episode now arouses in him? The woman will seem like a nebulous figure in a remote past! Why? For now she is viewed as she was even then—as an idea.

Thus we find in the illustrations offered by our changing dream selves some luminous hints about the mentalist nature of our wakeful self also, as we find the same truth through rigorous metaphysical reflection upon the varied course of time. Yet the one thing of which every man is certain, the one fact upon which he never wastes a moment to entertain doubts, is the unalterable nature of his own identity. "*I* am" is a proposition which he feels can be safely laid down as being beyond all refutation. The identity and continuity of his own personality, he asserts, must surely be as plain to the metaphysician as it always is to the common man. Unfortunately for such certitude, metaphysical analysis does not lead to confirmation of these statements. For they are made from the standpoint of wakeful experience alone. What about dream life? There his personality becomes a little blurred and may change altogether as when a beggar with a wooden stick dreams that he has become a king with a golden sceptre. Next, what about deep sleep? There he has not even any consciousness of *"I* am", no sense of personal identity at all.

The notion that the characteristics of his own existence as a particular individual (not of course the existence itself) can possibly be held in question strikes an ordinary man as absurd. But the metaphysician, simply because he seeks to reach his findings after accumulating all the available facts and not merely a portion of them, cannot afford to leave out of his purview the dream and sleep standpoints which the ordinary man complacently ignores. And from the totality of all three standpoints we have already seen how he is compelled to deduce that the ego's belief in its own complete and final coherence as a person is refuted by the facts. For we can say that a thing continues as such when it remains identical with itself and when it is fundamentally permanent. Both these characteristics are absent from the personality. It is perhaps pardonable for the "I" to see how fleeting everything in the whole world is and fail to include itself, to note the continuous change and flow of external experience and fail to observe its own flux and evanescence. For what is a man really aware of? He is aware of a series of physical sensations, separate changing mental states and fluctuating emotional moods which follow each other throughout wakeful life. But of a self *apart from* the totality of this series he is not ordinarily aware. As a person he is, in the end, what other things are—a thought.

It will be said however that he is aware above all of the body, that the body is an "I" which is always present and always identical with itself. Let us try to look into this self-identification with the body a little more closely. It is through the senses that we become aware of our own bodies, no less than of the external world. But it was earlier found that if we seek out the basis of all sense-activity we find that it is our own consciousness and nothing else. The man who has not analysed what happens when he sits in a chair or looks at a tree naively assumes that he is experiencing something outside himself. But he is *actually* experiencing something inside his own sense-organs. And the latter in their turn can yield their awareness of anything only by virtue of the quality of awareness itself, a quality which is utterly beyond their own capacity. Therefore the senses must themselves constitute part of the mind as much as the "I". But the senses are known to be parts of the physical body. Therefore even the entire human body, as a part of the external world, although the part with which we are uniquely related and most intimately associated, is something seen, experienced and known and therefore something which is associated with our consciousness (as are all other objects) as one of its ideas, albeit the most vivid and intimate of all.

It comes to this: that our sensations of the body are really activities of the mind. Sight, hearing, taste and smell are simply localizations of these activities. The senses are really the limiting and defining conditions under which mind works when projecting our space-time consciousness. They merely canalize the mind's own image-making power and do not themselves create the images. All the five forms of sense-experience are like spokes radiating from a single common centre; a single consciousness is behind them. This consciousness is pre-supposed in seeing, hearing, tasting, touching and smelling, a consciousness which unites all the isolated impressions into an orderly whole. Therefore it is also the basis of our bodies. What we understand by body is in reality something pertaining to the mind.

The materialist wholly overlooks the significant role played by thinking in his experience. He overlooks that he has to *think* the body into his consciousness before he can even know of its existence at all. Mind must present the man's body as an idea and then only is there awareness of it. The brain itself is but a mental product in a mentally produced world. It is the mind as the intangible invisible principle of awareness which makes us aware of the brain's existence, so how can the brain be the originator of this function? In short, the mind of the man who accepts materialism has forgotten to consider itself.

The consciousness of sense-impressions is not a property of the body because the latter is as much an *object* to consciousness as any other idea, for the body passes in and out of consciousness, as in sleep for example. How much less then must it be a function of the brain which is merely a part of the body? Consciousness indeed is a property belonging to mind.

The problem of the relation between the mind and the body disappears when we grasp these great truths that the body is only an experience of consciousness and that such an experience can be external during wakefulness or internal during dream but is actually as much a powerfully held thought in both cases as is the outside space which is set up to contain both the body and the world. The body does not stand for an actuality apart from the consciousness of it. All the long controversies and variable theories of the relations existing between the two are empty and misleading. For there are not two separate and separable substances—matter and mind—to be studied but only one. His body is as much a man's thought as the world outside it. In the body mind is conscious of itself as "body". In ideation, feeling and memory mind is again conscious of itself but this time as the thinking intellect. The whole mental life is a continuous flux and unrolling film of momentary thoughts. Those which are held most strongly within the focus of attention at any particular moment constitute the self at the time. The body-thought is only a part of it. The "I"-thought which man habitually associates with the body vanishes in dreamless sleep along with all the other thoughts. Therefore the sense of personality cannot fundamentally be a bodily one,* although it includes the body at intervals, and must be a mental one. In short, it is a man's ideas about himself, which of course include his ideas about his body, which constitute his personality. If this world extended in space and changing in time is really a thought-structure, and if the person is a part of the world, then it logically follows that he is just as much a thought-structure too. When mentalism reduced the world to an idea, it inevitably reduced everything and everyone contained within it to an idea too. The world-idea springs from the same root as the person-idea but both flower in contrasting colours.

The first of our thoughts is "I". All other thoughts follow its arisal. It does not stand alone but instantly associates itself with the thought which next follows. And this is the body-thought. Unfortunately it ends by limiting itself to the body too, which could never have come into existence at all but for its own prior existence. Thus this association has degenerated into a bondage of the "I"-thought to the body-thought. The only self man believes in today is his body. Consequently the original "I"-thought becomes converted into "I am the body". After this there arises the world-thought. The "I" unconsciously provides the particular space-time characteristics through which the world must first pass before it can emerge into its consciousness. Thus the "I" veritably holds as its own thought both the body and then the world outside the body. But because it began by deceiving itself about its own relation to the body, because it took the body for what it is not, it ends by deceiving itself about the things outside and around the body and takes them for what they are not too. Hence the arisal of a triple error: the world, the body and the "I" are all regarded as non-mental.

The "I" every man knows is indeed his self but it is not his ultimate self. When he discovers that his own personal existence is no less a thought-structure than that of his physical surroundings, that everything including himself has an imagined existence, he comes close, very close, to the gate of initiation into a higher world of understanding. He who witnesses the events of a dream, he who participates in them, and he who creates them are one and the same entity. Because the process which brings the wakeful self into being is as unconscious and involuntary as the process which brings the dream self into being, nobody notices at the time that either one is a thought creation. Just as a man who has been dreaming that he was a wealthy king finds on awakening from his dream that he is really a poor peasant and that his gorgeous palaces, respectful people and spacious country were only ideas, so it is the discovery during *wakefulness* that the wakeful personality is also only an idea that constitutes the first crucial

---

* That the sense of "I" does not ultimately reside in the fleshly body has been sufficiently demonstrated in a somewhat different manner in *The Secret Path* and *The Quest of the Overself*, so the same ground need not be covered here.

stage of his liberation from ignorance. Jesus told his disciples that when they knew the Truth it would set them free. They were already physically free so the liberation to which he referred could only have been a mental one. Gautama was called "Buddha", which means "awakened one", because he had awakened from the attachment to his own person which was as erroneous as the attachment of the dreaming peasant to his royal self. Then as now the mass of humanity were still so utterly sunk in their thought-made self as to take it for the final one.

The Wonder of Awareness.

We have found that thoughts and sensations constitute the person. But does the person constitute the whole of the "I"? Can we separate self from the ideas, the perceptions and the memories which it holds? We know that there is an "I" of some sort for it is our own thoughts that come into being and not another's. A thought is always somebody's thought. It has a personal background. Also, the expression "I" is unique inasmuch as it is the only term in every human language which cannot be literally used to stand for a class or group. Thus the meaning of terms "horse" and "house" can refer to any or all of a million horses or houses in existence whereas the meaning of "I" must always be referred to a single individual alone. He who speaks to another may legitimately speak of himself as "I" but the person who is being addressed may not also speak of the first man in the same way. Hence whoever uses this term does not ordinarily understand by it what another person using it will understand.

Although the "I" changes from instant to instant we feel somehow that it knows itself indirectly through its thoughts, acts and experiences, and that something remains constant and stationary through all these changes. If in one sense there is a continuity between what we once were and what we now are, then this persistent core must be a deeply buried mental one. What is this mysterious core? Can the "I" know itself directly?

Hume, the metaphysician, burrowed beneath his flux of multitudinous sensations in the hope of finding a definite and constant self lurking there but reported failure. He found only his own thoughts, varying from moment to moment, but no thing worth calling self. How could he have succeeded? For he overlooked that which made his burrowing possible, that out of which the very birth of his sensations became possible and upon whose hidden existence he unconsciously formed the thought of a self's possible existence. The fact that he could examine his own thoughts showed that there was something in him which was itself deeper than them, for it could not simultaneously be both the owner of the thoughts and the thoughts themselves, both the examiner and that which was examined. What is this "something"? It is, it must be a still deeper "I" which, although usually ignored, must matter most of all. And this, when traced through the conventional confusions and unconscious processes which habitually surround it, is nothing else than that intangible *principle* of awareness itself whose own existence makes the existence of all the multiple items of awareness itself possible.

Science can paint a plausible picture of the way in which the body becomes aware of the world through the senses and the brain. It can show how every sensation corresponds to a precise physical activity inside the brain. But it has never yet shown nor ever can show a brain activity which corresponds to that unique element of *awareness* which knows and feels all these sensations, to the consciousness which reacts by attention or inattention to such sense experience.

Those who would treat this principle as a sort of froth formed on the surface of matter, who would define it in terms of the physical brain alone and who would arrogate to a little fragment of bone-shielded flesh the whole marvel of consciousness, imagination, reason, memory and judgment, need to be reminded of Bacon's warning that Nature is to be interrogated and not interpreted. *"Hic Deficit Orbis"* ("Here Ends the World") was the inscription which ancient geographers put on their maps at the Pillars of Hercules, situated at the western entrance to the Mediterranean Sea. "Here Ends the Mind", says the modern materialist, pointing a cocksure finger at his brain.

Let him explain then those rare but authenticated cases in the annals of surgery where large portions of the brain have been cut out by operation or crushed to pulp by wounding or eaten up by disease—portions containing those nervous centres which, every physiological student is taught, give birth to or control the psychological functions of thought, sensation and memory—and yet the patients have continued to think, feel and remember like normal human beings. Let him also explain why, when the marvellous structure of the eye of a corpse continues to make retinal pictures of the scene before it and when consequently on his materialistic theory there ought to be a corresponding excitation of the brain, there is surely no awareness of the scene at all.

What the hidden teaching says is that the awareness is itself a separate principle. Part of it acts upon the body, principally through the heart and the brain. It has certain correspondences and relations with centres in the brain. The part which thus acts is the part which is projected into a particular space-time existence and which thenceforth *imagines* itself to be an entirely complete and self-sufficient being. It is indeed what we know as the person. It is this projected fraction of awareness which is what we ordinarily term consciousness, that is the sum of all our personal sensations, thoughts and feelings. It is this fractional consciousness—and not the mind whence it originates—that has its seat in the particular body with which it is so intimately associated, a seat which is largely located in the brain and hence the parallel workings of both, as noted by physiologists. But even then this limited field of awareness cannot rightly be limited only to the brain with which it is related, much less imposed as a boundary on the larger mind whence it emanates. It is not even confined to its associated body but, from that body's viewpoint, emanates and spreads outward in space. The area of such expansion varies with different individuals but in the case of an average human being this emanation extends to a distance of nearly a couple of yards. A sensitive person coming in contact with or close to another person may actually feel this emanation or aura, charged with thought and feeling as it is, merely by standing within it. But even without otherwise being particularly sensitive, people whose mental and emotional characteristics are sufficiently alike will absorb ideas and feelings from one another if they stand near enough to intermingle their auras. The political orator who conquers a large audience owes more to this fact than he realizes just as the passions which unite an unruly mob receive much of their strength from it too.

With what faculty does man dream of distant continents at night and with what faculty does he picture them in imagination by day? Is it not with the mind and does this not show that it can embrace the most distant places? At what point of the universe *dare* he say that any object, however distant, is outside his mind? Just because he is capable of thinking of the entire universe, of embracing the most distant star within its operation of knowing, we are entitled to say that mind is everywhere. It is like space of which nobody can say where it ends. Space is indeed the form which mind takes. But this is the same as saying that mind is formless. Mind occupies no definite position in space for the simple reason that space itself is its own production. Although all the thoughts which have existed in our mind and which still lie there latently are beyond counting, we know that we can use the phrase "in our mind" only in a metaphorical sense. If the thoughts had ever been there in a spatial sense they would have needed a very large place to accommodate them! What does this imply? There is no length and breadth for a thought and consequently no real length and breadth for the mind holding it. Whatever we do theoretically for the purpose of intellectual analysis and communication, we cannot actually divide the mind from the thoughts which it holds. All are one. Thoughts are only phases of consciousness. Consciousness is only a phase of mind. Mind is outside the limitation of any particular place. It is not really flesh-tied, but our belief about it is.

Were the mind actually in space, it would then be possible to assert that one part of it was above or to the left of another part. But such assertions are absurd and cannot be truthfully made, for the mind is not an assemblage of parts having position and distance; consequently it is not in space. For the same considerations mind is not in time. We cannot think of one part of our mind following next after another part. We can only think of its manifested thoughts doing so—which is an entirely different matter. That which materialists take to be mind is but their *imagination* about it. It is, therefore, incorrect to limit the mind in space solely to that portion of the body which is called the brain. On the contrary, because of this ease with which the mind assumes form and extends in space, because we can place no limit upon its extension, it will be better to say that the brain exists within the mind. But ultimately there is no such thing in point of fact as a geographical distribution of the mind, that is, it cannot be localized, nor can we say that it has an outside and an inside. Nobody can determine where the frontiers of the province of mind are. It is therefore utterly meaningless to look for its location, whether we look in our own head or elsewhere. There can be no question of a position for mind for it is positionless. It cannot have a seat. It can everywhere be mysteriously present. Its infinitude cannot be compressed into a little canopy of bone in the head. The materialist tries to squeeze mind into his head but fails. The mentalist tries to put his head into mind and succeeds.

Once again it must be repeated that it is entirely absurd to degrade the wonderful doctrine of mentalism into the nonsensical statement that it endeavours to prove the earth, mountains, sun and stars to be all contained within the narrow space of the human skull. We can only laugh at such nonsense and repeat that the brain is not the mind. It is a bit of nerve-stuff. The essence of this doctrine is that all these things are ultimately known by the mind, are known only as mental perceptions and therefore can only exist within such a conscious, immaterial and untouchable principle of awareness as we know the human mind to be. Science may rack its brains but it will never find a physiological basis for this awareness—although it can easily find a physiological outlet for it—and consequently never find any other path of further travel in this affair then the metaphysical or mystical enquiry into self. Neither the bodily sense-organs nor the physical brain nor even the two in combination yield the actual unified perception of a thing. This wonderful synthesis can be achieved only by the consciousness which observes and interprets the reaction of both sense-organ and brain. It is no use talking in terms of cerebral changes here for with the detection of this principle of awareness we depart from everything physical and enter a new world entirely, the world of pure mind. The sensations themselves are only the *objects* of man's conscious attention. What about their observer's own existence?

In the opening page of this chapter there was described the case of a man who wept during dream over the supposed sufferings of his family. What was the real relation during the dream itself of the wakeful man to this projected fraction of consciousness which was his dream itself? It was that of a mere spectator but, owing to his temporary identification with the dream self, this relation was concealed from him at the time. There were thus two aspects of one and the same man: the projected active dream personality of whom there was consciousness, and its spectator *of whom this personality itself was then quite unaware.*

Now the fact that such a double nature can exist during dream should warn us that it may exist also during wakefulness and that the waking self may be no less a mental construction than the dreaming one; that there may be a spectator behind it of whom—because of our temporary identification with this waking man—there is no consciousness; and that this relation may likewise be a concealed one.

We learnt from our studies in dream and sleep that these do not exhaust the whole existence of mind. They are not its only possible states. Deep sleep despite its unconsciousness hints at the existence of a still deeper mental layer within the "I" but beneath the personality. The mystery of self can consequently yield up its furthermost secret only when man also becomes conscious of what he is in this deeper part of his being.

When we think of the wakeful world, it is not seized as a whole because, as our object of present attention, it is separated from ourself and placed right against us in thought. When we think of the dream world, it is not as the waking self contemplating the dream self, but as the mind divested of its personality altogether. Thus an understanding of the simple experience denoted by the words "I dreamt" raises us to the level of a witness and clear above that of the personality. The waking self sets itself up as the criterion of existence and therefore speaks and thinks as though it has itself dreamt and slept. But that which brought both dream and sleep about is entirely beyond its control and consciousness. If the personal self as ordinarily known in waking did not originate dream and sleep then another "mind" must have done so and this second "mind" must be related to it somehow. This is the deeper mind we seek, which, itself neither dreaming nor waking nor sleeping, watches the production of these phenomena in its offspring the person.

The absence of thoughts during sleep does not prove the absence of the thinker. On the contrary, it has already been noted that the acknowledgement of their absence indicates the presence of an observing element which is aware of their arisal and disappearance. It is unfortunate, of course, that we are not aware of this observational activity until after it has occurred, which means that we know it only by remembrance and therefore at second hand. But sleep, mind, consciousness and the person being what they are, this could not have been otherwise. The wakeful state is simply the natural result of mind projecting a mere fraction of itself as the personal consciousness with the fullest force. The dream state is the result of the same mind projecting the person with partial force. The sleep state is the result of mind withdrawing the attenuated dream consciousness into itself and closing the personal aperture altogether. Then the individual being loses its awareness. But the mind, possessing its own peculiar kind of awareness, does not. The family "I" ceases to exist with its compulsory return to the mind because it cannot absorb what is beyond itself and must instead submit to being absorbed. The onset of sleep is a sign of such complete absorption as the onset of dream is a sign of its half-absorption.

This loss of personal consciousness during sleep is inevitable because the person itself is a nucleus of thought-structures temporarily lit into life along with the world-thought but both thoughts dissolve when their informing principle of attentive awareness is withdrawn. Nevertheless whether the person be asleep or awake, the mind itself does not change with the changing states of its surface being because it is the pure principle which renders possible all those countless acts of awareness that constitute the experience of the other states. After the onset of sleep the wakeful or dream self merges back into this innermost principle and consequently is no longer present to be conscious of anything at all. From its limited standpoint we are quite correct in describing sleep as an unconscious state. But from the broader standpoint of the principle of mind which observes it, we would be more correct in describing it as a state in which there exists a kind of consciousness which is frankly incomprehensible because beyond our finite limits. But we ought not therefore to deny the existence of this consciousness.

Indeed it is impossible to advance farther in this metaphysical study unless the ability is developed to separate analytically two opposing concepts—the self from the not-self, the observer from what is observed. The first step to advanced philosophic knowledge is this ability to separate in understanding that which is observed from that which observes it. So long as these polarities are confounded with each other—as they usually are in uninstructed minds—the higher metaphysics must remain a closed and sealed book. Such discrimination is easy where physical things are concerned for all conscious experience is twofold and obviously involves a knower and a known, a self and an "other", but it calls for a far subtler sense where abstract ideas are concerned. Hence we must now make our thinking sharper than ever to comprehend what follows.

The present examination of the wakeful self has shown us that it points beyond itself to a principle of awareness which makes possible all conscious experience—and consequently the personal "I" along with it—but which is itself hidden deep beneath the threshold of consciousness. Why do we miss noting the existence of this principle of awareness? Firstly, because it is a universal one. It cannot be experienced in the same familiar way in which we experience particular things because what is limited cannot get behind what is unlimited. Metaphysically we may obtain the intellectual and total conviction that it is there but actually we may not ordinarily become conscious of the principle which makes our own consciousness possible. Secondly, because it is itself the principle behind that consciousness, it cannot turn round to look at itself. We are compelled to take for granted that it exists but being itself the subject it cannot also be at the same time an object of our consciousness. This hidden observer eludes our most eagle-eyed introspection because it is totally beyond the introspecting consciousness. We are normally unaware of it not because it does not exist but because it transcends the familiar "I" himself.

When we believe that we are conscious of ourself we are really conscious of a heavy disguise, of the powerful complex of thoughts constituting the conscious "I" which the unknown self puts on and takes off. This deeper self is of course there beneath the disguise but we never know it in its undisguised state. Just as we do not see an invisible gas in the chemical laboratory but can detect its presence by smelling its odour, so we are ignorant of the hidden observer but can detect its presence by noting that something makes it possible for us to be conscious of the fluctuating states of the surface "I". Thinking, being itself a part of the field of our observation, unfortunately cannot break through into the consciousness of the observer which transcends that field. The consciousness which knows cannot itself be included in what is known. It cannot itself be known except as the conscious idea of it, which would be like knowing a man only through a photograph of him. For there can be no knowledge of the comings and goings of the "I" except by some witness that could be less limited than itself, which could precede it and be its final owner. The "I" is indeed a symbol which stands for something immeasurably wider than itself.

Again, the personal self is gradually changing through the years but the mental principle which informs it and makes it possible for us to be aware of the changing conscious and bodily states, is not affected by this process and remains ever the same. This principle is the relatively permanent element within us and the ultimate basis of all our kaleidoscopic states of consciousness. To become aware of the arisal and disappearance of all those thoughts which make up the totality of the waking self their witness must be relatively changeless, for it is only the striking contrast between them and itself which could possibly make it aware of such transience. The constant succession of sensations, the innumerable changes of perception and experience could themselves be evident only to some observer whose own mental permanence and unity must be pre-supposed or he could not notice the facts of succession and change. The consciousness possessed by the hidden observer cannot be a fitful one. Being the very principle of awareness, able at any time to shine through its projections, the wakeful or dream selves, it must therefore be an unbroken and unfailing one.

The Hidden Observer.

We are able to see things as lying outside each other and events as happening after each other only because there is in us something which itself is not in space or time. The consciousness of events would not be possible if the observing mind were itself involved in the same time-series. For the process of knowing these events involves the process of connecting them in thought. This in turn involves the working of a mind which cannot itself be one of the thoughts it thus connects. This mind must therefore transcend what it experiences and be outside the flow of our time altogether. It is only because the consciousness pre-supposed in experience is larger than the events that we are able to become aware of them at all. The fact that we are conscious of the changes which make up the stuff of time is itself possible only because there is something hidden in us which is above change and beyond time.

We may not in the movement of our thought as it traces out the possibilities of such a situation think of changes happening within this hidden observer. But even if we attempted to do so, the inexorable logic of consciousness would march us to defeat in the end. For even if there were such changes we would then need to bring in a further observer which itself *must* be unchanging in order to disclose the fact of these changes! The first observer could become a changing experience only by occurring in the larger field of awareness of the new one. And the latter must be unchanging, because if it were not then there must needs be a still further observer behind it able to note its changes, an observer which must itself relatively be majestically changeless so as to note their contrast. And even if this last one should tantalizingly prove not to be so, then it would need a still further observer in whose field of observation it itself existed and by which its own changes of experience would be noted.

Thus we could theoretically and exasperatingly continue without end to construct a psychological machine wherein one self revolved like a wheel inside another self and that again inside a third, but inevitably in this receding series of observers we would be forced by necessity to complete the mechanism by introducing one final unchanging observer of them all. However far we could possibly travel inwards in tracing such a series of self-duplications, however much the chimerical horizon receded on our mystical journey, we would always arrive in the end at the same position from which we started, that is, that there must be a limit to the series. And this limit would consist of an ultimate unalterable element in the mind which is the real if hidden owner of all the preceding observers. Nothing could ever bring this element, which is the very essence of mind, to an end. It would always be present and always the same.

Nor could such a psychological situation end in anything else. It must always repeat itself for no changing event could be an object of observation to a perceiving mind unless the latter were relatively stable. The mutable can be recognized only by a perceiver which is itself grandly immutable. The mind which made observation possible to the first ego in such a series would still be present to make it possible to the last one in the series. And although consciousness of the entire total of all earlier observers would be in it as their final owner, it could never itself be in consciousness.

But it will be asked, why should the ultimate observer be aristocratically outside ordinary consciousness? The answer is that as soon as we attempt to know the knowing self of the series, we attempt the impossible. For the moment we could succeed in knowing it, it would become the known idea, the observed experience, and no longer be the knower, the observer. Every fresh attempt would only repeat this situation. Let us therefore stick to our original observer. And let us not forget that all these different observers are and can only be different states manifested by one and the same mind, whose essence continues serenely unchanged.

It is indeed the pre-supposition and permanent basis of all our conscious experience because its products are present as that experience. But the very fact that it must be pre-supposed in order to explain experience shows that it cannot itself be known in such experience. Consequently, it is essential that we keep clear in our minds this difference between the particular thoughts which are ever succeeding each other in a flowing stream and the general principle of Thought which secretly makes us aware of them. If it perceives then it cannot be perceived, just as the bodily eyes are able to see everything else around them but are unable to see themselves. This is why we are never directly aware of pure Thought but only of individual thoughts, pictorial ideas or sensuous images. They are merely evidenced by it whereas it is the incontestable evidence for its own veiled existence.

As it is impossible to think of this mental stuff as possessing any particular shape in itself, we must conclude that whatever assumes form or takes shape, that is to say whatever is *seen*, must be only a mental *production* and not the mind itself. And this must apply equally to so-called material things which are presented to the five senses as to blatantly obvious mental things like episodes of the remembered past. Then if the mental constructions of experience are doomed to pass away as transient, the mental principle itself must remain throughout these transformations what it was and is. We must therefore be very careful not to think any element of particular or separate thoughts into our concept of this pure

Thought-in-itself, that which is here called mind.

In the last chapter definitions of the terms "brain" and "consciousness" were offered. In *The Hidden Teaching Beyond Yoga* a tentative definition of the term "mind" as being "that which makes us think of anything and which makes us aware of anything" was offered. To this definition we may now add: "and which reveals its existence in every thought but is unknown to us apart from such manifestation".

Thus we return to our hidden observer with the qualification that it must also be the final one. If we are unable to bring it into our field of observation nevertheless in its mysterious way it must contain both our outer world experience and our inner personal experience within its own field. It becomes very important for us to discover what is the relation between these two selves. How important this innermost self must be is deducible from that fact that whereas the person can see the world from outside but cannot adopt the same standpoint as regards itself, the hidden observer can stand outside the person "I" and thus obtain a more accurate and comprehensive picture of its character possibilities and activities. The total knowledge of the final self must indeed be far fuller in quantity and superior in quality to that of the surface self. It must at least possess fewer of the limitations and endure none of the mutations to which the familiar ego is exposed. It is never in the field of the person's observation whereas the person is always in its field. Is it not an astonishing commentary upon human ignorance that generally the personal "I" does not even know that this witnessing "I" also exists?

It follows from all this that the self which is in consciousness is like the island of Teneriffe which is the peak of a submerged mountain thrust above sea level, or like the visible tenth part of an iceberg whose vast bulk floats unseen beneath the ocean's surface. It further follows that when we use the term "I" and think only of the body we are talking a kind of nonsense—similar to that which a man would use if he always referred to a mere fraction of himself, such as his big toe, as "I"! There is thus immensely more behind this simple term than we ordinarily know. The mind cuts itself into two, the portion of which we are continuously aware being the observed person and the portion which makes us aware that there is a person being the observing mind.

Once we comprehend this situation then it becomes possible to find the answer to questions like why if the person is itself owned and is not the ultimate owner does it seem to own the self; and, why does it yield the feeling of being substantially our real self? The answer is that the witnessing self is present in hidden association or mystic immanence in the personal self and reflects into that self the feeling of its own real existence. Its presence in each one of us thus explains why it is that we have the sense of personal identity at all. But this does not warrant the materialistic illusion which substitutes the personality for what underlies and supports it.

Now we have learnt that it is useless to look for the whole self in the wakeful state alone and utterly ignore the other two beads on its string. For dream and sleep no less pertain to it than waking. It is useless to take only a fragment of experience and then expect a full answer to the question "What am I?" But the advance which we have now made in standpoint has advanced the result obtained. Self is thus shown to be a little more complex than it is commonly suspected to be. It reveals itself to be threefold: (a) The physical body, (b) the personal consciousness, consisting of feelings, thoughts, desires, images and karmic tendencies, (c) the impersonal observer whose presence is indirectly revealed by the person in the same mysterious way that the presence of magnetism is revealed by movements of iron filings. *All* these three elements combine together to make up the total "I". Whoever equates his "I" with only one or confuses it with only two of these factors commits a serious error and does not really know himself. For the physical body makes merely mechanical responses to its environment; its behaviour cannot possibly cover all that we experience when we utter the word "I". And the personal emotions and thoughts are only fleeting and ephemeral phases of the self. We are not angry all the time, for instance, nor do we always think of metaphysics alone, nor are we constantly wanting some pleasure either; that is to say, our personal states are different by turns. Our mental and emotional conduct, in short, is too contradictory to stand by itself for the true self. Both stable flesh and moody feeling *belong* to it. But they do not include that sense of unchanging identity of "I"-ness which runs like a thread through all of them.

The physical body, the personal thoughts and feelings are only *contents* of the self, not its real *character*. The sense of awareness accompanies every act, every feeling and every thought. It is their common factor. The acts, feelings and thoughts slowly or swiftly change their aspect until sometimes they are quite contradictory but the pure consciousness of them remains unchanged through all these endless mutations. We must not therefore make the common mistake which totalizes them alone as the self but leaves out the all-essential inner sense which strings them together. The common view quite evidently needs to be corrected. Were the "I" nothing more than this series of changing thoughts and fitful feelings it could not become aware of itself as an *individual*. Such awareness evidences a deeper principle in its own being. The presence of this principle may be inferred, even though it may not be separately experienced, from its being reflected into every thought image and perception as the stuff of awareness of them.

Thus we have advanced from the narrow personal "me" to the wider, more inviting and more inspiring "I". The final and most important member of the "I" family is this unseen and unknown one. It is the subject of which they are the object. It is the silent spectator of a play in which the others are actors. It is the mystical quintessence of the "I". The ordinary "I" is *a* thought, the ultimate "I" is pure Thought.

It should now be clear that this consciousness must be identical with the fourth state of consciousness which we earlier found to transcend sleep. It is the fundamental observer who notes the comings and goings of the other three states because it can stand aside from them in unbroken beatitude. It is our truest deepest self because it alone outlives unchanged the surface self of changing personality.

Thus the witness-self walks through this world *incognito*. Only the few to whom philosophy grants her earned favours find it out and know it by its true name. The rest regard it under the limited aspect of a particular personality. When they employ the word "self" they do not usually refer it to anything beyond this physical being who stands before them in flesh and blood plus his little psychological collection of bitter-sweet memories and transient moods, hot desires and cold fears. It is within such small limits that they confine the meaning of this term. But the man who has come to genuine self-knowledge knows what he really is *over* and above this named embodied individual; hence he may aptly adopt the expressive term "Overself" when referring to it. Theologians probably mean this when they speak of the "soul". But as our concept is as radically different from theirs in some ways as it is roughly similar to it in others, and particularly as it is not a theological theme for us, we prefer to call it the Overself. The person is only a projection from the Overself as a dream-figure is a projection from the mind of a dreamer. It is only a dependent creature which has forgotten its origin and now *imagines* itself to be the real "I".

A difficulty which troubles the student of mentalism sooner or later has to be cleared at this point. It could not have been effectively dealt with before. We have seen that each individual generates his own external world from his own subconscious depths, and that if he believes the world to be external to his consciousness, he is under an illusion. This implies that all other individuals, being themselves parts of the world's totality, also exist only as his thoughts too. Hence any individual can say to himself: "But if all other human beings are only sensations of my own consciousness, then all mankind become a part of *my* existence and my mental traffic with them becomes mere soliloquy. There is then no one left with whom I can talk or to whom I can write. I am forced to arrive at the conclusion that I alone exist! But this is to reduce social existence to a nonentity and social communication to an absurdity. Moreover other persons have just as much claim to sole existence as I have and these conflicting claims to complete isolation must end by cancelling each other out. Such seems to be the logical outcome of mentalist doctrine."

The most serious implications of this egoist error are twofold. First that nothing else exists except one's own thoughts. Second, that every other individual is a product of one's own creation. The consequence of this is that not only one's body but also one's mind is no less a creation of another man's mind than his is a creation of one's own. Were this true we would ultimately land not only in the semi-insanity of sheer egoism but, what is worse, in the full lunacy of pure nihilism, the doctrine that nothing exists at all!

Students must indeed beware of falling from the materialist pan into this egoist fire. It would be easy to mistake mentalism as teaching that the world we know is wholly the imagination of the individual mind and that it has no existence outside of our little ego. It was said in the earlier volume that the world of sensations is the only world man knows. Although the statement still remains psychologically correct, it does not go far enough. It must not be misunderstood to mean that nothing other than personal sensations exist. It is true that each of us lives in a closed circle able only to infer the existence of the others from our sense-impressions of their activities. But that the world-experience of two different persons can form a subject of conversation between them as if it were one and the same for both, is something that has to be accounted for. The possibility of this mutual understanding is a sign indeed. If man knows nothing more than his sensations, there must still be something in existence—even if hidden and unknown to him—to cause these sensations. A man absorbed in watching a cinema picture knows nothing more than the flickering sights and sounds which reach two of his senses from the screen; but there is also a projecting machine which is the hidden and unrealized cause of his sensations. The existence of material objects as the cause of sensations has been rejected. The existence of the similarity of these sensations in different individuals has already been accounted for by the existence of the World-Mind's master image. Each mind is certainly confined to its own sensational world but each sensational world is rooted in a common mental ground. Hence approximately the same world is experienced by several minds. The fact that two individuals can talk with understanding about the same external thing is equally explicable by the fact that the thing is mentally constructed and that there is a common consciousness underlying all the individual consciousnesses. It is this consciousness which brings all those different selves together and gives a similarity to all our sensations of the world and, because of our self-communication with and understanding of each other, enables us to assert the existence of other persons outside us, although it is quite impossible to experience their consciousness in precisely the same way in which we experience our own.

We have to think the world independently of whether we want to or not for the plain reason that this greater mind is thinking it into our own mind, is projecting and knowing the external world *through* the individual mind. Every object in the universe is held in the larger infinite consciousness, whether it is thought of or observed by the finite consciousness of any human being or not.

The World-Mind does not directly create the world but its presence makes it possible for both ourself and the world to rise karmically of themselves into actuality. The World-Mind must logically be prior to its ideas, that is to both the world-idea and the ego-idea. The person and the world lie latent within mind which unites and yet transcends them because it is their hidden reality. The two are always related to each other and never found apart. Yet this relation and they with it dissolves in a higher unity. For both are but the expressions of one all-embracing mind.

Thus mentalism breaks through these egoistic and nihilistic circles with its tenet of a mind which is cosmic in its operational field. Nevertheless the egoistic conclusion, however absurd it may sound, is not so far from correctness as first sight may indicate. For it is unconsciously struggling to express a profound truth which has been glimpsed as from far off. Its chief error lies in mistaking the "I" to which it refers. Not only does the person belong to something beyond itself, to the hidden observer, but when we shall finish the present enquiry we shall find that this connects it with all other selves. It has to be included in a larger self, where all are one and one is all. Certainly if this "I" be taken as the limited personality the conclusion becomes erroneous but if it be taken as a universal "I", a higher individuality, then it is metaphysically correct. Hence to utter the phrase "I alone exist" truthfully we must first transcend the level of personal existence and then realize a greater one.

His familiar "I" is simply the sort of person a man imagines himself to be, an imagination which he changes from time to time during life. All the other persons also exist besides ourself but, like our own personality, they exist as thoughts. Only when we or they find the truth behind personality do we or they attain an existence higher than that of a thought. For the person to which we all cling so stubbornly is after all but a mere shadow thrown by the Overself, a pale relic of its transcendent self. It may now become a little clearer why the egoistic approach to the world prevents us from arriving at truth, and therefore why the philosophic discipline demands the reining-in of the person. For the birth of objects as ideas cannot be accounted for and must remain incomprehensible and mysterious so long as we persist in thinking that the world-experience is solely *our own* experience. The egoist ignores the one World-Mind within which his little mind is itself contained, fails to perceive that his is only a semi-independent perception. Human experience is the final residue of a process of inter-action, a fabric conjointly woven with a common mind in which all human beings dwell and think and which dwells and thinks in them. The world itself is the outcome of a combined cosmic and individual imagination.

It comes to this, that there is *ultimately* only a single observer, the World-Mind, and only a single great world image and we as persons are contained within the great one. If we want an apposite analogy we may liken the World-Mind to a dreamer, the world image to its dream and the countless creatures within it to the various figures taking an active part in that dream. To make this picture more accurate we would have to add, however, a further factor which is missing from ordinary human dreams—the dreamer is perfectly conscious in this case that he is dreaming. Now each dream-figure is itself imagining its environment and yet beholds more or less the same world. This happens for two reasons: first, there is ultimately only a single master-image of its environment to which its own thinking has unconsciously and involuntarily to conform; second, there is ultimately only one observer functioning through and in all the innumerable individual observers who already exist within the dream. This of course is the dreamer himself.

But let the reader remember that this is only an analogy. It is intended to help him understand what, by its very nature, is difficult enough to understand. We are not here stating that the world *is* nothing more than a dream and that all of us are destined to be annihilated as soon as God wakes up from His world-dream. We are saying only that the world is *like* a dream and that the activity of World-Mind is *like* dreaming. In the end these studies will reveal that the truth behind the world is its essential enduring reality and that the truth behind ourself is our own enduring divinity. In what way the one is real and the other divine is something which has to be dug out by hard labour. An analogy like the present one is more useful to lighten this labour but cannot act as a substitute for it altogether. Let it be repeated therefore that because we are what we really are annihilation is not for us. The hidden meaning of the dream analogy has yet to unfold itself. Then we shall discover that there is no dream, that life is not meant for lotus-eating but for enlightened action, because its reality is immeasurably more wonderful than the make-believe of any dream.

7

The Scorpion of Death

WHEN Kee-Loo said to his teacher, "I venture to ask about death?" Kung-Foo-Tze replied: "While you do not comprehend life, how can you comprehend death?"

Such too is the philosophic attitude towards this matter and this is why in all our previous writing we have refrained from touching too freely upon the most melancholy of all topics. It is only now, when a modicum of light has been thrown upon the nature of existence, that the appropriate time has come for breaking this reserve. Otherwise why should anyone concern himself with the adventures of man in the dark spheres beyond death when he has not understood what has already happened to him before he arrives there? There problem of the spirit-world, which men do not know, can be satisfactorily solved only after they have solved the problem of the earth-world, which they do know. Those who accept any of the various accounts of life in the next sphere when they have not understood the present one, can and often do easily delude themselves?

Now, however, when we know something of the true ancestry of this world, something of the final fate of the twinkling stars and circling planets and especially something about our own human selves, we are surely better equipped to tackle this problem with a little more intelligence and a little less blind belief than is usually shown towards it. For just as mentalism has helped to fashion a key to a correct understanding of this world so it can help us secure a correct and rational understanding of the next world.

We all know what death will do to man's body. What will it do to his thinking feeling self? Does he become a "spirit"? The answer to this question is so important to all men as to demand and deserve extended treatment. Firstly, let it be said that the grim process of dying and its immediate aftermath are events upon which a little light can be thrown from the more advanced experiences of a certain yoga-path. For one of these experiences, which occurs in some cases but not in all, is an important state of death-like trance. From the accounts of those who have had such experiences, from the classic descriptions contained in ancient mystic texts and from our having personally passed through some of these phases, it is possible to procure a few hints as to what happens during and after this momentous transition. For the rest we shall draw upon a definite tradition about death in the hidden teaching which can be explained in a manner appealing to reason alone.

The pain which is so often associated with this event arises either from abrupt and violent physical changes or abrupt and violent mental ones or from both interacting together. Where, as is usually the case through ignorance, thought clings obstinately to the body and feeling clings obstinately to its desire, where there is over-strong refusal to let both go and an exaggerated fear of what is coming next, the physical pain is needlessly increased through a nervous reaction. But when the dying person is sufficiently enlightened to know that the body is his idea and to have disciplined his personal desires, he will naturally be prepared for this great change. Just as a fully-ripened fruit falls easiest from a tree so such a man will part easiest from his body. In the case of a highly-expert yogi who has made meditation a part of his life, and certainly in the case of a sage who knows his real self apart from the body, the passing out should be quite peaceful.

Dying itself—and we do not speak here of accidental or violent death—may fitly be compared with the squeezing of a saturated fruit for its juice. The dying person feels an intense pressure which begins in both feet and moves slowly up the whole body, leaving the limbs heavy, cold and numb. This in turn affects the activity of breathing, the flow of blood and the senses of sight and hearing. When, in the final crisis, the pressing process is completed the heart cannot expand properly. The sensation of being intimately identified with most of the body then disappears and centres within the heart itself.

If a strong emotional thought of some other person dominates the mind at this moment, as often happens when the dying person is far away from someone who is dearly beloved, this will be telepathically and automatically communicated. The latter may then experience a sense of great uneasiness, a feeling of something being wrong. If sufficiently receptive in temperament he may understand intuitively that the other person is dying. If sufficiently impressible in imagination, he may even clairvoyantly see an apparition of the dying person standing in front of him. When this happens the dying person himself also sees the living one at the same time. In other cases the voice of the one will be heard calling out to the other although nobody else present will be able to hear it. All these phenomena are really mental and indicate that the dying person has his mind fixed upon the living one and that his anguish, love or wish are capable when sufficiently strong of transferring themselves telepathically to a sufficiently intimate or receptive mind, which receives the stimulus and calls up within itself the image or voice of the other. It is the intense concentration dynamizing the original thought or emotion which acts upon and evokes an image within the second person, that is to say, the vision or voice is ultimately the result of the latter's own unconscious mental activity. This is just as wonderful a mental power as that which clairvoyance is commonly supposed to be.

A sense of utter helplessness next overwhelms the dying man. He may have been one of the most powerful potentates on earth during his lifetime. Now however he feels as powerless as an infant lying on its back. He senses that irresistible natural forces have taken hold of him and are drawing him, as through a long tenebrous and narrowing tunnel, he knows not whither, away from all that is familiar and friendly into a dark unknown territory or perhaps into self-annihilation. He yearns to express his feelings to those around the body which is now being vacated but he finds that the power of speech is paralysed. A terrible loneliness creeps painfully over him. This part of death descends on his desire-filled, possession-grasping nature like a shower of ice-cold water. But the man who has learnt the art of letting go, who understands the inner significance of Jesus' words: "Blessed are the poor in spirit"—with him all is well. At this fateful hour too the disciple of an adept in yoga or of a sage in wisdom will vividly behold the familiar form and feel the consoling presence of his teacher, whose image always appears at this moment to assist the passing over. The last thoughts of a dying man contribute to the complex group of factors which determine what form his next incarnation will take.

The ebbing away of consciousness which culminates in the death paroxysm provides the man with an opportunity he may not have had during his earthly lifetime to perceive what he has not hitherto been able to perceive. For from the moment when the pangs are over, and especially after the final beating of the heart, the "dead" man passes into a state of clairvoyant vision which to him may seem to extend over a few days but is really much less than that by the different standard of our earth-time. There now begins for him the discovery that a mysterious and deeper layer of his mind has kept a secret record of all the multitude of his experiences from prattling childhood to crabbed old age. Nothing has been lost but all still exists there in picture form. He will receive flashing glimpses of most episodes and many details, particularly those which were most intense, of his own past life. Persons who have accidentally fallen to the ground from a great height or who have suffered the pangs of drowning but escaped death often speak of the broken confused fragments of a similar experience which they are likely to remember ever afterwards.

The past returns fitfully in an unwinding web of impressive sharply-focused pictures which stand out as *external* to him. Nor does he re-live them in the same way as when he was in the flesh. For then time ran forward; here it runs backward. That is to say, he starts from the latest events preceding death and walks backward step by step until the earliest years are reached. Thus his past reverses itself. Again, when he was in the flesh time ran at the rate marked out by the earth's daily round of the sun. Here it rushes along with a hitherto unknown and unbelievable rapidity. And all this happens because he goes out of the body clinging to life, with his face turned towards earthly existence, wanting it and wrapped up in it. Such an imaginative return, such a living back through bygone episodes and ancient events is not merely a memory but something more vivid than that.

What happens next is that *a living being, which although he does not know it has already imperturbably observed the death of his bodily being, a hidden "I" which has always observed the surface "I", something within him yet something that he has not hitherto recognized as himself,* will now touch his consciousness. This being is none other than his own majestic Overself. Through his eyes he will gaze afresh at the total impression rather than the episodal detail of his earthly life. Through its revelatory eyes he becomes his own incorruptible judge. The purely selfish, purely personal point of view suddenly deserts him. For the first time, perhaps, he sees himself not only as others see him but also as the impersonal power of karma sees him. During this time he comes face to face with the *consequences* for other persons of his acts whilst on earth, consequences of which he was often quite unaware or in which he was often egotistically uninterested. He then perceives that many of his own misfortunes—so vividly depicted again in this amazing panorama—were definitely self-made and self-earned. By this diviner light of a conscience magnified one thousandfold, he *feels* that whatever happened to him was a just result, was traceable in the end to his own character and his own deeds. A great remorse overwhelms him. He puts passion aside and sees this surface "I" as the once-hidden observer sees it, without its own self-flattery and unconscious self-deception. He sees wrong-doing, sin and evil in some of his deeds where, previously, he hardly suspected them even to be present. He also sees other persons, with whom he had come into intimate relation, as they really are too and not as they pretended or as he believed them to be, and thus discovers how he has lived in a make-believe world of his own. Finally, he is made to ask himself the question, What have I done with this gift of life?

The second experience does not last long and is succeeded by a third one wherein the ebbing tide of consciousness turns all existence into what he now has the chance to understand as being the texture of a dream. All these episodes and persons of his past earth-life begin to seem curiously remote and unreal. The universal existence becomes mysterious and phantom-like. He has a chance to perceive the world's materiality for the fundamental illusion that it was. If he can realize this—and few do because it demands the putting away of personal desires and heavy attachments to do so—and if he can hold to this realization right to the very end, then he may definitely gain a spiritual profit which will show itself in the following incarnation. He must indeed be able to free himself from this very past whose contemplation he has just finished. Unfortunately man usually passes through this experience without a knowledge of its high potential value, that is to say although his earthly existence *now* seems like a dream he does not see that it was *always* like a dream.

When these revelations are at an end he falls into a welcome dreamless sleep, an utter rest of all his being within simple unconsciousness.

Only now is the transition of death really complete. An epoch of the individual's life is at an end. The flesh has fulfilled its task of providing through the senses the needed conditions whereby the consciousness which it enchained was able to gaze upon and be active in an outside world, thus obtaining contacts with external objects set in a particular kind of space and moving in a particular level of time. In this way alone could the little centre of finite consciousness which is the "I" gather experience at all, experience which will one day be distilled into the sublime discovery of reality.

In the Spirit World.

Those who pessimistically believe or teach that death is the unpalatable end of all for man have concentrated all their attention on the human body and merely exhibit their ignorance of what the human mind is, how it comes into activity and what course its evolutionary destiny must naturally take. They would be correct in comparing death, as they often do, to the change which a machine undergoes when its whirring wheels come to a standstill were it not that a machine lacks the unifying consciousness which a man possesses. When a machine ceases to operate we do not have to account for the loss of this consciousness but when a man ceases to live we do have to account for it. Why, if the body be their true self, do these materialists not insist on remaining alive instead of yielding it helplessly one day to the cold touch of death? Let them take a walk and refresh their fogged wits.

Those others, however, who have shed such materialistic beliefs and come to regard the body as an intimate form of consciousness to which the "I" is compellingly close but with which it is nevertheless not identical, will not find the next step in this teaching so astounding as it may seem to others. For, knowing the true relation which exists between mind and body, they cannot be deceived into melancholy acceptance of the materialist belief in human mortality. They can understand from mentalistic teaching that mind has fashioned a brain as it has fashioned the senses to suit its evolutionary needs, and that the five senses spring into activity at its bidding, not mind at their bidding. The sense-powers are mental ones as is amply demonstrated by dream-experience. The body merely brings together our five kinds of sensation into a single group. But what are the sensations themselves? They are experiences of the mind. Consequently the whole collection of them which we call the body is likewise something which essentially pertains to the content of consciousness. Every physical body must be a particular form of and within consciousness; it exists as an intimately-held thought for a containing mind, and so we can cheerfully understand the further truth that death can be nothing more than the cutting off of this collection from the mind itself. Its disappearance does not involve the disappearance of that which contained it any more than the cutting off of a part can destroy the whole. There is absolutely no necessity for the mind to cease its own existence when a collection of its sensations, an object of its consciousness like the body, ceases to exist.

There is one thing which the materialist has overlooked: *To what* have these ideas of both life and death come? They have come to the mind. In what do they appear and in what will they vanish? They appear and vanish in the mind. Therefore there will still remain something which cannot be lost, that is, the mind itself. It is the witness of the birth and death of these ideas. Even if the idea of life disappears at least it will disappear into the mind and be still contained by it. Even the world-idea disappears into the self. Why then should anyone fear death?

The unreflective man may deceive himself into believing that the world is outside his consciousness and that when he loses it at death he loses all possibility of further human existence. But the philosophic student knows that the world exists inside his consciousness and consequently knows that it is not lost at death, that it will come into spatial manifestation once more when consciousness becomes active again. In this sense his knowledge victoriously triumphs over death. Moreover the mind itself—as apart from its contents—is not in time, is not limited to the succession of "before" and "after", for these are in it and for it. Hence birth and death, which are ideas solely dependent on time, cannot apply to it. The mind, in this sense of not suffering from limitations imposed by time, is immortal. Only in the pitiful illusions of materialists can it go out like a quenched flame.

Let it be noted too that the mind must have existed before the birth of the body in order to receive those sensations whose conversion into sight, hearing and other perceptions constitute the body. No man who has thoroughly understood the tenet of the ideality of the body can ever again subscribe to the mistaken notion of materialism that death ends all. It ends something but leaves the mind, the veritable human essence, untouched.

If we consider the experience of dying once again, we find that when the short period of post-mortem blankness terminates, consciousness slowly revives—so slowly that the process is comparable to gestation in the womb—until the man finds himself once again as he formerly was. The higher viewpoint has vanished: the personal one alone remains. Once again he is a living self-centred creature surrounded by an *external* world. Nevertheless we must understand that what he feels to be external is, in reality, quite internal. For, as we shall shortly show, his new environment is produced in exactly the same manner as were his former dream environments. Its space is not physical but mental.

The question, Where are we after death? is an erroneous one and should be rephrased as: What are we after death? The spirit of the newly-dead man does not reach this other world by any sensation of geographical travel or spatial movement. He reaches it by a change in consciousness. The doctrine of mentalism especially makes it easy to comprehend what happens to man after death. It demonstrates physical life to be but a particular mental state; when the latter passes away the mind itself still remains and gives birth to a new and different state. It makes clear that if this earthly world is a form of consciousness the so-called next world into which we enter after death must also be a form of consciousness and not a place. It explains that such is the wonder of mind that it can create its own world by its own constructive powers. Whatever other worlds exist, they can only be mental ones, forms of consciousness too. These subtler worlds of being are not other-dimensional localities or geographical "spaces" but only states of being, psychological conditions. This is as true of after-death worlds as of mystically experienced "spheres". All the different states of consciousness, with their different time and space orders, constitute different worlds of being for the individual minds, that is "spirits" inhabiting them.

The newly awakened spirit first becomes aware of a succession of thoughts and hence of time. Only later does it become aware of space and the sensations of what may be called the spirit-body and then the awareness of other forms, other creatures and objects enter its field. But the so-called spirit-body is not at all a body as we ordinarily think of the term. It is not really different from the body—if we may think of it as such—which is formerly used on earth during its dreams. It is a psychological state. To think of it in the gross way in which we usually think of "bodies" is to deceive oneself. It must be repeated that all this is mentally constructed. There is really no such thing as "astral matter" from the ultimate standpoint any more than there is such a thing as earthly matter, both being only forms taken by consciousness. Those who have mastered mentalism will understand why this must be so. But the spirit which enters the next world in the materialistic ignorance which is so regrettably common in human life will naturally carry its old beliefs with it, and imagine that it is experiencing a kind of matter, just as it formerly did on earth.

It is not ordinarily possible for man to examine the condition of death from the inside, as it were, to understand by his own experience what has happened and yet return to life. But Nature has made it possible for all men to obtain suggestive hints about the state called death by making it possible for them to pass through the two states of dream and sleep. All three phases of man's existence are intimately allied with one another. We praise the wisdom of Shakespeare, and rightly. Writing of death, the poet asked: "And in that sleep what dreams may come?" It is unnecessary to resort to paid intermediaries in order to get at second hand a glimpse of what will happen to us after death. We get it every time at first hand when we dream at night as we get it every time when we are plunged in profound sleep! The psychological experience which we then undergo is up to a certain point the same as in death, but its theme differs in certain ways. If we can put ourselves in the extraordinary position of a man who dreams that he is taken by death and yet the following night dreams again that he is still alive, we can comprehend the position of the man whose earthly body actually dies but whose mentality revives later in a new earthly body. The likeness between death and dream is such that just as the dreamer unconsciously and involuntarily creates scenes, events, persons and surroundings, so the spirit unconsciously and involuntarily makes its own little world for itself. Each movement of its thought is simultaneously a movement of its environment. The unconsciously and involuntarily exercised power of selective attention makes and unmakes its new experience.

Although the spirit's state is likened to that of the dreamer's, there are however some important differences. First, it is much more prolonged. According to the new time-standard by which it now lives, years may and do pass away. Second, the wildness, incoherence and illogical disorder which mark so many dreams are not to be found here. Everything is presented to the spirit in an orderly connected and plausible manner. Whereas the dreamer cannot control his phantasies and usually experiences a wild jumble of incoherent episodes and incongruent figures, the spirit on the contrary finds its existence fairly logical and reasonably continuous.

Those who have grasped the central implications of mentalism will not need to be told that the world in which the disincarnate spirit finds itself, although an imagined one is nevertheless as feelingly real and as sensuously vivid *to it* as the one it has just left. Nevertheless the new world in which it now finds itself is not, as in the case of earthly existence, something which is shared in common with all other human beings. On the contrary, it is unique. It pertains solely to the spirit's own person. The truth is that just as the dream world is ordinarily a private world, so is the spirit world. All goals end in God. The spirit has begun its momentous return journey to the Great Aloneness of God and this first stage is a kind of precipitation into the aloneness of its own individuality. But being alone is not the same as being lonely. It is alone only in the sense that a dreamer is really alone with his own pictorial fancies and human figures, who are nevertheless quite real to him and may give him many crowded hours of experience. From this we may understand how the spirit is no longer in a public and common world as it was when on earth. Those who would make the spirit world merely a glorified second edition of the physical one, err.

Waking reverie, dreaming life, artistic phantasy and spirit experience—all these four belong to one and the same general species of existence. This after-death life is really a kind of intense reverie in which the spirit sees its own visions as if they were external to itself, visions peopled with images and scenes which are subconsciously constructed partly out of the ideas, feelings, tendencies and associations of its physical lifetime. The similarity of sensory human experiences in large masses on earth during that lifetime accounts for the similarity of spirit experiences in large masses here too. This does not mean that all the disincarnate beings are experiencing a common spirit-environment, however, but that they are each using and reproducing common materials for the construction of their private environments.

Next it must be made clear that both exceptional happiness and exceptional suffering in the spirit-world can come only to exceptional souls. Most people are not exceptional either in virtue or in vice. Consequently it may be stated that their spirit life will not involve any experience that need be much dreaded nor, on the other hand, any experience that will be highly alluring. The average individual is a lukewarm mixture of good and evil and consequently should not expect any such exaggerated experience after death. The "hells" of the wicked and the "heavens" of the virtuous are indeed sparsely populated. The new entrant will most likely fall into a state which is hardly different from that of an uneasy sleeper, a state in which unconsciousness is predominant but is punctuated with fitful scraps of dream-like consciousness. During these prolonged spells of awakening he recovers much the same personal consciousness, desires, emotions and thoughts which he possessed before. There is no startling change in him. His remembrance of the past returns. He finds it hard to believe that he is really dead. For just as his customary friends, work and pleasure, bulked largely in his ordinary dreams during earthly life, so will they bulk largely in this prolonged and extraordinary dream that is spirit existence.

But for the others who have been particularly virtuous or particularly bad, there are six fully conscious states in one of which the spirit will find itself by a process of natural gravitation and mental affinity; three being evil, dark and unhappy and three being good, bright, progressive and pleasant. The seventh and intermediate state lies between these two divisions. It is the one which has just been described and to which most people pass at death. Each state may be said to measure a different intensity of moral character. Thus the lowest state is a sphere of hatred and wickedness, that is a repulsive hell, whereas the highest state is indeed one of goodness, that is a blissful heaven. The forces of moral attraction and moral repulsion determine the character of the spirit's environment experiences and contacts with other beings.

The number of educated minds in the East or in the West which accepts literally the belief in the horrible infernos and smug paradises of popular religion grows smaller and smaller with the passing of every decade. Most of us would prefer soft couches in our present drawing-room to soft couches in a hypothetical heaven. Most of these stories of glorious heavens and painful hells are not to be taken literally but neither are they to be despised. They may usually be regarded as true in a symbolic way, provided they are first purged of the fanatical exaggerations which are intended to impress the masses and of the priestly exploitations which are intended to give power over the ignorant. What is the truth behind them?

The answer is that in the lower states the spirits become victims of their own extreme selfishness and extreme vices, which evoke by the same dramatizing power which the dream-mind possesses (for it must be remembered that they are dwelling in a world which is in every way equal to our dream world) a variety of forms, figures and continuous episodes of a tantalizing character. They dwell environed by the divinest spheres, to which only a change of thought is needed to lift them, yet they ignorantly gaze mesmerized on their own hideous or vicious creations. These illusions, which they hug to their breasts when momentarily attractive but from which they recoil in fear when later grown frightful, always begin with the promise of slaking desire but they always end with the torment of denying it. The spirit's imagination wears itself out with these struggles against its own self-created phantoms until finally it perceives the truth that hell is simply the hunger of its own unsatisfied passions and thus renounces the grosser ones. This act teaches it to keep its leering aggressiveness on a leash and liberates it to rise higher. The first and last lesson is that the next world is not a geographical place but a vividly prolonged mental experience. And like all mental experiences it can and does contain geographical places *within* itself. And like all vivid mental experiences it is real enough whilst it lasts. The truth is that neither heaven nor hell is actually a place but is only a state of the human mind, that both are nowhere to be located, and that all after-death existences are purely mental in the sense that dreams are mental. For example, the multitude of young and convinced Nazi Germans who were killed in the war—fanatically afire with the passions of greed, cruelty, envy, hatred and conceit as they were—were tutored in the most effective way. They were doomed to undergo a veritable nightmare in which they experienced in prolonged form the living *images* of the agonies they had brought to others. They became the scarified victims of their own debased thoughts.

The pictures of hell as a sulphurous realm of shades were not therefore without their use for keeping unenlightened multitudes within decent bounds. Their lurid details of torture and torment indicate that the priestly minds which painted them originally understood well the inhibitive power of suggestions given to the impressionable minds of the populace, especially the suggestion that evil-doing brings painful retribution. Those who denounce the doctrine of purgatory as mere superstition are only partly right for they have obviously outgrown the mental need of such a suggestion, but they are wrong from the standpoint of others charged with the moral instruction of mankind. We must remember too that such a purgatory as is here described is only a temporary condition after all. If people who believe in the dreadful doctrine of eternal damnation had either the courage or the competence to analyse their belief metaphysically, they would no longer believe it.

In the three psychological spirit-states which have affinity with what is finer and purer in man we may find the reality of the better side of those paradises which orthodox religions promise to their devotees. Truly no evil thought and no painful suffering can penetrate the happy blissful visions of these regions, which fulfil both the personal yearnings and idealistic aspirations of their inhabitants in a way that the past earth-life often failed to fulfil. Here they may recognize and meet their beloved ones, whether relatives or friends, who have passed on before them. If the love is really there it will certainly bring them happily together again. Nevertheless, from our earthly standpoint it will be only in the sense that two loved ones are brought together during a dream. Each enters the spirit-dream of the other. In both cases the second person will actually but unconsciously be reconstructed by the spirit for itself. Yet for the spirit it will be just as vividly felicitous, recognition will be just as blissfully spontaneous as in earthly life. The spirit in any of the seven states will meet other people and enter into relations with them, but these people are actually thought-beings and these relations are thought-weavings. Nevertheless these meetings in the three higher and heavenly states can be and are most emotionally satisfying to their participants. The fragrance of these affectionate communions, these beautiful interchanges of thought and feeling, lingers long in this wonderful region. For in such consciousness a stretched-out time standard yields a period which is indeed joyously spent, compensating in a way for much of the miseries of limitations which afflicted the earth-life that went before. Those personal, cultural and ethical higher hopes which crossed the skyline of their horizon on earth but which were denied realization, now find quick and easy fulfilment. The secret of this glorious existence is now a familiar one: the creativeness of thought working on a level where it can play largely unhindered.

What the spirit passes through in any of the after-death states is largely determined by the general tendency or habit-energy of what it thought, believed, desired and understood during its earth-life. There is no reason why anyone should not have his glorious picnics in paradise if he wants to. A dreamer may have them, so why not a disincarate spirit? The after-death state enables man to realize for a limited time his dominant longing. His thoughts and affections will inevitably gravitate to the mental sphere most in accord with them. The Asiatic philosophers have flippantly said that if cows have a heaven it will be full of green grass and if dogs go to heaven it will be full of white bones. This is understandable when we realize that the death-world is such a subjective one and so largely evolved out of the individual's own imagination. Hence a devout sincere Muhammadan who expected that he would find himself in a heaven with all the pleasures promised him in the *Quran* might well do so—but not for eternity as he wrongly believes. For just as he had to wake out of his earthly dreams each morning when alive, so the hour must inescapably come when he will have to wake out of his paradisaical ones also. Then he will ruefully realize that the whole experience, prolonged though it be, was created by his mind. There is always an end to the dreaming sleep of earthly life and correspondingly there is always an end to the dreaming activity of spirit life. Even though he meets his beloved ones again in the after-death state, it will only be to separate eventually a second time. Nature is inexorable. Therefore it is wiser to win the understanding that enduring union with others exists only in finding the enduring self.

The passage from this intermediate state to the next one, which is that of pure blissful dreamless sleep, is marked by a swoon similar to but without the agonizing features of the swoon which marks the passage from physical life to the spirit-world. The spirit now enters and dwells in a condition which is equivalent to what it formerly knew as deep slumber. Here it finds a merciful rest from the burden of personal consciousness, an utter oblivion of the self-centred memories, joys and pains which have inevitably accompanied it hitherto upon its earthly and unearthly existences. The peace and refreshment which the man found intermittently for a few hours at a time in physical life during the night he now finds again for a long uninterrupted period.

The post-mortem period may roughly be divided into three stages. The first is a stage where the dream-life is immersed in the darker side of personal existence and ignoble desire; the second is a stage where the dream-life is immersed in the brighter and nobler side of such existence; whilst the third is an entirely dreamless and unconscious rest. Thus the spirit passes successively through the phases of misery, happiness and that which transcends both. Most individuals skip the first stage, however, and start their spirit-career intermittently conscious in an unexciting neutral zone.

A question commonly asked is whether it is possible to communicate with spirits either through home seances or through sittings with professional mediums. The answer is that under abnormal conditions we may succeed in doing so. But in most cases it is unlikely that the communicants will be the spirits of those whom we believe them to be. Both sitter and medium are usually ignorant of the working of the deeper layers of their own minds, an ignorance which often causes them to ascribe to a spirit words and visions which emanate from themselves alone.

It has earlier been explained that Nature keeps a perfect record of everything that transpires in her wide domain. Where a medium is genuinely sensitive to telepathic emanations she may glean scraps of personal identity, description and history from the cosmic mental record and then pass them to her client in all sincerity as a definite message from a spirit, when it is really nothing of the kind. Again, even if a successful contact with a spirit is established the message will naturally and necessarily be interpreted by the medium in terms of her ordinary physical space-time perceptions and the belief that accurate expression of the communication is taking place will then be an illusory one.

But the most serious drawback is that there exists a sort of no-man's land, a psychologically criminal belt which surrounds this earth and contains the most degraded creatures, devoid alike of conscience and truth. Strange evil entities walk these border-lands of the dead. Nature has very sensibly put a curtain between us and the afterworld and whoever meddles imprudently with it does so at his peril. That lying and malignant spirits lurk behind this curtain is a fact admitted even by spiritualists themselves. Most attempts, therefore, to look behind it are attempts to look for trouble.

Modern spiritualism has rendered great service to mankind in convincing many people of the truth of survival and in consoling the bereaved but the public would be safer in being content with studying its literature for, generally speaking, it is a field of research which should be left to a few carefully selected mediums and a few prudent investigators who are sufficiently trained in scientific methods and yoga technique to work competently and safely in such a deceptive and dangerous field. There have been in the past a few earnest devoted and excellent Spiritualists who have broken the hard crust of materialism for many people and deserve every credit for doing so and there are living today a few Spiritualists whom we personally esteem for similar reasons, but their number is swamped by the multitude who have merely substituted a subtler form of materialism or who have ignorantly opened doors for lying spirits to come out of their lurking places or who have deceived themselves by attributing to outside sources manifestations from the underground part of their own consciousness.

By the grace of the Overself by the force of great love genuine communication is sometimes effected through a medium and does bring great comfort to a bereaved person. But whoever is so bereaved as to feel the overwhelming need of entering into such communication, despite the warnings here given, should remember that the only reliable method in the end is to enter it for oneself. It is also the only satisfying method because it involves one's own personal experience, not something got at second hand. And this can be done only in the stillness of mental quiet or in the vision of dream. The first demands some progress in meditation whilst the second demands the practice of a certain pre-sleep exercise which is given in "The Fifth Meditation" in Chapter 14. A pure love or a powerful spiritual affinity between a disincarnate person and an embodied one can break through from the spirit world to our own or *vice versa*. Truly a deep noble affection between two persons conquers the chasm set up by death and brings not only loving thoughts from the spirit to the receptive consciousness of the living person, not only a sense of its personal presence to a sensitive mind, but in times of danger may also bring by spontaneous reaction a protective gesture which may effectually help to ward it off. It is no idle saying that love conquers all things for at the very base of the universe there is this wonderful unifying power. But such communication can in the nature of things be possible only for a limited period. Any attempt to make it a lifelong practice is to ask too much from Nature and will lead to undesirable consequences.

The newly-arrived spirit will see his old home, city and family but he will not know that they are figures and scenes constructed by his own mind. They will not be the actual figures and scenes of the physical world. For communication therewith will now be as unnatural and unusual as it was from the earth side before his death. Hence a change in the selective space-time level changes the whole universe for the experiencing being. Just as living men are not ordinarily aware of the dead, so the dead are not ordinarily aware of the living. But just as the living may and sometimes do see a genuine apparition of the dead or intuit a genuine communication from the dead, so the reverse may also happen.

It was pointed out in *The Hidden Teaching Beyond Yoga* that man's space and time senses were expanding. But that is only half the story. For these senses are also contracting. Man is exploring minute worlds which are as unbelievably tiny as the macrocosmic worlds are unbelievably vast. He has to measure the lightning-swift rapidity of light's motion as he has to calculate the immense age of the universe. His thought has indeed to run up and down the scale when he tries to comprehend his environment, to such extraordinary extremes that his whole conception of time and space has to become equally elastic. From this it is easy to see that there are countless possible strata of mental existence, all of which must be relatively real to the conscious beings who dwell within them. Hence if our idea of "here" and "now" were to change then the particular world which hinges on it would necessarily change too. Time and space are elastic. They will differ to different beings in different planes. There is no fixed space and no fixed time. We are never conscious of them but only of our own space or time perceptions, which are variables. The mathematical theory of relativity has shown that different kinds of space are conceivable but the mentalistic theory of relativity shows why they must be conceivable. Consequently those who teach that the innumerable hosts of spirits are continuously in touch with and observant of our own physical world teach what cannot possibly occur in Nature's scheme of things. For when, refusing to keep company with credulity, we understand mentalism we understand too that time and space are the forms under which we cannot help perceiving the world. The different kinds of living creatures have different kinds of space-time perceptions. If such differences exist between the living creatures confined to our physical world, how much more must they exist between them and the so-called dead creatures of what is an entirely different world? Each creature can only possess experience in relation to its own particular level of space-time perceptions. To assert that all the millions of inhabitants of the spirit-world are co-conscious with us of this physical world is to assert what is metaphysically impossible. The belief that thousands of ghostly eyes are constantly prying into his private existence may be welcome to a naive and humourless person but must be repugnant to a sophisticated one.

All general descriptions of the next world which give the contrary impression are inaccurate merely because they are descriptions made from outside, as when a medium sometimes succeeds in passing on a communicating spirit's account of its experience. The spirit does not usually understand that its world is a dream world and the medium certainly does not even consider the notion. Each spirit will have its own private world just as each dreamer may be said to have his own too. Consequently there may be as many million spirit worlds as there are spirits. We can therefore describe with conscientious accuracy only the psychological condition of the spirit, not its particular environment. Whoever has followed carefully the foregoing explanation will understand why it is impossible to give in detail a genuinely scientific account of everything that happens to an individual spirit. We can no more ordinarily do so than we can cross the silent shore of sleep and describe what dreams other human beings are having. All that can be done here, if the reader is not to be misled as most people usually are misled when reading descriptions which purport to describe post-mortem life, is to provide an *outline* of the general psychological condition in which the spirit finds itself and the general destiny which faces all spirits at the end of a certain period.

The master key to understanding the psychological experience of death is to keep in view its identity with dream or sleep. Mind is immortal. It remains untouched despite the body's dissolution. We have no more reason to fear its death when the body is destroyed than we have to fear its death when we retire to sleep at night. Sleep affects the body but leaves the mind as active as ever in dream or as potentially active as ever in deep sleep. Death works upon the human being in a somewhat similar manner and the experiences which come to the soul after the flesh has terminated its living existence are nothing else than prolonged vivid dreams or unconscious deep sleep. If we can touch and see things and people without the help of the flesh during dream, we shall certainly be able to do the same during so-called death. And if we can take a benign rest from all the fret and agitation of personal existence at a later and deeper stage of sleep we shall certainly be able to enjoy rest at a later and deeper stage of death. That in us which can survive dream and sleep in the earth-world will likewise survive them in the after-world. Why then should any of us fear? If however we insist on believing that we must eventually perish which means that we insist on identifying ourself with the body-thought rather than its Thinker, then we must accept the fear and suffering which come with wrong thinking.

The Pageant of Change

Such is the human experience which follows after physical death. What of its metaphysical meaning. Above all else stands the fact than puny man no less than the vast world which surrounds him is subject to constant change. His own body bears mute witness to this irrefutable fact. The straight-spined, smooth-skinned, rosy-cheeked, brown-haired child seen again by someone returned after an absence of two generations has become a bent-backed, wrinkle-skinned, sallow-faced, bald old man. His life has been but a tale of powers, functions and appearances rising to their attractive zenith and falling to their uncomely nadir. When all the bodily changes culminate in a final crisis there happens what we recognize as death. Yet what are these earlier changes if not slow minor deaths? Does not the infant die to become a child and the child die to become a man? Does not physiology prove that every seven years the body is completely transformed anew owing to the process of cellular development? And even whilst science reveals that the chemical alteration of man's body is incessant, his own experience reveals that the general alteration of man's thoughts is a parallel one. If the first were not a fact then flesh and bone would not show the slow hardening and imperceptible thickening which come with age, whilst if the second were not a fact he would never ask himself apropos of his own self as it was a score of years earlier: "Could I have been so different? He seems like a stranger!"

What we can see through a microscope as an individual

blood-cell has a life of about one month and then dies in the spleen. Thus man lives by the death of his own blood corpuscles; they have to die if his body is to survive. Every piece of fleshy tissue, every nerve-tube and muscular fibre is in fact gradually dying daily but we do not stop to observe these minor deaths through which the body is passing; only relatively is its final death more important than these earlier ones. All constitute a continuous series of changes which are as inescapable as they are natural. The wearing-out of our bodies happens by the iron process of Nature, against our wish and without our will. Youth fades from them like light from the darkening sky and old age falls upon them like flakes of chilling snow. The hand of death mercilessly touches all things! Who or what has escaped it? The little plant which matures into a mighty tree cannot avoid either slow decay or ultimate destruction in the end. The flower shows its fair perfumed face only to wither miserably away. When we remember the countless millions of animal and human creatures which have gasped a last sharp breath and expired, we may well think of our planet as being a gigantic cemetery. Yet which among these pitiful millions who rushed out seeking passionate life paused to think that death itself was rushing after them? For only the man who attains some reflective moments awakens to the sad instability and depressing transiency which permeate the stuff of all human existence. Almost all conscious beings are lost in the fearful flux of time, which imparts a fictitious sense of death's remoteness to them. Such is the strong illusion which has taken root in their minds that they thoughtlessly regard as permanent what can exist for a limited period at most, although every day Nature is withering all things and taking all creatures away before their very eyes.

Everywhere the same process is happening. Countless rivers are daily losing themselves in great oceans and oceans are incessantly losing themselves in atmospheric vapour. Plant and animal bodies set up whirling cycles of carbon and nitrogen interchanges during their own growth and decay. All living forms on the planet are engaged in a perennial flow of change involving a turning wheel of life and death. Fossils indeed are the only organic forms which last for hundreds of thousands of years but even they must crumble and pass with the passing of sufficient time. Even the particles of the seemingly inert chair in which we sit are minutely changing from moment to moment, otherwise it would not be liable to slow decay through the centuries, but the process is so slow as to be imperceptible to our physical senses. It is hidden from our eyes by the veil of time, because the changes in the chair's particles are not immediately apparent to the eye. Is there any single moment, therefore, when the stuff of the chair can be said to be really stable? If there is, we cannot even calculate its duration, for the present is ever vanishing into the jaws of the past. No sooner is it in being than it is gone. Its disappearance is the appearance of a fresh and equally incalculable instant. Time itself thus illustrates the universal flow, the cosmic restlessness, the omnipresent ephemerality which are but other names for death.

The life of every form on earth is forever in flux, a fleeting phenomenon which is as brittle as thin glass and as transient as wind-blown dust. The dark stamp of mortality is imprinted upon all bodies, whether of crawling worms or mighty potentates. From the high Himalayas to the low ocean bed, from the protozoic cell to proud strutting man, all are subject to this divinely-ordained unending process of birth, decay, dissolution and death. There is no escape from such a flux, which is both the first and final feature of all existence. Whether it be a race of men or a range of mountains, every formed thing rises into being only to fall victim to this iron law of its own appearance. This very planet which coaxes its pigmy inhabitants to build towering edifices of great civilizations must one day, as science itself suspects, itself decline and dissolve into cosmic nebula.

In a group of tumbledown ruins a few miles from Lahore, India, and amid a heap of reddish stones strewn on a marble courtyard, there stands a crumbling sarcophagus. It bears the terse inscription: "Here lies Jehangir, Conqueror of the World." Where now art thy conquests, O Jehangir? Where art thou *thyself*? Dost thou not illustrate the verse of Persian Omar?

> Think in this battered Caravanserai,
> Whose doorways are alternate night and day,
> How Sultan after Sultan with his pomp,
> Abode his hour or two and went his way.

Music, the lovely queen of all the arts, alone can express this pathetic realization of the sad mutability of earthly existence in a way which words can never do. The unearthly haunting strains of Tchaikovsky's *Fourth* and *Fifth Symphonies* are such an expression. Change is the one certain thing which does not change! It is equally the foremost characteristic of all living forms, however much new pleasures may camouflage their transiency and however long the old doctrines of Heracleitus and Buddha may disappear. This restlessness of the universe might well make us question whether Change itself is not the ultimate reality.

What is the law behind these fleeting pageants, these endless changes? To answer this consider how many hundreds of crawling worms are killed and eaten by a single bird during the course of its lifetime and have thus in part become transferred into the bird's own living body? How many hundreds of dead birds have been eaten in their turn by living insects which have thus transformed them into their own living but different forms? And how many worms, birds and insects have rotted and mouldered in the ground until they fertilized the brown earth, nourished new vegetation and fed great trees into whose forms they were themselves absorbed? Consider too that the railway train which carries us comfortably from city to city burns coal which is the residue of trees dead for millions of years, which thus live again in the energy they provide to propel the locomotive. This ceaseless interchange of particles not merely within the same body but also between different bodies means that nothing can really claim as its own a single particle of the body which bears its name. Every particle, on the contrary, belongs to the All. Where, physically, is the real death in such a process of constant destruction followed by constant rebirth? Is it not rather an endless movement of *life*? Is death not ultimately a process of critical change whereby life passes from one shape into another? Is not everybody that dies somehow and somewhere and in some form reborn anew?

Thus the course of Nature circles infinitely. If she destroys it is only that she may create afresh. This is true of every part of her domain, whether in the life and fate of human beings or whether among the lands and waters of the globe; whether in the cyclic currents of human history or in the ebb and tide of animal history. Destruction and death are only part of her game; in the end they are but illusions, although verily quite often painful illusions to those who suffer them. The universe being what it is, death cannot be separated from life nor destruction from creation. The convulsions of Nature which engulf a whole continent through rolling flood or heaving earthquake are no less part of the World-Mind's work than the creativeness of Nature which brings millions of beautiful flowers to colourful bloom. Thus the World-Mind creates, sustains and destroys the universe in the materialistic sense although we know now that these three processes are but appearances in the mentalist sense.

"Nothing in the world perishes and death is not the destruction but only the change and transformation of things," are the irrefutable words inscribed on an ancient Egyptian papyrus. That death exists is but a one-sided half-truth. For it derives meaning only from the presence of life. And life is equally meaningless unless taken together with its twin.

"The rudimentary universe waited for life to appear," cried the scientific speculators of the last century. They pictured a planet whirling its hot career through empty space for millions of years until the first microscopic jelly-like living entity appeared, generated in the hot sandy inter-tidal mud of primeval seashores under frowning clouds which perpetually filled the violent sky.

"But there has never been a dead universe!" retort many of the scientific speculators of our own century in the brighter light of their later knowledge.

Thus we are cradled in a great mystery and cremated in a greater one. For all the lengthy and admirable explanations of science are explanations of the mechanical physical processes which accompany welcomed birth and walk with unwelcomed death; they do not touch even the hem of the elusive garment of life itself—the unique element which has passed from body to body, from ancestor to inheritor, from parents to child, as a flame was passed by runners from torch to torch in the old Olympic games of Greece.

The activity of the universe executes a perpetual cycle because it is the fundamental meaning of manifestation. When we gaze at the spectacle of the world-process in the way which we have been doing, the fact that it is a *living* process stands out pre-eminently. Its permanent reality lies not so much in the amazing multitude of forms which come and go as in their being alive. The flesh is always symbolic of something *more than flesh*. If death is only a transformation and not an annihilation, if the stream of life flows ceaselessly through a myriad different shapes, all this points to the permanence of the stream itself. Innumerable physical bodies may break up and crumble to dust and vanish from our sight, but the new bodies which they fertilize both before and after death represent a kind of continuity of the life-stream. And thus we arrive at the conception that the life involved in all these bodies must be something apart and self-existent and moreover must be something permanent.

Can we assign any beginning or end to this universal life-stream? We cannot. For even if we trace it back to the remotest and earliest thinkable form which it could possibly have taken, we realize that this form must have inherited its existence from another one which preceded it. This in its own turn must also have originated from a preceding one. Thus if we maintain a constantly questioning attitude we shall regress ever backwards in thought through a series of inter-related bodies but shall never be able to come to a legitimate stop. The living spark which flits through all this series is indeed as beginningless as it is endless. The life principle is greater and wider than the forms which it takes. It does not die with these forms but, like an everflowing river bearing all things uninterruptedly along its surface, bears them along without a break in its own existence. It is the common factor in all the countless little individual lives which have their little day, the single and stable principle which is implicitly present within and survives them all. It is their hidden driving force. Yet it is so utterly elusive that we cannot catch it within our mental or physical grasp for it is as mysterious as an algebraic x—a symbol which stands for an unknown quantity that truly exists but waits to be discovered. The essence of life eludes us because it is infinite and unconditioned. Although present in all atoms and all individuals it is not itself atomic or individualized. It is present in the eye, for instance, yet no finite eye could ever perceive it.

When we consider the innumerable times in which conscious beings must have taken birth in some form or other; when we remember the immeasurable series of variegated existences through which they must have passed; and when finally we consider the inconceivable endlessness of the life-stream which has flown through them, we are forced to arrive at the conception of the life-stream being itself the only reality, the only true eternity. But life is a twin; intelligence is always found alongside it. Life and mind are inseparable. Hence mind is equally the real and the eternal. If every embodied creature is subject to the death that eventually follows birth and yet bears a mysterious life-essence which is not subject to this limitation, then our experience as a flow of changes becomes intelligible. For we know that they are changes only because of the subconscious contrast provided by the existence of the hidden unchanging observer which is always present along with such experience. And whatever does not change does not die. Thus the very idea of immortality arises for us because there actually exists an immortal principle within us.

Is there any analogy which helps us to understand these difficult points? There is. Science has taught that there is nothing in space which is not perennially moving, from the mighty sun whose motion is doubled by the earth that circles around it down to the infinitesimal particle of dust which the most powerful microscope can barely catch but whose protons revolve at unimaginable velocities. Movement is thus the heritage of all existence. And movement means that something has passed from a particular point in space to a different one. But such a passage is only possible when it also occurs between two different points in time. Therefore we are compelled, along with Einstein, to recognize Space, Time and Motion as inseparables. Thus whatever moves must move spatially—be it a minute molecule or a vast solar system. And as its path is finite it cannot, in the end, escape from its starting-point but must eventually return to it, that is to say, all motion is shuttle-like. Every moving thing is really vibrating to and fro, however long in seconds or centuries its backward swing be delayed. In the activity of an ocean set astir by the wind we find an example of what such vibration really means. Wave after wave travels forward and each seems to be a separate mass of water as it heaves itself up to a crest and then falls down into a trough. But physics tells us that our eyes are deceived and that every moment the content of every rippling wave is leaving entering it and a second one. Each individual wave is constantly dying and continually being reborn. The only constant and continuous existence is the ocean as a whole. The universal life, seen through its innumerable manifested bodies is forever entering and leaving them like the water, in the waves, but seen as it really is in itself is forever constant and homogeneous like the ocean. This is only an analogy of course and should not be pushed too far.

The antique expositors of the hidden teaching in Asia, Africa and America symbolized the enthralling truth of this original oneness and eternal renewal of life under the pictured figure and fabulous story of a coiled serpent. For when this creature periodically sloughs off its old skin it appears with refreshed strength in a new one. Such an apt symbolism speaks of the repeated re-embodiments of all individual living things as well as of the repeated transformations through which seemingly inanimate Nature herself passes. Again, when a snake lies in its underground hole it usually coils itself into a pattern like a circle. Now it is not possible to mark when and where a circle really begins or ends, as it is not possible to mark when eternity and where space begin or end. Not only does life like a circle return whence it arises on itself but the entire universal movement is ultimately a circular one. The earth on which we stand revolves on its axis and when we glance up to the open firmament we see heavenly bodies which revolve around their orbits. Hence the ancient teachers used the whirling Swastika to symbolize the incessant vibratory movement of the cosmos and the circular serpent biting its own tail as a suggestive emblem of the self-renewal of the cosmos, whilst they used both signs to stand for its ever-living and endless character.

If life is a universal presence we cannot rightly confine it only to such forms as appear to us—with our very limited perceptions—to be living ones. Therefore the universe cannot produce a single dead thing although it may produce a seemingly inert thing like a mineral or a metal. The chemical division of forms into organized bodies and inorganic substances, the biological division of Nature into animate and inanimate matter and even, as we have begun to show, the psychological division of mind into the conscious and the unconscious, can only be dictated by practical convenience and not by scientific actuality. Indeed such a sharp division will sooner or later begin to look somewhat out of date and wholly arbitrary, when the latest investigations have run their full course. The incessant inter-atomic movement should alone suffice to demonstrate that *all* substance is living substance, that there is nothing really dead in the universe, whatever its appearances may be. Even the hardest rocks grow or decay with time, as is clearly demonstrated by the fossils embedded in them, and thus betray the world to be a living process and not a lump of finished matter.

From another standpoint, in so far as it is the succession of released karmic potentials arising and determining one another in a beginningless series that is at play, it is easy to see that the world must be a continuous process and not a stable thing. The universe is vibrant and alive. Death touches its appearance only and is the gateway to a fresh birth. Change itself is but a manifestation of the Changeless. This is the meaning of the procession of ever-active change which surrounds us. And because the principle of life is itself a power belonging to the principle of mind, whose essence is a deathless one, even our individual failure to know its existence does not deprive us of our share in its immortality. If death in the *immediate* and *individual* sense is to be seen all around us, it is not too much to declare that death in the *ultimate* and *general* sense is a notion utterly foreign to the man who perseveringly pursues his enquiry into the meaning of this universe and courageously faces all the inconvenient questions which arise on the way.

Now anything which is seen, felt or tasted, that is to say anything which is experienced by any one of three senses, must by its very nature distinguish itself from all other forms if it is to exist at all. It has to be separated out. Therefore it has to bear a particular form. And whatever bears such a form necessarily involves itself in height, length and breadth and therefore involves itself in space. But in actual experience space involves time and time involves space. Each idea is but part of a whole which includes both and which may be termed space-time. Space and time are inseparably associated together. And it is the process of change which provides us with our idea of time. Therefore this form involves itself in time too. From this point we may advance to the conclusion that whatever assumes a shape which can be pictorially imaged in the mind and whatever exists in the time-series—whether it be our own body or the things which surround it—*must* in the end become the victim of this process of uninterrupted change. This means that the form which it bears must be a fugitive one and necessarily impermanent. Such is Nature's abiding law. Death, as the most critical of all forms of change, is the necessary if heavy price which every incarnate being has to pay for living in this space-time world at all. But death does not speak the last word. For the twin truth to all this must clearly be that an existence which is formless and timeless, which is in Being rather than in Becoming, must also be an immortal one.

What am I? is consequently a question whose answer lies enwreathed in the fundamental distinction between the human being as we ordinarily know him and his hidden ultimate essence. There are certain aspects of his being which are obviously transient and these can be collected together under the designation of his person, but that out of which these aspects arise is ordinarily beyond our comprehension. It is here that it meets with stubborn difficulty for ordinary life and conventional education do not afford any ground for the concept of an existence which transcends both relativity and personality. It is also because of this inability to extend the mental horizon to such a concept that men usually end by degrading it; hence their eager desire for a perpetuation of personal life after death, not understanding that all its limitations and defects would necessarily have to accompany it too.

These studies will later reveal that not personal but collective satisfaction is the farthest goal of life. Those who want the first without the second are foredoomed to disappointment. This does not mean however that we are consequently condemned to misery. For man possesses a higher individuality and in it, in the realization of this Overself, there is also an exalted if less exciting satisfaction. All solely personal satisfactions must, by their very nature, be transient ones, whereas that got from the Overself is, likewise by its very nature, alone permanent. "Do not nurture the unreasonable wish that the changeful shall become unalterable," is the wise counsel of a Chinese text, *The Teaching from the Platform.*

To the question: "Is such a deathless, formless, timeless, infinite life anything more than a mere theoretical concept? Is it an actuality?" Philosophy answers in a firm voice: "Yes. It truly exists. It is reality. This universal principle exists in every man as his higher individuality." Because it possesses this power to manifest in changefulness without itself changing, it must be called a principle rather than a person. It is indeed the principle of all our life and all our consciousness. Nowhere in the cosmos can the two be found apart, the one without the other. Whatever lives, be it a rooted plant or a roaming animal, has its own field of awareness. This is because it is not life that produces mind, as materialists aver, but mind that produces life. Mind is at the base of all things. Life is but its dynamic aspect and hence mind itself is an unkillable thing. Metaphysicians of the East and West have wasted much of their time and created many puzzling but unnecessary pseudo-problems by differentiating between things and their properties, between substance and its attributes, thus setting up an artificial separation where one does not exist. This has led to the delusion that energy can have any meaning other than as unreal theoretical abstraction apart from the Mind or that Mind can exist apart from this particular property of being active. The world is not only an idea: it is also an activity. The latter arises because mind possesses its own energy.

Now mentalism says it is the thought that conceives the physical thing. And because all thought is in constant flux, because it is a successsion of conscious moments, all things themselves are experienced as if they were in a constant flux of existence. For what is the first characteristic of any thought? Is it not always and without exception doomed to die and vanish as surely as it has arisen? It may live for a few seconds as an inner fancy or a few years as an outer thing but it will surely pass again. Nothing that is formed escapes from the relativity which is perpetually imprinted on all earthly existence and this relativity is explicable only on the basis of its being mental. Every thought that disappears thereby *contradicts* its own earlier arisal. Moreover the stability of material things is contradicted by the discovery that they are mental constructions. There is no finality anywhere, neither in things nor in thoughts. For the forms of things perish and their inner reality escapes the grasp of thoughts.

Mentalism has assured us that both thoughts experienced as being external, namely sense-impressions, and those experienced as being internal, namely what everyone agrees to be thoughts, that is to say, the images present to the mind as physical things and the images present to it as its own fancies, are constructions built up solely within our mental activity. The first seem permanent and the second seem ephemeral but this difference arises more out of the self-deceptive power of consciousness than out of anything else. For it is merely a difference in time, and time itself is merely a form of consciousness. Both are simply two different forms of a single basic activity. This mysterious principle of mind which makes their appearance possible is not only uncontradicted by such appearance but must relatively be their permanent background. Hence it is uncontradicted either by any changes of its own nature or by any later changes of human experience. Therefore all material forms and all mental constructions, being liable to death, are called "the uncontradictable" in this school of thought, which by contrast names as "the uncontradictable" that mind which is their everlasting Essence. Yes! This statement evidences that it accepts a definition of mind which has no materialistic reference. Beneath the changes there is something which never changes, which indeed holds them all within itself. That which spreads itself out around us as a physical world and that which is felt within us as a thought-world constitute a unity in the end. Such a position seems to involve a curious duality. Intellectually this is necessarily so but the philosophical consciousness does not find it so. For it unfolds the ultra-mystic insight which actually unifies all experience when it is at work. For it the sharp contradiction between appearance and reality which besieges less advanced faculties disappears. Hence it is said to be the fruition of "the yoga of the uncontradictable", the deathless prize of those advanced methods of yoga which seek to enter into the conscious realization of this sublime oneness.

Rebirth.

But a voice of protest breaks in. "What are all those impersonal abstractions to us? While death chants its mournful dirge across the planet, martyring millions of broken beasts and crushed ants who perish helplessly to its tune, where is the hope for mankind? Is the universal everything, the personal nothing? Is the creature itself forever immolated on the altar of its species, its race? Must we accept the consequences of this chill truth which so offends our human feelings?" These complaints are reasonable ones but let us remember that if life is sadly stamped with transiency, death is so stamped too. The one is thus always a preface to the other. If anything changes and passes away, this is only because it turns into something else.

Next let us note what is seldom seen; that if the creature is being immolated for the sake of the universal evolution, the universe itself is being immolated for the sake of the creature's evolution. The universe is not useless. The experiences it provides make the individual confront it one day and ask, "Why? Whence? Whither?" When at long last the creature finds the answers to these questions, it finds itself, its true eternal self. Those who ask for personal survival after death during an endless eternity are unconsciously asking for the everlasting survival of all their moral faults and defects, all their mental incapacities and limitations. This in turn implies that they are asking for the fixation of error and the stabilization of evil and ignorance. How much better to ask for the progressive change of personality, for evolution from the worse to the best, even though this involve the gradual letting-go of the imperfect characteristics and traits of a particular personality and its gradual transformation into a diviner and grander being? There is no need to fear this passage from our inferior personality to our higher individuality. It is not a retrogression towards less than that what we already are, that is towards annihilation, but an advance towards more than we now are, that is towards true self-fulfilment. The individual consciousness is not lost. It is expanded, increased, enlarged.

Again, all this ever-renewed unrest, this universal proclamation that life is an ever-active Becoming leads the creature to ask: Is there a changeless existence anywhere? And if there is, can mankind hope to liberate itself from the thraldom of this incessantly-turning wheel and participate in it? Thus the pressure of constant change forces it to seek the Immutable. The depressions of carking illness awaken it to yearn for the Undecaying. The agony of unexpected loss arouses it to seek for the Peaceful. The touch of chill death drives it to look for the Deathless. And in the end even the perplexities of self-conscious ignorance goad it forth in quest of the True. All these roads will meet and finish in the conscious discovery of the mysterious principle within itself which is undying and universal.

But even so these complaints are justified only from a certain standpoint. For the released consciousness is only partially released by the critical transition of death. The multitude of impression which it has gained during its incarnation have worn certain furrows of desire and habit. These tendencies attach themselves to it and colour it completely. Not having yet understood that there is an ultimate and impersonal purpose to be attained in passing through these experiences in the earth-world, it has developed an excessive interest in them. It has formed strong passionate attachments to the more pleasurable ones and strong personal dislikes to the distasteful ones. And it has come into contact with other persons, some of whom are greatly loved but others greatly hated.

All these are mental ties, and so long as they exist the

"I" necessarily continues to feel the need of the physical body in which it formed them. And thought being creative, it will be driven by its own forces, that is its own karma, sooner or later to return to earth again. All these ties need a new incarnation for their working out and adjustment. No world becomes real for us until we experience it, which means until we think it. That is to say, it does not become real until we make it part of our consciousness and thus absorb it fully into our self. Therefore the spirit is inwardly impelled to think the space-time characteristics which will bring the earth back into its consciousness. Before this can happen, however, Nature so ordains matters that it has to pass through the intermediate period corresponding to dream wherein the earthly experiences just completed are first mentally digested. This interval is followed by the further one wherein the entire being rests and recuperates in deep sleep for its next return to earth.

The individual stream of mind flows in continual circulation through the incarnations and is not exhausted by any one of them. We were and we shall be. No life is a finished one: we must continue somewhere and somewhen. Hence the birth of every baby is never a biological accident but always a psychological necessity. Sexual union brings two cells together, which unite into a single germ and grow, but it does not create new life. It merely creates the new conditions in which an old life can express itself. Karma links an act to its consequences less because of the fact of reward or punishment than because of the profounder facts that mind is continuous and that all things are mental things. If it works through a succession of apparently different persons this is because all are connected by this continuity.

Both the rosy successes and bitter failures of life arise naturally. The mentalities of men differ greatly and their perspectives of life must likewise differ, because the width of the second depends on the quality of the first. Both mentality and perspective are, in the final analysis, results gained from former births. No experience is ever lost. All the innumerable memories of innumerable lives are subconsciously assimilated and transmitted into wisdom, into conscience, into tendencies and into intuitions which spring from men know not where but which nevertheless influence their characters and lives. However, the process is long and slow. We cannot jump the hurdles which bar us from the winning-post. Who knows how many repetitions of the same sharp experience, how many sojourns in the stumbling flesh are needed before these aims are fully and effectively accomplished? The one essential is right direction. There is no standing still. We must develop or degenerate.

There is no fixed interval between the re-incarnations. The individual karma, modified by the evolutionary karma of the planet, decides its length in each case. Consequently a man might be reborn after one year or after a thousand years. But a new body cannot be taken until the flesh has totally turned to dust. It is a wise hygiene which cremates rather than buries it.

The possibility of rebirth is strangely shown by the analogy of sleep. In sleep we disappear into dream or unconsciousness. In death we do exactly the same. Each morning we reappear out of apparent blank nothingness with all our personal character and particular tendencies intact. The marvel of rebirth is thus not different from the marvel of waking up the same man each morning. The dogma of the Christian Church which says: "I believe in the resurrection of the flesh," is without reasonable meaning unless it means a renewed appearance on earth in this sense.

We who crowd the modern scene are witnesses unconsciously testifying to death's defeat. Those who can grasp the inevitability of repeated human re-embodiments on earth need not fear death. Here in rebirth they can find again, if they want it, the comfort of personality as others can find in the Overself the aspiration to a higher individuality. Here too they can find their loved ones once more. Thus in the history of the human body we have taken on a fresh fleshly garb not once but innumerable times. The connection between these different births may best be understood by understanding the connection between the different aspects of the same human being at the ages of two, twenty, forty and seventy respectively. Just as it cannot be asserted that we find precisely the same man at each age and yet it must be admitted that each is the inheritor of the preceding one, so the succeeding re-incarnation is not precisely the same as the preceding one but only its inheritor. In each there is summed up all its previous existences, all Nature's previous endeavours along a particular line.

The course thus run is long but not endless. With the last lesson of this earth well learnt and the first principle of being well assimilated, we finish the weary round of reincarnations. And then, according to the temperamental and ethical tendencies previously developed, we shall take one of three paths. First, we may elect to merge finally and forever in the universal mind and lose the burden of the little self in the larger peace. Second, we may leave this star for a higher one where the forms and grades of existence are finer and fairer. There are other inhabited globes, some lower and some higher than ours in the evolutionary scale. Any human being who has developed so highly that he has personally outgrown the usefulness of our Earth has thereby earned the right to reincarnate on a globe bearing more advanced beings. But this is an uncommon event. Third, we may, actuated by an all-embracing pity, silently take on the terrible sacrifice of abandoning the rewards rightly won and remain here in constant reincarnation to help those who grope in the darkness of ignorance and bewilderment. In that case, self-doomed to descend again and again amongst suffering mankind, we must expect to remain always uncomprehended and often unthanked by those we seek to serve. Whereas it is strongly-felt desire which leads the ordinary man into a course of repeated earthly existences, it is strongly-felt compassion which leads the sage into the same course too.

Sometimes an advanced god-like being from another planet has deliberately reincarnated himself on our Earth so as to help its benighted humanity before, during or after a critical time; this happens mostly when human character sinks into deep materialism and has to endure its attendant sufferings. Such an act is necessarily wrapped in a mantle of mystery. It represents a tremendous sacrifice, *a veritable crucifixion of consciousness.* If Jesus was a "man of sorrow" it was not because of what men would do to his body—but because of what they thought in their minds.

For lesser mortals who have to reincarnate willy-nilly there is always the opportunity to mix a little altruism with the desires which force us back into the tempting flesh. The aspiration to serve will then play its part in modifying karma and in dictating the character of the next incarnation. A powerful intuition of the existence of such a path, interpreted though this intuition necessarily was in a narrower non-reincarnatory and non-physical sense, was expressed by the young nineteenth-century French Catholic mystic St. Thérèse as she lay dying on her bed. "The beatitude of heaven does not attract me," she exclaimed. "I want to pass my heaven in doing good upon this earth. My wish is to work here again." To her sister's orthodox objection: "You will look down on us from heaven?" this blessed and beautiful soul answered: "No, I will *come* down. Would God have given me this everlasting desire to do good on earth after my death unless He had meant me to fulfil it?"

It was explained in the fifth chapter why humanity can attain its fullest spiritual Self-realization only in the wakeful state of the physical world. Because the after-death regions here described are the equivalents to the dreaming and sleeping states only, it becomes needful for the imperfect spirit to return to earth again, where alone it can find the adequate conditions for its further progress. This is the final justification of rebirth.

It is the business of philosophy not to avert death, for it cannot constrain what is so inherent in the very nature of things, but to give us a clearer understanding of the significance of death, a profounder courage with which to face the final adventure and a rarer calmness with which to witness what few can escape witnessing. It reveals death to be but a change of dress, such as we have gone through many times before and will probably go through many times again. It teaches us to get away from the conventional attitude, which is based on ignorance, and to understand that both birth and death are part of the process of educating mankind. When we identify the "I"-thought, which always arises first, solely with the body-thought, which always arises second, we turn the scale of values upside down and limit the larger factor to the lesser one. Through this initial error we not only strengthen our sorrows and increase our grief, but also fill our hearts with unnecessary fear. But when we become conscious that we *are* conscious and that this is the most direct thing of our experience, we have reached the momentous turning-point of understanding the difference between both thoughts. For the need of making this miracle—and it is nothing less—clear to our own understanding itself puts us on the right path to achieving it.

Is it not better to believe that death is the eternal friend of man and not his bitter enemy? That it comes into his existence from a beneficient source and not from an evil place? That it stays him from wandering into further evil courses? Is it not better to think with Plato that "the mere preservation and continuance of life is not the most honourable thing for men, as the populace think, but the continuance of the best life whilst we live?" Death reminds man that physical well-being *alone* can never suffice, as it sets him free when physical burdens prove all too heavy. If it ends his cherished hopes, it also ends his worst diseases and his chronic pains. When the wife of the Chinese mystic Chuang Tzu died, he told one of his disciples: "If someone is tired, we do not pursue him with shouting and bawling. She whom I have lost has laid down to sleep for a while. To break upon her rest with the noise of lamentation would but show that I knew nothing of Nature's sovereign law."

After "love", the word "death" is the most misunderstood and most misused one in the language. Man makes much alarm when the body ceases its action but never sheds a single tear upon the millions around him who are spiritually already almost dead. His alarm is needless. When he will have answered the riddle of his living self he will have answered the riddle of his dead one. For he will then discover the grand truth that he is infinitely more than he seems. Thoughts and things will pass, but his own essence will never pass away. He is ultimately made of such stuff as reality is made of. When he shall come into consciousness of his own estate he will not be afraid of reaching the grim terminus of earthly things. The black-coated men may thrust his heap of bones and flesh into a wooden box, but they cannot thrust *him* therein. No grave has yet been dug than can hold a man; it can only hold his discarded decaying flesh and nothing more. For no knife has yet been made which can dissect him.

When our life has reached its westering glow, we find no nutriment in the idea of total annihilation. Both animal instinct and human reflection tell us that the journey from cradle to crematorium cannot be for this. Let us not give our assent to this gloomy postulate. The more so when we understand that the principle of life is everywhere present and that it takes an infinite variety of space-time forms beyond our present perception. It is only our lesser part which can vanish; the higher one survives forever. Annihilation is not our fate. Therefore it is better to believe with Nature that death is as necessary as its twin brother birth, and as helpful as the respite of friendly sleep. It is truer to believe that it is an episode in life and not an end of it, an instant amid eternity and an incident amidst a series. It is a long dream and a longer sleep. He whose body is eaten by worms or burnt by fire remains untouched and unharmed. His personality returns as surely as tomorrow's sun, whilst his essence has neither gone nor come: *it is*! And we write these words not in theological hope but in solid certitude. For science, mysticism and metaphysics combine to speak with united voice on this point. This is something which is not only true today but must also be true always for it transcends historical and geographical conditions. Time can never cripple such a truth.

We shall certainly survive the sharp sting of this scorpion of death because the "I" owes nothing to the body for its own existence, but draws its life from that higher individuality which lies above it unchanged and unaffected by both birth and death—the Overself.

8

The Immortal Overself

JUST as it has been necessary to purify our ideas of what is meant by "I"; just as it will later be necessary to purify our ideas of what is meant by God; so it is now necessary to purify our ideas of what is meant by immortality. We did not deny the "I". We shall not deny God. We are not now denying immortality. But fallacious conceptions of it must be got rid of.

It has already been learnt that personality is a changing series of thoughts, a moving cycle of states of consciousness and not a permanent fixed self. Just as the body is a complex of component parts, so is the "I" a complex of inter-connected thoughts, sensations, perceptions and memories. So long as these thoughts stream after each other in a series, so long can the personality endure, but when the stream stops flowing then personality cannot survive. We witness this even during lifetime for in deep sleep there are no thoughts and then we lose our sense of "I".

The personal "I" is but a bundle of impermanent hopes and transient fears, a little sheaf of cravings that change with the changing years. Nothing that we know among them is immortal even during this present earth-life; how then can they be immortal through all eternity? To cultivate a belief in a personal ego that will permanently survive in a state of fixation is to prolong the illusion that even now blinds our eyes to truth—unless of course we choose to regard the series of continuous reincarnations as a kind of immortality which, in one sense, it certainly is. But this conception will not satisfy those who demand conscious unbroken continuity as a characteristic of their immortality. We shall certainly exist after death, whether in the dream-like stage with which it begins, the sleep-like stage with which it ends or the new reincarnation which completes the whole circle of personality. Yet in none of these shall we have done more than achieve a mere survival. Let this satisfy those who want it but it is not the same as true deathlessness which can be achieved only by transcending the transient personality.

It is here that once again the importance of our discoveries about the mind-made nature of time becomes apparent. For the question of immortality is tied to the question of time and cannot be separated from it. In its common form, it is naively supposed to be the perpetual continuance of the same personal self in eternity. But this is metaphysically impossible. The mere fact that a person appears abruptly in time makes him inescapably mortal. For whatever has a beginning must have an ending. This is an inexorable law of Nature. Yet, the notion of the eternal existence of the same person in a world which is itself subject to eternal change, a notion which constitutes the orthodox concept of immortality, is one of the fond delusions which man has always liked to harbour.

This popular notion which is based on the powerful hope of continued personal existence in time is not the metaphysical one. Immortality is not to be honoured by its being a prolonged time-series, which is merely a quantitative gauge, but by its mode of consciousness, which is a qualitative one. Its value is in us, not in time. We may live a million years as a worm or a brief day as a man. Is the worm's immortality to be preferred to the man's mortality?

Men ordinarily love their own fettered existence more than they love anything else. Consequently their notion of a worthwhile after-death state is one wherein they continue that same bondage to the surface life of the senses in which they were held on earth, just as their notion of a worthwhile goal of human evolution is one wherein they can personally enjoy perpetual bliss. They do not comprehend that this is only one stage farther than the materialist view which would make man but an elongated ape and which would limit his experience to whatever manifests itself to his bodily senses alone. They do not comprehend that if they are to experience egoistic existence after death it will have to include all the pains and disappointments of egoistic existence before death. There is no freedom from suffering anywhere in the universe so long as there is no freedom from the ego. Hence even those who fondly believe and ardently hope for such a personal survival, such an endless continuance of the miserable limitations and unsatisfactory defects of their earth-life, will *even there* have one day to wake up and start in quest of the Overself. For the call of the inner life can nowhere be evaded although it can often be postponed. It is the final purpose of human existence, wherever the drama of that existence be set. Hence they too will one day have to seek escape from time to timelessness. We may mitigate the apparent harshness of this doctrine as we please in order to help those unable to bear its full brunt, as theologians and priests have mitigated it with their theory of a permanent personal soul arbitrarily made static at a certain age of a certain earth-body, but we can do so only at the cost of its truth.

An endless prolongation of personal existence with all its narrow interests and parochial experience would be as unbearable in the end as an endless prolongation of waking life uninterrupted by the boon of sleep. And yet even in this widespread longing for personal continuance we can detect the beginnings of what will one day grow into the nobler longing to live forever in the true immortality. For it is an unconscious perception that human existence *does* possess something within it which is unaffected by events in time and is therefore genuinely eternal, something which stands apart from all the miserable mutations of the flesh and the "I". It is indeed an unformulated intuition which, hiding among the perishable elements of personality, affirms that there is an imperishable principle which cannot be brought to an end with the end of the body. The popular error which transfers what it knows, namely, the characteristics of the physical body, to what it does not know, namely, the mind for which that body is but a cluster of ideas, must be corrected. When this is done the desire for the endless continuance of a body-based "I" naturally sinks to a secondary place. When the mind-essence is recognized as the true ground upon which the whole structure of this "I" has been built, it will also be recognized as something which is never born and consequently never dies, as what was is and shall be. It can then be seen that if all our memories involve time, they also involve as a background the existence of something in them which is out of time. This view of immortality as belonging to the higher individuality of Overself rather than to the lower personality will then replace the former one, which is ultimately doomed to suffer the anguish of frustrated desire whereas the true view bathes a man in increasing peace the better it is understood. When man continues firmly and unfailingly to identify himself in thought with this, his higher individuality, quite naturally he comes to share its attitude. And from this attitude the belief, "I shall die eventually" is entirely absent. To imagine is to create. That which a man thinks, he becomes. Rightly thinking himself immortal, he consequently attains immortality.

The common conception of immortality would make it an indefinite prolongation of personal existence. The mystic conception would make it an indefinite prolongation of personal bliss. The philosophic conception, however, transcends both these notions because it discards the personal life and replaces it by its ultimate non-egoistic root, the individual Overself. The first two are still within the time-series, albeit it is not the kind of time we ordinarily know on earth, whereas the third is beyond any possible consideration of time or succession. It *IS*. Such true deathlessness can be attained only in the Overself, for this does not derive its life, as the body does, from another principle. It has life of itself. Consequently, the body has to give up in death what it has previously received, but the Overself, never having had anything added to it, has nothing to give up. It cannot but be immortal for it is part of the World-Mind and what is true of that must also be true of itself. That which is forever in union with the World-Mind must itself be forever free from a change like death.

What is meant when it is said that the Overself is man's higher individuality must now be explained. We know that the World-Mind must be everywhere, yet it is certainly not everywhere, the personal consciousness. There must be a point-instant in space-time perception where the latter can meet it. In most mystical experience such a point is *first* felt to exist within the heart. But the World-Mind cannot be confined within such a limited perception. And later mystical experience always transcends this centre within the heart and largely detaches the consciousness from the body altogether. Yet the finite self can never bring the World-Mind in its fullness within this experience simply because finitude would itself merge and vanish while trying to do so. This mystical meeting-point, the Overself, represents the utmost extent to which the finite self can consciously share in the ultimate existence. It is that fragment of God which dwells in and yet environs man, a fragment which has all the quality and grandeur of God but not all the amplitude and power of God. The difference between the World-Mind and Overself is only one of scope and degree, not one of kind, for they are both essentially the same "stuff". We may climb as high as his highest self but not beyond it. Thus our personal life is a phase of the Overself's life. The latter's existence in its turn is a phase of the World-Mind's existence. Through his chain of relations the little self has an everlasting kinship with the cosmic one. It can become aware through philosophy of this kinship but it cannot transcend the relation itself.

The World-Mind apparently breaks itself up into an endless multitude of such higher selves but after it has done so it paradoxically remains as unlimited and as ultimate, as un-diminished in its own being as ever. The notion that the Infinite Existence has divided itself up into such units is correct only if we understand first, that this division has not involved any reduction in its essence, and second, that it has not meant any real parting of them from this essence. We can best understand this by remembering what happens in our own mental activity. Our innumerable ideas are a kind of division of the mind but do not really involve its exhaustion for the ideas not only arise but must vanish back into it. Although the mind perpetually empties itself into thoughts, it is never less itself, never less its own single presence. Nor are these thoughts separate at any moment from the mind. In the same way, except that it is not affected by the transiency which affects all thoughts, the Overself is not separate from the World-Mind. Every Overself exists in the World-Mind just as different thoughts exist in one and the same human mind. The World-Mind's consciousness may multiply or divide itself a million times but its stuff is not really divisible; it only appears so.

It may be noticed that the term Overself has here been used only in the singular number. Yet if it is not the World-Mind itself but only a refracted fragment of it, a spark from its flame, should it not be right to use this term in the plural number also? The answer is that this would tend to give a wrong impression that the Overself of one man is actually and eternally as separate and isolate from that of another man as one reincarnation is as separate and isolate from another. If there be a slight technical confusion in using the singular number alone, there would be immeasurably more confusion if, in using the plural, this dire error of any radical difference existing between them were to be authenticated. The Overself of each man is historically distinct from that of another man but only in the sense that each has overshadowed or animated a different series of reincarnated persons and presided over their different destinies. Just as there is no intrinsic difference between individual sunrays themselves, so there is no intrinsic difference between one Overself and another, but just as each ray will have a special *relation* of its own with the objects it encounters so each Overself will have a special relation of its own with the cycles of reincarnated personalities. Like a single ray it shines down upon a particular person whereas the World-Mind like the sun it also shines on all persons alike. Each Overself *in itself* is exactly the same as and all one with another. In other words, the difference is only relational and not intrinsic. There is certainly *not* the separateness between them that there is between two persons and yet there is not entirely the likeness which exists between two identical things.

The experience which one man has when he first comes into the consciousness of the Overself is absolutely identical with that which all other men have when they too come or shall come into it. There is no difference in any detail. The contradictions which exist in recorded mystical experience arise either because of the mistakes, illusions and misinterpretations made by mystics who lack philosophical training or because they have not had an authentic experience of the Overself at all. This will become clear when we reach the subject later in this course. Nevertheless the memory-content kept latently within an Overself is absolutely distinct in every case because the series of personalities projected from it has necessarily been distinct from the series projected by another. This memory-content cannot be abolished; it is there and from our space-time standpoint must be recognized as establishing a claim to individuality of a sort on the part of an Overself. Consequently we say that the Overself possesses a higher kind of individuality but it does not possess personality. The Overself of one man is distinct from the Overself of another but not separate from it; at one with it but not identical with it. Hence if two men who deeply hated each other were suddenly to come into the realization of their own Overself, they would just as suddenly mutually love each other. If they could sustain this realization then there would be perfect and permanent sympathy between them instead of the strife which formerly engaged them. The Overself is consciously divine and can never lose its really universal nature any more than the sunray can lose its real nature as light, divided a millionfold though the latter be. We may no more impose such personalistic limitations upon it than the single and simple corpuscular cell in the body of a vertebrate animal—which would be but one out of many millions of such cells—may impose its particular limitations upon the central consciousness of the animal itself. From the human standpoint the Overself is the deeper layer of mind where man can become conscious of God. It is the timeless spaceless immanence of the universal being in a particular centre.

Why am I myself and not somebody else? This is an important question which can find a final answer only when we can penetrate into the consciousness of the Overself which projected this particular "I" into incarnation, for an entire tangle of evolutionary necessity and karmic history would need to be unravelled. Meanwhile it may be said that the Overself projects itself into a series of separate beings but instead of holding its light they hold its shadow. Although the Overself is but a segment of the one World-Mind its expressions during cosmic manifestation, that is personalities, will each possess traits of their own which differentiate one from the other. These are the transient differences which divide the innumerable living beings but they all exist on a lower level than the Overself which eternally unites them. And just as each of the figures in a dreamer's mind lives a characteristic life of its own in a semi-independent way, so the personalities projected by the Overself largely follow their own course once they have been placed at its starting-point. The Overself within the person is always the same and always aware of its relation to it, even though the person is so ignorant of this relation. The memory of the essential characteristics of all former related incarnations are registered and preserved within the Overself, although it does not need to sit and brood over this knowledge, which is kept latent.

This higher self does not itself evolve through widening experience like the personal self which it sends forth to taste of the fruit of the Tree of good and evil. Each reincarnated "I" may be symbolically thought of as being but a point dwelling in the superior self's infinite and eternal experience. The body provides the *field* of experience, thought and feeling provide the *means* of experience, whilst the higher self is the ultimate experiencing being in man, the mystical "Word made flesh". It is the inner ruler of the ignorant personality, the divine deputy to profane life. It stands to its related successively reincarnated persons in the relation of a sun to the planets which circle around it. In this sense, as that which exists behind and above his sensation-emotion-thinking being, as a thread-soul by which all the innumerable reincarnations are joined together, we may call it the real being of a man. And although as the hidden observer it owns the ego it does not do so in the sense of personal ownership. It is as disinterested and as impartial towards this reflected shadow of its own being as towards all others. The explanation why the division involved in such self-fragmentation was the only way in which any "I" could come into being at all is a most metaphysical one and consequently a most subtle one. It may be understood better by understanding what is involved in the everyday act of seeing. If we were to see white alone in everything and everywhere and always; if we were never to see a red or a blue or even a faint grey; if we had never known at any time any other colour than white, would it be possible for us to see anything at all? For without the experience of contrast we would not even be aware of white as such. Where everything is always white and where we have never known existence without it, we would not only be unconscious of all other possible colours and chromatic variations but we would also be unconscious of white as being white. For the blackness of coal would be meaningless without, say, the whiteness of snow with which it could be contrasted.

Now the Overself's original consciousness is a single and undifferentiated one. This means that its only awareness is of existence but not of personal existence. It is conscious yet not self-conscious in space and time. But such a consciousness is in a certain sense equivalent to having no consciousness at all. For experience can only begin when we can begin to distinguish between something that is, be it our own self or an object, from something that is not. We can know anything, whether it be our own self or an object, only when we can oppose it by a second thing. Therefore a single undifferentiated consciousness is, from a merely human standpoint of course, like having no consciousness at all.

Thus self-awareness can arise only when there is awareness of a contrast between two things. We become aware of the existence of anything only in and by becoming aware of what it is not at the same moment. For unless we can distinguish it in this way we cannot distinguish it at all. Now the very first of such contrasts must necessarily be that which exists between the self and what lies outside it. That is to say, the opposition of the idea of "not-me" must arise if the mind is to become aware of the idea of "me". If there were no second thing there could be no conscious existence for the "me". The existence of "me" implies the imperative need of a co-existing and contrasting "not-me". Self-consciousness must limit and restrict itself by "not-me" if it is to be at all. The one must always presuppose the other. For to know anything at all is to draw a clear circle within which consciousness must lie enclosed and outside which there will simultaneously lie whatever is to be known as not itself. Knowledge can only come into being if it is knowledge of something which is not the knower. Hence the very idea of a self implies its being distinguished from what is not the self, which means from what is *outside* it.

Now if the Overself is to set up the opposition of an "other" which is separate and distinct from itself, its first step must necessarily be to limit a part of itself to less than what it really is, to contract away part of its own infinitude and freedom. Its second step must be a narrow and intensive concentration on that which it thus presents to itself and which is now seemingly independent and apart. Every concentration of mental power involves a self-forgetting proportionate to the intensity with which attention becomes absorbed in the thought of that which is external to it. Its third step must be to provide this limited ego with a field of experience to complement and complete it, of which it can become conscious as something *outside* itself.

Thus the projected person has come into being. It exists through what is external to it and the latter exists through it; both are inter-locked. The two are inseparably coupled in each indivisible moment of individual consciousness. Thus the person's world-experience is born and in so far as the one confronts the other, self-consciousness is aroused, just as the electric current which meets with the obstacle of a piece of carbon during its onward flow strives to overcome the resistance and this striving generates light. This resistance which the "me" requires is got through the limitation provided by its spacetime perceptions and sense-operations. In the case of man the setting-up of the five senses produces the externalization of his perceptions and consequently of experience, thus producing objects for his consciousness and "matter" for his belief. Nevertheless we must not fall into the easy error of forgetting that this felt opposition does not render consciousness independent of the world. It has already been shown that both the "me" and world unfold from a common source, the hidden mind. Their opposition must therefore be only outwardly apparent and not inwardly irreconcilable. They are still related and not isolated. For although *felt* in experience as separate and opposed, they are *known* in analytic reflection as joined and united.

Self-awareness must be bought at the heavy price of such a splitting up. Those who ask why the ego be not Overself-conscious from the first do not know what they ask for. It could only be born at all at the cost of having some neighbouring existence in reference to which it could have a meaning as a distinct entity, as a personal self, and from which it could be differentiated. For both personality and personal consciousness are modes which limit the pure being of the unlimited Overself. The ego could only have its separate experience by losing awareness of the unique and universal principle that underlies it. We can know that we exist only by knowing that some thing or some thought other than ourself also exists. This is a supreme law which must bind all intelligence, both that of the tiniest gnat and of the Overself alike. This is why the unlimited Overself must delimit its horizon, must make a descent from its own transcendent Oneness into separate selves and must reduce itself to setting up relations with them. Consequently, when the universal and infinite Overself both limits and differentiates itself in order to acquire self-consciousness, the portion of itself so limited and finitized forgets its infinite character. In revealing the "other" it veils a part of itself; in setting up an object for experience it has also set up a subject shrunken and dwarfed through this lapse into personality. This is why nearly all creatures in this space-time world have forgotten their divine origin.

Nevertheless we must never forget that the infinite World-Mind through its intermediary the Overself dwells in every one of its innumerable finite centres just as they dwell in it. The roots of all creatures are planted in the ground of a universal being whose life is common to them. Not one can isolate itself from the World-Mind in fact although it may do so in belief, any more than it can isolate a reflected image from the light itself. Ultimately it borrows its very life from the Overself, never has been and never can be disconnected from it.

The Hidden Side of Selfishness.

The overself is truly an eternal image of World-mind. Therefore it is written in the Bible that God made man in His own image. The reference here could never have been to the lower aspect of man, the petty creature who frets and fumes his way through life. The phrase fits finely however to the immeasurably higher aspect of this twofold species. The fact that men have turned round and denied their person, nay, even sacrificed their person, points to the presence within them of something which is different from the person, points indeed toward the overself. Each man therefore has two faces. One is downturned toward the earth but the other is upturned toward World-Mind. The first is the "person" and the second is the Overself.

Why do we so pathetically feel our cramping limitations, our shameful weakness, our saddening mortality, our mocking finiteness? It is only because we *unconsciously* possess a point of view which transcends our normal one that we are able to see how limited our little self is at all. It is only because we are subterraneanly related to the infinite that we know that we are finite beings at all. It is only because there exists something in us which goes beyond us without losing its hold on us that we are troubled by any aspirations at all. It is only, in short, because the Overself is present behind its limited expression the person that the latter can understand at all how limited it is. The quick satisfaction we derive from material things, the prolonged absence of the thought that one day we must inevitably die, even the very reality which we attribute to the external world—all these when rightly understood are symbolic promises and remote reflections of the sublimer satisfaction, the genuine immortality and the intuited reality which the presence of the Overself within even now unconsciously yields us. They speak not only of what we secretly are but also of what we may openly become.

Every individual is necessarily incomplete because of his finitude. All his endeavours, whatever direction they take, are expressions of his unconscious quest for completeness, of his repeated search for self-satisfaction. Hence all his characteristics bear an illusory resemblance to those of the Overself, and necessarily so, for he is unconsciously and often distortedly trying to express what truly belongs to him.

When we can come to regard the limitations of the surface self as ephemeral ones we open the gate to correct understanding of the hidden dimensionless mind at its centre. The various distinctions which arise within this mind, the innumerable thought-forms which are perpetually being born in it, do not diminish or exhaust it. It is useful to consider each human incarnation to be like a tiny wave of water upon the surface of a limitless sea. Each wavelet has its individual and unique shape but all are formed within one and the same sea. Each may think of itself as being but a tiny wave and nothing more or it may think of itself as being not only a wavelet but also as being not different from the sea itself. Similarly each incarnate creature limits itself unnecessarily when it refuses to realize that it is really not different in *essential nature* from the Overself. Each is potentially grander and greater than it knows. If man is slowly learning the hard lesson that a human life is a wavelet upon the ocean of being which must sooner or later level itself out again, there is still left the water of which the wave is composed. This idea may be regarded as eternal death and hence undesirable from the limited point of view of the person but it is eternal life from the larger point of view of those who have analysed the person and find it to be like a flickering shadow which rises and sets with the rising and setting sun.

A metaphysical lesson drawn from the dreaming state may also help us here. What is the true status of a number of different persons who are convincingly seen during this state, who speak in clearly heard voices, who carry on conversations with one another and take up different standpoints in discussion but who finally vanish when the dreamer himself awakens? He then knows that they were dramatized out of his own mind-stuff and that therefore they were all essentially one and the same in essence. He knows too that his mind never really differentiated itself into these different figures but only *appeared* to do so; that is, its own continuity and selfhood remained unbroken throughout. In the same way the Overself has always been the single being out of which the many reincarnations have appeared, the sublime unity which always escapes the doom of these multiple and perishable personalities whose separateness is as much a surface illusion as the separateness of all those dream figures. It is their truly abiding nature. It contains the highest form of immortality. Again, because separateness vanishes during sleep the selfish strife and evil born of it also vanish. The peace which then suffuses a man and which is testified to by the lingering after-echoes felt immediately upon awakening could be his during wakefulness too if he would deliberately and consciously subordinate this separateness.

It was earlier noted that everything throughout the universe is sentenced to be forever in motion and forever in flux. But what do such changes mean unless they mean that everything is forever making changes and thus modifying its own identity? And in the case of human beings where—even leaving out the equally definite but less perceptible bodily changes—the thoughts and feelings alter so quickly that the conscious being of a few minutes ago is not quite the same as the present one, the change in identity is not only inescapable but also irretrievable. The mental state or emotional mood which has passed away can never again be got back precisely as it was. Do what we will we cannot keep a fixed unbroken identity but must submit to a perpetually changing one. We are continually forced to surrender the "me" from moment to moment. *Then why not yield to Nature's bidding and surrender it altogether?* Why run vainly after something we can never even hope to catch? To comprehend this universal truth, to accept its inflexible lesson, to cease trying to cling only to the transient identity of the personality, in short to refuse to allow the "me"-thought to arrogate sovereignty to itself and thus dominate its own thinker—this is the necessary prelude to opening the heavy door which bars our way to discovery of what exists behind the "me". For this reason every illumined religious mystical and philosophical teacher has voiced the need of self-surrender.

It may be objected that we feel the personality as the basis of all our conscious existence, that to be conscious at all we have to pay the price of finitude and that try as we may we cannot divorce consciousness from the personality. How then can it be annihilated unless we want to annihilate our own existence completely? The answer is that man first of all is called upon to understand that the world in which he lives consists of various levels of being, each one providing through the *forms* which it takes a perpetual space-time suggestion for the creature within it. This done, he is not called upon to deny his own personal being but only to deny his false *conception* of that being, that is to recognize it to be only an underself. He is not even asked to say that it does not exist but only that its existence is thought-constructed. He is asked to admit that his present understanding of "I" is incomplete and must be perfected. Do what he may man cannot give up the "I" for it is that which has brought him to birth, but he can give up the illusions about it which hold him captive, the wrong concepts wreathed around it which lead him astray into sin and suffering. Strive as he may man cannot disentangle himself from desire for his earthly existence depends upon it, but he can, when he becomes the personality's witness, disentangle himself from his habitual enchainment to desire. He is asked to dwell again and yet again in this strange new world of thought until it eventually becomes as familiar and as intimate as his daily self.

If we assume that by metaphysical probing he discovers and by ultra-mystic practice he sees at last that the "I" is not in the body but the body is really in the "I"; if he realizes that the personal "I" like everything else within his ordinary experience is really a thought-construction which feigns a permanent and stable entity of its own; if he penetrates deeply beneath it and uncovers its hidden essence as mind, what has he done? He has got rid of a mistaken idea—however powerful, however hypnotic and however over-confident his belief in it formerly was—and he has substituted for it the contrary idea of his higher individuality, the Overself which can never be annihilated, which forever remains what it was, alike in quality but distinct in characteristics from the World-Mind. The personal consciousness which he has evolved after so many incarnations, with so much effort and through so much toil, is not swept away. It remains. Only, it takes its proper secondary place. It becomes subordinate to the Overself. Both are there within the same zone of awareness. He keeps this sense of his own personal transience alongside his sense of a sublime ever-abidingness in the Overself.

If therefore he is seemingly called upon to part with the personal, he is really called upon to receive consciously that unfettered peace-fraught existence which is its origin. If he is seemingly asked to surrender the Many, he is really asked to take full possession of the One which is their background. If he is seemingly led to deny all formed and felt experience, he is really led to accept the ultimate principle which permits such experience to be possible at all. If he is forced to negate the products and constructs of mind it is only that he may affirm the pure mind itself. If he is asked not to assign an exaggerated value to a self which is transitory by nature, it is only that he may perceive the unique value to be assigned to an individuality which is permanent and real. Thus whatsoever he seemingly loses is returned again to him deprived of nothing but its transient shapes. The supersensual whole cannot be less than its sensual part. Why then should anyone fear it?

If it be further asked how a man can play his part in the world's work and fulfil his obligations to society unless he stand solidly upon the feet of his own personality, the answer is that he who has unfolded this insight has not altered his actual existence. For practical purposes he remains the same man as before and plays the same role in society—more likely, he will play a much better one. He is not deprived of the slightest capacity for useful action, but on the contrary his discovery beneficially influences his ethical standards and improves his external life. He is not called upon to suppress personality but to suppress that blind *infatuation* with it which is the source of so many practical mistakes, moral sins and social injustices; he is not required to submerge the needs of self but to submerge their satisfaction at the cost of injury to others. What has such a man lost in the end? His personality has not been destroyed but only purified; his consciousness has not been paralysed but only disciplined to understand itself better; his responsibilities have not been deserted but rather fulfilled in the most conscientious manner; his possessions have not been scattered but only turned into a trust to be used wisely.

But is it actually possible to take up such a philosophical attitude towards one's own ego? it may finally be asked. Surely the feat of witnessing its activities quite impartially must always be a theoretical and never a practical achievement? We may discover the answer for ourself. When we become intensely interested in an exquisitely beautiful musical piece unfolding itself on a concert platform, what happens to us during the deepest moments of such concentrated rapt attention? Do we not actually drop the entire load of our own personal memories, ambitions or anxieties, hopes or fears and thus stand aside in temporary freedom from them? Is this not a practical if involuntary and temporary achievement of that philosophical attitude?

Admittedly no one wishes to lose the sense of "I-ness"—this powerful instinct which is the driving force back of all animate Nature. We have yet to see a single case where those who denounce the ego as a fiction and disbelieve in its existence act upon their belief. From the meanest worm to the highest mammal, everyone loves his own existence. Why not? Why should we pretend to be other than what we are; why should we prate of desiring to lose our self or prattle of its unreality and non-existence, when we cannot get away from it even if we wish to? Every living thing, whatsoever has the faintest trace of consciousness within it, feels this deep desire: "*I* want to exist. *I* want to live." But the mistake it makes is the failure to comprehend that to satisfy this intense craving it is not necessary to cling only to the limited and fragmentary form of self with which it is acquainted, for it can receive full satisfaction only when it lets the latter go and reaches towards the perfect being that is its inmost essence. If we think down deeply enough we shall see that even the desire to give up selfishness is itself prompted by a subtler selfishness and motivated by a nobler egoism. We may put aside the "me" but we cannot get rid of the "I". We can however expand its circumference. We can also deepen its centre. More, life cannot ask of us and yet let us remain in the kingdom of man.

The personality is indeed "I" but it is not the ultimate "I". For we are not selfish enough? The trouble is not that self is merely an illusion, as some claim, but that our present knowledge of it is only a broken fragment which has still to be supplemented and completed. It is wiser to possess firm faith in the infinite resources behind self and not waste time decrying its present life as purely phantasmagorical. A man is not to be blamed for acting upon self-interest. This is natural. He is to be blamed for failing to see that he is taking only a surface-view. Just as the many little wheels of a great machine are unaware of the general direction in which the machine itself is moving, so the great multitudes of men are unaware of the general direction of all this cosmic activity, wherein every incarnation is a movement from the less to the more, a minor stage in man's major quest of the Overself.

We barely know our self; we clutch a more surface-fragment of it and remain content. We do not live but merely keep alive. We fulfil our own being only when we enter into this higher self. God's deputy to us being the Overself, it should constitute our supreme value, that which is most worth while in life. Loyalty to this larger self is not mere sentimentality but practical wisdom. Selfishness is simply the ignorant opposition of the limited personality against its proper and superior self. If we have the courage to pull the bleeding roots of this opposition out of our own nature without waiting for karmic experience to do it for us, we may advance to the next and higher stage at a bound. The "me" which recognizes and submits to this truth, the "I" which is educated to keep to its proper place and not to claim a higher one, the ego which perceives that its existence although a distinct one is not a separate one, the personality which is willing to be ensouled and inbreathed by this impersonal being of the Overself, will then become purified of its own littleness. Henceforth it will be an unhindered channel for a power light and being superior to its own. Henceforth the individual will enter into a sacred union with the cosmic will.

Now because the World-Mind is everywhere present, every individual entity partakes of its life and consciousness through its ray the Overself to however small a degree. Nobody is ever inwardly separate from it however outwardly distinct from it. We dwell with it in a mystic togetherness, in a secret continuum. The recognition of our intimate relations with the World-Mind brings a new interest into the dullest life and provides a fresh urge to the weariest one. The ultimate mental essence of all the multitudes of human beings, despite their varieties, diversities and differences, is through the Overself a shared existence. On this view life becomes an enterprise rich with significance, for we are privileged co-partners with Deity and not merely the puppet automatons of Deity. Here indeed is a thought which gives height to a man.

Thus it is for man himself to rise into the grade of philosopher and make his partnership a conscious relation instead of an unconscious and stunted one as it is at present. When we can comprehend what life is seeking to achieve in us, then the universe will cease to oppress us and become more acceptable. An important value of such a message is the peace which the larger outlook brings through bringing a proper proportion to human outlook. So long as the surface self torments itself unendingly with unsatisfied and unsatisfiable desires which experience in death both their final and worst frustration; so long as it oscillates excitedly in time only to be given ironically its own final quietus by time itself: so long does it display ignorance of its true relation to its own hidden source. When we can lift ourself to this higher standpoint, rebellion against life as it is dies down. We learn the wonder—for it is nothing less—of total acceptance and learning, widen out such peace as may already have become ours. And if we share in the activity of the World-Mind we share also to some degree in its wonderful possibilities. Not that the ray can become more than it is—a representative of the sun on earth—but that it can draw from that which pervades it the affirmation of its divine quality.

We not only need a purpose in life; it must also be a satisfying purpose; and what could be more satisfying than such a sacred co-partnership?

When we understand that the World-Mind is the basis of all existence; when we realize that it is the sustaining and uniting principle of our own self as well as of all other selves, our prayer and our efforts will henceforth be for the welfare of all creatures, not merely for our own. For we will know that in the universal good our personal good will necessarily be also included whereas if we selfishly seek our personal good alone the derisive irony is that we shall fail to attain it. Our duty is to consider ourself not only as a part living for its own sake but also as a part living for the sake of the Whole. Put into plainer language this simply means that if men were to consider the welfare of the All *as well as their own* (for they are not excluded from the All) they would gain greatly for this attitude would bring more and not less happiness. They practise selfishness because they honestly believe such to be the way to satisfaction. They disdain to consider the common welfare because they honestly believe such to be the way to the loss of happiness; but when their ignorance is removed they discover that satisfaction is ultimately rooted not in the person alone but rather there where all persons may meet in a common centre. For they all share the greater life of God who is in each of them as a unity and not as something which has been broken up into little pieces. Mankind's interest includes their own as the larger of two concentric circles includes the lesser one.

The contrast between "I" and "you", the differences between one man and another are plain and clear; it is consequently natural for both to accept the reasonable conclusion of their separateness. What both do not see however is that the same powerful misapprehension, the same suggestive force which prevents them becoming conscious of the ultimate reality behind the world's multiformed appearances also prevents them becoming conscious of the ultimate unity which in the end lies between their separateness from each other.

When the inter-connectedness and inter-dependence of all existence is grasped, the quest of a purely individual salvation is seen to be an illusory one. I am to be saved not for my own sake alone but because *all* are to be saved: this is the proper attitude we should adopt. We can now begin to understand what Jesus meant when he uttered the words: "Whosoever will save his life shall lose it." For this wider self, which was the Christ-principle in Jesus, is the secret thread which ties man to man. It also offers the scientific basis of Jesus' beneficent injunction: "Love thy neighbour as thyself." It lives in the "I" as the latter itself lives in the body. We can begin to understand too what Paul meant when he pronounced that truly mystical sentence: "I live, yet not I but Christ liveth in me." The Overself is indeed the Cosmic Christ to which we are silently called to dedicate our lesser existence.

9

The Shadows of Evil and Suffering

WHY does Overself permit the sin of moral evil to exist in its offspring, the person? Why does the World-Mind allow the suffering of physical pain to mar its universe? are questions which always arise. Who that is living today when Pain, like a moaning wind, has passed across the face of this earth in the wake of the onrushing victories of Nazzidom, has been free from the distant sight or even personal experience of the horrors of violence, disaster or accident; of the afflictions wrought by dishonest, brutal or depraved men; of the miseries inseparable from poverty, privation and social degradation; and of the agonies borne by sick, diseased and deformed persons? Nay, most creatures are born amid their mothers' pain; lacerating anxiety in some form eventually becomes their intermittent lot; and finally pain once more often attends their exit from the world's stage!

Such dismal sights, such saddening experiences, raise occasional doubts about divine benevolence in the minds of religious people, if they are not too craven to question the words of priest and scripture; such wounding terrors may even disturb the smooth ecstatic moods of the contemplative mystic, if he is not too enamoured of his own spiritual enjoyments to heed what is going on around him; and they will certainly trouble the thoughts of the rational metaphysician if he really is one such and not a mere parrot-like repeater of what he has read or heard.

When the thoughtful survey the havoc and misery that have now relentlessly pressed the wonted gaiety and common goodness out of present-day humanity's life there come to the strongest hearts moods of heavy despondency, nay, even of tragic despair. It is then that the old plaint of Job rises to expression on twentieth-century lips. "What is the meaning, what is the use of all this suffering? Why do the virtuous endure unmerited anguish? Why do the wicked flourish?" are the bitter cries wrung from them. The seeming waste and stunning wrong of so much human suffering may well make us critical of divine wisdom. Those who cannot reconcile the contradiction of the presence of evil and suffering with the presence of a benign and peaceful God are not to be blamed. Most of us feel that if whatever gods there be had consulted us when making a universe, we would have eliminated these two bugbears of the human race and thus have made a better job of it! It is not too much to say that these twin problems of evil and suffering are perhaps the oldest ones which have ever confronted knitted human brows. So difficult and so gigantic are they, however, that most answers have apparently been inconclusive, otherwise humanity would not be raising them again to-day just as they were raised five thousand years ago.

For the purpose of literary convenience let us treat these twins as a single topic. The contradictions which beset it can vanish only in the air of a subtler way of thinking. Such a standpoint may be found. Let us descend to particular instances to understand its meaning. Let us imagine that we have given up the human body for that of a tiny fly and that we have comfortably settled ourself on a nice patch of plastered wall. There we surrender ourself to a busy, pleasant activity with our funny little proboscis. Suddenly there is a lightning-swift rush, the grotesque and baleful head of a lizard looms over us, he gobbles us up and the next thing we know is a fall into the death-swoon of unconsciousness. Now that lizard represents for us *as a fly*, not only the cause of our suffering but also the principle of evil in this universe, Satan if we like to call it that.

Imagine next that we are once again a human being with a much larger body than that of a fly to take care of. We live in a tropical country. Day and night we have unendingly to defend ourself against mosquitoes—those humming plagues of the hot lands. They torment us whilst we work and attack us whilst we play; they will not even let us sleep unless we hide behind a barrage of net curtains. But this is not all. For some of these mosquitoes are often the bearers of malarial fever and a single sting may suffice to render us helpless for weeks at a stretch, or intermittently so for the rest of our life.

Now the same species of lizards which attack and swallow flies in the West will greedily attack and swallow mosquitoes in the East. For the mosquito, therefore, a lizard is definitely an evil thing, a source of suffering and a well of wickedness. But for us as a human creature the lizard is highly virtuous, indeed a genuine benediction, for it helps to remove the vigorous vectors of malaria from our environment. The question then arises; which viewpoint is the correct one—the fly's, the mosquito's, the lizard's or the man's? To assert that any single one is *absolutely* true is to adopt a rationally untenable if emotionally justifiable position. What is a source of pleasure to one creature brings misery to another. What is desirable in some particular connection proves the reverse in a different one. The impartial enquirer has no alternative but to admit the principle of relativity into his conclusion and to say that ultimately both good and evil are wholly relative to the mental standpoint taken, and that the latter must essentially be variable. This is as good as saying that both good and evil are only relative mental conceptions and that from the point of view of the universe itself, which must necessarily mean from the World-Mind's point of view, there is nothing in it which is useless or unnecessary.

Let us try therefore to desert the common and conventional standpoint for a while and see what a universal one may yield us.

Firstly, let us frankly acknowledge that there is much in this varied cosmos for which we humans may well be thankful, much that is truly good, beautiful and useful in Nature, life and man. The assertion that all life is suffering is an exaggerated one. For we cannot form an idea of suffering except in relation to its opposite, which is happiness; hence the two must exist simultaneously. And experience confirms that both are found together in this world. The very existence of life's joys implies as an inescapable corollary the existence of their opposites too, no less than the existence of light implies that of darkness. The unborn infant which floats blissfully in the fluid of its mother's womb lives successfully with collapsed lungs, although the same condition in an adult would mean his death. When the infant is born it takes its first breath and signalizes the event by crying out with pain. Henceforth the rhythm of taking in and giving out its breath will symbolize the rhythm of experiencing pleasure and pain which will mark the entire course of its life until the end. Life is never all pain nor all pleasure. Moreover, conditions could always be worse, cold consolation though this seems. All conceptions of happiness are relative ones. Everybody would like to be in someone else's shoes. Indeed, the Arabs say, "I had no shoes and I murmured, till I met a man who had no feet."

Secondly although we may certainly blame man himself for some of the evil and suffering in the world quite obviously there remains a large portion for which we cannot blame him, as for example the sufferings inflicted on each other by wild jungle beasts which have no contact with him at all. Where then can we ascribe the final responsibility except to the World-Mind itself? When we understand that this whole world and not merely a part of it—the part which pleases us—is a divine manifestation we understand that God must be in the gangster too. It may be that the gangster has misdirected his will through ignorance, misused his opportunities through self-deception and misinterpreted life through greed but this does not make his innermost actuating force any the less divine. We must face facts bravely and realize that the divine will is ultimately behind the whole universe and consequently must even be behind its horror and agony and wickedness too.

Not that these things have been deliberately created but that they have indirectly been made inevitable through the inner necessity, the karmic continuity of the universe which made the infinite Overself refract out of itself a succession of finite incarnate lives. The "fall of man" was the fall into separation, multiplicity and limitation. Strife and its consequent sufferings were inherent and latent in such a division of being. The universe, being an effort to manifest infinite Mind in finite mental centres, the limitation of being thus involved inevitably leads to limitation of moral outlook and this in turn leads to the arisal and existence of what we call sin. This again brings consequent suffering to others and also to the sinner. Struggle exists in the world because of the world's diversity, because life has been fragmented into innumerable creatures who are all struggling blindly in the endeavour to attain some want. From the very moment of their birth they begin an acquisitive process, adopt a grasping attitude. Hence the moment the myriads of separate finite centres came into existence their warring future could be foretold. Their strife is the tremendous price paid for their birth. For when, in the course of its natural evolution, the conscious being came to distinguish itself from others and recognized its separateness, its power of free choice awakened and the possibility of discord with other beings was introduced. For such a moment was a tremendous turning-point in its consciousness. Its karma as an individual began to generate. Hence we read in Genesis: "And the Lord God said, Behold, the man is . . . to know good and evil." For each finite being had to be given a certain amount of free play within the world scheme. None could be unalterably confined to a fully pre-ordained plan of movement. The Overself had to leave us free to pursue paths of wickedness rather than compel us to pursue paths of righteousness. The first was alterable through suffering into permanent and profound goodness whilst the second could produce only a worthless robot-like superficial and ephemeral goodness. A universe of innumerable creatures who were not merely automatons but entities free to develop had inevitably to become a universe of contending creatures. The cosmic evolution could not be so fixed and fore-ordained that there would be no room in it for individual initiative.

The ego is at first unable to look beyond its immediate selfish interests. This inability leads to a situation where there is set up between it and other individuals of like limited vision a melancholy inevitability of discord. Out of its sense of separateness there slowly arises a conflict which culminates in sin and consequent pain. It blindly seeks its happiness at the expense of others and thus introduces suffering into their lives and later by karmic retribution into its own life too. Evil-doing is the price of its freedom. It is part of a divine manifestation, and because it is free within certain limits it has also been free to deform this manifestation, which is what all of us have done at some time or other. Moreover, the tension between every individual's present imperfection and innate possibility and the unconscious yet imperative need of realizing this divine possibility results in a strife which in its turn generates both pleasure and pain. Its life is torn by the tension between what it actually is and what it feels it ought to be. Such a tension is the inescapable consequence of its double nature. For it is personal and finite on the one hand but universal and infinite on the other. In its indistinct endeavour to fulfil itself the individual self tries a hundred different roads most of which are at first anti-social and egoistic.

But the sharp thorns are mingled with delicate roses. If we may become villains we may also become virtuous men. Ethical flowers and intellectual blossoms are in the end our rewards for the pains we have suffered. Moreover the thorns pass, the flowers remain. For the ego's sojourn in the world will through the course of gradual evolution elicit from within it all the latent possibilities which are hidden there. That which is without will thus enable it to reveal that which is within. And when the ego comes to self-knowledge and feels its pristine peaceful oneness with others, the strife ends. It is certain that so far as suffering arises out of the evil deeds of men, the cosmic evolution will through continuous rebirth and karmic tuition purify and ennoble all mankind eventually, even if the process requires millions of years. For the ego wrongs both others and itself only because its self-knowledge is grossly limited and its world-understanding lamentably incomplete. Its sin consists in this, that it misapplies its power, misdirects its feelings and perverts its will through ignorance. The human heart is perfectly right in obeying the instinct which drives it to try to secure happiness. But it cannot rest in external satisfactions alone. It will be led by their limitations and insufficiencies through the religious, mystical and philosophic quests successively. Hence it does not come into its own until it comes into this recognition of that which underlies its own self.

If it be true that the moment man dissociates himself from the Overself, evil is born, then the only radical cure for it is his re-association once again with the ever-waiting source. The divine hunger to get out of this dissociation discloses itself in the hungers of a lower level which so palely and sometimes so ignobly reflect it. He may not and usually does not know it, but in every quest of amusement where man seeks to forget his cares and miseries, he seeks to forget himself in fact, and thus to transcend himself. He runs agitatedly hither and thither in quest of one material boon after another only because he feels the inward void and seeks to fill it. In every desire which sends him running hither and thither, he is seeking the satisfaction which in the end he will find only in the Overself. In every effort to hold on to his mutable possessions he is seeking the ultimate and immutable reality. In every incarnation he shows by his acts or hides behind his thoughts this terrible truth that he is sadly out of harmony with his true life-aims, that he is pathetically self-estranged. He hunts for wealth, looks for love and tries to climb the ephemeral eminence of fame when all the while he is really seeking the Real. For its attainment confers a wealth which can never be lost and a love which lasts for ever.

When we understand that we are all children of the Infinite Parent, that our love for it is as natural an affection as is that of flesh-born children for their earthly parents, we begin to understand that love enshrines a great mystery. There is no doubt that at certain rare moments of a mortal love—especially at its beginning—it is bereft of the gross flesh and touches something that transcends its low earthliness. For a few interludes it is an activity of the Spirit, a sacred quest of two lonely mortals each seeking the Overself in the other, an embrace of God under a lesser guise. Many poets have perceived this. Stephen Phillips has phrased it finely:

> Not for this alone do I love thee; but
> Because Infinity upon thee broods.

But alas! what man seeks and hopes to find in woman, what woman expects and yearns for in man, can only be found on earth subject to the limitations of place and time, which means subject to loss of freedom and to cancellation by death, to the corrosion of decay and disease and to all those fitful evils which shadow emotional moods. For this notion of love is a sadly limited one. To bestow it only on a wife or a child, a sweetheart or a sister, is to bestow it in anticipation of its being returned. Man finds in time that such giving which hopes for a getting is not enough. Love cannot stop there. It seeks to grow beyond the restricted circle of a few friends and relations. Life itself leads him on to transcend it. And this he does firstly, by transcending the lure of the pitiful transient flesh and secondly, by transforming love into something nobler and rarer—compassion. In the divine self-giving of this wonderful quality and in its expansion until all mankind is touched, love finally fulfils itself.

But such a lofty tower is not quickly climbed. Only when he has seen his most cherished hopes wither and die, only when he has vividly felt the appalling transiency of external existence and only when he has felt in advance the prick of sharp thorns beneath every tempting rose, does he become reflectively self-aware. Then he perceives how he has misdirected his efforts and with this perception his life will take its most crucial turning-point and one more soul will have begun its quest of the Overself. And the more he pursues this quest the more will peace fall upon his harassed soul like dew upon parched earth. When at long last the ego widens its knowledge and perfects its understanding then this same creature which had formerly been a living centre of partial evil becomes transformed into a living centre of benevolence. There is no greater or grander moment in its life than this moment when such self-recognition dawns. Henceforth it brings to others no less than to its own self happiness and not pain. The two contending forces in the universe, the so-called good and evil forces, are not, as is often believed, those which draw man down into matter and those which abstract him from it, but those which generate and stimulate a selfish personal attitude and those which generate and stimulate a selfless impersonal one.

Each ego strives to complete itself, to enlarge itself by an acquisitive process in the unconscious quest of its hidden unity with all the others. Hence it follows an evolution which eventually develops into a threefold stream during its long course: a movement which manifests as the physical, the intellectual and what may for the moment be called the spiritual. In the physical it proceeds outward and touches low dark depths of ignorance and evil, losing itself for a time in the illusion of so-called matter. This is the so-called descent of Spirit in Matter. But all matter whether it be the root-matter of the Hindus or the electrical-matter of the scientists is in the end but the appearance of a particular thought to a particular thinker or of the cosmic thought to the cosmic thinker. It is Thought contemplating itself under a disguise or through a coloured window as it were. It is not a second and separate substance.

Desires wax mightily on this first path but wane on the third one. The intellectual evolution provides the longest course and the greatest struggles. For in the first stage the ego is merely acquisitive but in the second stage it adds the further quality of being inquisitive. From being merely avid to seize life it becomes curious about it. Out of the union of these two qualities still greater evil is born, the insidious evil which can be wrought by human cunning. Yet out of it too there comes after much suffering and much pain the first dissatisfactions with itself and with life, the first discovery that the way to overcome them is to overcome itself. Thus it reaches and passes the turning-point of its long evolution, the point where through the unfoldment and use of its own intelligence it turns its face around and begins the homeward journey. In the spiritual evolution the ego proceeds inward and finally effects the sought-for unity when it returns with full consciousness to the Overself.

If limits had not been set to the ego's movement, if its will were wholly free, then it would throw all things into confusion and end its own existence in self-destruction. But if it had been wholly controlled by destiny, if it had not the partial free will which it does possess, then it would become a mere automaton, a puppet, and end its own existence in a living death. Herein we may perceive the infinite intelligence which makes our universe what it is, that is a cosmos, an ordered system. All separateness, all evil, all strife, all selfishness and all ignorance arise during this outward objectifying movement of the mind. All unity, all goodness, all harmony and all wisdom arise during its inward and returning movement. The conflict between these two forces, between the separative and the unitive, is continuous but at certain critical transition periods of evolutionary karma it becomes openly magnified in scope and historically momentous in importance. Such a critical period is what great numbers of mankind have been passing through during our own generation. The world war in fact marks a tremendous evolutionary turning-point for millions of human beings.

These facts—unknown or unregarded as they often are—inform

us that the surface of life does not show the real truth of it. When we read the book of experience by their light, when we connect the everyday deeds of existence with the quest of this far-off divine goal, then both this experience and these deeds must unquestionably be completely altered on our entire scale of values.

The Triumph of Good.

If the infinite intelligence knew that the constant play of antagonistic forces had to become an inevitable feature of manifested life; if it had to permit what we humans regard as evil and suffering to exist; and if the universe itself was to be permitted to exist at all as a karmically controlled self-developing and self-actuating system, it knew also that the evolutionary process would bring all these sinning and suffering creatures to a point where they would shed their sin and become self-sacrificing co-operators in the cosmic order and thus the disappearance of the karmic causes of suffering would lead to the disappearance of suffering itself. If a world-process necessarily involved separateness and separateness at some of its stages involved selfishness and selfishness in its turn involved evil and pain, it would be equally true that in the earlier as in the later periods of this process, the selfishness would not be present and consequently the evil and pain would vanish too. They would not be eternal but only provisional phases of existence.

We may be assured therefore that the World-Mind has set limits to these two bugbears. Evil is ephemeral. In the end it defeats itself. It has only a negative life. It represents the not-seeing of what *is*, the not-doing in harmony, the not-understanding of truth. Evil is, in short, a lack of proper comprehension, a too-distant wandering from true being, an inadequate grasp of life. When insight is gained and these deficiences are corrected, it ceases its activity and vanishes. The mystic who penetrates into the profound core of being finds no evil there. In these troublous times philosophy bears its calm assured message of hope to us and bids us have the conviction that in every evil there exists the cancer of its own ultimate self-destruction. Evil is present but it is not eternally present; it will be transmuted, let us not doubt that. We are too preoccupied with ourselves to comprehend that if pain and evil play a dominant part on our miserable planet, there are other planets where they may be and indeed are utterly unknown.

But why is it, if really ephemeral, that evil itself seems to have been inseparably present throughout the history of the universe? There is a twofold answer to this question. First, this earth provides a theatre for life's evolutionary activities and thus ultimately for man and that evolution is the orderly unfoldment of latent possibilities. But the scientific story of evolution from a primitive savage humanity is only a partial truth and nothing more. The doctrine of a historical human evolution from ancient barbarism to present superiority is self-flattering, but not quite correct. For beings of every grade from the lowest to the highest appear at one and the same time upon earth and those who contribute the evil but later evolve out of it do not vanish entirely as a type. They are replaced by other beings who have come into manifestation later in time. This however is true only for a limited period for an hour strikes when the upward passage of lower types will cease altogether on this particular planet and the evolution of the others will then hurry forward. From that hour evil will wane and sink out of sight.

The cosmic existence renews itself in successive reincarnations, as it were. It is itself eternal and infinite but these recurring cycles are necessarily timed and finite, however inconceivable their periods and however unimaginable their bounds be. Thus there has never been a starting-point which was the same in degree for all beings, for the simple reason that there has never been a sudden creation out of nothing but always the projection out of Mind of a beginningless and endless self-repeating serial universe. There is no such thing as an unbroken ascent, a smooth and merely mechanical progress. The evil in man is strong enough to prevent it. But the ascent and the progression themselves are true facts. Only, evolution has a spiral structure. It is not a straight step-ladder. Life did not begin on this planet with any single group alone and will not end with it. Hence owing to the cyclic operation of repeated re-embodiment not only of living beings but of the whole planetary system itself, there was never a time when primitive humanity was merely an assemblage of wild savages. On the contrary, culture and civilization, intellectual development and ethical aspiration, science metaphysics and art were developed in every large population group throughout the pre-historic world and existed alongside of quite primitive conditions. The religious myths and legendary traditions which have come down to us from earliest recorded times carry faint distorted echoes of the memory of these facts. Hence too there has never been a time when social groups were either all evil or all good. Humanity has always been a peculiarly mixed lot. Those who eventually subordinated self and refrained from evil-doing were more than balanced by younger souls who had themselves to eat of the bitter-sweet fruit of the Tree of Knowledge of good and evil in their turn. Thus it happens that so-called savages have always shared the planet at the same time with civilized peoples. Thus too a situation develops such as has existed within historic times, when it has been as though the newcomers started to read the serial story of human life somewhere in the middle, a particularly difficult process for them and a somewhat disturbing one for those already reading it.

We have already learnt that when the One Existence threw off a myriad minor existences, evil sprang up naturally as one of the temporary relations between them. When the formless Mind reflected itself into countless transient and contrasting forms, selfishness—with all its melancholy train of sins and sorrows— came unavoidably into being for a while through attachment to those forms. But we must note that evil forms part of the ego's experience of the world not because it is inherent in the world itself as because it is in the illusions generated in the ego by the contrasts and limitations of the world; in short, that it is in the person, not in the environment. When it is overcome by the person within himself and he passes away to higher worlds more fitting to his higher space-time perceptions, there is necessarily a continued predominance of others left on the planet in whom evil itself still remains strong. This predominance becomes accentuated by the natural increase of population in geometrical proportion, with the unfortunate consequence that the quantitative mass of evil likewise increases because of the multiplication of those who are under the sway of selfishness.

Second, although good triumphs ultimately over evil when the ego's journey along the third or spiritual path finally terminates, we do not see this ultimate triumph of the natural processes of development because it occurs in a realm beyond our sight. For it cannot be fully accomplished whilst we are yet in this low-grade space-time world. The fruits of victory are handed to us only on a level of higher perception. The hard ordeals of earthly life are compensated for in the end in a super-earthly one. The belief that absolute perfection can be achieved whilst man is yet tied to the finitude of flesh and must needs live under the conditions of sensuous limitation which this imposes on him, is validated neither by facts of past history and present observation nor by affirmations of the hidden teaching. He can certainly achieve a wide measure of freedom from certain limitations and approach close to perfection along certain roads, but beyond this the very nature of our pitiful planet bars his way. The ugly struggles and appalling sufferings of life upon it are matched on no other one. And these in turn arise because our perceptions are so poor, so finite and so circumscribed—in short, because we are so *ignorant*. All that is finite, which includes everything formed on our particular space-time level, is necessarily imperfect. Hence freedom from all limitations can be man's, if he has earned it, only when he is divested of the present earthly body and has come to the consciousness of a supersensual changeless life. For then only he can he become utterly freed from all time and place considerations. Only when he has solved the mystery of time, which essentially pertains to his earthly life, will he be permitted to solve the mystery of Infinite Duration, which essentially pertains to his unearthly life.

We are always looking at the universe in little bits and broken pieces whereas the World-Mind looks at it as one Whole. In popular language, God alone knows all. The cosmic process has a significance in this integral sense which our eyes always miss because of their concentration upon the bits. It stands complete and instantaneous in the World-Mind's consciousness. The history of man is the attempt to realize in time and space what already exists as a harmonious unit in the World-Mind's consciousness. Both the evil and its extinction exist simultaneously in it and could we but share that incomprehensible consciousness we might then justify the dark ways of God to despairing man. In this consciousness there is the incredible All-time where everything is happening at the same moment and not split up into before and after. When we understand what time means, when we know that past, present and future are terms that have a practical rather than philosophical truth, that they are graven images whose worship causes us to forget the timeless reality underlying them, we begin to emancipate the mind from ancient illusion. We begin also to understand that to think of the universe as having once started suddenly into existence out of nothing at all cannot be correct.

The universe's existence in time must be looked at, if it is to be looked at aright, as the unity of an eternal Now, Then and Everywhen; its existence in space as the unity of a boundless Here, There and Everywhere. There is no real beginning as there is no real end to its history. An unbegun and unending universe is by the very fact of its nature not a stable thing created in time but an active process working simultaneously with time, an eternal act of World-Mind. And because it is really an active mental process and not a fixed material structure, all things and all beings within it without exception, whether in utter unconsciousness or in full awareness, are striving to attain their inner reality, a striving which will necessarily lift them, as it proceeds, beyond this terrestrial sphere of limited space-time perceptions.

If the World-Mind views the end alongside of the beginning, the enterprise along with its fulfilment, the achieved goal along with the temporal struggle, let us not fall into the error that this makes us mere automatons. We are what we are—super-sensuous beings temporarily fascinated by our own sensuous space-time perceptions. Mind is the only reality. All human ideas return in the end to the particular mind which generated them. All human individualities must likewise return in the end to the World-Mind whose ideas they in their turn also are. The universe is nothing but the eternal activity of Mind in its finite ideas. Human life is nothing but the travail of those ideas to reach and realise their infinite Source. The spiritual or third path of the ego's evolution is indeed called "returning home" by a Chinese sage.

The Overself being by nature pure and benign, how is it that these thoughts of evil are able to arise at all? We do not perceive the tremendous complications involved in such a disarmingly simple question. For we live tied by a relativist outlook to the half-understood single space-time order of wakeful experience and yet demand a perfect and complete explanation of mysteries like suffering and evil, whose full relations we cannot perceive because they transcend all the possible time-orders of relativity. The only answer at all comprehensible to a human mind is that evil thoughts arise only on the Mind's surface, only in the innumerable but totally transient forms and appearances which it takes. Mind's celestial nature itself remains unchanged, undefiled and untouched by such thoughts. It is like an immense ocean whose surface is the playground of myriads of waves rolling angrily to and fro but whose vast body is quite still and unmoved. Just as the sky's nature remains the same however many black clouds may pass over it, so the Overself's original purity remains undisturbed by the human thoughts, emotions and passions which pass over its projection, the personality.

After all, what if the finite ego does involve a seeming self-limitation for some fragment of the infinite Overself? It is only our illusion that there is this limitation anywhere in such an exalted being. We may and must regard it so from our lower human standpoint but this is not the Overself's standpoint. To get a better view of the matter we must look again at the illustration of dream from two distinct standpoints. From the first, a dreamer becomes involved in his own imaginations, entangled in their patterns and deluded by their seeming reality. From the second, he does not change his own intrinsic nature at any moment of the dream for it remains as the underlying basis. The first view is true but transient whereas the second is true and permanent. We must apply this analysis to our consideration of the Overself. Some part of it has gone out to be dwarfed apparently by its own self-imagined limitation as a single human being. This part is fascinated or hypnotized by its own projection of the universe which provides a background for the operations of the personality. But on the second view we must remember that in all this the Overself is still experiencing itself when it experiences the world and is still seeing itself when it sees its myriad personal lives.

Amid all the horrors and all the grossnesses of this planet's life, we need to remind ourselves again and again of their leaf-like transiency, to remember that the mind has fallen into error, has misapprehended its own experience. Evil and suffering, strife and opposition make their appearance only on the level of form, separateness and illusion. They are not present in the Overself's own ever-perfect being. It dwells in a region of ideal unity where no discord and no conflict could ever enter. Man may overcome them therefore *within* himself by rising to its sublime level. We need to remember again and again that there exists behind the veil of our present space-time perceptions an unsullied world of being where these dark shadows have themselves not the slightest existence at all. There is indeed a secret kingdom of heaven where our finest and fairest hopes may find genuine realisation. Inexorably if imperceptibly the flowing tide of evolution is moving us all toward this grand goal, perfecting us through the very pains and errors which are temporarily inseparable from a certain stage of existence. *This* is our glorious destiny and nothing less nor lower shall be able to hold us in the end. Salvation is for all, not for a self-flattering or self-righteous few.

When we remember the enormous sufferings of our century it may be hard for us to believe that there is a God, but it is harder still to believe that this universe was put into being and that the formative (rather than creative) power behind it then went off and lost all interest in it. The Mind that visualised this universe must surely be aware of the cries of the sorrowful, of the sins of the wicked and of the struggles of the virtuous. And if this Mind be a beneficient one, as every seer proclaims, it must surely be desirous of bestowing help and light wherever these be needed. Shall it not therefore eventually remedy all wrongs and mend all defects? We fume and fret however because we do not understand its inscrutable ways, its infinite patience. It knows that if its own differentiation into innumerable finite centres brought discord among them for a limited time, the evolutionary return of those centres to itself will, with accumulating experience, bring harmony among them again. Why all our pother to arrive at perfection? There is plenty of time stored away yet in Nature's calendar. She herself does not appear to be in a raging hurry. She spent millions of years merely to bring the human body into existence; how much more time must she spend to bring the human mind and character to perfection? Time makes our minds old and our wisdom mellow. Life needs plenty of time to effect its high but hidden purposes. Therefore it needs rebirths and plenty of them to make man what he ought to be. The gulf between palaeolithic man chipping flints and Immanuel Kant shaping metaphysical history is stupendous and explicable only in the light of repeated re-embodiments. The perfectibility of man is ensured through this long series of renewed experiences but for this very reason he had to be left a large liberty to introduce his own evil, his own pain. The removal of this liberty would have defeated the inner value of the entire process.

> The wine of life keeps oozing drop by drop,
> The leaves of life keep falling one by one,

wrote the old Persian philosopher-poet, Omar Khayyám. When we turn our eyes towards our own past, if we have lived much and felt deeply and therefore sinned much and suffered deeply, we begin to re-echo the well-known words of Gray's verse:

> Yet, ah! why should they know their fate?
> Since Sorrow never comes too late,
> And Happiness too swiftly flies.

So many of our years are altogether gone; perhaps a third, a half or three-quarters of our life lies buried beyond recall. Can we show any receipt in terms of inner progress for the time that we have spent? Let us at least make something of the days yet to come that we might later look back on them and find permanent worth wrested from their grip.

The Freedom and Fate of Man.

When we come to consider the problem of human evil and human suffering more specifically, we find it exceedingly complex and involved in thorny difficulties. But here we can be helped by using the method which we have already used in connection with the instances of the lizard and the mosquito, the same method which Einstein used in dealing successfully with the problem of the velocity of the earth on its travels through space. And this is to apply a form of the theory of relativity.

If we look along a tree-lined avenue the trees which are farthest away seem closer to each other than those which are nearest to us. If however we take up a position in an aeroplane which is hovering above the same landscape and look down at it through a pair of binoculars, we see then that the trees are really placed equidistant from each other. The illusion has been corrected by changing the point of view. It is possible to regard our present problem in a broader perspective and thus effect a similar change of view. We shall then perceive that evil may be offset by an equivalent good. Consequently our attitude towards it may become greatly modified. Again, we count pain in the lists of evils and seek quick deliverance from it. Yet suffering may be regarded not only from a partial point of view but also from that of the whole, when the moral or metaphysical instruction which it may impose on the sufferer will be seen as its obverse half. Here again we shall then have to modify our attitude towards it. From the hard but high standpoint of a metaphysics which refuses to accept materialism, the estimation of an unfortunate event or unpleasant person as evil is our human and limited way of looking at events and persons in time; it is in short really an idea in the mind.

Our parents give us much of the form and force, the health and disease, of our body when they give its germ with the genes. Thus from the very beginning our physical life is fated for better or worse to follow a predestined course and time merely unfolds and often mercilessly unfolds our individual story. We are then merely hapless spectators listening to the tale. Where is the chance here for those born to be struck down sooner or later by maladies resulting from the defective physical organizations with which they start? Where is the hope in this dread finality for the victims of imperfect genes?

The answer will depress some, exalt others. If despite the best efforts our body refuses to yield amendment of its maladies; if our life is crippled to this extent; we may turn for relief to religious faith or mystical experience or metaphysical thoughts that enlarge our horizon but diminish our self-centredness. Our sorrowful experience will not then be valueless. There will be some ethical or philosophical lesson to be learnt indirectly through it. 'Know that sorrow, being the means of convincing man of the need of inner life, is a spiritual teacher,' says a Tibetan text, *The Rosary of Gems*. Those who have suffered deeply, whose hearts have been broken and whose hopes have been withered, will listen sooner to a spiritual message than others, no matter how clever or how intellectual the latter be. Most of us must usually pass through the miseries of frustrated worldly desires before we can pass into the ecstasies of satisfied divine ones. We are forced to revise our values only when the senses have lost something of their savour.

All apparent evil is not real evil. Who has not known someone who has been turned from a wrong course by sickness? The same hardship which weakens one man's virtue strengthens another's. Tears do not always tell us the truth. We have for example impartially to ask ourself how booming guns and bitter oppression serve as anthropological instruments which shape the souls of men and serve the ends of super-physical evolution. We must begin to admit with Eckhart, however grudgingly, that: 'The swiftest horse that bears us to perfection is suffering.' A man may be suffering what is really good for him and yet he will weep, as though it were really bad for him! Too much good fortune has already ruined too many good men. All experience tends to educate the intelligence and discipline the emotions. Consequently if suffering brings men back to the blessed life that transcends it, then if only for that reason and to that extent its existence is justified.

It has earlier been pointed out that the universe could not be manifested without manifesting the pairs of opposites, such as light and darkness or life and death. This duality is inevitably inherent in its very structure. Consequently it is an inevitable accompaniment of our own human existence too. In the physical body pleasurable nerve-reactions lure us on to eat and sustain its existence, but painful reactions are equally provided for to repel us from drinking poisonous acids, for example. It is useless therefore in a body built on opposing tensions to expect that we shall be so fortunate as to experience only one of them—that is the pleasurable one—during a lifetime. A similar duality applies to our mental and emotional life, as a little reflection will reveal. To look for impossible one-sided perfections is to invite disappointment. Just as the forces of winter wither the foliage of trees but are not therefore evil forces, so the destructive element in Nature withers the forms of individuals, nations, civilizations and continents when they have outserved their utility and the appropriate time of disintegration arrives. This is not to be taken as a victory for evil powers but as a manifestation of one side out of a pair of opposites.

It would be senseless to ask for a world free from suffering. Imagine what would happen to a hand accidentally put into a fire if there were no nervous system to provide the owner of the hand with a warning signal of pain. It would be altogether destroyed and its use lost forever. Here the pain of being burnt, severe though it be, would really act as a disguised friend if it persuaded the owner to withdraw his hand from the fire. So far as suffering protects physical life, it possesses a justifiable place in the universal scheme of things. Then what about protecting moral life? Pain fills a place in the present evolutionary stage of our ethical existence which is hardly less and often more useful than that filled by pleasure. But our egoism blinds us to this fact. If it does no more than arouse us from the stupor of understanding into which most of us habitually fall, pain will have done something worth while. Plato has even pointed out that it is a misfortune to a man who has deserved punishment to escape from it. After all, the punishment may cause him to recognize that wrong has been done and thus purify his character. Again, it is through pain that man's cruelty and pride and lust may best be broken, they are hardly amenable to correction by mere words. The pain inflicted on a swollen sense of "I" for example by karmic compensatory working is not really punishment any more than is the pain inflicted by a surgeon who opens an abscess with his knife. The coils of karma which entwine themselves around the wrong-doer are primarily there as a natural consequence of his own acts, not as a fiat of punishment. Time is educating and developing him to perceive the right. When he has the humility to face the responsibility for his own past errors, he may see how many of his troubles were self-earned. Where he cannot trace the cause to his present personality, he must needs believe it to lie in his previous ones.

Nobody likes to impose a discipline upon himself and that is why everybody has to submit to a discipline imposed by karma. Hence pain and suffering come to us principally through the operations of karma. Their seeds may have been sown during the present life and not necessarily during a past one. The first error which most people make when accepting the tenet of karma is to postpone its operation to future incarnations. The truth is that the consequences of our acts come to us if they can in the same birth as when they are committed. If we think of karma as being something whose fruits are to be bourne in some remote future existence, we think of it wrongly. For every moment we are shaping the history of the next moment, every month we are fashioning the form of the month which shall follow it. No day stands isolated and alone. Karma is a continuous process and does not work by postponement. It is indeed incorrect to regard it as a kind of post-mortem judge! But it is often not possible to work out these consequences in terms of the particular circumstances of this birth. In such cases—and in such alone—do we experience the consequences in subsequent births.

Even those who accept the twin doctrines of re-embodiment and self-made karma, which are the most reasonable of all doctrines claiming to explain the principal vicissitudes of human fortune, are not infrequently hazy about the proper practical attitude to adopt as a consequence of this belief. It is necessary for them to understand first of all that although whilst evil endures we must accept the fact of its existence as the price to be paid for the self-limiting of an emanation from the Infinite into the finite, we need not therefore complacently tolerate its activity. Because we believe that karma operates to bring about sometimes approximate, sometimes adequate justice in the end, we must not therefore for example stand indolently aside from aggressive wrong-doing in passive trust to its operation. For karma needs to utilize instruments and its effects do not spring miraculously out of the air. Hence we must not shirk if we are called upon to co-operate with its intended educative effect, to work with its intuited operations and to set those causes into motion through which its reactions may be produced.

The second point for their understanding is the place of free will in the practical application of this doctrine. For we weaken ourself and injure truth if we believe that all events are unalterably fixed, that our external lives are unchangeably pre-ordained and that there is nothing we can do to improve the situations in which we find ourself. It is true that we are compelled to move within the circumstances we have created in the past and the conditions we have inherited in the present, but it is also true that we are quite free to modify them. Freedom exists at the heart of man, that is in his Overself. Fate exists on the surface-life of man, that is in his personality. And as man himself is a compound of both these beings, neither the absolute fatalist nor the absolute free-will position is wholly correct and his external life must also be a compound of freedom and fate. No man however evolved he may be has entire control over his life, but then he is not entirely enslaved to it either. No action is entirely free nor entirely fated; all are of this mixed double character. The student of mechanics who strikes a parallelogram of forces is able to arrive at the resultant which has been born out of the commingling of their totality. Similarly all those elements of heredity, education, experience, karma (both collective and personal), free will and environment conspire together to fashion both the outer form and inner texture of the life which we have to live. We sew the tapestry of our own destiny but the thread we use is of a kind, a colour and quality forced upon us by our own past thoughts and acts. In short, our existence has a semi-independent, semi-predestined character.

The materialists paint a terrible picture of the universe as a vast prison where man's fate, thoughts and acts are wholly determined by his physical environment. The ignorant among Orientals live in a locked-up world where man paces helplessly to and fro—a prisoner to divine predestination. Karma refutes both these dreary contentions and assigns to man sufficient freedom to shape himself and his surroundings. By his own development the individual affects or enriches his environment, helps or hinders Nature, and the reverse is also true. Karma does not say that we must stand waiting like ragged beggars before the door of fate. Our past free will is the source of our present fate, as our present one will be the source of our future fate. Consequently the most powerful factor of the two is our own will. There is therefore no room either for foggy fatalism or over-confidence. No man can escape his own responsibility in the matter of shaping his internal outlook and external environment by laying the blame on something or someone else. Everyone who is struggling with obstacles should drink a cup of the wine of inspiration from the hand of Beethoven—master music-maker. He who sought to hear the elfin strains of music was himself struck stone deaf. He whose life was completely dedicated to melodious composition for others one day became unable to hear his own compositions. It disappointed but did not discourage him. Facing this problem with a stout heart, he declared, 'I will grapple with Fate; it shall never drag me down!' He went on with his work and gave still greater and grander things to the world, for what he learned in suffering he taught in song.

Every man should study his mistakes in action and ascertain their source in himself. Let him frankly admit his partial responsibility at least and set out to make what amends he can. This is painful but it is better than continuing to dwell in illusions from which severe checks or sustained disappointments may later bring him down to earth. For once a thought-series or deed is strong enough its karmic resultant is as inevitable as a picture on an exposed photographic film. When karmic force has attained a certain impetus its onward movement can no longer be stopped although it may be modified. This is why it is a philosophic maxim to nip undesirable growths in the bud and thus extinguish karmic energies before they become inexorably decisive. A thought which has not attained a certain fullness of growth and strength will not yield karmic consequences. The importance of nipping off wrong thoughts at the time of their arisal is thus indicated. The way to fight a bad tendency in oneself or a bad movement in a nation is to check it during the early stages before it has gathered momentum. For it is easier to scotch it at the start when it is relatively weak than later when it is relatively strong.

Nevertheless the philosophic student must understand that if he should fiercely resist karma's decrees at some times, it is also right that he should bow resignedly to them at other times. For if he has not learnt the lesson of letting go when it is wise to let go, then every mistaken effort of his fingers to hold on against those decrees will only bring him further and needless pain. He should not rebel against them blindly. How to comprehend which course is to be taken is something which he has to deduce for himself. No book can tell him this but his intuition checked by reason or his reason illumined by intuition may do so.

Such an intuition must be carefully distinguished from pseudo-intuition, which is a mere echo of his own emotional complexes, innate prejudices or wishful thinking. The former is the authentic whisper of his own Overself. The ageless Overself holds all the innumerable memories of its related personalities in solution, as it were, so that they are and yet are not. It wills only what is karmically earned by him during these successive lives, which is always what will justly compensate him for the characteristics he has manifested through his actions. And because the Overself is the source of this karmic adjustment, it may be said that each man is truly his own judge. For it must never be forgotten that fundamentally the Overself is his own central self; it is not something alien to or remote from him. The real nature of karma is not grasped if it is believed to be a power external to the self, ruthlessly dictating its decrees for our helpless submission. On the contrary by virtue of the fact that the whole world is mental it is a power working in everything and everyone. This yields the clear implication that what happens to him happens by the secret will of his own innermost being. From this standpoint the sufferings he may have to endure are not evils in the ultimate but only in the immediate sense and what appears as a blind external and ruthless force is really a conscious internal and purifying one. Sooner or later evil challenges man to obliterate it, provokes him to overcome it as pain provokes him to seek for peace. Thus he turns to the quest of the Overself. It is well to remember that in the end evil in the life of every individual is an unstable and insecure phase only. It is certain to perish, for it bears within itself the seeds of its own destruction. Through constant adjustments effected by karma the surface self eventually and inevitably ceases the misdirection of its intelligence and force and brings them into harmony with the divine.

On this larger view the best karmic recompense for right actions is the upliftment of character which follows them, just as the worst karmic punishment for wrong ones is the degradation of character which is increased by them. Mentalism makes thought all-important in the end and it is so here too. For karma has a twofold character. Every deed creates both its physical reaction and the psychological tendency to repeat the deed.

It was mentioned in the earlier volume that thought tends to be creative and that sooner or later it produces karmic fruit in man's general environment. This is also true of his moral life. Here, it is not always necessary for his thoughts to translate themselves into deeds before they can become karmically effective. If they have sufficient intensity and if they are prolonged over a sufficient period they will eventually bring appropriate results even in external circumstances. This can be made clearer by an actual illustration. If a man persistently and intensely hates somebody, even to the point of ardently wishing his death, but if through fear of the consequences he lacks the courage to slay the other person, then his murderous thoughts will one day react upon himself in an equilibrated form. He may then himself experience a violent death or fall victim to a fatal accident or suffer from a disease which is as corrosive to his body as his hatred was to his character. Thus although not actually guilty of committing murder, he undergoes a physical penalty for *thinking* murder.

For similar reasons diseased habits of thinking may manifest themselves as diseased conditions of the flesh. The physician may rightly see the immediate physical cause of such a condition but he will not see the ultimate mental one, which may be excessive anger, morbid hate, overpowering fear, inordinate lust or habitual spite. We must not, of course, leap to the illogical conclusion that everyone who suffers from a disease has been thinking negatively in the past or present. The body has its own hygienic laws which cannot be transgressed with impunity, although most transgressions usually occur through sheer ignorance.

All this is possible because the entire basis of existence is a mentalist one. The creative factor in the karmic process is the mind itself. Consequently a mental change is needful if its operation against us is to be radically and favourably altered. Those who cannot bring themselves to conceive such a possibility should consider how frequently the hair of emotional women has turned grey either on hearing unexpected bad news or on suddenly being confronted with a terrifying situation. The change itself is purely physical because hair, skin, flesh and blood are formed and nourished out of a common root, whereas the cause of the change is purely mental because all that really happens before it is the entry of a new idea into consciousness. Let them consider also the rare but well-authenticated cases of Catholic women mystics whose intense meditations upon Jesus suffering on the cross have incontestably produced stigmata—the reproduction on hands or feet of bleeding nail-wounds. That this demonstration of the mind's power over the body extends even to the higher animals may seem still more fantastic, yet research among Indian peasants will soon reveal evidence of it. For when a cow catches sight of a cobra which has merely touched her udder by accident but not hurt it in any way, the fright affects her so deeply that she will never again yield any milk.

Man acts in the end according to his knowledge. If it be said that many intellectuals are notorious for shaming their knowledge by their deeds, we reply that what they possess is theory, not knowledge. Therefore when the teaching that he will inevitably receive the results of his actions wins acceptance through thoroughly satisfying the rational need of knowledge and the emotional need of justice; when this idea attains a certain degree of heartfelt force and intellectual clearness; when its innate truth is recognized as credible and its fairness as consoling, and when it begins to become dynamic in the world-outlook of a man; it will then not only begin to exert influence on his exterior life but cannot even be stopped from influencing it. Where it apparently fails to do so, it is always either because the acceptance is merely superficial and vocal or because innate selfishness and undisciplined passion assert themselves in the subconscious character. In the first case the doctrine is known only by decayed tradition or by parrot-like hearsay, as so often happens in the East. Through its conventional acceptance it has never been turned into profound conviction and consequently has lost much of its ethically disciplinary edge. In the second case the complexes are at work without a man's awareness and prevent him from giving full weight to the doctrine. This said, it is axiomatic that man tends to do ultimately what he thinks and feels.

With the significance of his sufferings properly understood and the needful adjustments in action, character or intelligence properly made, he may seek and keep that mental equilibrium which is inner peace. In making these truths his own he will face the hardships of life with fortitude and the inevitability of death with serenity. Thus he can learn to move with an undaunted heart amid earthly troubles and with an unruffled mind amid earthly joys not because he seeks ostrich-like to forget the one and reject the other but because he seeks sage-like to understand them. For in the words of a Mongolian text, "Whoso bears joy and sorrow with even mind has spirituality, although he may outwardly seem a worldling."

It would be easy to mistake such a serenity either for mere smugness or for shallow optimism. It cannot be the first because it is too conscious both of the defects of its possessor and the miseries of mankind. It cannot be the second because it is born of truth, not of emotional self-deception. It is a quality which emerges after long philosophical practice. It smiles only because it understands, not because it is emotionally basking in the rays of temporary good fortune. Every flower has such serenity because every flower is a philosopher. When it is born it finds itself smothered in the dark earth, with gloom all around and obstacles hemming it in. Nevertheless it struggles bravely upward. It has a natural faith, an inward urge (as all true philosophers have) that somewhere ahead there is welcome light and cooling air. And it is patient. Whilst it is growing upward it is calmly waiting. And so one day it adds its quota of vivid colour, its measure of heart-catching beauty to the common good. Now if it were a materialist, if it continually looked downward and believed only in the darkness around, then it would never live to see sunshine. Every man who adopts a materialistic attitude puts himself in this position. He is born to see and to welcome the Light, the Good, the Beautiful, but stubbornly remains in self-bound darkness. He is born to co-operate with Nature, to work with her and secure her abundance of latent gifts yet he opposes her everywhere and endures endless suffering because of this divorce. There are moments when something within tells him that whatever exists, there is yet a better, that wherever he finds himself there is yet a land of promise and that the best of all is intangible and invisible. Nevertheless he denies the voice because he cannot immediately see the Better and cannot instantly realize the Promise. So long as he will not listen to it but prefers to listen to the voices of other men as blind and as ignorant as himself, so long must he perforce remain agitated by sorrows today and joys tomorrow, so long shall he be a stranger to the serenity of a divine life.

The Miracle of Grace

The dark karma of sin and suffering which most of us carry is too heavy to be carried alone. For alas! we have to face the fact of what we are, not in serene essence but in bitter actuality: we are weak ignorant moody despondent creatures. We are unable to remove intellectual doubts, overcome moral temptations or solve practical difficulties. We cannot grow angel's wings overnight. A struggle must take place; a struggle directed first against what we know to be our vices but later against what we once believed to be our virtues! This conflict is inevitable because the person will not lightly let go its hold. Therefore we need something on which, quite frankly, we can lean for help until the day arrives when we can stand up sufficiently strong to bear our own burdens. We need help. Most of us are like frogs in a waterless well and must implore something outside to come to the rescue and lift us out of our helpless state. Recurrent problems and repeated failures tend to break the ankles of our self-reliance so that we feel no longer able to walk by our personal strength alone. We must then needs look elsewhere than to our own resources. We must indeed look for effective help to a higher power. Something greater than our ordinary self must take a hand in the complicated game of living.

This is true of most human beings. But those of us who have started in quest of the Overself and who ardently long for a divine enlargement of experience, have even more about which to be melancholy. Many of us are not strong enough even to discipline ourselves nor to mortify our selfhood; the heritage of karmic handicaps hangs like a millstone upon our backs and tends to smother the yearning to better our character. And support and sympathy are human needs. Consequently to depend on ourself alone may lead to little satisfaction. Moreover, our intelligence is often too poor to comprehend the subtle metaphysical truths round which so much of this quest revolves.

For all these reasons there is room in life not only for self-effort but also for divine effort, that is to say for grace. Although the enterprise of getting insight has to be started by a man himself, it cannot be ended by the man. Thus the person reaches a stage one day where it has to call in the help of its Overself. Such help manifests itself as grace.

There are intellectual doubters who regard the doctrine of grace as one which, however much it may appeal emotionally, has no metaphysical merit. The rationalists laugh at it and the atheists scorn it. This is their error. The possibility of receiving such help exists because there is a universal element in which we all exist. There is indeed such a thing, as those of us who have experienced its working well know.

What is grace? It is a descent of the Overself into the underself's zone of awareness. It is a visitation of power as unexpected and unpredictable as it is welcome and gratifying. It is an unseen hand stretched forth from the world-darkness amid which we grope with unsteady feet. It is the voice of the Overself speaking suddenly out of the cosmic silence with which we are environed. It is like a glorious rainbow of hope which suddenly appears when all seems lost.

More precisely, grace is a mystical energy, an active principle pertaining to the Overself which can produce results in the fields of human thought, feeling and flesh alike on the one hand, or in human karma circumstances and relations on the other hand. It is the cosmic will, not merely a pious wish or kindly thought, and can perform authentic miracles under its own unknown laws. Such is its dynamic potency that it can confer insight into ultimate reality as easily as it can lift a dying person back to life again or instantaneously restore the use of limbs to a crippled one.

Because the Overself exists in every man, grace too exists potentially in every man. When its power awakens within him he is immediately conscious of a tremendous change in the particular direction it takes, whether that change be mental or physical, emotional or eventful. Such indeed is the force of grace, that in the emotional or intellectual spheres its touch often over-stimulates him and may temporarily affect his balance.

The Overself is not far away, no farther in fact than a man's own heart and as near as is the life that sustains his days and nights. If it is felt as far away that is his illusion. He must cure himself of it by metaphysical enquiry and mystical practice. The statement that God dwells in the heart of man is not only a poetic one but also a scientific one. Shakespeare's perceptive power recognized this and hence he could openly speak of "that Deitie within my bosome" in his most mystical work *The Tempest*. Therefore the birth of grace is *first* felt in the heart, not in the head, because the heart is its most intimate habitat in the human body.

Grace manifests itself in two ways: first, a sense of dissatisfaction and insufficiency with the exterior life alone; second, a yearning for inner reality. The birth begins by a gentle indrawing of attention to the breast. The force works by a centripetal movement which attracts his attention away from his external life and physical environment. To the degree that he obediently yields to this centripetal influence and centres his attention more and more on the interior direction to which it points, to that degree shall he find his reward. He begins to feel that something lies hidden within himself of which he must come into conscious possession and that without it he will suffer the miseries of privation and frustration. What this "something" is does not form itself clearly in his mind but he feels and intuits it to be the sacred element, the divine soul. The ultimate effect is, first, to cauterize the *personal* "I"-thought in the man's heart, and, second, the way being thus prepared to confer an insight into ultimate reality. The first effect is accomplished by stages, which may spread out over several years, but the second one is always accomplished instantaneously.

He may understand that the first activity is taking place within him because of the agonies caused him by spiritual yearnings and aspirations which begin to spring up unbidden within his heart in consequence. They are preceded by anguish and tears. Consequently grace often comes as the climax of an emotional struggle. In some cases it originally manifests as a vision of mystic light. The vision is momentary, however, and may not be repeated. In this sublime moment when a higher power takes possession of the ego and leads it into itself, he may know that grace has been granted. He must give his ungrudging acquiescence to the divine leading. But although the glimpse occupies but an instant in time, its consequences will work themselves out during the ensuing weeks and months, sometimes during years. Once the grace has been granted the aspirant's road takes a turn for the better. It then opens up for him a perspective of possibilities hitherto unglimpsed.

It is perhaps in the moral sphere that the memorable touch of grace is first felt, and that with an abrupt force akin to a revolutionary one. Psycho-analytical professors and their followers are apt to regard what they call the unconscious mind of man as a bottomless well swarming only with shapes of lust and lewdness.* They have yet to learn that it holds also an infinite fund of goodness, truth and beauty such as would overwhelm them with its grandeur could they become but momentarily aware of it. They have made much of the torments caused to man by his suppressed sex desires. Do they know of the torments caused by his

---

* The school of analytical psychology founded by the keen Dr. Carl Gustav Jung must be exempted from these criticisms. It was learnt with pleasure during talks at Zurich with this gifted man that he disowned the materialistic views of his master Freud and that he had arrived at a view of man which took proper account of the mystical side.

unconsciously repressed longings for the higher life, the inner reality? Do they know that there is a deeper and grander "unconscious" than that which they have allowed him and which waits for its full recognition?

Even in the heart of the worst sinner there is this hidden core which remains unsinning, unstained and unpolluted, the soul which is always safe and which silently beckons him to pursue goodness and wisdom. Therefore its grace is as much if not more for those whom a self-righteous world despises and whom a formal frigid society rejects. The flower sheds its fragrance on all who approach it. It does not withhold the gift from a single person. The Overself is not less noble than the flower and will not withhold its grace from anyone merely because he cannot obtain a certificate of moral worth from his disdainful fellows. At its mystical touch the memory of bygone sin is banished, the agony of present suffering is softened, the ugliest past slips away, the bitterest resentment dies down and the hurts of frustrated craving dissolve into thin air. The weak are sustained, the afflicted consoled.

All our best faculties and nobler qualities, all our higher functions of thought, imagination and feeling themselves form a link with this link between man and God, this intermediary which is able to share in the life of both the person and the World-Mind and thus connect the fleeting with the eternal. For man it constitutes a goal toward which his intellectual efforts may direct themselves, a focus for his ethical aspirations, a light on his daily path and an inspirer to lift him above his animal side. It prompts him to practise virtue and instigates him to appreciate beauty. It is a keyhole wherethrough he may get a glimpse of reality. It is his central self which he has to find if he would know what he really is and what God really is. It is also the inner guide to which some mystics allude.

Hidden behind all human striving, often followed or denied all unknowingly there is this unseen light and unheard bidding of the Overself. All things are indeed unconsciously striving to realize their inherent divinity, to progress toward their own ideal self, to actualize what they already are in hidden principle and final possibility. Why should its existence guarantee that man will turn one day and become a humble suppliant at its feet? Because when, like the prodigal son, he has eaten his fill of the husks of divine estrangement he will experience a reaction. Be he fettered slave or pampered sovereign, a divine nostalgia will sweep over his heart. He will be driven by home-sickness, if not by the sour frustrations and nauseating defeats of life, to turn his face toward the one last yet one best hope left him. Every finite being is unconsciously and imperceptibly drawn onwards, like a moth to a flame, to the infinite being that is its Overself. There is no real happiness, no true peace, no enduring satisfaction until this goal is reached. None of us would aspire toward the divine if it were not already present within us to prompt the aspiration. None of us would feel this lacerating nostalgia for the beatific life if the latter did not really exist. Here then lies the guarantee that every ego will one day turn its face toward the light and ultimately be saved and finally be redeemed.

The Overself does not always play the part of a witness however. Still and unmoving though it be, nevertheless its presence paradoxically makes possible all man's activities and movements. In a broad sense it is not only the hidden observer but also, by virtue of its being a function of the World-Mind, the inner ruler of the person. Thus it arranges the karma of the coming incarnation before birth, for it contains all his karmic possibilities out of the past, and it is the secret actualizing agent which passes them down into time and space for his ultimate progress. At critical moments in the personal life it may suddenly and dramatically interfere by engineering unexpected events or by imparting a powerful urge towards a certain decision. This also is an act of grace. In the result the man is super-rationally guided or miraculously guarded.

He who submits to the Overself and receives its grace will be roused from a moral or mental torpor and will experience, usually for a time but in some cases for all time, a noteworthy change in his character. Not only will his heart be affected but also his head, not only his feelings but also his thoughts, not only his desires but also his will. For the Overself is the higher conscience of every human being because it is in very truth his guardian angel watching over him from on high. Hence the degree of development of acknowledged conscience in a man betrays the degree to which he is able to hear its voice. If a moral course which is very injurious to self or others is being pursued, sometimes it interferes in the personal life with a clear and unmistakable warning. It lifts the person for a few minutes into its own exalted viewpoint and lets him see the hidden truth of the situation with wonderful clarity. A sense of strange exaltation will necessarily accompany the experience, which will be so intense as to take on the character of a deep reverie. But alas it soon fades away and the recipient often subsides into his former and familiar viewpoint, with its artificial resistance, and thus continues to decieve himself. He may justify himself by a process of rationalization, not comprehending that passion, emotion, self-interest, appearances or narrowness of experience may be blinding him to the actual state of affairs. Hence it is necessary to recognize such uncommon opportunities and assay them for the pure gold that they are. They should be repeatedly pondered over and taken deeply to heart, these rare visitations of our diviner self, for if we fail to heed them the Overself will next speak with a sterner voice—that of unloosed karmic suffering. We may rightly look for further help in our difficulties—and sometimes miraculous help—from the Overself if we follow the better path it always points out, but hardly otherwise. He who will not heed or does not recognize it will soon find that the grey dawn will come and default on his rosy dreams of the night.

If the man's egoistic resistance is stubborn or if he is excessively preoccupied with business or pleasure so that his mind does not relax for a moment during his waking life; if he is unwilling to forget for a while the contemplation of his own affairs in order to remember the contemplation of the contemplator himself; if the spurious prestige of his personality is unfavourable to its reception in any way, then the Overself may have to pass its message or warning or arousal during his sleeping hours. In that case he will receive the communication in his conscious mind sometimes during a dream, which may or may not be symbolic, but more often immediately after awakening from dreamless sleep. It is important therefore to attend carefully to the ideas arising during any exalted state of mind coming unexpectedly at such time and not to miss their serious significance. For then we entertain an angel unawares and may regretfully realize this only long after the event.

The Overself works quietly and surely and changes life in an untheatrical manner. It lays its grip on a man without blatant advertisement of the fact; all other conversions are only emotional disturbances. The divine self works deeper than that. It wells up quietly within a man and silently holds him to its higher purpose by an inexplicable concatenation of circumstances. Why does not the Overself demonstrate its power, interfere dramatically in the life of every man on earth today and forcibly make him its conscious channel? The answer is that just because it knows its own deathlessness and the person's transiency, it can afford to wait with a wonderful patience for the growth, ripening and decay of the person's conceit and strength. This explains why we cannot force the coming of grace. It appears at its own time, not ours. It comes suddenly, unexpectedly. It is a gift. We cannot get it by scheming or struggling. We can make ourself ready for it, however, and so profit by the visitation immeasurably more than we might otherwise have done.

The touch of grace can be felt in an unmistakable manner but only after a man has been humbled, chastened and made lowly. When he finds that the net results of self-help on the secret path are often doubtful in value and sometimes even dangerous in result through the pursuit of an erroneous course; when he discovers his own weakness after many a futile attempt to break his bad habits or to enlighten the darkness of his passage through life; when in short he feels that he cannot help himself any more, the time has arrived to call on an outside source for such help. The gracious current of a stronger power than his own must be introduced into his inner life. But it can only be introduced if he calls on it, if he aspires towards it and if he gives his devotion to it. The basis of attraction between those who seek and that which gives is and must be faith and love. All the way from the aspirant's initial dream to his final achievement, he must resolutely resolve to stand or fall by his faith that this higher Self truly exists and that its realization is the hidden purpose of his incarnation.

We must alter our attitude and habitually look up with love to the Overself. We must become as devoted to it, as attached to it as we are devoted and attached to nothing else. That power which runs the universal life can also run our personal life—if we will let it think, feel and act through us; if we can learn to agree: "Thy will be done." The fact is that grace falls from heaven as freely as dew from the sky but men receive it not.

Nothing but utter humility towards this higher self will lift the heavy bar which confronts us at the doorway into the Pyramidal King's Chamber wherein it dwells. The surrender of arrogant self-will, ignorant personal desire and blind egoistic motive is both a pre-requisite to and the consequence of a growth into this larger life. It is a pre-requisite because when the grace starts to work we automatically if intermittently give some external tokens of such surrender; it is a consequence because when the grace has proceeded farther we develop a more impersonal outlook quite naturally.

Grace is wholly the operation of Overself but man may help to call it forth by his yearning and prayer, by frequently turning his gaze from his little person to this larger self. Hence no sincere and sustained cry that goes out during a crisis into the seeming void goes unheard by Overself. But it must be sincere in the sense of being uttered by a man's acts no less than by his thoughts. And it must be sustained in the sense of being a continuous aspiration and not merely the mood of an hour. He who sincerely invokes the higher power will not invoke it in vain, although its response may take an unexpected form sometimes not altogether to his immediate liking, sometimes beyond his fond hopes, but always for his real rather than apparent benefit. It is often a waste of time to beg for undeserved favours, sometimes not so. But it is practical wisdom and ethical sincerity to take to heart this truth—*repent and be redeemed.*

In the end all our values of good and evil are relative ones. They are only our progressive but transient ideas. But here in the Overself we find the supreme and absolute value because it transcends the plane of ideation itself. The Overself cannot separate itself from cosmic karma but it is not subject to the working of personal causality because it is not subject to personality, change, relativity; being beyond the limits of these ideas which appear within it. When we come to examine the nature of ultimate reality we shall learn why this is so. Hence personal karma cannot operate in such a sphere of absoluteness, however rigidly and inflexibly it operates within the space-time world of relative existence. This fact that personal causation does not exist in the profoundest plane of existence offers a great hope for mankind. For it makes possible the introduction into human life and vicissitude of this totally new and unexpected factor of grace. It is like a lifebelt to which despairing mortals may cling. The worst sinner may receive what he has not earned if he will sincerely repent, make all possible amends and turn his face around in sublime faith. Regardless of what his past life may have been if, by change of thought and deed, he can succeed in making his voice heard in that higher region it is always possible that there will descend this gift of grace. That which mystics sometimes feel in the depth of their trance as the presence of immeasurable love does not exist for them alone. It shines upon all beings. Therefore salvation is for all. Jesus' doctrine of forgiveness of sins is a simple expression of this truth, put into terms of morality and made easily understandable by untutored minds. The newer principles of quantum mechanics and the formulation of the law of indeterminacy are scientific expressions of the same truth in terms of physics, but understandable only by technical minds. These principles however must not be misunderstood. They do not abrogate the impersonal karmic forces which govern the universe, which bring it into primal being and which dissolve it into final non-entity. These remain as powerful and dominant as ever. Only, we must complete the circle and perceive that the truth about *human* life has room enough to include both the clutch of karma and the freedom of that out of which karma itself originates. Which is to say, in the end, that we do not attain our aims, whether they be physical or spiritual, by self-earned merit alone or by God-given grace alone, but by both together. The first fits us to receive the second.

Therefore nobody can afford to omit grace from his scheme of things. Consequently, nobody can afford to omit the yearning for it, either. Nobody need be too proud to pray. This raises the question of the necessity and utility of prayer. Prayer is not to be scorned by anyone. We minify the power of the Overself if we do not accept this statement. So long as we are imperfect so long may we find it necessary to pray. So long as we find lack of anything so long may we have to pray. Only the sage who is integrated and desireless does not need to pray, although even he may pray for others in his own mysterious unconventional way. No, can we say it is always wrong to pray for physical things: sometimes it may be right. But a prayer which is merely a petition to a supernatural Being to remove self-earned afflictions from the petitioner and nothing more can bring no other result than the psychological comfort it gives him. It will certainly not alter by a single jot the karmic requital which is being suffered. It will merely be a noise in the air. In vain does it protest at fate. But a prayer which combines with itself the repentant effort to alter the character-defect which gives rise to the afflictions and which is the complement of an actual attempt to make reparation if someone else has been wronged, may not be a vain one. Repentance and reparation are the all-important factors which can make a prayer successful. They will then be a force which may affect personal karma because they introduce *new* and favourable karma. Nothing could be more self-deceptive than the phenomenon which may be witnessed among Buddhists, Hindus and Christians alike, the automatic and apathetic muttering of formal prayers read by rote from a book or learnt parrot-like by heart or revolving incessantly on a piece of printed paper inside a mechanical contrivance. It is useless to flatter God, to bribe Deity or to exhibit a merely mechanical and ephemeral fidelity.

If people make such a wrong approach it is clearly not only because they do not understand the karmic implications which flow out of events but also because they misunderstand the nature of Deity, attribute their own all-too-human feelings to it and see it through a haze of sickly sentimentality which may be comforting for a time but can only end in disillusionment with further time. Let it be noted then that the God to whom man prays dwells first in his own heart. When his prayer produces an after-feeling of relief or peace, it is probably a sign that he has prayed aright, but when his perplexity or distress weighs on him as heavily as before it is probably a sign either that he must pray again and yet again or that he has prayed wrongly. In so far as a prayer exalts a man's thoughts above his petty personal concerns, it is sure to be helpful for his progress. In so far as it is a purely materialistic or utterly hypocritical appeal to an anthropomorphic deity to shower material benefits of a particular kind, it is sure to be useless either for spiritual or practical purposes. The best way for man to appeal against the principle of karma when it is exacting painful tribute is not to pray but to change his thoughts. The more he can alter for the better the general trend of his thinking, the better will his external life ultimately become.

Prayer comes to its finest bloom, its loveliest florescence, when it can utter four short words: "Thy will be done." Their meaning is not a fatalistic acceptance of karma, not a reference to some power remote from the one who says them. Only towards the close of this course will their wonderful significance become apparent. But meanwhile we may anticipate it by re-reading them in the following way: "Thy will be done *by* me"—not "*to* me". Nor is it enough merely to say them. They must become vivified by inward experience. The effort to lift consciousness up to the higher self must be made at the same time. The success may be only momentary but in that wonderful moment the sentence will assume authentic significance; its utterance will be heard on a higher level. Then—and then only—will something descend and enter into its speaker to enable the burden to be borne. And this mysterious suffusion will be that power of grace which answers and rewards genuine self-surrender. From the moment when, sensing the impalpable inter-relation of man and God, he agrees to work with the universal order he shall know peace.

10
The War and the World

THE chequered surface of history is largely a tale of tears and chance but its depths are a revelation of evolutionary unfoldment working alongside of karmic readjustment. There is a just logic in the sequence of historic events but it reveals itself only if we examine them by the light of the doctrine of karma. We must recognize that there is a common national karma from which neither prince nor pauper is exempt. It is not outside the business of metaphysics to trace the historic workings of karma through the complicated web of world events from present causes to future effects and from visible consequences to invisible origins; to understand and reveal the general direction in which society and its systems are consciously or unconsciously moving at any particular period and to judge whether this trend should be resisted or assisted, retarded or accelerated. It is thus that philosophy—of which metaphysics is but a part—can prove its usefulness as being not only an enlightening explanation of life but also a practical way of life. The need of a metaphysical understanding of social existence is not felt by most persons and even despised by many persons. Yet they possess one all the same. Only because it has not been deliberately sought for and thought out, it has not come to a sun-clear consciousness of itself. And because of its unconscious character it is primitive, crude, imperfect, unbalanced and faulty. It is a comfortless but uncontradictory fact that the consequences of an erroneous and materialistic world-conception reposing on shaky metaphysical foundations which have been faulty to a degree are to be witnessed everywhere in the hideous havoc and personal disasters it has brought upon our own epoch, in the widespread sorrows and unparalleled sufferings through which humanity is slowly beginning to learn how deceptive was its belief that it either understood or controlled life. We have witnessed this self-deception in its most arrogant and exaggerated form in the case of Hitler himself.

Hitler however has been only a monstrous symbol of the extreme growth of the materialistic tendencies of our time. His downfall could become a signal that materialism has exhausted its most useful potentialities. His affront to human dignity has brought the world to its most terrible predicament, but the severe crisis and supreme sufferings to which it has led are themselves signs of the disruptive forces which have arisen of their own accord within materialism and could destroy much of it as they mature. Through Hitler's instrumentality the worst of the latent evil in mankind's character has been brought like scum to the surface, only the better to be recognized for the hideous thing that it is and repudiated. For when a world-view has ceased to suffice for mankind it begins to germinate its own destruction through the karmic woes which it breeds. Thus those who will not walk willingly along the road to ethical and mental enlightenment have to walk it under the compulsion of self-earned sorrows. The fact of the failure of the materialistic outlook, the lesson of their own experience, bids mankind distrust and denounce it. Thus materialism is being destroyed not only from without by the superior offerings of mysticism and philosophy but also from within by the cancerous consequences and miserable failure of its own ethic.

They must take a different road and seek redemption from their past thinking. If they could get hold of right principles they could not go far wrong in practical details. Action is but the reflection of attitude. The solutions of all our sociological and economic problems, for example, do not ultimately lie within sociology and economics alone but much more in psychology. Indeed, it may even be affirmed that without a re-education of mankind in meditational practices and philosophic truth—which includes psychology—all reformers labour largely in vain. The roots of our troubles lie in the imperfections of human nature and in the fallibility of human knowledge. Philosophy is not an aimless useless study: it leads to right thinking, which is one of the most essential precedents of right living. It can offer not only a profound analysis of the past but also sound proposals for the future.

Hence when the pressing need of today is to secure complete victory over the deluded materialists who have ravaged this planet and misused the ancient mystical emblems of the Swastika and Rising Sun for their own selfish purposes, and when the pressing need of tomorrow will be the reconstruction of the world's physical resources and social edifices after the devastations of history's worst war, it need not seem to many a mere waste of time, energy and brains to show that the abstruse doctrines of an unfamiliar teaching can be applied to help us carry out these heavy tasks more wisely. Even wandering philosophers and meditative mystics may have something to offer out of their composure and compassion to their gloomy contemporaries which may possibly be helpful in this confused period. It will not be a luxury then to consider their ideas which, instead of being remote from present problems, are actually very near them. For the illuminations gained in moments of meditative or metaphysical retreat can be brought into relation with the contemporary issues which face us. The dust will soon settle on the piteous tears that have dropped on the bodies of so many slain men, women and children, but we should profit by the mistakes of the past as well as by the misfortunes of the present to prevent avoidable suffering for the future.

Our generation has seen the smoke of battle, the spread of

rapacious destruction and cruel desolation; it has listened to the dissemination of hate in all five continents and has watched terror and tragedy stamp their brutal feet upon the multitude. Those who were satisfied with their environment, their house property, family, social status, political and economic beliefs, have begun to discover with the abrupt loss of some of their possessions that something more is necessary if life is to be supportable. A process has started, at first beneath the threshold of consciousness but gradually rising above it, which first awakened them to the *fact* of the transitoriness of things and, second, aroused them to the sense of spiritual lack in their outlook. They have begun to feel the need of inner help with which to bear the strain of all these painful upheavals. Only now are they more ready to question life as to whether it possesses a higher purpose than the merely materialistic one. Where words have failed to arouse torpid spirituality and teach the lesson of non-attachment, the roaring torrent of events has succeeded in doing so. Until now many necessarily stumbled in darkness or, what is worse, walked by false lights. The tremendous area, imposing scale of tragedy and colossal merci-lessness of what has proved the most destructive of all wars has affected men and women everywhere and aroused them from their habitual ethical and mental torpor. The very uniqueness of the historic circumstances attending it has invited universal attention and fostered some reflection thereon, however little. It has begun to purify them from earthly attachments in the sense that they are forced to witness vividly the tragic transiency, the utter instability of earthly things as they are forced to experience the terrifying insecurity of their own persons. They become aware of the radical hopelessness of a materialistic outlook, a hopelessness heretofore disguised, as it so often is, by passions, enjoyments and luxuries. They are awakening to the realization that the nature of the chains of attachment is not altered merely by covering them with the flowers of pleasure. Hence the war has acted also as a practical and terrifyingly vivid initiation of the whole race into this need of inner support and deeper under standing.

After all, man is but a pilgrim upon this twilit planet and were it not for the harsh goad of sorrow he would often fall back into the soft arms of sense-satisfied ignorance and lose all sight of the high place to which he is wending. We must lament as much as anyone the nerve-breaking suffering and mind-torturing adversity which has gripped mankind like the talons of a merciless tiger for years. The moral rottenness of the Nazi hierarchs may have been the immediate cause of this agony but nevertheless we cannot be blind to the ultimate fact that mankind generally largely contributed to this horror themselves. Hitler thought that he laboured and warred and deceived and plotted only for himself or at best for Germany, but he partially acted as an instrument of collective karma. The world's condition at any time and more strikingly so at such a time, is both an index to the thoughts of man and a reflex of his passions. From this aspect the war is an external objectification of the greeds, selfishnesses and animalisms which prowled within the hearts and suffused the thinking of many millions. Let us face the stark fact that it has always been going on, only it was going on inside ourselves. We have always had to struggle against our own evil attributes and irrational instincts. What we first tolerated and then fought in the Nazis is but the visible exteriorization on a mammoth scale of feebler vices which we were already fighting on a smaller one in our own character. The tiger and the reptile still lurk beneath the surface, albeit most of us have sought to enchain them. But there are others who have sought to liberate them. The aggressive and grasping mentality, the selfish and materialistic outlook are not confined to Germany alone but have their lesser representatives inside most other countries. For most other countries have men who hate others because they belong to a different race or different class as they have greedy aggressive creatures who despise ethical standards and strive to secure their aims by trampling down whoever stands in their way. Wherever there is maniacal exaggeration and gross distortion of mental perspective, wherever men have made the little "I" their god, wherever there is fanatic racial or religious hatred, wherever there is belief in mere militaristic violence, wherever there is selfish worship of industrial achievement in brutal indifference to the human factors involved, wherever there is extreme nationalist cupidity, wherever there is complete animalistic lack of conscience—there are evil forces. Only, in Germany the psychologically diseased Nazis rose to the top, infected the unfortunate people wholesale and turned their country into a lair for criminal lunatics.

Hence in the hours of world-accounting, karma's retribution did not descend on the Germans alone but also on many other peoples. It is an old truism that mankind must learn through suffering what it refuses to learn through reflection. No deliverer, no Messiah has yet appeared who can place his people in perfect and permanent happiness. For they must learn the error of their ways and the best learning comes from bitter adversity. The chronicle of a nation cannot differ from that of an individual. Every man must run the course of sorrow as well as pleasure, of trouble as well as joy. So every nation must experience similar cycles too. In this stupendous world-drama which has been playing itself out before our eyes, each country has been allotted a special role by destiny. But the role is largely self-made and arises out of character of its people and the collective karma, good and bad, which they have earned.

This said, we must recognize the terrible fact that the struggle against Hitler is not less a struggle against malignant denizens of the nether world who have used him merely as their human instrument in an effort to prevent or destroy the iconoclastic universal awakening which they well know is impending in our century. The host of hard Nazi leaders and officials wandered into birth untamed by their experiences in the lower hells, putting their faith again in the power of violence and bloodshed and bringing a red harvest as the final offering to their deluded followers. Hence the utterance of Field-Marshal Smuts, whose wartime advice weighed so much with Churchill: "Before I did not think there was such a thing as anti-Christ, but I believe it now. I see what incarnate Evil means in the world." To understand this we must first understand that all war is really fought out on three different planes. First, the technical, which involves the clash of physical weapons. Second, the mental, which involves the clash of intellectual ideas. Third, the moral, which involves the clash of karmic forces. But this war is unique and has not only been fought out on these three planes but also on a fourth one. It is a struggle against unseen evil spirits for both the soul and the destiny of the multitudes who dwell on this planet.

We have learnt from ancient American, Asiatic and Egyptian sources the startling story of a great continent which lies wrecked beneath the grey rolling waters of the Atlantic Ocean. Deep in the silt beneath them lies the best proof that a great continent and a developed civilization have sunk from human sight. Modern science however is patiently collecting facts which show that there is much more than mere probability in the theory of the existence of Atlantis, as Plato named it. The Athenian philosopher claimed that it had been peopled by a race who raised an advanced civilization. Be that as it may, the tradition of the hidden teaching is emphatic on the point and speaks also of a vast transcontinental war which split the Atlanteans into two camps. Memories of the same struggle have been preserved in mythological form in the undated Indian narrative of the *Ramayana*. How many know that the world war which preceded the destruction of Atlantis was similar in essence and importance to the war through which we are passing today? Both represent struggles between the good and evil forces, colossal conflicts for the mastery of the internal and external life of mankind.

During the course of our long planetary history, the general moral evolution rises and falls like a series of ascending arcs, but the terminal of each arc is spiral-like on a higher level than the terminal of the preceding one. Consequently collective humanity always tends periodically to show forth its worst characteristics before it shows forth its better ones. Such a terminal is being passed today and it is the business of the evil powers to make the most of their chance. Those who, through selfish bias, wishful thinking, undeveloped intelligence or unawakened intuition cannot understand the deeper significance of the present war will not also understand that the essential forces operating on both sides are far more than merely nationalistic, political or military ones. It is still more a climacteric war of ideas and ideals, of the unseen powers of Light and Darkness. On its results the cultural, religious, ethical and material fate of mankind are to be settled for better or worse for centuries to come.

It has been told, in our study of death, how there exists a psychological belt around this planet which contains the scum of the spirit world, the most degraded of its creatures, the most malignant and untruthful of its inhabitants. This is the real source whence Hitler and his gang have drawn their inspiration, this is the mental lever whereto an unnatural abnormal and dangerous gap has been opened by the Fuehrer and with which he has held frequent communion during his secret semi-trances. We may see in the sinister efforts of these forces of darkness which, working through him, have sought by sheer violence to press the minds of all men in a single ugly mould, an illustration of their profoundly sinister character. For the ultimate basis of man's being is freedom, is the illimitable infinitude of the Overself. And we may see in the vicious attempts of the same forces to maim the lives and despoil the possessions of so many different classes and races, through willing human agents who have been stirred up to aggression or hatred that they might climb to eminence on other people's misery, an illustration of their profoundly selfish character. For the truth, which the world-wide character of the danger and struggle of the war must now begin to impress upon everybody, is that all mankind is moving, however slowly, towards the time when it shall eventually form one great family of nations, that is a united commonwealth. But this truth is utterly obnoxious to these materialistic instruments. Hence their attempt to secure earthly dominion has been intended to hinder the physical, the intellectual and the moral evolution of mankind.

There is still another significance of this titanic effort by the forces of darkness and destruction to enslave the bodies and dominate the minds of the entire human race. It is more hidden and more important than the previous one although to some extent intertwined and dependent on it. These powers have made their firm stand against the dawning both of higher general intellectual enlightenment and of diviner ideas on our spiritual horizon, a dawning which has become historically and karmically due. They have seen in it their own inevitable weakening and compulsory retreat. Hence they have sought to eliminate every man who has held even a mere fraction of such ideas, whilst bludgeoning the minds of all others with titanic falsehood or forced co-operation. They have even side-tracked the simple-minded by utilizing the prestige and stealing the very idea of unity, towards which mankind is irresistibly if slowly moving, and by presenting compulsory enslavement which is their own ugly caricature of this ideal, as being the reality itself! The totalitarian governments have cunningly sought to pervert sound spiritual instincts into false materialist ones. The profound if unconscious aspiration to attain inward unity with all men through realization of the Overself has been twisted into the compulsion to sink individuality into the grotesque mass mould fashioned by the dark elements! In other words the ideal of materialist uniformity has been substituted for that of spiritual unity.

Those who fail to perceive that the course and consequence of this war have been utterly unlike the course and consequence of all preceding wars fail to understand its essential character. The world-drama which is being enacted today *and which will continue even after the war is unique.* Its highest significance is that the powers which make for darkness, ignorance, evil and the powers which move us toward light, wisdom, goodwill are fighting their age-old battle anew. Everyone must take his side in this sacred struggle. Nobody can be neutral without deceiving himself. There is no place for mere spectators. This is a war in the heavens as well as on earth.

The Social Crisis.

The old belief that progress has an automatic character, a belief which the West acquired in the nineteenth century, began to explode in the twentieth century with the explosion of shells and bombs in the two world wars. It was thus that we began also to remember that history has shown time and again that mankind rises to the heights only to fall again into the abysses. Mankind's story is not a narrative of mechanical progress but of arcs rising and falling through varied peoples and civilizations which serve Nature's purpose during the rise and, failing to do so any longer, perish during the fall. It is an historical process of the epochal and interrupted development of men and their systems successively rising to culture and power and later, with their degeneration, making way for others. But through all these ups and downs there is a recapitulation on a higher level and consequently there is an evolutionary self-unfolding and the coming into fuller expression of latent possibilities. Let us not look for smooth straight-line progress when all history, whether of a race or of an individual, shows it to be zig-zag or rather spiral-like in character.

What we perceive in human life may also be perceived in the life of the starry worlds overhead; every astronomical revolution, every return of a wandering planet to the same point in the zodiac which it has touched and re-touched before, pre-figures for us this truth of cyclic alternation as a universal law. Thus those who object to change and insist on living in the dying past are laughed at for their pains by the very planetary system itself, which never ceases to revolve and carries them too in its own onward and circular movement. One insect, the worm, gives silk to man, but another insect, the moth, destroys it. Throughout Nature we find this double characteristic, construction on one hand, destruction on the other, co-operating with the work of time. Cosmic equilibrium calls forth at one time that which it crushes at a later time. This is why the history of both the inferior and superior kingdoms of Nature moves through a series of well-defined epochs. Yet every return is only relatively the same because the whole cosmos is undergoing a mysterious movement in space. For it has already been mentioned that the end of each evolutionary arc is intersected by the beginning of a new one, which eventually rises to a far higher level in its own turn. Owing to this overlapping both the decaying and nascent phases of civilization exist for a time side by side. The conflict between them precipitates a state of peculiar confusion and sharp crisis. Such a state exists today.

Such is the mutability of social existence. Only mental coward or the emotional weakling will refuse to recognize this fact when once he has discovered it. Why then should we regard our own epoch as immune from this prevailing periodicity? Those who have a philosophic perspective and can trace the thread of causal connection between historical events have not been taken unawares by any of the major international changes during the past couple of decades. They knew what was coming and understood why it had to come. Thus for those who have eyes to see, the factuality of national karma is verified by the actuality of history. Only those individuals who are biased by the desire to keep in comfortable ideational ruts and those groups who are unwilling to subordinate their sectional earthly interests to the common welfare will naturally fail or refuse to perceive that we are moving through a transitional period which marks the decline and finish of an outworn era alongside of the commencement and growth of a new one. But this blindness does not help them for the changes proceed all the same.

The epochal decline is brought about by an increasing manifestation of all the evils and maladies which have been inherent or latent in the passing phase. Thus materialism—the belief that reality is solely contained within a matter which can be seen, smelt, touched and tasted, the dogma that the mind of man is solely contained by a lump of meat in his head, the denial of the existence of a super-sensual Mind in the universe, that is of God, and the setting up of a set of selfish values for the conduct of life based on these views—represents the essential culture and actual practice of mankind on the declining arc, whatever its pretended culture and hypocritical practice are supposed to be. During its early and middle phases an historic-karmic cycle proceeds slowly but when it approaches its culmination the momentum of change, dissolution and destruction increases with dramatic speed. At the general turning-point when a new cycle is about to open the disturbance of conditions becomes like an irresistible avalanche, men and their methods going to devastating but temporary extremes. This process of planet-wide disruption brought about by swift-acting karmic forces moves a stage further with the coming of World War II. The movement of events and with them the movement of outlook is no longer slow and uneven but jumps forward erratically like a horse out of control. We are covering the changes of centuries in a period of a few years, the movement of many years in as many weeks.

We are confronted today by such a terminal period, such an abrupt closing of an entire cycle of planetary history. At the same time the ascending arc has also started its career, so that we really stand in a transitional phase between the two. Hence the presence at one and the same time of two contradictory currents in our civilization as, for example, an insensate desire for sensuous pleasure continuously occupying one group of human minds the moment it is relaxed from its inescapable responsibilities and duties, on the one hand, and an earnest desire for super-sensuous understanding and upliftment of consciousness occupying a different group, on the other hand. Life, these last few years, has seemed a bewildering chaos, a meaningless maze, a nonsensical pattern of events. But there is really a perfect logic behind these events, a hidden significance within them, an undisclosed chain of causation which has linked them into rational shape. The crisis has been an integral one, involving the whole of human ideative and practical activity. Because the structure of civilization has become organic what happens on the economic side, for example, affects the cultural side too. An entire chain of widely different factors stretches across it and all of them are firmly interlinked, so that links like religion and aviation which seem so dissimilar are actually influencing one another.

Humanity stands at the cross-roads of its social existence, not sure in what direction to move its feet. It is confronted by one road which is merely the continuation of that which it has hitherto been travelling already and which therefore appears easier. It is confronted by a second road which leads through hitherto untraversed unknown territory and therefore appears harder. The first demands self-sacrifice in the beginning but will take very much more in the end. The second demands much of it in the beginning but will return very much more in the end. In one sense it is free to choose which road it will take but in another sense it is not. That is the new epoch cannot become a mere replica of the vanishing one because both evolutionary pressure and karmic adjustment are also at work. If humanity chooses the first road then the new age, which has been inaugurated by the blood and violence of strife, will continue to be inaugurated by this same terrible couple. If it chooses the second one, then both will subside and a real peace will be established.

Philosophy believes that we shall best find our way not through the ugly horrors of revolution but through the peaceful changes of regeneration. A new order of society which brought less freedom, less kindness and less truth instead of more, is not worth having and is indeed an insult offered in the name of progress and an outrage perpetrated in the name of justice. The belief that justifies immediate tyranny as a road to ultimate freedom, presents falsehood as a road to subsequent truth, temporary terror as a road to permanent peace and contemporary cruelty as a road to eventual welfare is held by those who begin by deceiving themselves and end by deceiving others. Long ago Jesus pointed out that one does not gather grapes off a thistle tree and it is still true that one does not gather the fruit of human happiness off the tree of human barbarity.

But unfortunately there are not many philosophers among mankind. It is therefore the behest of prudence as well as the dictate of idealism that a generous reconstruction should be initiated by those in a position to do so. For if those who have power and influence bungle their chance to take the lead in this matter of making the needful adjustments to the new tempo; if they wait for events to push them, they will wait until events will not only push them but angrily push them to a calamitous degree.

We need a new way of looking at economics and religion, at society and history, at politics and ethics, at education and art. If civilization survives the crisis it will either arise Phoenix-like with a nobler form or it will fall into the marsh of increasing decay. Its past errors, recognised and remedied, will either form the foundation of a better-ordered life or they will be allowed by a blinded people to grow worse and thus bring down twilight upon itself. The choice between advance to a newer epoch or retrogression to an expiring one must be made, the decisive situation which confronts mankind must be recognized for what it is and the significance of the shocks of the past years must be understood. For the possibility of continuing more than a little way along the old road has come to an end. A transformation of human life must occur. If we grasp this then reconstruction will not seem so fearful for the alternative to it is truly fearful. We must rise to the historic occasion and place the general welfare above narrower interests.

Mankind is emerging from tradition which served it but now hampers it. The collapse of a debilitated culture, the break-up of a small-hearted economic order, the disintegration of an effete social order and the decay of an outworn political order are inevitable historical processes, however excellent and worthy all these orders may have proved themselves in the past. Within the structure of these systems, valuable as they originally were on their own level, a *spiritually* progressive human life has now become less and less possible for the two thousand million human beings on this planet. The bases of the old industrial age in the West and of the old religious age in the East are being uprooted and scattered. It is useless to refuse to recognize these catastrophic facts, to seek to hold on to that which is being ruthlessly torn from our hands, to be blind to what is passing before our eyes. Whether we like it or not it is better to open them to what is inevitable rather than shut them and suffer the consequences. A new world will be born out of the old one. This is an event which one can avert. It will be worse in some ways but better in others. To the extent that we plan this world unselfishly to suit worthwhile ideas and ideals, it will be a better one. To the extent that we let the crucial situation selfishly take its own course, it will be a worse one. The mind that takes the initiative in searching for and securing new ideas, the "blitzkrieg" mentality which has been so greatly needed to achieve successes during the war, is also needed to achieve successes during the peace.

The single outstanding practical idea among all these ideas is that whether the new age will also be a better age depends on ourselves, on how much our comprehension has caught up with these titanic events, on how far and how fast we have travelled in outlook through this grim experience of planetary war; on how bravely we can endure having artificial values wrenched out of our lives in consequence and on how readily we have let karma train us even whilst it tortured us. Civilization must change; it is best for us to co-operate with destiny in determining the nature of that change. That the transition must meet and overcome Himalayan obstacles is plain and depresses many. It is easy to fall into the pit of despondency and adopt a negative attitude towards them. But if a man has a difficult task to perform and considers only the difficulties which confront him, it is unlikely that he will ever succeed in doing it at all. Just the same, if he finds himself in a difficult situation and considers only its difficulties, he is unlikely to get out of it. Philosophy says the truth of a situation or of a task can be seen only by seeing all its sides, the bright along with the dark, the shadows along with the sunlight, and that the correct understanding of the principles of life should persuade us to look to our latent resources and not sink into ignoble inertia. We can, if we will, transform the theoretically possible into the actually accomplished. Hence the way out of world suffering need not be into world despair but into world hope.

Mankind's crisis has been fateful but it need not be fatal. "Be firm and patient in adversity and throughout all periods of panic," is the apposite advice of Muhammad. Much of the bitter karma which brought us to our present condition has been largely worked off. The remainder may be modified by creating and introducing an opposing current of new karma which, if we make it sufficiently strong, can affect the old one. Nay, were we astute enough and self-renouncingly repentant enough to foster the new factor until it became overwhelmingly powerful, some (not all) of the old forces could even be inoperative. For changed thinking co-operating with remorseful amendment sets new karmic causes in motion which, if they are of an opposite character, may soften the hard effects of old karmic misdeeds or attenuate their otherwise prolonged results or offset their unpleasant direction or at least check the stream of negative thoughts which they generate.

We must bring our minds and morals abreast of the tremendous happenings which have shaken the world. If we do not or cannot, then we are doomed to become darkly depressed. If the evil forces represented by Hitler and inspiring his insincerities have striven to impede our transition into a better civilisation by proffering a pretended new order in its place, it is for those who comprehend what the genuine new order should be like to strive to precipitate mankind's progress toward it. If no epoch has ever been comparable with our own sufferings, it is equally true that none has been comparable in its opportunities. The groans of the wounded upon this planet's battlefields and the tears of the womenfolk in its bereaved homes will not be utterly in vain, at the very least for coming generations, if with aroused conscience we turn the catastrophe of war to subserve the nobler end of making a *better-based* civilization. The war will not end with the last bomb which falls or with the last shell which is fired. It will not only have to be fought to a finish: it will also have to be *thought* to a finish. That is we must re-think the social principles and cultural foundations upon which many of our existing arrangements, beliefs and habits are based and use the destruction of war to prepare the way for a worthwhile reconstruction of peace.

Philosophy believes in constructive service. It believes that the squalor of the labouring masses, the diseases of the close-packed Western slums, the semi-starvation of the toiling Asiatic peasants could be got rid of and the consequent mental degradation of these men and women averted. The means are here, the brains are available, the machines have been and shall be invented. Shall the will be absent? This renovation of human life would demand much but would give back more. There is, for example, potential abundance on one side and actual want on the other. A wise and efficient statesmanship would try to bring the two together. The paradoxical state of affairs which permits the masses to live in misery or poverty when the material resources of the earth are ample, when properly organized and scientifically developed, to maintain them in comfort must surely be improved. The shame of mass unemployment should touch the social conscience. Our planetary storehouse needs to be better tapped and better organized for the benefit of all mankind. If the advanced countries and classes help the backward ones, all may benefit. A tremendous all-round expansion of production, trade and consumption is possible. The world's potential wealth is immense. The little-developed but vast tracts in Asia, Africa and South America would alone suffice to provide the land and material whose co-operative working along modern scientific lines on a joint East-West civilization could greatly help to remove destitution, hunger and the causes of economic conflict from the face of this planet.

We shall begin to understand what is now happening to the world only when we begin to understand that there have been more dynamic transformations in the physical basis of human life, more fundamental alterations in its intellectual basis, more iconoclastic shifting in its ethical, social and religious basis during the past generation than in all the preceding two thousand years put together. We can interpret these plain facts in but one way. The world-reconstruction is here and we are actually in the midst of its first lap. If the vast untouched possibilities and the immense unexploited resources of Nature on this planet were properly utilized; if the time and labour of millions of persons working at antiquated tasks or not even able to obtain work at all were wisely organized and efficiently directed, starvation could be eliminated and sickness reduced, human life dignified and human existence made more worthwhile. For we have reached the opening of an age in mankind's long history comparable with the opening of the age when they discovered the plough and the wheel. There were more new practical discoveries and technical inventions during the nineteenth century than in all the preceding centuries put together. Industrialism began to transform the way of human living. But it was only a crude and cruel beginning. We are now technologically right in the first stride of history's most epoch-making time. Why should not the world, with all its scientific ingenuity, grow richer and not poorer in the future?

Not that the post-war world can be turned into a paradise. The idea is but a mirage. No miraculous millennia can arise suddenly. It is a long road from the acquisitive instinct of the first and second evolutionary paths to the altruistic one of the third path. Those who look for the overnight conversion of a race betray a vivid imagination but a faulty knowledge of man. But if as philosophic students we refuse to be carried away by emotional enthusiasms for utopias which cannot be materialized, this is not to say that we must refuse to exert all energies to make this the best possible environment we can. The world can be turned into a better place to live in for the millions of men, women and children who have hitherto known only the degradations and discomforts, the miseries and sadnesses which accompany a society without a conscience. And it comes to this, that a coloperative friendly world will be immeasurably superior to a haphazardly drifting one. And one certain characteristic of the post-war period is that there will be much levelling up and much levelling down throughout society, The chief consequence of this will necessarily be that the coming era will be chaotic and confused.

The so-called lower classes could for the first time in history live above the poverty-stricken level and enjoy a more dignified and more spacious life. And the coming inventions, which will transform social and industrial life, will help to make this so. Men, women and children everywhere could be fed, clothed, sheltered and educated, could live so fully and so leisurely in a material sense, as they have never lived before at any time. The new opportunity, backed by the staggering new inventions which are coming, that faces the human race today is colossal. On this view the war will not end with the signing of peace. It will need to be carried on against all those diseased physical and mental conditions which made the rise of the twin forms of totalitarianism possible. So long as they last so long must many still remain warriors. But it should be a war waged in the spirit, not of hatred or acquisition but of altruistic service.

Civilization will need to be largely made anew after the stirring events which are leaving such a terrible mark upon it. But when the powerful tension of discipline which is imposed by a great war relaxes, when peace arrives we find that it is not peace after all. For the reaction is often indiscipline, that is anarchy and chaos. The coming of peace will necessarily release forces of an iconoclastic unrestrained and chaotic character. The confused storm-clouds which lowered over the European scene before the war were already indicative of deep changes in the social and intellectual climate. The post-war ferment will unleash energies that require to be directed into the right channels if they are to bring more happiness and not more misery to mankind. For it will be as dangerous to be swept away by unbalanced demagogic appeals to the passions as by selfish reactionary appeals to the instincts. It will be an urgent task to keep aloft of sanity and wisdom during the inevitable clash between an epoch that is perishing and an epoch that is being born, or else we shall become a squirming heap of struggling men who have spoiled a planet. Consequently those who lead groups or direct thought ought to meet present situations not only with adequate understanding but also with kindly understanding. Neither hate-inspired outbursts and the advocacy of brutal methods on the one side nor reactionary refusals to make needed changes on the other will avail. What the world needs today is not a quicker revolution but a quicker evolution. For it may accomplish the second with sweetness and sanity but the first only with blood and tears.

When it is asked what kind of post-war world should be set up, between two extremes we should choose neither! It is better to effect a compromise between them but it is always best to rise to a view which is above them. Philosophy alone, both because of its utter lack of partisanship and because of its non-materialistic outlook, can offer such a view. Comprehension is better than conflict. The attitude of mutual help could felicitously solve all the problems of reconstruction.

The little experiences of everyday living largely determine men's outlook. Given better physical environments and more effective and timely religious, mystical or philosophical instruction, they would once more begin to display the diviner nature which underlies their defects and which can never be destroyed; they would once again fulfil finer hopes and not fail them. Consequently we must change external conditions if we would change the internal ones and we must change the mental conditions if we would change the physical ones. We must clear out the slums in human cities so as to help clear out the slums in human minds. Men whose bodies are enwombed and bred to maturity in dark slums naturally possess dark slum-like minds. They have no horizons. Hence we must attempt to make it easier for man to relax from the sordid struggle to keep bodily alive and to give some thought to the nobler struggle to keep spiritually alive. He must have enough food to eat, enough clothes to wear, a sufficiently suitable dwelling-place and enough work to sustain him and his family. If he lacks these things he will be without the energy for philosophy and without the time for mystical life. If he is wholly enslaved by this struggle or set free to starve in old age, he is at best but a half-man. What hope of a higher mental life exists for him?

We have the chance not only to enter an age of plenty but also of leisure. The growth of leisure makes the growth of culture possible. The brain of man reduces the slavery of man. The elimination of unnecessary physical toil gives him a better chance to think and feel above the animal. The inventor clears a pathway for the spiritual teacher who wants to help his fellows realize their higher possibilities.

But just as plenty misused may lead to more materialism and not less, so leisure misused by being spent wholly in sensuous pleasures may lead to more spiritual ignorance and not less. The question of their right use is primarily a question of a right mental attitude. Such an attitude can be got from the contemplation of right ideas. For the tangible values of economic and social forms are not the only ones that concern us. These are primarily of value in so far as they render human living on this earth at all possible but they possess another significance, a profounder and intangible one. Therefore we should beware of entering into inner relationship with any materialistic school of economics which subscribes to the sordid thought that reverses Christ's command and proclaims that man needs only his bread and butter and the kingdom of heaven will be added unto him. This is like trying to grow flowers without roots. We must indeed make a better world for the masses but should refuse to raise such an effort to the status of a single all-sufficient cause. The failure of all such economic materialism is its failure to realize that man does not exist primarily for the body. This arises out of its lack of new perspectives rather than out of its lack of new arguments. Not for the bread's sake nor the body's sake nor for any State's sake as exemplifying these things in our days was man put down here on earth to win his bread and use his body but for the grander sake of realizing his Overself.

The liberating study of philosophy tends to counteract such one-sided views. It reveals that the practical and contemplative factors are both essential to a balanced life. Those who regard the two lines of conduct as logically irreconcilable are refuted by history. Our mistake, for example, does not lie in the wide use of machines, the amazing application of technology or the quest of comfortable living. It lies less in the practical way we live than in the moral ends for which we live. It lies in the ruptured equilibrium between the satisfaction of bodily needs and the satisfaction of spiritual and aesthetic ones. It lies in accepting the lack of those ethical restraints and exalted inspirations which the religious faiths of our time have so largely failed to give. When the practical unites with the contemplative, then only will a civilization be born upon this planet inwardly sounder and outwardly more magnificent than either alone can conceive or create. Taken separately in total isolation they are both unsatisfying because of the missing opposite factor. Moreover contemplation tends historically to enervate the will and to throw the dark mantle of pessimism over this world, whilst practicality tends to glorify the gold nexus at the expense of the ethical and thus commits a grievous mistake. But were deep thought upon life and the devotional attitude towards it to be linked with energetic development of the earth's material resources and a co-operatively organized society, the resulting synthesis would astound all.

Co-operation is certainly a vital need of the coming age. It should extend between classes within the same nation, between the nations themselves and even between the five continental groups of the planet. In this world where form and differentiation are supreme there can be no complete harmony and agreement. The notion of making all people think alike is a foolish one. But the unity which cannot be found outwardly can however be found inwardly. Mentally, we can all agree to differ. Morally we can all try to feel for and with one another. The consequences in happier living of doing so would be tremendous both for ourselves and for others. Our unsuspected avarice and respected acquisitiveness, however, prevent us from seeing this truth, indeed prevent us from seeing many other truths. This is why philosophy inculcates a course of self-discipline for emotion, egoism and thinking before revealing its major truths.

What will emerge for the thoughtful observer from all the post-war conferences and congresses, therefore, is that no satisfactory solution of the practical problems which harass modern mankind can be found on any other basis than that of a broadly co-operative one. All other solutions will be partial at their best, mistaken at their worst. This will not only be true of the different classes, castes and groups which compose a nation but, more strikingly if to a lesser extent, of the different nations themselves. The walls which Nature has built between the different races and peoples will change only with the slow changes of evolution but the walls which man's thought has built between them are falling to pieces before our eyes. We are learning at last how to share our lives on this planet together. For only when we can come to see that the peculiarities of nations and the prejudices of races are irrelevant, that the prime fact is that we are human beings first and Dutchman or Fiji Islanders only after that, shall we begin to cease this age-old worship of the flesh and thus to cease our hate-breeding materialism. World society must one day become one society. But as this structure is beyond mankind's present capacity, the preparation of its groundwork is not. If they cannot get over their body-based prejudices quickly enough to attain this goal at a single leap, they can at least attain it by a series of single steps. If they have grown so used to their leg-irons that sudden freedom would frighten them, then they can drop the irons one by one.

Mankind is being shaped to live as one great commonwealth on earth; the nations will sooner or later have to work together, peacefully if they possess goodwill but forcibly if they lack it. History and circumstances conspire to this end, for their future is henceforth one. The evolutionary tide is sweeping them into the direction of forming a functioning whole. This means that eventually all existing man-made boundaries between countries will break down and vanish, that a regional autonomy will replace the old narrow nationalisms and that each people will contribute to *as well as profit by* the common welfare. The inhabitants of this planet will, at some distant time in their history, begin to function as a single unified entity. This process will be helped by the coming new inventions which will profoundly alter transport and communications.

This is the goal held before us. How quickly or how slowly we move towards it will depend on how much or how little we profit by our past experience and our present sufferings. But the goal itself is inescapable. For it will be a physical expression of what already exists as a metaphysical fact. Whoever throws a pebble into the ocean of present-day world existence at any point whatsoever starts a ripple which spreads everywhere. This may be better understood by considering the doctrine of karma more deeply than has hitherto been done. In *The Hidden Teaching Beyond Yoga* it was hinted that beyond the scientific and practical form of it as there presented there existed also an esoteric and philosophic interpretation. This interpretation will now be given.

We live in a regulated world-system, an orderly cosmos, and hence one in which things are related to other things and beings to other beings in a vast network that stretches through all time and across all space. The universe is both a collection of forces which are unable to exist separately but act and interact upon each other, and a collection of things which do not stand by themselves but are intrinsically linked as parts of the whole. The belief that any particular thing or being stands absolutely alone is based on deceptive appearances. Separateness exists only on the surface; it is our illusion. Independent existence is indeed our fantasy.

Human life, particularly, is like a gigantic moving wheel which contains within itself countless tiny cogged wheels revolving continuously against each other. The great wheel is God, the World-Mind, whilst the little ones are individual men. And just as the imperfect or irregular working of a single wheel affects the working of its neighbouring ones, which in their turn pass on something of the trouble to their neighbours, so does the daily life of mankind feel the benefits and disadvantages of its own inter-dependence. The to-and-fro flow of exchanges—mental, emotional and physical—between a man and his human environment is constant and unavoidable. He literally shares life with others. The belief in the existence of a completely separate person is really a superficial one. When we examine still more sharply into what we mean by the disarmingly simple word "I", when we settle its innermost significance, we free ourselves from the second great illusion which after the illusion of matter hides the truth about existence from us. To carry reflection to its farthest possible point is to see that it is impossible to confine any being within the bounds of personality as we earlier found, when considering the beginnings of the world, that it was impossible to confine any event within the bounds of causality. We shall find that because personality is only a part of the universe, it is not and cannot be an ultimate fact. We shall find that the strands of inter-dependence and inter-relation which tie up into the knot that makes a single person extend infinitely in space and infinitely in time. When we try to follow up all these strands we are led from the part to the whole, from the personal to the universal. Any attempt to isolate more than its surface-side is foredoomed to failure. For a separate ego cannot exist alone, cannot stand without the universe behind it.

The "I" is therefore not so simple but, on the contrary, much more complex than it first seems. We can stake out no permanent boundaries, fix no final limits to mark where one ego really begins and where it really ends. Not one may be rightly thought of by itself apart and detached from the others. Nothing and nobody is really self-existent but everything and everybody is inter-dependent with others through an endless series. If therefore we regard an ego as really being existent in itself and in its own right, we fall into illusion through ignorance. Physically we are all so inter-dependent on each other in the present, so intimately related with the entire procession of all mankind in the past; mentally, we are all so constantly inter-changing our ideas and so frequently inter-circulating our feelings; and karmically, all our historic lives are so inter-penetrating and linked in such a large network of circumstances, that it is more correct to view the person as being only one particular aspect of the total unified existence out of millions. Such is the relativity of every creature that its proper significance can finally be determined only by reference to the significance of all. Any adequate meaning of the "I" must not be so narrow as to omit its cosmic reference. No thoughtful man can look on life, therefore, as a purely personal affair but must inevitably come to regard it as a whole, as essentially one. Just as all the countless cells in a human body really belong to its single existence, so all the countless creatures in the cosmos really belong to the One Existence in a similar way. He who can go further and realize this oneness in full consciousness rather than in mere intellection, permanently rather than intermittently, basically rather than superficially, has found the hidden secret of an undying self and united with the mysterious flux of an eternal life.

If therefore we wish to think truly of ourself we must think of it in terms of the Whole. Consequently the esoteric interpretation of karma recognizes that a wholly isolated individual is only a figment of our imagination, that each man's life is intertwined with all mankind's life through ever-expanding circles of local, national, continental and finally planetary extent; that each thought is influenced by the world's predominant mental atmosphere; and that each action is unconsciously accomplished with the co-operation of the predominant and powerful suggestion given by mankind's general activity. The consequences of what he thinks and does flow like a tributary into the larger river of society and there mingle with waters from innumerable other sources. This makes karma the resultant of *all* these mutual associations and consequently raises it from a personal to a collective level. That is to say "I", an individual, share in the karma generated by all other individuals, whilst they share in mine. There is a difference, however, between both our shares in that "I" receive the *largest* share of the results of my own personal past activity and the smallest share of the results of the rest of mankind's activity.

Hence our hint in the same book that not all sufferings are merited ones but that compensatory good fortune comes accordingly into play. If owing to mankind's inter-dependence we have to suffer what we have not personally earned, it is equally true that owing to the same inter-dependence we are able to receive unearned benefits from the general good karma. Thus this collective operation of karma is like a two-edged sword which cuts both ways; the one painful and the other enjoyable. The esoteric view puts a fresh face on the popular form of the doctrine, and if it has generally been kept in the background this is only because men are more interested in their own personal welfare than in the common welfare. But the world-wide effects of the war which have caught almost all mankind in their net, help to vindicate the truth of this view better than any verbal explanation could do so.

For they have brought both the fact and need of human inter-relationship out of obscurity into the light.

We live in common with others, sin in common too and must be redeemed in common. This is the last word, dismaying perhaps to those who have out-stripped their fellows but heartening to those who have lagged behind. On this larger view karma makes us suffer for and rejoice with society as a whole. Hence we cannot divorce our own welfare from the social welfare. We must escape from inner isolation and join our interests to those of All-Life. There is no need for antagonism between classes, nations and races, no need for hatred and strife between different groups whether large or small. All are ultimately inter-dependent. Their separateness is as great a delusion as separateness of individuals, but only philosophy and history prove this truth. The situation in which we all find ourselves today compels a recognition of this challenging truth in our mutual interest.

The Personal Crisis.

Mankind need to free themselves from the sharp spiky clutch of war more than ever before because science has turned it into an unbearable catastrophe. They will consequently devise political schemes to prevent it. Such schemes are necessary and may go far but they cannot go all the way. For war is first bred in the *thoughts* of men before it is born from their hands. It is therefore equally necessary to set their thoughts right. When they awaken to a more metaphysical outlook they will perceive that by starting a war against those thoughts and feelings which breed external clashes and conflicts they can penetrate to and cut at the very roots of this perennial problem, which has turned history into a tale punctuated by falling tears. Political conferences can bring about verbal peace. But this may yet leave millions of men hating each other. An invisible war will thus continue. Therefore we must keep this thought steadily before our eyes, and present it to such as will care for it, that real peace can be achieved only when it is achieved inside men's hearts. "Each day I believe less and less in the social question, and in the political question and in the aesthetic question, and in the moral question, and in all the other questions that people have invented in order that they shall not have to face resolutely the only real question that exists—the *human* question. So long as we are not facing this question, all that we are now doing is simply making a noise so that we shall not hear it," wrote a wise Spaniard, Miguel de Unamuno.

All these numerous errors in action and sins in ethics are traceable to the single initial error in thought, the first fundamental misconception in understanding. The real roots of fratricidal troubles lie in human nature and all the social, political and economic roots are but secondary. Thought is creative. The lusts and hates, the greeds and jealousies which afflict frail man materialize sooner or later into such ugly external forms as we have already witnessed during our own century. Whoever deplores them must realize that the most effective way is to penetrate to their deep causes. Not that the secondary reliefs afforded by external measures are valueless; on the contrary, they have a most important and essential place; but that a poisoned blood-stream must be purified at the same time that its consequent skin eruptions are tended. The best way to help mankind is to discover and spread the truth about mankind. After all, man's institutions are drawn out of his heart and mind. If his thinking is imperfect and his emotions debased by selfishness, his institutions will share this imperfection and corruption. Therefore they will fulfil themselves only as they become expressions of nobler attitudes and as they become voices of his higher unearthly yearnings, of his mysterious aspiration toward Overself. If people were half as enthusiastic about truth as they are about political readjustments, they might have a better world more quickly, more surely and more painlessly. For in the end every social problem becomes the personal problem. It is because each individual member has gone wrong that society as a whole has gone wrong. If we try to get a new and better world without trying to get new and better men to inhabit it, we shall find in the end that we have succeeded only in getting a new edition of the same old and defective world from which we want to get away. But most men are unwilling to transform their character. So life, to the dread accompaniment which Mars has played as an overture, has itself undertaken the task for them.

War is an awakener. One of its functions is to quicken the blood-flow of new ideas, whether they concern the technicalities of military armament, the industrial arrangements of society, the fundamental forms of educational literary, artistic and religious culture of the conventional standards of morality. The economic, political, technological, social, cultural and religious cobwebs are brushed away by the brooms of war merely because men are too timid or too stupid to brush them away earlier by reason. But apart from this, war tests mankind. An instance of this is the way it forces those who deal in vague generalities, whether military, metaphysical or industrial, political, religious or mystical, to face the grave and specific problems set by hard facts and definitely do something about them. Mere verbal heroics, glib wordy theorizing, futile and illusory perfectionist babbling are tried in the furnace of war and found wanting. It unveils pretences and shows up things as they are. It strains our characters to the utmost. Its stress and danger bring out both our hidden strength and disguised weakness. This enforced psycho-analysis also reveals whether we are making real or sham progress. We may make alarming or assuring discoveries about ourselves, we may even find that we have been living in a world of make-believe illusions and mistaken valuations, but in any case we shall know better both what we really are and what is the intrinsic worth of our social and cultural institutions. There have always been recurring periods of history when society and its systems, culture and its ideas, religion and its beliefs, rulers and their subjects are put, whether they like it or not, through a sifting process which slowly and abruptly revaluates them and their traditions, but there has never been a period when this process has been so widespread and so thorough as now.

After all, this world is but a contrivance to draw forth latent perfection. The situations in which we find ourselves and the social upheavals that surround us are but instruments to develop character and capacity, whilst the relations we contract are the tests, temptations, opportunities and privileges to turn our latent possibilities into realized actualities. During the last few years humanity has been standing at the cross-roads of its own character and consequent destiny. Both its individual members and its collective sections have had clear-cut issues thrust upon them. There could and can be no evasion. There could and can be no standing still. There could not even be any compromise, save a sham self-deceptive one which would soon end in failure. All have had to make their particular choice of direction and begin to move forward to greater things and grander ideals or to degrading events and lower standards. It has been a time of the utmost importance in human history, a veritable crisis. The entire war period, including the years which immediately preceded it and those which will immediately follow it, has created out of its strife, agony and destruction abnormal physical situations and unique practical experiences which have had to be faced, met and mastered by millions of people. And to others it has presented hitherto unasked questions and unthought-of problems concerning religious or metaphysical matters. It has raised to the surface all those hidden pre-suppositions, attitudes and values which secretly governed their thinking about life. Few persons could evade the issues which have confronted them, just as few could escape the necessity of new orientations. Disagreeable, troublesome and painful though this usually has been, it nevertheless possesses a profound significance. For it has provided mankind with the opportunity of making distinct progress of a mental, ethical or physical nature. The tragedy of our time has entered deeply into individual lives and made the need of finding an inner rebirth in order to avoid an inner collapse something that itself can no longer be avoided.

Just as groups and governments attempted in their ignorance of its inevitability to escape from the coming war by methods of appeasement of isolation but found their attempts vain, so individuals in their self-ignorance attempted to escape by methods of pleasure-seeking or indifference from facing their inner poverty until bursting bombs or vanished supports, until all the torment and terror of our epoch brought on an inner crisis and forced them to face themselves. Hence in a little book written seven years ago we published the prediction that "the hour approaches when your world shall meet itself, shall see its own face unveiled. This is the time of weighing all things in the balance". Thus the churning operation of war brought us nearer to self-knowledge, showed up our unsuspected moral heights and depths.

Philosophically the most important effect of the war is less its alteration of artificial values than the series of shocks which it has given to the consciousness of mankind. Although these shocks were karmically originated, they have also been cosmically co-ordinated in time. That is to say, the evolutionary pressure from within has been synchronized with the karmic pressure from without, the call of the Overself harmonized with the logic of events in such a way as to make both force themselves abruptly and sharply upon mankind's attention in repetitions which have struck like hammer-blows deep through the surface consciousness. They have shaken up the thoughtless habits and selfish traditions which have so long fortified a materialistic outlook. The most important effect of these psychological shocks has been to awaken deeply-buried memory.

The profound importance of memory is widely overlooked. This is because of the prevailing materialistic belief that memory is a physical faculty. It is not. It is a metaphysical, that is, a mental, one. We have seen that it is nothing less than revivified memories which the World-Mind brings into play when the karmic hour strikes for the rebirth of a universe. When we come to consider the individual mind we find that in the end it is nothing less than a defect of memory to which all its moral evil is due. For man, having forgotten his divine origin through long enslavement to transient things, fails to recognize his hidden oneness with his fellows and acts for personal self-interest alone. Forgetfulness prevails but it shall not always do so. Underneath this sin and evil, this ignorance and materialism the true self-knowledge still exists and the true goodness still inheres. Both await their chance to show themselves. If therefore moral evil is to be cured, the complete remedy must be as twofold as the disease. First, it must show up his enslavement for the degrading thing it is and call him to *repentance;* second, it must reveal to him his higher nature and call him to *remembrance*. In his spiritual history there comes a time when bitter bereavement, heavy loss, the failure of ambitions or physical illness temporarily weakens his zest for the world and enfeebles his will to live. He turns away from sensuous pleasure for a while and lets brooding melancholy settle over his soul. The mood passes of course but out of its darkness there is born his quest for inner reality, his yearning for an abiding satisfaction which is independent of external things.

Something like this has happened to multitudes of men and women everywhere through the war. Even if they have not already lost a loved one, endured starvation and oppression or suffered wounds during the conflict itself, life after World War II will necessarily be harder for them, much harder, than it was after World War I. Those who had high standards of living will have to replace them by low ones. Those who had steady incomes will have unsteady ones. Those who could earn enough to keep themselves in modest comfort will find themselves with the wherewithal for modest discomfort. And those who had little before will find they have nothing at all. Penury will succeed prosperity. Simplicity will succeed luxury. Serious reflection will follow pleasure-seeking. The awful truth of the transiency of earthly things will thus be burnt into the hearts of men and women who formerly gave it not a thought. Such is the first wide initiation of mankind, abrupt and brutal though it be, into the need of being unattached.

But what does this non-attachment mean? Monks and ascetics glibly use this word but their sense of its meaning is not the same as the philosopher's. It does not mean that we are to prefer being well-emaciated to being well-nourished. It does not mean that we should deliberately choose dirty hovels in which to dwell, uncomfortable chairs in which to sit, ill-paid menial work by which to earn our livelihood or poverty in preference to prosperity. And it certainly does not mean that we are to turn our backs on wife, child, parent, friend and social status. Those who say it does mean these things make the mistake of confusing different levels of ethical reference, of propagating for universal practice a moral attitude which is perfectly right for themselves alone, perfectly right for men who have outwardly renounced the world and become monks. All such public advertisements of piety, however, leave the philosopher cold. He practises non-attachment by understanding the transiency of all things and therefore by refusing to look for *permanent* happiness in this mundane sphere, by ever keeping at the back of his mind and in the inmost recess of his heart a secret reservation against dependence on any earthly thing or living creature for final happiness. He will take the best that this world offers him, if he can, but at the same time he is fully prepared to take the worst. For he knows the real nature of the world and puts his ultimate faith in That where no person and no formed thing can dwell. He is, in fact, really attached only to one thing—the Overself.

It was observed by the old Asiatic sages that four types of persons search for the ultimate Reality: first, those who thirst deeply for knowledge; second, those who yearn ardently for happiness; third, those whom wide experience has made wise; fourth, those who are in grave danger, which naturally yields the emotion of fear. Now fear is not only an instinctively-directed psychological mechanism for protecting the physical body but also a stimulus which prods the mind to profounder thinking. Through the impact of war enormous numbers of people in many lands have been involuntarily placed in this fourth category. For many months or perhaps for some years they have not dared lay their heads down without the haunting dread that this might be their final sleep on earth. Even the younger men and women have een stimulated to serious thought by the fact that death, which had formerly seemed so remote from them, has so widely and so tightly wrapped its ghastly black mantle around this planet.

That death is the great tutor of man is obvious, for all his property, relatives and body leave him at a single stroke: he has then to face *himself*. In the poetical phrase of an ancient Tibetan text of this teaching "he is as distressed by death as a lotus torn from its stalk". Mankind have forced willy-nilly by the turmoil and devastation of war to face up to this fact of the ever-existence of death and hence to reflect, however slightly, upon its meaning. Such reflection automatically sets their feet on the quest of the Overself. Thus they illustrate the dictum that the war has not been all loss and that some spiritual profit will emerge from its destructive machinery. Now because different ethical and mental strata naturally exist among people, the first step on this quest is religious, the second mystical or metaphysical and the third philosophic. Hence the present has been a period of increased interest in all these subjects.

The masses more easily seek relief for their earthly despairs in religion which offers a veiled recognition of Reality. Religion appeals more to the senses of man than mysticism and hence it is easier for him to grasp. The price of this of course is that it can only offer him less than mysticism. Yet he who, lacking the guidance of true metaphysics of the consolation of genuine mysticism, is deprived of the hope amid world despairs which sincere religion gives, the support in world trouble which it yields, is forlorn indeed. If, for instance, any sceptical Englishman did not during the dark bleak night of the Dunkirk crisis relax his reasonings and feel the profound need of God, in the sense of a supreme power behind the universe which upholds righteousness, then there is hardly any hope that he will feel it at all during the remainder of his life on earth. But those who clung to their faith in Faith got their reward and came to see that England, as the sole free survivor in the old world fighting the forces of incarnate evil, had indeed something to live for. For if England had fallen all Europe would irretrievably have fallen into the abyss too. Religion has flourished in time of war because it satisfies the pressing emotional need of immediate consolation and elementary enlightenment without demanding any intellectual labour in return. "From despair we learn prayer" is one of the tritest but truest of European proverbs.

This is the first step in the right direction, but it is still far off from the further positions which await man's visit. The second stage occupies him either with mysticism or with metaphysics, depending on whether he is emotionally or intellectually inclined. But not a few persons have something of themselves with the two interests at the same time. Mysticism offers a practical and personal super-physical experience through the pursuit of exercises in meditation whilst metaphysics offers a rational super-physical explanation of the universe in terms of abstract conceptions. A life which has not time for mental quiet and no time for right reflection is a life which is cheating itself. Fortunate indeed are those who are sustained by the peace gotten from the one and by the understanding gotten from the other.

Because it is immensely easier to find reasons for our feelings than feelings for our reasons and because the search for personal satisfaction is immensely more attractive than the search for impersonal intellectual truth, mysticism has always received many more adherents than metaphysics. The period of anxious suspense before the war, the dramatic surprises and unpleasant strains of the war itself—no less than the chaotic uncertainties which will come with the post-war period—have particularly brought about an urgent need of mystical satisfaction. These have indeed combined to create a more or less pathological state in large masses of people. The need of bandaging their bleeding emotions, soothing their jangled nerves and healing their mental distresses is more urgent than the need of providing intellectual food. Consequently their initiation into the valuable practice of regular meditation, which brings such a peace-fraught benediction to the personality, is becoming increasingly important. All over the world isolated individuals and little groups have begun to recognise this importance and are taking to these practices. Not only so but a movement for a dedicated minute of "going into the silence" for daily prayerful meditation has actually been linked up with the Government-controlled broadcasting systems of England, Australia and New Zealand since the war began, in the correct hope that this observance will help both the invisible and visible wars against the forces of Darkness. Indeed if the terrible strain and tremendous burden of our times will have driven mankind to take notice of and place a proper value on meditation as an essential part of their daily programme, if their failure to find outer peace will have driven them in sheer desperation and through this way to seek inner peace, then the war itself will not need to be written off as a total loss in history's balance sheet.

The third and highest stage in the long pilgrimage of man is philosophy. This also has found its recruits through the impact of our planetary upheaval but they are necessarily much fewer in number. For they seek not only a satisfaction of the religious need of reverential worship, the mystical yearning for inward beatitude and the metaphysical search for rational understanding, not only to attain and synthesize all these different-coloured elements and then bring them into balance with the further element of altruistic practical activity amongst mankind, but also to attain the transcendent fourth state of consciousness which is nothing less than insight into ultimate Reality. Here man directly meets God face to face as it were, and not at second hand through the screen of his beliefs, emotions or thoughts *about* God. This is the hidden goal which, whether truth draws them or sorrow drives them, whether peace lures them or reason persuades them, is one and the same in the end for all men. Whoever completes his passage through this stage can view all peoples and their wars not merely by the light of contemporary politics but also by the light of eternal laws. He can recognize the divinity in sinful creatures where none else can do so. He can see in the very midst of violent strife that there is yet something sublimely beyond all strife. He can compassionately regard all men and women as children of the same Father, albeit when some of them slay others in war to gain a little more land they are naughty little children. If there is a long way from the first bud to such a bloom it is also true that the finest fruits ripen slowly. The quest upon which the awakened amongst mankind have now embarked is the most worthwhile in their history.

The terrible feet of Mars have not tramped all over this planet for nothing. All through the tragical transition of this war there has been going on a silent but incessant movement of thought away from materialism. Not till the tension of actual fighting comes to an abrupt end with the coming of peace can we expect this movement to show its important consequences in the conscious mind of mankind. The aftermath of this unique war when the cannons once more point their silent unused muzzles in the air, must inevitably be the widespread self-discovery of an ethical, religious and mental crisis in the individual no less than of a cultural one in the community. For the outward state of every people reflects the inward state of each component member. He cannot shift responsibility solely to his guides, rulers and leaders. For in so far as he acquiesces in their acts and principles, he must share that responsibility and consequently the karma that follows after it.

Behind the grave significance of our times stands a further fact. We have learnt already that from the moment when a separate centre of consciousness was projected out of the Overself, its eventual struggle against other separate centres could be accurately predicted. So long as the person denies its own divine source, so long must it live in perpetual if hidden conflict both with that source and with other persons. This must be related to the fact that there are limits set in space and time for every evolutionary world cycle, although these limits are so vast as to seem non-existent to our limited human powers of conception. The consequence of this is that the number of persons who come into existence during such a cycle is necessarily also finite and limited. The mass of conscious beings follow their historic course of development collectively, rising and falling with the evolutionary tides more or less together. Those who at present compose the human race stand generally at a point on the second of the three great stages of its planetary life, that is the intellectual, which is itself midway between the entirely externalized or physical and the entirely interiorized or spiritual stages. It is on this second stage that the process of individualization reaches an extreme limit. Such a limit has now been reached by the human race generally. The unfoldment of its latent possibilities through the medium of separateness can go no farther, except it be to go towards utter self-destruction. Therefore the evolutionary impulse has begun to turn it away from its present excessive pitch of individuation and to direct it towards the ideal of union, both with its source and with the rest of its kind.

Such is the unprecedented planetary situation today. The same process which projected the ego from the Overself into that exteriorization of its own consciousness which we believe to be a material world is now at work to withdraw it again. This reversal of directive force necessarily involves a certain abruptness in its operation. We have indeed reached the most tremendous spiritual turning-point in humanity's long history. It has found itself here today not only because of its past external actions but also because of its present internal needs. If conflict was the inevitable outcome of the original movement towards separateness it is equally true that the cessation of conflict, the restoration of harmony will be the inevitable outcome of entering the present movement away from separateness. If both the ascent of man and the relations between man and man have been marked by the spilling of blood, his further course will be marked by increasing bloodlessness. The bitter biological struggle will lose its crudeness and be replaced by the recognition of values higher than merely animalistic ones. It was in this general sense that the brief but optimistic reference in the last chapter of *The Hidden Teaching Beyond Yoga*, that mankind was coming of age before our eyes and that there was no need to lose ourselves in despair over its future, must be understood.

Nevertheless this does not absolve us from the immediate task of passing this critical bend in our evolutionary road, nor does it dictate whether we shall effect this passage peacefully and painlessly through understanding and acceptance or stormily and painfully through ignorance and rebellion. How far and how quickly the drift away from ingrained selfishness and olden materialism is travelling today and shall travel tomorrow with the cessation of war becomes therefore a matter of the utmost importance. If it has not travelled sufficiently far the near future of mankind will be dark indeed. We have been walking perilously close to a precipice. If enough men and women do not react to the impact of these terrible events by setting out to seek redemption, if culture does not acquire a soul instead of pretending to have one, if the falsehood and hypocrisy which have prevailed for so long and so deeply under the veneer of public life and social systems do not yield sufficiently to the cold breezes which war is blowing through them, then everything will sink with a sinking civilization. Society has been sick for a long time and has passed into a dangerously critical state. It must better itself or else make way for a better one.

Mankind may rend the apocalyptic veil of this problematic future for themselves. If they can quickly produce a sufficient minority of men and women who will dedicate their inner life to one of the three stages of the quest of the Overself for the sake of the common inner welfare not less than their own, or if they can produce a sufficient minority of leaders who will be permitted by their peoples to implement in action a constructive social idealism based on a return to non-materialistic principles, their safe passage into a brighter new age will be assured. Not many indeed are needed for this grand purpose, for it is rather the concentrated quality than the diffused quantity of the thought or action of these few altruistic souls which will count most in such an historic effort at world-redemption. Thus the social crisis returns always in the end to the personal crisis. Every man who makes his deep irrevocable choice whether he will live only for selfish and sensual aims or whether he will live for altruistic and purer ones is affecting not only his own fate but also the immediate destiny of our civilization. That such souls exist and that such leaders have begun to make their appearance affords a basis of hope amid the terrible world darkness today. The problem still remains, however, whether enough will light their lamps and light them quickly.

In this connection there must be repeated, however wearisome the repetition may seem, that we can help others and ourself to pass through this crisis by a change of thought. Our thinking is creative. The most immediate and urgent form which such creativeness should take is the opening up of a mental channel between blinded, suffering, deluded mankind and their supreme sacred source, not merely for self-benefit but to attract higher forces to our earth, that they may uphold us in the terrible conflict against the powers of Darkness which menaces our present existence and future hopes. Such a channel may be opened by detaching a fragmentary part of our daily programme for the simple purpose of stilling the mind, "going into the silence" and aspiring intensely for the divine Light to pass into and through us for the blessing of mankind. This practice is best done in an unobserved place, or at the window of a room whilst seated in a chair with legs uncrossed for it should be followed at dawn or sunset, facing towards the sun. It should be continued until a feeling of living response arises, which feeling may come within ten or twenty minutes in most cases.* Here is a chance for those who have felt the need of a high and holy Cause in whose service they could lose themselves and for which they could forget themselves.

Can we afford to sit any longer like a blind boy sitting profitlessly with a book before a shining lamp? Humanity, marred and maimed as it is through trying to live in the old selfish and materialist way, must begin to turn with the cold dawn to higher laws for its governance. Erring grievously as it has been, the war has at least shown its wrongdoing as in a mirror. With the arrival of sanity's hour it must scourge itself with higher ideals and turn to amendment. If grace for the individual man is procurable only by a change of thought, that is a veritable repentance, it is equally true that grace for a whole people is procurable on the same terms. The muddy tide of materialism—whether crudely blatant or pseudo-religious—which submerged the finer instincts of our human race must move backward on the ebb. Everything depends on how strongly, after the sufferings of this terrible planetary purgation, this vast purifying fire of war, a better and repentant mood will arise in a people who, having gained an insight into the consequences of their own blunders, will comprehend the inevitability and inescapability of karma's retributive working, who, perceiving that the fate of all units and groups is now inter-locked, will sympathize with others where once they hated or stood indifferently aside, and who will bring the ready assent of their instincts to revere the reality of the Overself where formerly they ignored and despised it. This would necessarily lead them to re-value thoughts and things, actions and achievements, men and institutions, ethical codes and cultural qualities.

If we have seen the horrors of the past few years, we also see opening before mankind a perspective such as was never before known in their history. They possess today an opportunity not only to put wrongs right but also to attain a truer view of life, to comprehend that it is not meaningless but has an exalted purpose, that it is their privilege to co-operate in securing the fulfilment of this purpose within their own lives, and that their brief hours on the stage of universal existence could become the prelude to ineffable ones. Mankind have been estranged from the inner sources of truth and hope for so long that the more sensitive are now beginning to experience the thirsts and hungers of a veritable drought. For materialists may say what they please but it is really unnatural to live in and for the body alone, unnatural to be nothing better than a piece of timber in mind or than a fox in feeling. It is easy to see in recent world history the thick darkness which envelops the minds of men but the keen-sighted may also see in it the thin rays of light which are widening as they extend farther.

---

* For full detailed instructions see *The First Meditation* in Chapter 14.

Human life is not a stagnant pool. There is a sacred Something back of us which demands and must have expression and growth, which must break through as inevitably as tomorrow's sun must destroy tonight's darkness. And the tragedy through which our own generation is passing has precipitated such an event. As though this were a holy day of ordination, younger men and women feel the birth with their own mind of new ideas which are spiritually exciting and intuitions which revive their fading faith in mankind's future.

There is a wider groping amongst men for a fresh conception of their own personal existence alongside of a sincere struggle to see the larger vision of a less selfish mentally-helpful society. The cry for divine fellowship has begun to go up from this earth. There are now the first clear signs of an immature understanding that man's true business in life is something more than making shoes, growing corn or receiving dividends although it may include these things. There is rising to conscious realization the knowledge that grander than the moments which wealth, fame, sex and all those transient pleasures of the senses which constitute the best values for so many, may offer a man is the wonderful moment when he can commune with his hidden source. There is beginning a belated recognition that the characteristics of earthly life—transitoriness and change—will remain forever stamped upon it, however much the old doctrines disappear and however much newly invented pleasures may camouflage their resulting sufferings. There is growing up in the hearts of intelligent men and compassionate women who have suffered deeply (for themselves or for others) during this war a nostalgic yearning for what may be called the kingdom of heaven, the reign of goodness, peace, truth and divinity. The only question is: Are there enough such persons to affect the crisis as a saving leaven or are they still too few?

The doctrine of historical cycles has warned us that there is no unimpeded progress toward perfection, that stagnation and retrogression inevitably make their contributions too, human nature being what it is. But it has also shown us that although there are always periods when mankind degenerates morally, there are at least as many other periods when it advances morally. And it is the latter which, in the ultimate reckoning, will have the last word. For karma tends to educate a man and his own Overself tends to draw him to itself. The sinner of today becomes the saint of tomorrow. After all, despite the unpleasant testimony of contemporary events it is not that mankind are really as evil as they appear to be but only that they get caught in a vicious circle of self-made errors which generate bad karma, which in turn expresses itself in hard grey and ugly environments. These again breed hard grey and ugly thoughts which inevitably lead once more through a habitually malformed outlook to further errors and bad karma. The world crisis affords them the chance to break up this circle.

All that wars against moral truth, that would turn the hand of man against his brother, will one day infallibly perish. None of us dare hope to see such a day, for quick millenniums are the cheap delusions of wishful thinkers, but all of us may hope to find within ourselves *even now* this same sacred principle and thus assure ourselves of its truth. We may safely take our stand on the oneness of essential being. We may wait quietly for the World-Mind to reclaim its own progeny. For we are ever moving towards the morrow. If, meanwhile, we endeavour to co-operate reverently and intelligently with its Idea, and at the same time aspire toward that region where the atmosphere is timeless, our patience will not sink into lethargy.

This is the grand goal towards which all living creatures are moving. This is the last residue which shall justify all their groans and tears. This is what saves life from the charge of being useless. This is the never-ceasing heavenly melody which even now may be heard beneath all our transient cries by those who have ears to hear. There is no need to lose heart. No single defeat of true ideas and no violent devolution of revered ideals could ever be really definite in this ancient war of light against night. Hope is the beautiful message of the unknown goal, the star that blazes when all else is dark, the encouragement of the sublime Perfect to the struggling Imperfect.

11

The World-Mind

IT is now needful to formulate our ideas about the Supreme power, to unveil intellectually a little of the mystery of the World-Mind. But before we can comprehend what it is we must first comprehend what it is not. Before the builder of a house can proceed with the actual putting-up of the edifice he is compelled to clear the site of all obstructive debris. He who would build the house of a true God-idea must likewise first clear his mind of all false conceptions and false beliefs. How is he to achieve this? He must begin by doubting. He must doubt every principle and every fact which has been hitherto carelessly shoved into the storehouse of memory under the suggestive influence of environment, heredity or education. It is only by struggling through such a wilderness, where the explorer must needs feel lonely and comfortless for a time, that he is likely to reach the promised land. Hence we must first free ourselves of defective conceptions which may once have been quite useful but which now prevent us from perceiving truer ones. Despite a lack of taste for theological terms, it will be better to use the popular word "God" whilst we are examining the popular ideas and resume the chosen term "World-Mind" when we examine the hidden teaching's own conception.

Mankind in their infancy and adolescence have made queer fantastic and grotesque gods for themselves, have set up half-anthropomorphic, half-animal and even animal forms for their worship or solace. But with the increase of age they have slowly become imbued with the belief that God is a bigger edition of their own self—more powerful, more knowing, no doubt, but still somewhat human in outlook and understandable in behaviour. The utter simplicity of this anthropomorphic concept of God renders it available to the most primitive members of an aboriginal community no less than to the broad masses of a civilized society. It suggests that God is a kind of gigantic man existing among a multitude of little men. For if we take this elementary view we have to set up God complete with eyes, ears, hands and so on. We have to endow it with personal likes and dislikes, temperamental caprice and arbitrary conduct. Mankind then become its mere playthings. Such usage makes God a contradictory mixture of omnipotence, benevolence and omniscience on the one hand, and of racial favouritism, arbitrary cruelty and petty praise-seeking on the other.

The illiberal and illogical belief that God could act capriciously towards mankind, distributing special favours to some and special misfortunes to others, arises partly from the fact that the doctrine of karma was originally a semi-esoteric one and hence sometimes taught in a veiled form. The vicissitudes of good and bad fortune, happiness and misery were attributed to the arbitrary will of God who could be annoyed, angry, prejudiced or pleased with a particular individual. It was easier for practical realistic or primitive mentalities to believe this than to believe in the subtle mentalism involved in karma. Resignation to receiving the karmic results of their actions was consequently taught under the form of resignation to God's will. In the former public religion of most European peoples, such as the Romans, Greeks, Gauls and Anglo-Saxons, the doctrine of karma was originally not stressed partly for the same reason. But that it should drop out of Western teaching altogether when it was banished from Christianity along with Gnosticism was a calamity.

The anthropomorphic view is comforting and acceptable to most men because it brings God so near them inasmuch as it makes God so like themselves. But what they do not see is that it also brings God near them in the wrong way. They have merely substituted a human thought-image for the human stone-image used by aborigines. God has indeed sadly declined in stature and nature if we accept this view.

The question is: Do we want such a temperamental God who is merely a projection of the human mind, that is, an idea, or do we want God as it really is? The plaint against the God of vulgarized religions is that theirs is not God at all. It is unworthy of an intelligent man's best affection or highest hope. It is fit to receive only his worst fears and abject squirming. Its contemplation does not ennoble man but degrades him. Let us have the courage to face the fact that all the anthropomorphic gods are mere will-o'-the-wisps of man's own vivid imagination, gigantic phantoms of his own creation and priestly fictions which were useful to primitive peoples but are useless to twentieth-century minds nourished on developed reason and broadened experience. Our very notions of existence, being based on the five different sense-contacts, are imperfect and incomplete; hence liable to falsify the Supreme Power if we seek to bring it within the limited range of human ideation based upon them.

Again, if we think of God in this way as a glorified and expanded man, we shall have also to think of him in the same space-time order as ourselves, as running about from one duty to another like an overworked business executive! Those who stand in adoring awe of such a dwarfed humanized God because they cannot conceive of a better one do well. Philosophy would never blame but rather praise them. Those however who have kept the awe but lost its object are entitled to find a better one. The moment we try to reduce the Supreme Mind to the finite space-time form by which we ourselves are conditioned, we betray it. It must primarily exist for itself and not for something much less than itself. We have no right to confine its character within the limits of man's little field of personal consciousness. Who are we to drag it down to such a level? The Supreme is infinite and cannot satisfy finite demands.

If we begin to talk of this cosmic mind as "He" and "Him" we begin to turn it into an idol. The use of a masculine pronoun anthropomorphizes God and reduces this loftiest of all possible concepts to a wretchedly stunted stature. For this reason we refuse in these pages to call God by such a pronoun. The term "It" being neuter and impersonal, is a fitter appellation than "He". Those awed by conventional thought may at first feel such a neuter pronoun to be sacrilegious or derogatory but when they become accustomed to its use they will realize that it is, on the contrary, the use of a masculine pronoun which is sacrilegious and derogatory. How lofty, how pure, how austere is the conception of God which lifts it above the need of fawning flattery and which honours it as the sublime and sexless Principle which it really is!

The second error to be corrected sets the Deity far away from earth and far beyond the skies as an extra-cosmic being, turning it into a Creator who made the universe out of nothing and made it only a few thousand years ago and that by an outburst of sudden activity rather than by a process of slow evolution. Were God an infinite being standing alongside a world so arbitrarily created, and were the world something really isolated, then God's infinitude would no longer be possible, for the world's independent reality would limit God from the outside. Again as our earlier studies have hinted, the universal activity has never had a beginning. It never started *in vauco*. It has always been in intermittent existence. Hence there has never been a sudden and special "creation" of the universe as an act which took place once upon a time. In that case the concept of a creator outside of and apart from the universe becomes a superfluous one. No god-like being or man-like God has made the universe. For it is not a thing to be shaped but a process to be re-started. But even if we did postulate an external God as a creator of the universe, if we seek to discover its origin we are obliged to proceed further and postulate a second God who is the creator of the first one. Nor can we stop even there. We shall be forced to postulate a third God who created the second one. And so we shall get ourselves involved in a series of creators which must be extended endlessly backwards.

This is a most unsatisfactory position because it offers no final solution of the problem of the world. Yet so long as we think of the universe as such and not as it is in essence, we are driven to think of it as brought into being by some self-existent power, call it God or anything else. The only rational way to think of their relation is to place the universe as a thought within God and God as the life within the universe. God then gazes at its own images, which are within and not outside it, and thus gives them life, even to the extent of making them *appear* self-sufficient.

The third belief to be bettered is that God is a separate personality, an individual creature among other creatures only bigger and better than all of them. This is related to the anthropomorphic error already mentioned, only its intellectual level is higher and its sweep is wider for it includes all possible and imaginable super-human creatures. In our studies of the human "I" we have seen something of the limitations which beset the notion of personality. But the basic objection to the ascription of personality to the Supreme Existence is rooted in the fact that this necessarily separates it out from a second existence which is not itself. It chalks out a dividing-line which says: here God is, there God is not. When we consider God from this standpoint we unconsciously set up some point where its own being begins and that of all other creatures ends. A personal God implies therefore one between whom and other creatures there is a line of division. But when we set up such a division we deprive God of a title to omnipresence, universality and infinitude.

The conventional religious error is to turn the infinite into the finite, the impersonal into the personal and the cosmic into the parochial. This is done to suit the need of the insignificant inhabitants of a tiny planet but it does not suit the need of ultimate truth. An infinitely enlarged being is not the same as a truly infinite being. The first, no matter how far it be stretched out, however vast its world-enclosing sway may seem in terms of our delusive spatial way of thinking, is on an altogether different and lower level than the second. If God is to possess a personality, if it is to exist alongside of and outside other beings, then it will necessarily possess all the limitations which we usually associate with a personal being. But it will then no longer be the Supreme. If our faith cannot go out to a personal God because personality implies limitation, then it must go out to a God that is unlimited and therefore impersonal.

Now we know everything as *a* thing. The term "tree" for example must carry the picture of a particular tree or the ideas of particular trees if we are to think at all. We do not even know abstractions like justice or generosity unless they are translated into concrete acts or instances. In the same way we know living conscious existences only as particular existences. But whereas all other inanimate things and living existences can be thought of in terms of some other thing or existence on which they depend or out of which they arise or into which they merge, God alone requires no such relation because it is itself the pre-supposition of all possible relations, things and existences. Everyone and every-thing else is *a* thing but God is neither a particular being nor a mentally produced idea. But personality implies a particular being. Therefore God is not personal. It is divine Being but not *a* divine being; Love but not *a* loving Father. It has not a personality although, containing the total of all past, present and future personalities, it has eternal existence. With all this it must be clear that God cannot be a person. It must consequently be a Principle. It must, in this mentalist universe, be the Principle of Mind itself. God is indeed the World-Mind.

If this be so, it may be asked why has God been described in the religious and mystical revelations of every people and in every age as a personal Being? The answer is twofold. First, such is the mercy of the World-Mind that for the benefit of those—and this means the millions who make up the masses—who cannot hope to enter into its direct transcendental awareness it reveals itself indirectly and imperfectly through forms which meet the requirements and suit the capacities of their limited minds. That is to say it enables them to receive its grace. Through visions or intuitions, feelings or ideas, dream-experiences or mentally-impressed messages, it speaks to them in the way they can best understand. Hence the variety of its world-wide transformations, each bearing a different label, under which its messages are received. The Nameless responds out of its mercy to any and every name. To those who cannot grasp its impersonality it appears as an object to be worshipped personally. It manifests in the particular form sought after by aspirants, that is to say, the form which makes most appeal and is easiest understood.

This does not mean that the World-Mind divides itself into various beings, however, any more than the sun divides itself into the myriad sunbeams which it reflects upon the surface of the ocean waves. The World-Mind's own self-existence remains intact even when its response goes forth like a thousand varied echoes to a thousand varied calls.

Second, it is because the first promulgator of the religion often has to present the conception of God under a form which the masses can comprehend and such a form is necessarily a personal one. But if he does this he will usually have secretly taught his closest disciples at the same time that God is a Principle and not a person. Thus the outer teaching becomes a kind of device used to help the multitude, a device intended to induce a particular state of veneration in them. Unfortunately those who come after him in later centuries and who have not entered into the tradition of secret explanation, do not know that the presentation of a personal God is really an instructional device and consequently insist on turning it into a cast-iron dogma for all alike. When this happens the device loses much of its value; indeed there may come a time when it becomes obstructive to the growth of many mentalities.

We cannot visualize the World-Mind. It has no form of its own by which it may appear to us, for any form whatever would put it in space whereas it transcends space. But it can and does make token gestures to aspirants to indicate its existence and these gestures may take a personal form. Such appearances however are necessarily but transient images and temporary allegories under which it represents itself. The mental attitude of the seeker is here of much importance. His sincere faith and earnest devotion have something to do with the results he achieves. For when they impinge upon the World-Mind a spontaneous action immediately manifests itself and returns to the seeker in precisely the expected way by a mysterious device intended to help him in the familiar form under which he unconsciously worships it. Thus it may spontaneously formulate a human mental image and appear as Jesus, Buddha, Krishna, or even as a living and contemporary spiritual guide to instruct, inspire or assist them. This is hinted at in the *Bhagavad Gita* in the sentence: "I reveal my grace in the different forms and aspects solicited by the different seekers."

Thus the sinners and the sufferers, the ignorant and the illiterate are not excluded from its help. It responds in that shape which will best help their troubled hearts or seeking minds. The unphilosophical however cling to their inward revelation or intuitive feeling as being exclusive to themselves or their sect. They do not know that the Divine adopts as many different ways of appearing to those who call upon it as the latter themselves use. Now if an artistic style is to our taste, we get the experience of its beauty, but not otherwise. If a religious form is to our emotional taste, we get the experience of its sacredness, but not otherwise. The quality of our taste itself in both examples depends of course on how far we have climbed up the evolutionary hill. It really represents the state of thought and feeling induced by the artistic style or the religious form. Whether taught by an inspired man or felt in inspired moments, the idea of a personal God receives its value from our own responsive belief in it. It is the last stage on our upward way to the ultimate comprehension of the real God-idea, but it is not such comprehension itself.

It should be understood of course that when we speak here of the World-Mind responding to human needs, such response with a single exception really comes from the Overself. For this is the World-Mind's deputy in our human sphere. The exception is when the World-Mind also manifests itself indirectly not only in the diversified forms of visions, etc., but also at rare intervals in the flesh. At critical moments or crucial turning-points it responds to the needs of a portion of benighted mankind. But the popular beliefs that God can withdraw from the world to become imprisoned in a human body, or that infinite Being can be confined in the finite flesh, are useful only to those who cannot rise intellectually higher. Such a divine manifestation, such a Messiah, Avatar or Son of God is not a direct Incarnation in the narrow sense of the term, but a being from a higher planet whose purity or wisdom fit him to be a channel for its power.

A Philosophical view of Religious Worship.

It may now be seen that although this teaching refuses to

caricature God by humanizing it nevertheless it equally refuses to dismiss God by denying it. Although the foregoing lines have denied lower concepts of God in favour of higher ones, they have not denied the general concept itself. This is the error of the atheist. The idea of the existence of God is a true one. Men have not been deceived in giving their belief to it, although the *form* of this idea may be and often is a false or incorrect or incomplete one. The term God has indeed by such hypocritical misuse, thoughtless repetition or semantic variation become a coin of debased currency. When in the earlier volume we ventured to point out that there were many conflicting and contradictory meanings assigned to it this was done to assist the student to shake off his bigotry and purify his own conception of God; we certainly did not want to imply that there was no God at all. We did not protest against belief in God, which is justified by the acutest reasoning, but against belief in a magnified man as being God, which is absurd.

The sceptic who opposes the rational to the revelational and passes cynical judgment on God and the cosmos is perhaps right from his standpoint. Unfortunately, his standpoint is a limited one. He sees a part of the picture—and the dismal lower part at that—but does not see the whole picture. Hence even if he believes in evolution he also believes that evolution is a blind force. Atheism is justifiable only as the attitude of a vigorous reason shaking off traditional superstitions, but if its denial of conceptual caricatures of God denies also the abstract concept of God it is not and never can be a correct metaphysical attitude.

And here is one of the great services which this teaching can offer to sincere religion. It begins by pointing out that we may believe but we do not know whether God exists; what we do know is that we ourselves and the world do exist. It builds upward from these positive facts rather than from debatable dogmatic beliefs. And inasmuch as it demonstrates self, time, space and matter to be mental, the presence of the whole world within human thought becomes nonsensical without a World-Mind to think it, because human thinking has never voluntarily created such a world. To believe that these ideas can exist separately without a thinking being to generate them is to believe an absurdity. We get the knowledge of the world's existence through the five senses only because we also get the knowledge that we ourselves exist. Ideas cannot hang in the empty air. They must have a ground upon which to rest. That ground is there always, whether it supports thoughts or not. It is this mental principle which enables us to doubt the face-value of material appearances because their own existence refers to it. To think of the world at all pre-supposes the simultaneous existence of a thinking mind. The error of every materialist is to ignore the cosmic mind for which a world must exist and from which it cannot be separated. And so long as the world has existed so long at least there must have been such a cosmic mind. Such a deduction is stringently demanded by the most inexorable necessities of rational thoroughness.

It is impossible for anyone who properly understands mentalism to be an atheist. For the world as idea silently proclaims the fact of an intelligent and conscious World-Mind as the ultimate co-thinker of this idea. *In other words, there has never been a time when the world was without a supreme God in this sense.* The inevitable and natural corollary from this is that *man has never been bereft of the presence of God.* Thus the very existence of the world must depend upon the immanent presence of the World-Mind as the very existence of each man must have it as his secret inner Ruler. How then can a man be called truly cultured who passes through his earthly sojourn without making an attempt to understand, if not to commune with it? Human arrogance must inevitably bend the knee in submission before the World-Mind. For it is not only the first state of matter, but also the first source of individual being. Hence but for its very presence the atheist would be unable even to voice his denial, the agnostic unable to utter his doubt.

It is impossible to construct a sound metaphysics of religion which shall successfully resist criticism unless it is constructed upon the basis of mentalism. For this is the only possible scientific basis upon which religion can safely rest. All other bases must be merely dogmatic and appeal in the end to faith rather than reason. If the metaphysics of truth could do no more than demonstrate this stupendous fact of divine existence to the human reason, it would have done enough. But it can do much more than that. For its crowning service is to provide the basis for a higher yoga which will show man how to enter into conscious discovery of the One Mind for himself, and that not merely during moments of meditation but during the whole of his everyday existence.

The confusions which hang around the idea of God are necessarily reflected in the confusions which hang around the idea of religion. Those atheists who show their scorn for religion by uttering impatient epithets show also their ignorance of what the term really stands for. A religion usually represents a threefold attempt on the part of an interiorly illuminated man to give the masses some intellectual comprehension—however remote and symbolic or elementary and suggestive it may be—of the existence of the Overself and the World-Mind, that is of the soul and God, some means of bringing them into indirect communion with divinity and some practical guidance in the ethical conduct of life. He introduces such a belief only like a temporary mark to indicate the beginning of a circle, only until the masses can rise to a higher and better comprehension and communion during their slow growth with time through the reincarnations.

It is here that we may see how wise, how practical and how compassionate were those vanished sages who *gave* humanity its greatest religions, as distinct from those lesser vain and ambitious men who *exploited* it in the name of religion. For the sages who had themselves realized truth and who had experienced the ultimate beatitude were not content to hoard the one and enjoy the other in self-centred indifference to the ignorance and sufferings of the masses. They knew that the common people would be bewildered by the abstract subtleties of philosophy, frightened by the disciplinary difficulties of asceticism, saddened by the lack of time and opportunity to practise meditation and wearied by their constant struggles to earn a livelihood for themselves and their families. How then were the sages to bring within their reach some fragment at least of their own treasure? They solved the problem by creating religions. For through religion it became possible to appeal suggestively to the popular imagination. The primitive mind felt vaguely that the ornate image which confronted it in a temple was a partial embodiment of some supernatural entity which was otherwise remote and unreachable. The image and the ceremonial services centred around it spoke to it in an inexpressible way and the communication seemed to penetrate to the depths of emotional being, arousing awe, fear, wonder, humility and hope. It was in this manner that the sages succeeded in arousing uncultured mentalities and self-centred characters to the first recognition of an Ultimate Presence in the universe, a recognition which would only attain full consciousness when it had passed through all the stages of development embraced by mysticism and philosophy. All attempts to derive religion from animism alone are fundamentally false since they ignore the vital element of religion—the electric experience of conversion, of a "second birth", of an emotional earthquake with the resulting transmutation of worldly values.

The popular conceptions of God are not worthless, therefore, but in their time and place subserve an excellent purpose. Therefore the yearnings of millions of worshippers down through the ages have not been in vain; they were not deceived when they gave their belief to a higher power. Every religion has its measure of truth and holds its meed of usefulness.

As the inner significance of this wonderful universe begins to unfold itself before the student he cannot help but give it his reverence, cannot help but become more genuinely religious than the nominally religious people. For he knows now with unshakable conviction that the divine force is here in the very midst of humanity upon this earth, not far off in some remote sky or unseen world. He knows that beneath the dark exterior of human misery there is a secret brightness beyond telling. A man is all the better for believing in the existence of this higher power.

We must however set up a dividing line between pure religion and the man-made institutions which claim to represent it. Religion as the personal and private worship of a supernatural Power is an essential need of mankind whereas religion as the institutionalized and public worship of the same Power is something which may or may not be needed by mankind. When men come to comprehend that true religion is belief in the existence of this supreme power demonstrated by practice of a genuinely virtuous life and not necessarily belief in a religious institution demonstrated by practice of formal religious rites, when they come to regard true worship as being the effort at private self-communion with this power in contemplation and not necessarily the public utterance of fixed prayers in buildings, they will begin to understand what was in the mind of Jesus, Krishna and their like. When the early Christians were bidden by Paul to "Let this *mind* be in you which was also in Christ Jesus," they were clearly bidden to arrive at an inward and personal experience.

Not that the churches, rites and prayers are non-essential. The rites for example have more than a merely symbolic value. Here we must remember the earlier reference to the similarity of artistic and religious taste. What a worshipper gets out of them depends upon what he puts into them. If his faith, earnestness and attentiveness are large enough he will draw from the everywhere-present World-Mind, through his Overself, a response which although very limited when compared with what a mystic may draw from meditation, will nevertheless be something tuned to his understanding and feeling. If the one who officiates in a church and directs its sacred services is himself informed and *inspired,* then those services may be utilized as a means to exalt the thoughts of the worshippers and help them start the process of communion with the divinity within themselves. And the prayers have more than a merely formal value. If they are uttered from the heart they can become the expression of a reverence which is the humble acknowledgment of the existence of a higher power and to that extent begin to build a bridge between the person and the power. But when the rites degenerate into hollow mummeries and empty formalities and when the prayers decay into phonographic repetitions of mechanically-mumbled formulae derived from traditional conventional liturgies; when religious belief has lost its content and vigour and only dead dusty dogmas remain; when religious worship itself is nothing more than the constant unreverent begging for personal and physical favours and the attempt to cajole the Deity by memorized flattery, then the religious institution has become a useless affair or what is worse, a hypocritical one; finally, when the ecclesiastical structure of a religion becomes more important than its ethical values as manifested in actual conduct, then it has begun its worst descent.

Now and then there arises a Man who has gone far from the common track, who has discovered the Absolute Being and returned to share the discovery with his fellows. But he soon finds that only a few can absorb what he has to tell them, the few who become his closest disciples. What he brings to others appears to them like the blazing sun at full noon, so dazzling that they raise their hands to shade their eyes, preferring the more comfortable half-darkness to the dazzling light. The consequence is that within a century or two, sometimes within a generation or two, the comprehension of the half-illumined many supersedes the comprehension of the wholly-illumined few. The ripples of influence spread into ever-wider circles amongst those who, because they lack the faculty of properly comprehending the true doctrine, misunderstand and mangle it. The meaning of his message becomes narrowed, the emphasis is laid upon the letter rather than the spirit. The forms of doctrine, the organizations of men become more important than the living truths behind the doctrine, the personal character of those men. Righteous deeds become of less account than hypocritical acquiescence in erroneous dogmas. The means are revered but the end is completely forgotten. Finally the religion becomes a shell, half-empty inside but impressively ornate outside.

There are three chief justifications for the existence of a religion: (a) its intimation of world meaning with a consequent practical influence upon the character and actions of people for the better; (b) its affirmation of the existence of a higher order of existence than the material one; (c) its proclamation of a way to communion with the divine power. It should inculcate in mankind a belief in supreme Being as a preliminary to their step-up into conscious if dim communion with that Being through real prayer, and it should elevate a section of mankind in character and inspired services and set restrictive bounds on their baser attributes. But when an institutional religion fails to achieve these principal aims, fails to prevent wickedness or to convince men that their physical existence contains a higher purpose, it begins to fail in its own purpose. The recent history of large parts of Europe and large parts of Asia proves plainly that institutional religion has begun to fail on both these counts in those regions, for atheism and wrong-doing, both open and masked, have become common. Large numbers among mankind have seen too much distress in this epoch of gigantic upheaval and widespread change, suffered too much personal disappointment to accept such a situation blindly.

In this age of growing intellectual enlightenment there are many persons who have advanced beyond the appeal of such elementary ideas and who consequently need stronger pabulum. It is for such only that we venture to write, for we would not unsettle the faith of others even if we could. The most illiterate aborigine who worships in his own primitive way is perfectly right in doing so and is acting in the best possible manner for himself. He has started an attitude of veneration towards the World-Mind, even though he does not yet know that it is the infinite World-Mind, which he is remotely worshipping as from afar off rather than the grossly finite form with which local tradition has provided him. It would be unwise and unmoral for anyone to disturb such a religious attitude. Nobody should disturb the aborigine but rather encourage him. The same boy who is taught at school that the universal stuff is constituted from a certain number of different chemical elements is later taught at college that it is really constituted from electrons. Why? For the same reason that those who begin with popular religious belief are later led *by life* to mystical experience or metaphysics. All men worship the hidden reality but most men worship it in ignorance; only the philosophical do it understand-ingly. Thus they begin as religionists by bestowing superstitious adoration upon the Deity and they end as philosophers by giving it both intelligent understanding and reverential homage.

The aborigine's uncomprehending loyalty to his carved wooden fetish is admirable only for the quality of veneration which it shows, not for the direction which it takes. If he attempted to impose its worship on a civilized man he would be doing wrong. And if the civilized man attempted to impose his own more developed form of worship on the aborigine before the latter had begun to have doubts about the efficacy of the fetish, then he too would be doing wrong. There is no universal standard for all because people are not alike in mental reach and moral capacity. The philosophical objection, therefore, is not to anyone's belief or worship nor even to the anthropomorphic conception which would make the Supreme Mind an angry, spiteful or racial God, but to the foolish attempt to impose any form of belief or worship on those who are mentally outgrowing it and are becoming dissatisfied with it, or the intolerant attempt to persecute those who now cannot accept such a narrow idea as being true in the absolute sense. When such bigotry arises it becomes a duty to expose its narrowness and falsity. If it insists on giving God a shape, a form and a personality which the World-Mind by its very nature could never have, all right. This is an early view, but it is the only concept of ultimate reality which most immature minds can grasp. And we must let them keep it, if this is all they can comprehend, but they in their turn must not attempt to graft it upon the minds of those who have passed out of this early stage, those whose intelligence is growing and who begin to perceive that the idea that God is apart and separate from one's own self is an idea which is born of ignorance. It is not wrong to give the masses images to worship, unreasonable dogmas to hold and a personal God to believe in, provided they are told as they get older and reminded periodically that these are tentative, that higher views exist and must be respected, and that they need not necessarily cling always to the lower view throughout life. It is quite proper to teach such elementary views to the young in mind and body but it is quite improper not to teach them more advanced views if they mature in mind. The original object of creating orthodox religious institu-tions was to serve truth, whereas the object of some selfish prelates or ignorant clergymen has been to suppress it. For if these early symbolic ideas are allowed to remain so long-standing that they become deeply rooted in man's mind, then what was intended to be a foreshadowing of higher truths becomes a vicious superstition. If he is to spend the whole of his life as a mere worshipper of dead stone images, dead irrational dogmas, dead uninspired priests and dead unheeding personal gods, then truth turns to untruth and what should have helped him bridge the period until he is ready for a higher conception of divinity becomes a definite hindrance. From such superstition bigotry is born, from bigotry come quarrels and sectarian strife, and these finally issue in persecution and bloodshed. If religious guides will really and willingly help their flocks, some at least among the latter will by and by grasp something at least of the grander ideas not kept hidden from them. It is for the benefit of such advancing but bewildered and baffled persons alone that we wish to *purify* the conceptions of Deity and worship, never to annihilate them.

Another noteworthy error on the part of most religionists is to assume that in their available orthodox scriptures they have everything which their Master taught. For no master could have taught the multitude what was fit only for the comprehension of the few.

He who has fathomed the philosophic significance of what occurs within incense-wreathed or image-filled temples or what is preached in bare simple halls comprehends that these forms are speaking in their own fashion to simpler souls and conveying elementary lessons which will one day be developed in their fullness in the philosophy of truth. He understands well that there need be no quarrel between philosophy and religion for what the former expresses in abstract concepts the latter expresses through concrete symbols in its modes of worship and forms of belief. The inner meaning of those symbols is a philosophic truth. Man's intelligence rises by successive stages through the incarnations from the symbol to its reality, from the letter to the spirit, from the hand-built exterior sanctuary to the unwrought unshaped interior stillness. It is hard for an unpractised or unprepared mind to rise to an abstract mystical or metaphysical concept of God. What it can do, however, is to form a concrete picture for itself which can correspond to the abstract idea. That is to say, it can take hold of and understand an *image* of God by an act of imagination. Such a picture for worship or meditation is provided by religion. Then in the course of its own gradual evolution it one day develops the capacity to *see through* its own image into the profound concept of which this is a mere representation.

It is this reality of the World-Mind which popular worship unconsciously exalts but actually misconceives when it accepts the sentimental dross of superstition, fanaticism and intolerance along with the gold of sincere religion. "Whom ye ignorantly worship Him I declare unto you." These words, uttered by Christ's messenger at Athens, may properly be uttered by the philosophy of truth to it. He who would make a mere idea, a mere finite mental image into the true God blasphemes and materializes God, not he who doubts or denies the blasphemy itself.

The unparalleled bitterness of the times through which we have been passing indicates that we need the support of God more than ever before. And if, in most cases, we cannot obtain this support on a basis of knowledge but only on a basis of faith, let it be at least a rational faith and not a superstitious one. Let it not be a faith which sooner or later we shall abandon in disillusionment or despair but rather let it be one in which every advance of growing reason, every episode of widening experience will only confirm and strengthen. Atheists, seeing nominally Christian nations fighting each other in the West and nominally Buddhist nations doing the same in the East, blame religion for this moral degradation into insincerity. They are mistaken. It is not real religion but the absence of it, on the one hand, and the defeat by vested interests of those who would preach its *primary* truths, on the other, which are really responsible for these deplorable conditions. The disappearance of genuine religion from the world would be a great calamity as the disappearance of false religion would be a blessing.

This then is the message of philosophy, which today might well be accepted as the friend of institutional religion, were such religion more loyal to its founders and ethics and less to its bigotry and errors. For humanity needs more faith in a Supreme Power during such dark times, more faith that goodness is eventually rewarded and evil-doing eventually punished, more faith that we are not merely a bunch of greedy animals but also have a higher and finer human purpose to outwork in life. The future of mankind rigorously requires the further development of an anti-materialistic trend.

Thus we have seen that as mankind progress they develop different ideas about God. The same also occurs to their ideas about its relation to the universe. The earliest group of civilized ideas set it up as the *World-Builder*. This theory is based upon the observation that a house does not arise of itself but is constructed by some being—in this case a human being—who belongs to a higher order of existence than the house itself. It adopts the belief that the sun and stars and the whole of Nature could not have come into existence of themselves but must have a Maker. And just as a house-builder uses bricks for his work so God is believed to have used a substance called "matter" for the manufacture of this universe. God is one thing and matter is another. Consequently God stands apart from the universe. And as man is a part of the "made" world he looks up to his Maker with awe and reverence to be worshipped as something utterly remote from himself.

The value of this view is its acknowledgment of the existence of a higher order of being. The defect of this view is that it conceives God under the form of a magnified *man*. This makes him a particular object among other objects and sets him apart from us. In its highest form this belief regards God as an infinite Being but still places it outside of an apart from the universe. Such a view is better but still metaphysically unsound. For if God is outside the world, it is limited by the world and thus loses its infinitude.

When the ripening human intellect rises to a higher stage, however, the second group of ideas is born. it sets up God as the *World-Architect*. This represents a transition to the recognition that the harmonious movements of the sun and stars, the orderly arrangements of Nature point to a higher power which not merely makes the world but also plans it with an ultimate and benignant purpose in view, a power which is not merely existent but is also all-embracing, all-merciful and all-knowing. God is thus the life of the world through and through, its very soul. This removes the defect earlier mentioned by removing the anthropomorphic image under which the supreme was conceived. It puts a positive purpose into the universe, a beneficient plan behind it. It places the universe within God, who thus becomes its immanent principle. Its followers no longer look outside or afar for God but within themselves as their inmost soul.

The defects of this view are that it still has not annulled matter but retains a duality of spirit and matter; it still keeps two separate principles as co-eternally existent and co-eternally conflicting. Only when human intelligence reaches its full maturity does it evolve the third progressive idea of God, that of the *World-Mind,* an idea which takes into itself all that is true in the earlier ideas and at the same time transcends them, an idea which expresses completely what the other ones were struggling to express so partially. The belief in a God who is outside the universe is as natural for unmetaphysical minds as the belief in a God who manifests as the universe is natural for metaphysical ones. From this loftier standpoint the universe is a veritable self-revelation of God, not merely something made by it. There is only a single reality. There is not matter. Mind is the only being. Thoughts and things, men and universes are but manifestations of Mind. The Frenchman Malebranche came close to this truth when he declared; "we see all things in God." The World-Mind therefore *is* the universe.

Just as it was not right to expect a Class I schoolboy to grasp higher mathematical explanations, so it was not right in former centuries to expect the struggling masses, pre-occupied as they were with the daily toil for subsistence, to grasp such a lofty philosophic doctrine as this, which needs abundant leisure and trained mentality for its adequate understanding. This was one of the several reasons why the doctrine was hidden from them and why it became the esoteric property of a privileged few. Today most of these reasons have become noticeably antiquated in consequence of the tremendous changes which have come over the world scene during modern times. Therefore after the present storms have subsided and before the present century closes, we shall witness the release of a staggering knowledge, of which the ideas sketched out here are mere precursors. The mystical and philosophic enlightenment of mankind will then spread over the horizon to an extent unknown in ancient times.

Actually the teaching has always been open to anyone who, wishing to get at the essence of things, cared for it sufficiently to devote the needful time, energy and self-discipline to its mastery. For the best amongst the higher order of priests in antiquity were also mystics and even philosophers. They made it a part of their duty to watch and stimulate the spiritual growth of their flocks rather than to prevent it. Consequently they were always observant of those who could be led to superior doctrines and interiorized practices and such were fully encouraged to advance into them. Thus religion, mysticism and philosophy formed a functioning unit, as they would today were our spiritual guides more awake to the grave dangers to which their institutions will be exposed after the tensions of war have relaxed unless a new spirit and a new flexibility enters them. When the entire universe is subject to the law of constant change, when everything in this space-time world is stamped with relativity and transiency, how can the human expressions and applications of truth hope to escape changes and adaptations themselves? Religious worship is needed. It has an essential place to fill in human life. Rightly understood and rightly expounded it attracts faith, ennobles character and protects society. But when its influence wanes, when its ideas are no longer vivid, and when its practice becomes widely ignored its sponsors should ascertain why this is so and remedy the causes.

God in the Universe.

When we understand mentalism we understand too that the World-Mind does not exist separately alongside the universe but in it and as it. The world was not arbitrarily created by outside intervention but was periodically self-born through the hidden activity of karmic forces under an ultimate law. The impressions of all objects in the universe lie latent within the inner depths of the World-Mind, until they become active by the general working of karma when they are externalized in the familiar space-time level which we call the physical world. The world-series is not only self-actuating but also self-determining. There is no intervention of an outside being simply because there is no outside being. Thus it is the heritage of karma which really brings the appearance of a universe into being and not a personal creator. We must not personalize the World-Mind in relation to its activity. It does not make the world like a man making a boot. It does not create the collected karmic potentials but only offers the ground for their existence. They form a self-active system. The belief that all these karmic energies are like the parts of a vast machine which is alternately set in operation and stopped by a machine-tender and that their operator is a separate personal God sitting in solitude beside them would not be a correct one. For they do not need any separate entity to 'work' them. The karmic forces are set in motion spontaneously, not by the arbitrary fiat of a personal power. The mind-substance of World-Mind is their inseparable ground and from it they derive their self-actuating power. According to our human way of looking at things they have existed since the beginningless past and their very nature constrains them to self-actualize themselves as a cosmos when they rise out of latency and to dissolve this cosmos when they subside. There was no special reason why an external power had to make a world out of matter but there was every reason why it had to make it out of its own self because the latent karmic impressions within it *had* to manifest themselves.

Hence for this superfluous concept of a special creator mentalism substitutes the superior one of a principle which being nothing else than Mind, reproduces the universe out of its own substance, contains it within itself and is thus both immanent and transcendent. The universe is as inseparable from the universal mind as a man's ideas are inseparable from his own mind. Thus mind is moulded and yet Mind is the moulder. Mind takes on a myriad forms and holds them as though they were other than its own self. When we know fully by insight the essence of the tiniest ant, we know also the essence of the whole universe. For the mind-stuff which is behind the *form* of an ant is one and the same mind-stuff as that which is behind the form of a universe. The mind *is* the world. He who can perceive this has travelled far.

Thus instead of an absentee God we have an everywhere-present one who is the very essence of the world. The cosmos is nothing less than the self-externalization of the World-Mind which is self-existent and needs no second thing *in* which to reside, no matter *from* which to make a universe. Thought in its pure ultimate single essence is the substance of the universe. Those who cannot comprehend this may perhaps do so if they will remember that during one and the same dream, at one and the same moment, they can be immediately conscious of a tiger, a tree and a crowd of people. What is it which has thus manifested itself in all these different figures in this manner? Is it not a single mind, their own?

Thus mentalism renders it easier for us to understand three great truths. First, that the universe is God made manifest; second, that God must be immanent in the world just as our own mind is immanent on every one of our own thoughts; third, that because it has a mind behind it, the universe cannot be a senseless affair but must possess a consistent meaning. The world is so intimately connected with the World-Mind that it becomes meaningless and unthinkable apart from it.

The universe expresses infinite intelligence and possesses meaning precisely because it is a manifestation of infinite mind. The presence of World-Mind invests the whole world-process with sense and sanity. We may translate this into the statement that God is the secret and original source of the universal mental and biological activity, the basis and bedrock of the whole world-experience.

We earlier found that the whole universe is alive and mental. But if we understand the implications of the unconscious, we must add that the whole universe is also conscious. One fundamental error which is often made by those who approach this subject, whether they do it as materialists or religionists, is to picture consciousness only in an anthropomorphic form. They cannot get away from the view which limits the activity of awareness only to the way in which we humans think, know, feel and experience things. Even if mind be denuded of consciousness *as man knows it* this is not to say that it is denuded of consciousness as it itself knows it. We must give up this anthropocentric definition. We must make a sharp distinction between mind and human awareness and as pure awareness.

If bright flowers and grey minerals have no brains this means not that they are unable to be conscious but that their consciousness is of a different form and inferior to the human kind. The way in which some plants distribute their seeds no less than the way in which they protect those seeds against premature destruction is as much a tribute to the presence of universal intelligence as the way in which external forces are brought in to sustain life on this planet. The materialist theory that as soon as biological forms developed a brain the process of knowledge came into being is simple and plausible. But it is unable to account for the discoveries of Bose which demonstrate by strict laboratory methods that plants react to events in their environment in a manner which shows a certain measure of understanding. It is unable to account for the intelligence revealed by minerals and their salts when their molecules group themselves into seven precise crystalline patterns. For although they exhibit intelligence, neither crystals nor plants have evolved organized brains! The consciousness is not only in the colloids of animal organisms, where science has begun to detect its presence, but also in the cells, where science has failed to detect it; and not only in the visible brain but also in the invisible mind.

If we can appreciate this, we can proceed further and comprehend that the fortunes of living creatures are not left like straws to drift in the wind. Evolution is guaranteed because some fragment of the cosmic mind is itself the life-force which strives upward through all the muffling veils of the four kingdoms of Nature, a striving to attain self-maturity which is inherent in every finite form from that of a so-called dead mineral to that of a living man. Consciousness too develops along with the life-force, attaining conscious sensation in the lower animals, conscious thinking, that is intellect in the higher animal and lower human stages, and spiritual self-knowledge that is insight in the higher human stage. Therefore we need not fear that the cosmic purpose in its creatures is doomed to final failure.

Anyone can see how, if we take the kingdom of living creatures alone, consciousness slowly expands as it evolves from the lowest coral insect to the higher mammals, but this is only a fragment —although one of the most important fragments—of what the universal evolution entails. If the more reflective and more advanced scientists say that we cannot rightly leave out the mineral, the metal and the plant whose rudimentary consciousness stand at the base of this movement, philosophy adds 'nor the sage who stands at its summit'. The mind-essence is as much present in a piece of stone as in an animated human being. But whereas the stone cannot rise to the consciousness of its own essence, the human being has always the potentiality of doing so.

The intelligence in control of evolutionary processes can come only from a fundamentally mental basis underlying those processes. All this explains why biologists discover an amazing intelligence at work in the intricate formation and orderly maintenance of living organisms. It also explains why physicists find an extraordinarily sagacious behaviour in the energies they investigate and why Nature reflects a rational functioning throughout its vast domain. We may detect not only the intelligent system at the base of Nature but, in the graceful forms taken by mineral, acid, snow and ice crystals, for example, her artistry too. The presence of such orderliness in the cosmos shows that it could not have been born from an unintelligent source. The most microscopic and elementary of protoplasmic cells in the human body exhibits as rational a sense of discrimination in selecting its food as any ever exhibited by our modern Rationalists when they sit down at the dining-table! The materialist who sees only blind and unreasoning forces living in the universe is to be pitied for his own blindness and unreason.

Thus the world evidences a hidden mainspring of life and mind, will and intelligence. Although we must not restrict the World-Mind by believing that it works like an architectural planner or legal statute-maker, for these are purely human in outlook, nevertheless anyone with an eye to see can see that the universe reveals that it is being held in intelligent and intelligible order. Arbitrary caprice did not create the world once upon a time. Blind disorder has not ruled it since then. There is true meaning, there is strict law, there is genuine coherence, there is a movement through stone to flower, through beast to man, through higher and higher levels of integration in this universal existence. When this is understood, it can then also be understood that karma is not merely a law of inheriting previous impressions or of self-reproduction or of moral retributive justice but is also something much larger. It is an eternal law which tends to adjust the individual operation to the universal operation. It works for the universe as a whole to keep its innumerable units in harmony with its own integral balance. Retribution merely falls inside this activity as a small concentric circle falls inside a larger one. The results of each individual's existence, his heritage of thought and action have to be controlled so that they shall in the end obey the larger regularity of the cosmos itself. Every part is bound to the whole. Everything thus tends to ultimate rightness. It is indeed comforting to perceive that the universe has such significant equilibrium at its secret core.

There now arise the questions: Why was the world brought into existence at all? Why such prodigality on World-Mind's part in bringing to birth vast universes through tremendous geologic periods, only to disintegrate them again afterwards in the boundless abysses of spaces? Why this brown earth, those moving men, this golden sun, these speechless animals and those twinkling stars? An intelligent man is driven to seek for an intelligible purpose in the universal existence as much as he himself seeks to put one into his own individual existence. To pass from cradle to grave without either the belief or hope that some secret mainspring is driving the world onwards and upwards, without being able to interpret some kind of a meaning in its endless movement, is to turn his life into an unsatisfactory wilderness. The *Bhagavad Gita* rightly points out that those men are on the lowest level who regard the world as devoid of significance and without a superior cause.

One of the most prominent of the traditional schools of Oriental metaphysicians and mystics would make the universe a game of make-believe which the Infinite Self plays with itself, to and for its own great selfish delight. Were this view true then the universe could rightly be regarded as a vast torture-chamber with God as the chief torturer of swarming multitudes of hapless victims. It would also deprive existence of ultimate sense and rational significance. But such a dismal theory finds no place on the hidden teaching.

These problems are intractable unless we first understand that the universe is not *brought* into existence, that it is not created, and that it arises because it must. The World-Mind obeys the everlasting law of its own being and periodically manifests or reabsorbs the world-image. What is this inner nature which so compels it to do so? It is karma, the ultimate and eternal law governing the perpetual movement of its own activity and consequently governing the rhythm of universal existence and non-existence. This however is not a law set up from outside, for there is nothing outside World-Mind. This perpetual rhythm is beginningless and endless because the World-Mind itself is a beginningless and endless force. Hence the question why the world was brought into existence is one which we put only so long as we do not know what the world really is. When we understand that it arises in obedience to the general law of karma, that it is a perpetual self-reproduction appearing intermittently in cosmic cycles, that it has never had a beginning or will ever have an ending, we see that there can be no *ultimate* purpose in it but only an immediate one. Such questions are based on the untenable attitude of the questioner in taking for granted (*a*) that sudden creation of the universe in time is ultimately true, (*b*) that the universe was formed by an independent outside Creator. A universe formed on the basis of these two factors would naturally have purpose inherent in it. But there is no separate Creator. The collective karmic impressions rise of themselves within World-Mind. This is because there has never been a time when they did not exist for, although their forms may change, they are as eternal as the World-Mind itself. Indeed, they are part of the World-Mind's nature. Hence they constitute a self-actuating system. Because we can set no date for the World-Mind's own beginning nor any terminus for its own life, we must consequently refrain from the illogical attempt to set a beginning or an end to the universe itself. And the World-Mind has not *made* the world but only afforded the ground for its existence, the receptable for its mutually acting karmic potential forces, the stuff for its general karmic manifestations and the life-principle for its ever-moving activities which take place of their own accord. But we must not fall into the error that this view makes the universe a mere machine. For the ground receptacle forces and stuff all being mental, the world also is a mental activity and not just a mechanical movement in matter.

The world was never brought into existence but has always been in existence, however intermittently it reincarnates itself. In one sense, it is like a revolving wheel which forever circles on itself. No sage has ever calculated, no seer's insight has ever penetrated the primordial darkness around the beginnings of this process of ever-becoming which constitutes our universe simply because there are none. We can only say that it is the very nature of the universe to exist eternally in the sense that it is the very nature of everything else to exist only for a time. And because this is its own nature, because in this sense it is utterly outside the transiency of the time-series and has never had a beginning inside it, it is useless to ask why it was created. The question becomes unanswerable because it is unaskable; it no longer arises and consequently can no longer be put. The fact that the world is a perpetual self-actuating process, is something which precludes us from asking such a question. We have to accept that the universe *is*. And whatever really is can never cease to be, just as whatever never was cannot really come to be. Where the opposite seems to be true that is our sense-born illusion. If we see the universe dying and disappearing, it has merely been transformed into latency as a man's thoughts disappear into his mind, where they lie in a latent condition. What the universe is here for is a query which becomes meaningless by this light.

The problem as stated is a false one, a pseudo-problem. The world movement will not deprive the World-Mind of its own wonderful being if it stops or add to it if it continues. Alternate space-time manifestation and withdrawal of the universe are as inseparable from its nature as breathing is inseparable from human life. We have to accept the necessity of such mysterious self-manifestation as an integral part of its nature and as an eternal law of its inherent being. Consequently we cannot strictly and metaphysically say that there is any deliberate teleological purpose as such in the universal scheme when everything is thus happening of its own accord under a hidden karmic self-necessity. Again when we understand that World-Mind has its eternal existence outside of time whereas the cosmic process takes place inside time, we understand then that the World-Mind could not possibly pursue a cosmic purpose with some self-benefiting motive. There is no gain for itself in evolution, no purpose to fulfil for its own benefit, no profit to get to satisfy its own desire.

The All-Knower.

But if the universe has no ultimate purpose inherent in it this is not to say that it has no immediate one. And if the World-Mind has no self-motive, no special purpose on its own behalf, this is not to say that it has none on behalf of the innumerable creatures within the universe. Its own presence provides adequate significance to life from their standpoint. In these matters we are not left in the dark. We have quite enough to do to comprehend what the immediate evolution is working out in the universe and what it is seeking to do with the teeming multitude of creatures. And here the hidden teaching on the basis of ultra-mystic insight can quickly tell us much that we need to know. It can tell us something about the end which the cosmic evolution seeks to secure in mankind. It can tell us what human life is for and consequently provide us with worth-while practical aims.* And this is a long step forward. Our own existence is not purposeless. We humans have been given a goal to struggle for. We may clearly know what it is. Is this not enough?

The World-Mind abides unchanged and unaffected by the general movement. The cosmic process goes on therefore not for

---

* The Scientific Editor of the *New York Times* frankly confessed in conversation that even twentieth-century science can really say nothing about the purpose of life.

the World-Mind's sake but vicariously for the sake of the individuals within it. Hence the inner necessity which calls it forth into existence must not be misread. It is purely karmic. If we are called upon—as we are—to become co-workers in this process it is not really for the World-Mind's sake but for mankind's sake. Let us not make the mistake of imagining that our participation in the divine work is needed to help the World-Mind's interests. It is not. World-Mind is not struggling against great odds, is not calling for man's puny help. Being itself the source of the All it is not in want of anything. 'The divinity requires no aid,' announced Roman Seneca. The interests which shall profit are ours—not individually but as an inter-dependent whole. Nor let us fall into the speculative error of those theologians who imagine that it is struggling against an antagonistic satanic power and that our help is needed here too. Such satanic forces certainly exist and we of this unfortunate generation have had plenty of painful evidence of their handiwork but they are not supreme. They are merely centres of finite life and intelligence which have misdirected their will and thought to extremes of time and extent. Consequently they have doomed themselves to ultimate destruction. There is ultimately no other supreme power than the World-Mind.

From the practical standpoint, which is that of the part and not of the whole, when we comprehend that every living creature from protoplasmic cell upwards is seeking to realize its own existence and that this quest becomes a conscious one in the higher forms of man, we may however speak of the universe possessing a final purpose. In this sense only the World-Mind is forever producing and perfecting out of its own substance and under the necessary conditions of time and space a universe whose members will grow in consciousness through a series of planetary wanderings towards a sublime goal. The value of the cosmic activity consists in the general upward direction along which its individual centres move. The universal movement is destined to raise life and intelligence to ever loftier levels. This is the immediate and immanent purpose behind it. The development of self-subduing conscience and the unfolding of higher consciousness are the chief ends and best values which Nature is working out in man. For the personal self there is always a goal toward which it can aspire, hence there is always a purpose underlying its own existence. It will progress in its own intermittent way precisely because it is finite. The stretch of its little space-time existence is too narrow not to bring it half-muffled reminders of the illimitable infinitude whence it came forth.

What kind of perceptions, what kind of consciousness has the World-Mind? The attempt to answer this question is a useless one unless we change our way of viewing time. So long as we regard time as something operating independently apart from consciousness, so long will it be impossible even to form the merely symbolic conceptions which represent the limit of an intellectual answer to such a question. Our remembrances of the past, our anticipations of the future, even our moment-to-moment living in the present, are all mentally constructed. This would sound incredible were it not that our faith in time has been sadly sapped by the mentalist and dream investigation into its real character, as well as into mind which is the root of time. The present event seems real and the past one unreal only because our full concentrated attention is being focused upon it but is absent from the other. The immense power of either attention or inattention to build, eliminate, quicken or slow down different spheres of experience is hardly known and seldom noticed by the multitude but the yogi who has successfully trained his mental powers of rapt absorption soon ceases to be astonished at the extraordinary modifications in his space-time experiences of events and persons which thenceforth occur. It is quite possible for anyone who has the requisite concentration or sufficient interest and desire to develop the requisite intensity of concentration to convert his own past into the present for instance. A man who has lost a well-beloved wife may do it frequently when sunk in reverie over remembered episodes. Any expert yogi can do it at will by bringing into the centre of his mental focus a thought, theme, person or picture. Where then does the fixity of time lie? Where is the difference between past and present? Both lie within our mind and nowhere else. Both are ideas.

If during dreams it is possible to pass in a few minutes through a series of episodes which would require several weeks of wakeful time, and if during the influence of a drug it is possible to experience a single half-minute episode in what seems several hours, then it is clear that the order in which we experience events in time can be fantastically quickened or fantastically slowed down. If this is possible in the case of a human mind, if the attempt to impose our common standard of waking time upon a dreaming or drugged man is futile and absurd, is it not equally futile and absurd to attempt to impose any time standard at all upon the World-Mind? When we understand that no limit can be set to the number of different time-orders which can exist, we may understand that one second of our wakeful time may be equal to one thousand years of time in another type of consciousness whilst one thousand years of our wakeful time may be no more than one second in the existence of a superior consciousness.

We may go even further and declare that not only does the mentalist nature of time make it a variable thing, that not only must there be within the World-Mind several different time-series, but that although the time-perceptions of a creature belonging to one of them will be unknown to a creature in another series, the World-Mind itself will necessarily be aware of all these possible variations. How easy must it be for the World-Mind to quicken its own time-sense so immeasurably that it can embrace the happenings of a whole cosmic cycle of millions of years in a moment? Or to slow its consciousness down to the level of a creature whose whole long-drawn lifetime is to us but a few hours? Or to experience in one-millionth of a moment what we can experience only in a million years?

And this, unimaginable though it seem to a limited human being, is indeed the case. The successive happenings of our own time-order so appear for our benefit, not for the World-Mind's. Our finite way of observing events in time, of experiencing changes in succession, is not the cosmic way. Our time-order is simply one particular dress out of many which the cosmic world-idea wears.

The infinite World-Mind sees the universe in itself and itself in the universe. It is not unaware of what is happening here below. Its consciousness is perfect, which means that it embraces all possible time-series. Every event is indeed present to it but not in the way in which it would be present to a finite mind. For World-Mind grasps its world-idea in what to us is an all-timed fixity. The accomplished world, not less than its countless tiers of evolutionary change, suffering and joy, is simultaneously and infinitely present to this unconceivable consciousness. It is erroneous therefore to believe that what is now dead past to us is the same to the World-Mind. The latter views the universe not only in succession but also simultaneously. Such a state, such a higher dimension in which past, present and future time are co-equal can of course no longer be called time in the human sense of the term.

What are the World-Mind's space-perceptions? Just as, during a single act of attention in our finite way, when we enter a hall in the midst of a concert we can take in the hall itself, the crowds of listeners and the strains of music and yet attend to the business of walking down an aisle to our seat, so the World-Mind in its infinite way can take in the entire universe in a single act of its own attention, can make everything and everyone in it the content of its consciousness. From this illustration of what the mind of feeble man can accomplish we may derive a mere hint of what the infinite World-Mind can accomplish in the way of embracing the entire universe in a single all-comprehensive thought. Every place in the whole universe is equally present to its perception. Its experience is all-pervading, being always in contact with all objects at all times. If anyone who ascends to the observatory at the top of Empire State Building can see so much of New York City and so many different objects all at once, it is not too far-fetched to assert that World-Mind can see the whole cosmic process all at once.

The World-Mind's consciousness embraces the ALL, else it could not be what it is. It perceives the world without having to perceive it in bits and pieces as we humans do, that is it perceives integrally, holding everything in a single vast vision. This means that the parts are seen in their true relation not only to each other but especially to the whole. There is nothing outside its experience, but we must not make the mistake of imagining such experience only on the very low and restricted level of human perception, which can only string events like beads on the thread of time and hang things in space like fruits on a tree.

What is true of the time-perceptions of World-Mind is therefore equally true of its space-perceptions. Because it is the consciousness common to all beings, because it is present everywhere in everyone and everything, its experience is necessarily all-inclusive too. It completely embraces all possible space-orders because it is conscious of the universe as being *within* itself whereas we are conscious of it as being *outside* ourself and can function only in one state at a time. Nothing external can circumscribe the activity of the World-Mind simply because nothing external to itself exists. Nevertheless although the number of forms in the universe seems to us to be beyond computation this is only because of the limitations of the human mind. Actually it is measurable because an ordered universe is inseparable from a numbered one. For although the World-Mind is not itself bound by laws of individual causality, time and space, its manifestation in the world of appearances is necessarily bound by them.

The World-Mind's totalized all-inclusive single idea of the universe may be whole, perfect and accomplished from its standpoint but from the standpoint of the individual centres of conscious life within that great idea—being unable to expand their restricted experience—every event has to develop successively in a special time-order and every object has to rest in a special space-setting if it is to be present at all. Hence the World-Mind has to set up mental divisions of space and time within the individual in order to set up its infinite variety of karmic actualizations. We, its products, enter into those divisions and feel their reality like mesmerized subjects. But the ultimate truth is that they are ideas, no more and no less. Dreams seem to occur within time and space for they contain both events and things but if we consider them from the philosophic standpoint we discover that no fundamental change has occurred to the mind of the dreamer; it has neither moved at all in space to the distant city seen in dream nor hardly moved in time to the numerous happenings within that city experienced during what is but a single second of wakeful time; it has remained in reality motionless in time and space. This may help us to understand how the World-Mind appears to manifest a particular space-time-substance world but is itself actually all-pervasive, all-timed, all-spaced and all-substanced, eternally self-conscious being.

The notions that the all-conscious mind of this universe can be unconscious, as Von Hartmann believed, or mere blind will, as Schopenhauer thought, are untenable. Both Schopenhauer and Von Hartmann saw quite correctly that this deeper mind did not use the conscious thinking process which we humans are accustomed to use. But they made the mistake of deducing first that in its essential state it does not possess the attribute of any consciousness at all, and second, that human consciousness was *essentially* different from it and consequently separated from it by an eternally uncrossable barrier. They would have done better to point out the incapacity of our present consciousness to know what is beyond its range and to indicate that other forms of consciousness may exist. We must clearly grasp this point that space-time consciousness is the off-spring of mind, which must at the very least be allowed what its offspring possesses—the capacity to know itself. And if the greater must contain the lesser, if that which exists cannot possibly arise out of that which is not, then mind must possess a consciousness which at the very least must equal that which we ordinarily call such and at the very most must unimaginably transcend it. Hence if the World-Mind failed to recognize itself in every form in Nature, however low, however bestial and however circumscribed, it could not be the soul of the Universe. To the World-Mind all things and all knowledge and all orders of consciousness are equally present at a single glance for they are all one to it. Its own existence is therefore an eternal Now, an endless Here. This is esoterically expressed in the very name of Allah, the Muhammadan God: Al signifying the beginningless, La meaning the endless.

If the World-Mind knows anything at all it must also know the way in which the space-time world appears to and is experienced by its space-time creatures for the greater consciousness being co-extensive with the All, includes and does not exclude the lesser. There is no particular form of experience which it cannot take into itself. Every place is its 'here' and every time its 'now.' It does not leave out what is finite, it embraces all the possible finites and yet it is *itself* infinite.

All experience involves things seen in space and changes made in time. We must know their 'when' and 'where' if we are to know them at all. It is however only from the human point of view that we can make this assertion. There is another possible point of view wherefrom the world is embraced as an everywhere-ness and an everywhen-ness. This of course dissolves the very meaning of time and space, as *we* understand them. For just as an ant crawling over a sleeping man's body cannot stretch out its own intelligence widely enough to comprehend what that man, at his own narrowest stretch can easily comprehend, so man himself cannot stretch out his space-time perceptions even to a fraction of the extent of the World-Mind's. Time has acquired an exaggerated value among us. The theory of progressive evolution has given rise with some Western metaphysicians to the theory that Deity is actually evolving, that with more time we shall have a grander God! The ancient sages were not so superficial. For they knew time to be a mental product and they knew that Mind itself transcended it.

The condition of human knowing is the setting up of a relation between 'I' and 'not-I'. All our knowledge is thus relative to our consciousness. How can we hope to know in truth the ultimate nature of a consciousness which totally transcends all such relativity? We cannot rightly judge its consciousness by human standards. It is unphilosophical to try to force the infinite World-Mind into our little circle of finite space-time experience. What is an immeasurable cosmos to human experience is brought to a single point in the World-Mind. If we with our limited human faculty cannot grasp such a truth let us not deny it. What is an eternity of time to human outlook is brought to a single instant in the same all-thinking mind. It has already been pointed out that the ancient sages represented the ideas of infinity and eternity under the emblem of a circle returning on itself, sometimes modified into the figure of an ever-revolving Swastika-wheel. In this light, we may meditate on the mysterious saying of the cosmic Christ speaking through Jesus: 'I am the Alpha and Omega, the first and the last; for what was first comes at last and the last is the first.' If the World-Mind can manifest and operate in a multitude of different space-time orders without making us aware of what it is doing, we must be prepared to accept the fact that the inevitable limitations of our own perceptions cover those other orders with a veil of blankness for us. If one of our demands be that it display to our consciousness the method and manner of its universal working, we ought not to complain that it is ignored. All this majestic monism is truly and literally incomprehensible to human conceptual thinking. It is inconceivable to us precisely because we are finite and human but that is also precisely why we should not commit the error of denying such possibilities altogether.

We first imagine a humanized personal God who sits caught in the same web of space and time relations as ourself, and inevitably every succeeding thought about this God made with our own hands becomes filled with falsity. And because the universe is itself spun out of God's very self, our thoughts about the universe naturally suffer from the same falsity. We do not see that the moment we make the initial error of putting God in our own or indeed any space-time order, we have to regard its self-manifested universe as some thing born suddenly in time and appearing suddenly in space, and therefore with its prior existence still left unaccounted for. We need to lift our concepts of both right out of space and time—making God the unpicturable formless Mind and making the universe beginningless and endless. If this is a notion which we have never clearly appreciated before we should remember that Nature lays no banquet of obvious truths for us at her table. That which we require to feed us must be dug out by ourself with blistered hands and aching head. Everything that is worth while is recondite, unobservable and hard to come at.

12

The Unveiling of Reality

THE World-Mind is bound up with the universe not only so far as the latter is born of its activity but also because mentalism shows that it *is* the universe itself, from the ultimate standpoint. Whatever point in this measureless universe that we can think of, the World-Mind is there. The man on our globe, the man on distant Mars and the man on still more distant Neptune ultimately derives his inward consciousness and outward experience from it. There is no point in space from where we can possibly conceive it to be absent. This is what is ordinarily meant when we call God omnipresent and infinite. Such a view is true so far as it goes but it does not go far enough. For here a word of warning is needful. It has earlier been explained that if God is regarded as universal *only* in the sense of possessing colossal amplitude, as being self-multiplied to an unimaginable extent, we err. For we put it *in* space whereas space is only an idea *for* it. And if we deem it to be world-conscious *only* in the same sensuous way that we humans are, then we merely succeed in forming a refined anthropomorphic concept.

For the universe is in space and time whereas "the Mind of the World-Mind", if such a phrase may be used, is not to be wholly subordinated to its own emanation but must claim its own freedom, which means that it is not to be subordinated to time and space. These two states of its own existence are as far apart as black and white. The incessant movement of ideas which constitutes its manifestation of a cosmos does not represent the course of its own life. When reflection and yoga lift the curtain we are at last able to see earthly life for the show or appearance that it is. Everything which is in this universe is a perishable show of itself by the imperishable World-Mind, but it is a show which hides immeasurably more than it actually reveals. Just as a dreamer's mind remains perfectly intact, unlessened and whole even after it has emanated a widespread dream-universe, so the World-Mind remains perfectly intact, unlessened and whole even after it has emanated an illimitable physical one. Nothing of either the dreamer's mind or the World-Mind is really lost by such activity. Just as an author's ideas are not destroyed even though the paper upon which he has projected them is destroyed, so the World-Mind is unaffected by the appearance or disappearance of the images whose total projection constitutes a cosmos. And just as the artist's mind remains as whole and undivided after its labours of creation as it was before them, no matter how numerous the creative thoughts to which it gave birth, so the World-Mind remains unlessened and unweakened in all its incomprehensible integrity after the creative giving-forth from itself of the myriad units which compose the whole world-idea during a period of cosmic manifestation.

The One becomes a multitude. The World-Mind continually and spontaneously throws its being into living universes and living creatures. But that can never exhaust it for it never really loses anything by this process. The One has produced the Many out of itself, not out of some extraneous material, and cannot be measured by its expression in the universe, for this is always an incomplete one. We cannot arrive at Reality by stitching together millions of little pieces. It is not the whole in this sense. It is not only the totality of things but much more the essence of things.

We can easily comprehend how one human mind becomes many thoughts in succession yet still remains beyond them as its unlessened self. We can also comprehend how the same mind exists in all these different thoughts. Thus we can more easily comprehend how the World-Mind can manifest in a million forms and yet remain its infinite transcendent self. It is not contained by the universe, unbounded though the latter seems to be, in the sense that all space is not contained by an empty jar. The jar can only give us through what it holds a bare hint of what space is and the universe too can only give us through what it holds a bare hint of what the World-Mind is. The World-Mind is not only in the universe but also metaphysically beyond it. The finitude of the world points to the infinite which transcends the world. The fact that it is but a changeful Appearance suggests the unchanging Reality which underlies it. If the cosmos is truly a self-revelation of the World-Mind, it is nevertheless neither a full nor exhaustive revelation but only a fragmentary one. Thus the world is exhibited before us as self-revelation of Mind's immediate *presence* but, until we enquire more deeply, not of its *nature*.

We cannot stop with the dynamic conception of the World-Mind alone. For so long as it is conscious of its relation to the individual centres, so long as it is active in the out-breathing and in-breathing of universes, so long as it has to work with time—however far beyond and beneath our human range its own amazing time-sense may extend—so long is it in the realm of appearance and not reality, so long is it in the sphere of thought-forms and not of undifferentiated Thought itself. We cannot stop with this conception therefore if we would know intellectually at least what is absolutely ultimate, what is definitely final in existence. We must proceed on our way. And indeed it is the World-Mind, the living God Itself, which bids whoever comes to the comprehension that it does exist, whoever understands it to be the ultimate ground of all life and being, to look beyond it to THAT which alone possesses the uttermost reality. He must understand that although mentalism reduces the world to idea, it does not reduce reality to idea. Thus we arrive at the problem of the World-Mind's own nature. After the problem of matter it is the deepest and darkest one which confronts us. And because it is the ultimate source of everything it is likewise the ultimate key to everything. For we have reduced all human beings to cells in this cosmic mind and all material things to the co-produced thoughts of both. Everything exists within an ocean of mind just as all waves exist within the watery ocean itself. Cosmic Mind therefore is unique and like nothing else in existence. It is the ultimate. It is irreducible to anything simpler than itself. The importance of getting even an intellectual insight into its nature and meaning is such that it must simultaneously yield an intellectual insight into the nature and meaning of God and of reality, that is into the most fundamental problem open to human reflection.

Many may object to our use of the term "mind" in this connection. We have no quarrel with the use of other words in its place if it be understood that they are not descriptive enough to be anything more than mere conventional labels, useful only to help us think and read about something which lies beyond thinking. But earlier semantic studies have shown the futility of merely making pleasant noises in the air or black marks on white paper without some corresponding comprehension of them. Wide experience has proven that no amount of words will ever make the meaning of "Spirit" for example clear to a man who lacks all mystical experiences. Therefore we have usually discarded its use as a synonym for the highest existence. Few words, on the contrary, are needed to make the term "mind" meaningful to him. This is because he finds its derivations continuously present within himself. He can no more escape its manifestations as consciousness, imagination, thinking and memory, for instance, than he can jump out of his skin. His own mind above all else known to him bears the nearest or at least some sort of resemblance to the great Mind which sustains him. True, in his case its scope is immensely reduced and its actuality immensely dwarfed. *Nevertheless it is a resemblance* and therefore can help him in his effort to understand what would be otherwise so incomprehensible. This term "mind" is so suggestive, so much easier for those who have studied these pages to interpret correctly than any other which might be used, that we shall deliberately employ it henceforth to stand for the ultimate reality of all things, the absolute principle of all life But to differentiate such an employment from the common unreflective usage which makes it merely identical with one of its activities, that is consciousness, and to prevent its confusion with the mere sum of conscious thoughts, we shall here henceforth always adorn the word with a capital initial letter. Sometimes we shall vary its use by the synonymous term "Thought" capitalized as it is here, not in the sense of the *activity* of thinking, which remains uncapitalized here as "thought", but as its background.

Just as every human being possesses an outer life of wakeful activity and an inner life of passive dreamless sleep so does the World-Mind possess a corresponding twofold life. Its outer and active one is of course bound up with manifesting the cosmos. What is its inner and passive existence? The unity of the so-called unconscious with the conscious self in man provides us both with a key to the unity of these double aspects of the World-Mind and with an image of what reality is like. Man can turn his mental gaze outwards, when he sees a fragment of the universe spread out before him; or he can turn it inward during deep sleep, when he sees nothing at all being wrapped up in himself. Similarly the World-Mind can look outward and contemplate its own manifested ideas; or it can look inward and be absorbed in its own self utterly bereft of those ideas. Actually this analogy does not represent the whole truth however. For whereas man falls unconscious when he enters so completely into himself, the World-Mind does not but remains in a continuous and conscious, timeless and spaceless self-contemplation as pure absolute Mind.

Thus the World-Mind is not solely and entirely wrapped up in the cosmic image. We must distinguish between its exteriorized existence and its interiorized life, that is to say between the foreground of its attention concentrated upon its space-timed activity and the background of its attention concentrated upon its undisturbed stillness, between its terrestrial meditation and its celestial contemplation. The point may become clearer by considering what happens at the beginning and end of a cosmic period, the curtain whose rise and fall reveals or hides all things. When the World-Mind externalizes its attention, the karmic forces spring to life of themselves and evolve a cosmos; when it turns its attention inward the same forces retreat again into latency and the period of manifestation closes. During the ensuing disappearance of the cosmos the World-Mind contemplates its own absoluteness alone and knows nothing else. The first aspect is the World-Mind in alternating activity whereas in the second it is in primal repose.

The sharp distinction between the two phases exists only in existential expression, not in essential nature. It is in one sense like the sharp distinction between a man in sound sleep and the same man busily thinking and active. He himself remains essentially unchanged but what he is doing in one state and what he is doing in the other would make him seem to non-human beholders a different creature. Just as we have to treat man as a single being (mental) for philosophic purposes but as a twofold (physical and mental) one for practical purposes, so we have to treat World-Mind as a single entity from the philosophic standpoint but as twofold from the practical one. Both aspects are for us simply different ways of viewing it. This does not make one less important or less real than the other. They are distinct but not different from each other. Nevertheless this analogy is suggestive rather than exact. Whereas these two courses exist side by side perfectly in World-Mind they do not co-exist in a human being but hold sway in an alternating rhythm. Again, human thinking and activity are based on the five senses which in their turn have an extremely limited range. But the World-Mind's range goes far beyond and is above the senses. Consequently we must remember that the phrase "World-Mind thinks" means immeasurably more than it seems to mean. It is the movement of an infinite wisdom within an unlimited range.

To differentiate our thoughts about this double existence of World-Mind it is necessary to have separate expressions for them, but to avoid falling into the error that there are two different beings it is equally necessary to keep these expressions related to each other. Hence the hidden teaching simply drops the prefix from the name World-Mind and all limitations with it, leaving the simple truthful name Mind to stand for ultimate essence, absolute reality.

Thus Mind exhibits two aspects: the first as self-contemplative wherein it is aware solely of itself; the other as self-evolutionary wherein it progressively manifests the world and thus limits its own life and consciousness. The first aspect is sheer Mind-in-itself. The second aspect is Mind as it stands in inseparable relation with· the universe. The first we call Mind and the second World-Mind, but both are really one. We can arrive at a correct notion of God only by thinking of it in these two ways. If we regard it only as an infinite and transcendent being wrapped up in the static contemplation of its own perfection, remote and aloof from this finite world of ours, we see only a half of the truth. If we regard it as the universal energy working actively within every cell and every star, creating, preserving and destroying tier after tier of its space-timed universe, inspiring an evolutionary endeavour in countless series of conscious creatures, we see the other half. The World-Mind possesses both characters and is at once power active in the universe and absolute being withdrawn in rest. The immense difficulty of reconciling these two opposed factors exists however only for the undeveloped intellect, not for the unfolded insight. For the sage may discover by personal experience that his innermost self is static even whilst his outer person is active, and thus comprehend how the same opposites exist at the same time in the World-Mind.

Mind is the one thing which can produce a thousand other things which are all different from each other, and yet remain what it is in itself. It is in essence the Formless but by reflection the Formed. It is both the One and the Many, whichever way we wish to look at it. The universal existence therefore is a unity in diversity and a diversity in unity, a rest amid movement and a movement in the midst of rest. The world-picture is ever-changing but the screen on which the cinema picture is projected is ever-still.

Psychologically, all this may be summed up as follows: When

Mind is active in knowing and distinguishing one thing from another, it is finite consciousness. When it assumes forms and qualities, it is the things themselves. When it is centralized as an individual observer of these presented objects it is the "I". When it is centralized as the observer through the Overself of all the innumerable separate observers, it is World-Mind. When it is passively at rest, it is itself, Mind. The universe cannot help eventually but move from the Many to the One. This is why all life tends to the grand climax of blessed unity in the end.

The Fourth Gospel.

If we turn to the New Testament and particularly to that part written by St. John and commonly called the Fourth Gospel, we shall find some of these same thoughts expressed in another way. Its opening sentences: "In the beginning was the Word, and the Word was with God," plunge us immediately in the deep waters of the metaphysics of truth. For the universe is nothing but the outcome of divine ideation. The entire world is but a thought held by the World-Mind. But the World-Mind itself arises at the beginning of a cosmic period as a luminous thought in Mind. It is the first and last of all possible ideas, the one idea which includes and contains every other idea, however diverse it be.

Now every idea implies a corresponding meaning. The meaning of the universal process, that which gives significance to all existence and thus redeems it in the end, is the World-Mind. Furthermore, words are the expression of ideas. A word is a sign or a sound which stands for an idea. Hence the World-Mind is represented in St. John's sentence by "the Word".

Let us consider next that when human lips are shut and still there is silence and inactivity. This represents the ineffable silence and utter inactivity of Mind-in-itself, as well as of World-Mind in the state between two cosmic cycles. When the same lips open and speak, the silence is broken and the spoken word comes forth. This represents the opening of a cosmic cycle when the World-Mind arises and creative activity spontaneously begins anew. Until then the Supreme rested in its own mysterious timeless spaceless being, unbroken by events and therefore unbroken by any succession of past, present and future. But the manifestation of universal activity signifies the entry of some part of itself into time. That is to say, simultaneously with its own arisal the World-Mind holds the thought of a time and space order for the benefit of its creatures. Hence John's succinct phrase, "In the beginning was the Word."

Mind is the ultimate essence of everything, of every idea from the World-Mind itself downwards. John therefore equates it with the ultimate term which he knows: "God". Now whether the force we call the World-Mind lies concealed and latent in the illimitable and absolute essence out of which it arises periodically under an immutable law of its own being or whether it is actively engaged in the work of emanating a cosmos, it is as inseparable from that essence as the sparkling lustre is inseparable from a cut diamond. It forever abides with Mind. Hence John says, "And the Word was with God."

We found earlier that life and mind are twins, that the immense stream of energy which expresses itself in innumerable and diversified forms throughout the universe is one side of a coin of which consciousness is the other. Therefore John goes on to say: "In him was life; and the life was the light of men." For the World-Mind through its intermediary the Overself gives both life and consciousness to its projection, the person. This however is only the human application of this truth. There is also a universal one. When with the swing of the karmic pendulum the universe moves back into dissolution the World-Mind, *in its aspect as sustainer* of that universe only, moves back into dissolution too. The World-Mind as the activating intelligence behind the universe, appears and vanishes together with its manifestation. All that is left between two cosmic cycles is only its essence, Mind. The universe is its projection but it itself is also a projection, albeit the primal and *spontaneously self-originated* one. The World-Mind as such exists only therefore through all the millions of years that the universe exists. The two indeed rise and set together. Thus the whole universe exists originally as a germ inside the World-Mind and the World-Mind in its turn exists as a germ inside the Absolute Mind. This analogy however must not be taken too far as there exists at least one important difference. The Absolute does nothing to bring forth the World-Mind but the World-Mind appears spontaneously and periodically by itself according to an eternal law whereas the universe is emanated by the World-Mind's own active force. When the latter lapses again however it becomes the pure stillness of Mind.

The gradual unfoldment or evolution of the universe is really a gradual manifestation of the World-Mind itself, a mutual interplay of its own mental projections. So John says, "All things were made (i.e. manifested) by him." It is noteworthy that John does not say all things were made by *God*. Why he does not do so should be understandable in the light of the foregoing words. For the absolute Mind is concealed in everlasting repose. Mind in its own nature is inactive and self-sufficient, without need of anything, not even of self-expression. It abides utterly in and for itself. The active and expressive principle is something which arises out of it, the World-Mind, the "Word". We are not to think of World-Mind as having been deliberately created by Mind. That would be to think wrongly of it. We are to conceive its origin as self-born: it arose of its own accord.

Before a cosmic cycle begins there is literally nothing in existence, no forms of any kind and no conscious beings. This may be symbolically depicted by the darkness of night. The beginning of a cycle would then be symbolized by the sun's rising and its activity by the light of day. We may picture to ourself a point of light appearing in this boundless darkness and spreading itself out as an ever-expanding circle. There is nothing except our own limitations to stop this process of expansion going on to all infinity and to all eternity in our picture. In this analogy the primal point of light is the World-Mind at the dawn of its manifestation, while the ever-expanding circle is the universe as a process of Ever-Becoming. The whole cosmos exists potentially within this point, a possibility which our studies in the illusoriness of space must be drawn upon to vindicate. Hence the universe is continuously expanding and incessantly amplifying itself until the reverse process sets in and the cosmic cycle exhausts itself and finally closes. The vast ocean of light eventually retracts until it becomes a point once more. Then even this point vanishes.

We have spoken of these things as being symbolic. There is however a certain genuine actuality about this analogy. For the creative energy of the World-Mind is a force whose grosser manifestation we know as the various energies of the physical world. Light is the first of these energies. They are indeed its radiations. The fiery nebulae and the atmospheric electricity, for example, are generated in the end out of this primal Light. The seers of ancient Egypt, India and Iran knew the truth. The scientists of modern England, France and America are beginning to know about it.*

"In the beginning Ra (the Sun) raises himself," is the announcement in the Egyptian *Papyrus of Ani* anent the world's creation. The hieroglyphic characters for light and speech are identically the same. Hence in the Papyrus sentence just quoted Ra represents precisely what St. John calls "the Word". "Light thought, 'Would that I were many! I will create.' " is the announcement of the same event in the *Chandogya Upanishad*, an Indian text. And every high-caste Hindu is supposed to worship the Sun because it is the vesture of God. "God has created the world out of His own substance, that is His own thought, and the thought becomes Light," declared the prophet Zoroaster in Iran thousands of years

---

* See the author's *Discover Yourself* or *The Inner Reality* for recent experimental results quoted in confirmation of this tenet. There may here be added the following testimony of a distinguished scientist, Sir William Bragg: "Our distinction between radiation and matter becomes one of degree and not of kind. This widening of our view of the nature of things is surely one of the most remarkable consequences of modern research. Light, visible and invisible, electrons, matter itself, are now seen to have common properties and to be united in some manner we do not yet fully understand." Thus transcendental perception and laboratory discovery meet and verify each other. We live indeed in a veritable light-universe. This statement cannot be comprehended unless it is understood that there are two kinds of light-radiations: (1) the visible, (2) the invisible. The visible light-rays which form part of our familiar experience are feeble and fractionary when contrasted with the high-frequency rays—such as ultra-violet, X, gamma and cosmic rays—which are pouring throughout space. Hence the word "light" is used in a wider sense by modern physics than merely visible light. The spectrum which we can see forms but a small fragment of the entire range of electro-magnetic radiations. Therefore we must not misinterpret the word by narrowing down its meaning only to a concept drawn from our unaided human sense-experience.

ago. Since then his followers have worshipped light as being the one element of Nature in this gross material world which is nearest to Deity.

According to the present teaching this ever-luminous ultimate energy, this inexhaustible radiation from the ultimate reality of Mind is the World-Mind. It is the Original Light of which our sun is merely a single expression. Everything in the universe without a single exception has proceeded from it. This is why mystics who succeed in attaining sense-free intensity sometimes actually see this effulgent Light, either as a speck in the heart, a flash within the forehead or as an all-enveloping ocean. Such a vision, if authentic, is always accompanied by a great bliss but it rarely repeats itself once its significance has been grasped.

The space-time perceptions of human beings are too limited to comprehend that which is their infinite principle of life and thought. Most men are indeed totally unconscious of its existence. Few ever develop the insight which is needful to perceive that this is what makes their own existence possible and their own thinking possible. For the others, the multitude, there is only darkness where the few see light, only the failure to comprehend that the so-called non-existent is not only the concealed source of their own wakeful and dream consciousness but is also All-knowing and All-present being. This is what John means when he continues: "And the light shineth in the darkness; and the darkness comprehendeth it not."

We may summarize the situation so far reached by the statement that the fundamental principle of any and every existence may be thought of as sheer Mind when it is in repose and as the World-Mind when it is in motion; that Mind exists in and for itself whereas World-Mind exists in and for its manifested finite creatures; that Mind holds no object or second thing within its consciousness whereas the World-Mind manifests its cosmic idea as though it were an "other" not itself; and that Mind remains unbrokenly and timelessly the same whereas the World-Mind is active for tremendously prolonged periods during cosmic manifestation and then returns to latency according to an immutable law inherent in its own nature. According to the ultimate teaching, the length of each cosmic period constitutes one eternity. In this sense only can we say that the cosmos is eternal. But as the World-Mind itself spontaneously arises and disappears with the cosmos it too is eternal in this same sense. Hence the saying in the Egyptian *Pyramid Papyrus:* "I myself am Re, the Son of Eternity, abiding in all beings."

Although the World-Mind itself transcends all our human waking and dreaming standards of time, these time-orders still have a meaning and importance for it because of its progeny. Whilst it is thinking of its manifestation for their benefit, its own state is not timeless for timelessness is not the same as the totality of immensely varied time-series. Nevertheless the World-Mind never forgets itself in the innumerable forms it has taken; it always experiences the full measure of its own blissful repose. Paradoxically and to human intellect incomprehensibly, it is simultaneously self-aware as the pure principle of Mind. In the first state it contains all past, all future, hence no time-distinctions at all. The World-Mind as such endures eternally and pervades everywhere but as Mind it cannot even be thought of in connection with finite time and finite space! It transcends them utterly.

Time without events happening in it has no meaning. And time stretched out to the tremendous length of a cosmic period, that is to an eternity, will also have to be filled in with events of some kind. But it is still confinement within the time-order, however long-drawn-out it be. Timelessness is something quite different. It is that Infinite Duration in which Mind exists. "Endless Duration, Great Time swallows all the poisons of this world, otherwise the world itself could not exist," said an ancient Oriental Sage. The World-Mind is everywhere in space and everywhen in time. Mind is nowhere in space and nowhen in time. That is, World-Mind is eternal whereas Mind is timeless.

This principle of existence, whether as Mind, as World-Mind or as the series of manifested universes, is without beginning and without end. When the student takes to the path of enquiring: "What is the meaning of the world?" he reaches at length this perception of its endless nature as a cosmic process. The next step follows naturally and he then perceives that its essence ever was, is and shall be. But he himself is a part of the world. Consequently his own essence too shares this endless nature. It has not a perished past nor an approaching future but only a timeless Now. *It Is.* We can add no predicates to these short words. But why should our human weakness tremble at this inability? The Old Testament phrase "I am That I am" emphasizes the timeless Now and repudiates the "was" or "shall be" of the fleshly life. The timeless Now must not be mistaken for the passing present. It is that condition which is outside all time, outside all contrasts of past and future. It is not the same as the prolonged present. The latter belongs to a triad of before, now and after, the former belongs to a unity—infinite Duration. The old conceptions of time disappear before such serene contemplation. Once we understand that finite time is a form of thinking we may begin to understand that infinite Mind cannot be confined to any of its finite and transient ideas but must exist even when there are neither the thoughts nor the sensations to create time. Those who can comprehend this will also comprehend why it exists changelessly and timelessly. The Egyptian temple Mysteries symbolized this same timeless being under the picturesque figure of the impenetrably veiled goddess Isis, and it was ordained that no uninitiated man might lift this veil.

When we turn to time's twin we find that a similar extension of significance becomes needful. Infinite Duration is separable from Infinite Space. We know from our studies in dream and relativity that finite time and finite space vary according to the way in which they are experienced. That is, they are only ideas. Metaphysics takes all these notions and examines them. It finds a fixed time to be inadequate, a fixed space to be contradictory, a fixed material substance to be inconsistent, and therefore it rejects time and space and matter as being nothing more than appearances and as not being ultimately real. But just as finite consciousness points beyond itself to the Infinite Consciousness whence it roots out so do these three ideas point beyond themselves to their infinite ground. All spatial-orders therefore merely hint at but never exhaust the beginningless and endless character of Infinite Space itself.

Thinking outwards as far as we possibly can, imagining the utmost stretch of universal existence which we dare, that which remains will always still be as boundlessly vast as before. Whatever distance we may measure in cosmic space, that which is unmeasured will always remain unmeasurable. That is to say, Infinite Space is the easiest picturable *aspect* of the ultimate reality as Infinite Mind is its easiest understandable *concept*. For whether a cosmos exist to fill it or not, whether the ever-Becoming flows through it or not, Infinite Space *must* always exist. Whether we ourself are here to think it or not, it *is*. Although it eludes both senses and intellect nevertheless even the mere thought of it does offer a hint about the undimensioned ever-enduring and self-sufficient existence of reality itself.

Once we form a correct idea of Infinite Duration we know that it cannot be divided in any of the ways in which we can divide time itself. Duration transcends all possible measurement, multiplication or division. For the same reasons it is impossible to impose any measurement or division on Infinite Space too.

We gaze at the world through the coloured mental spectacles of "when" and "where" and do not comprehend that we see nothing as it really is. Such are the limitations under which our knowledge is received, such the conditions under which our thoughts arise! A further way in which we have to experience things and events is in a cause-and-effect connection. From a practical stand-point these three forms constitute the way in which we come to know the external world. In the case of the first two forms we have just learnt how when we ascend to the philosophical standpoint the matter assumes an entirely different aspect. This also applies in the case of the third form of experience. For then there is but a single real entity to be considered and nothing else. And when there are not two separate things existing there can be no twofold relation either and hence no such relation as causality, which depends on the prior existence of both a cause and an effect. It is easier to understand this by understanding what happens when we dream.

All the dream figures, events and things are after all nothing but the single essence—mind—out of which they were constructed and to which they were visible. From the standpoint of this mind it alone reigned and there never were two things at any moment; therefore causality could not have really reigned during dream and must be dismissed as a fiction. No real change occurred in the mind and no causal relation consequently ever came into being. But if we descend to the lower standpoint and consider matters from the point of view of the individual persons and things within the dream itself, then we admit the existence of a multiplicity for we perceive one thing acting on another and producing an effect and then we are forced to admit that causality does reign here. The same results follow analysis of wakefulness. Thus from the standpoint of the person causality exists but from standpoint of the person's essence it does not. If we accept the materiality of the world we have to accept the ultimate reality of all that goes with it, that is the personal entity and the relation of causality. If we ascend higher and regard the Overself alone, then the world is seen to be not different from it in essence and consequently the causal relation is seen to be an illusion. Hence personal karma, being based on causality, cannot operate here and the descent of grace which nullifies it becomes a possibility.

The Mysterious Void.

From these conceptions we may next ascend to the enigmatical climax of all this metaphysical teaching. It should now be clear that God is nothing that can be caught in our personal space-time net, nothing that can be seen, heard or touched; and we must think away all limitations from World-Mind's *essence* if we would catch even a hint of its true and perfect being. We must not try to put the ultimate into a strait-jacket by particularizing it into a shape, a time-order, an attribute or a creature. It is, so far as our human perception goes and so far as our human reflection can go, not this, not that. A world of changing phenomena cannot be a self-sufficient one, a world stamped by relativity cannot be an ultimately real one. Therefore the real world must be an absolute one where there is no change, no relativity, no time, no space, no thing that can change, no time interval between events that can be measured and no distance that can be calculated. But such an absolute thingless, timeless and spaceless world would be utterly empty when viewed from our side. Thought would come to rest not in a particular something but in a seeming blankness of being. If we think away all the form and solidity, the texture and taste, the smell and colour of any object, what remains? When every attribute and quality has thus been thought away, we are left with what is apparently an empty negation. There is nothing in this boundless empty silence for an observing intellect to take hold of. As there is no particular appearance in space or time and no intellectual image by which we can think of it, it looks like a blank nothingness bereft of all content. There is here no space for any shape and no time for any event simply because there is here no space-order and no time-series at all.

When we probe deeply into the nature of Mind we find that it is ultimately inconceivable, except by negating all its properties, which leaves a vast Void that is paradoxically the only existence. When the World-Mind is by itself in between the cosmic periods and has withdrawn its emanations, it too merges in this unfathomable Void. In this, its own ultimate state, the World-Mind comes to final rest. The sublime Silence which holds it, hears no sounds, sees no forms, observes no movements and performs no actions. There is here no distinction between one thing and another, one being and another, one creature and another. If therefore it be asked what was before the World-Mind the answer must be not nothing but No-thing-ness. For we cannot call it existence because there is nothing and nobody at all here to exist either as an experiencer or an experienced thing, either as a thinking being or as the ideas thought of. There is no room here for personality whether sub-human, human or super-human, for all separateness is utterly obliterated. It transcends all the relativities inseparably associated with such personality. Because this conception of the ultimate being deprives it of any kind of form in space and of any kind of existence in time; because it divests it of all relations with a second thing and of all that self against not-self background which is what *we* mean by consciousness, it seems indistinguishable from complete non-existence.

The intellectual conception of the Void at first always seems repulsively austere to human sense. It is associated—although quite wrongly—with conceptions like cold death and silent cemeteries. This reaction arises from the ingrained materialism of human sense, the incapacity to look beyond what it can see, smell, taste or touch. In the beginning few can face the concept of this vast Void without shrinking back in fear and fright. Yet it is necessary to face it until it becomes familiar and acceptable before we can pass on to the next higher degree of understanding. For it would be an error to interpret the term Void in a negative and nihilistic sense only. However paradoxical it may seem, there is a positive sense within it too. If the Absolute is so remote from all that we know of as existence, nevertheless it may not be rightly described as nothing. It positively is, although it has no individual existence. This notion of a formless and featureless Void is indeed ungraspable by the intellect and can only yield its profound meaning to a higher faculty of insight. For if it is the real nature of us all and if some in the past have come into its knowledge they were certainly not nothing nor was that which they knew non-existent. It must possess some kind of being therefore. According to a Tibetan text of this teaching, "Men created time out of Voidness: they themselves are Void. Those who understand this can dive deep into the element of Nirvana, which transcends relativity.''

It is admittedly not easy for our form-ridden consciousness to accept this notion that Nought is the equivalent of Reality, that Emptiness is the basis upon which all our wakeful, dream and sleep experience is built and not a solid ultimate material stuff, but once we thoroughly comprehend it we comprehend also that it solves the final enigma of existence. We must deny everything before we can understand everything. We must first find and affirm the Ultimate to be not this, not that, before we can find out what this and that really are. Nothing that is measurable, nothing that is finite, nothing that is formed can possibly be it. It is by leaving out all that is transient, by negating all that is familiar, that the final concept of all can be grasped. The Void is really un-nameable, for even this word itself is entirely a negative one and does not hint at the positive "Be-ness" which fills the actuality it represents and which has a real if mysterious existence of its own.

The mind cannot successfully represent an absolute void to itself for even when it believes that it has reduced everything to total blankness it is itself still there to think this blankness. At the very moment of thinking the Void the mind is actually itself filling the Void: By the very act of declaring nothing to be there the mind declares its own presence. By asserting that all is darkness it asserts the existence of its own light. We cannot think of a non-existent thing, for even if we declare it to be such we are at least thinking the idea of it. The notion of an absolute void is equally unthinkable for even if everything else were eliminated the thinking mind would still be there. The metaphysical meaning of thoughts lies in Thought. The fact that Mind appears to be a "nothing" is only our illusion for it is the final irremovable reality left when all else is thought away. The notion of utter non-existence is therefore fictitious and illusory. The idea of *absolute* annihilation is equally an illusory one. Even beneath the negative thought which we entertain there is an affirmative sense—the subtle sense of sheer being itself, the mysterious element of awareness whose mere presence enables us to utter this very world-denial. Thus there paradoxically *is* a residuum—the Mind-stuff out of which it is born—and this continues to exist unaffected by the disappearance of the particular forms into which it was temporarily moulded by our space-time consciousness, but without which it is *like* but not really no-thing. For all these properties which we have thus thought away are also limitations. That which is left over is Mind in its own pure intrinsic nature. Thus we see that this unlimited and infinite being must be unconsciously presupposed before we can know its limited and finite manifestations within and around us.

The Void is unique inasmuch as we cannot even set the idea of

Fullness against it even though the latter is contained in it. Thus everything we see around us has come forth out of the Invisible, which cannot therefore be a mere nothing. The Void is empty only of individual and separate appearances but not of the universal reality which is their original nature. The materialist notion of a stuff called matter which spreads out to fill empty space as water spreads out to fill an empty vessel may be matched against the mentalist notion that the Void itself is both potential stuff and potential space. Were we to remove every vestige of the universe with all its creatures from the lowest cell to the highest man, from the subtlest proton to the bulkiest star, ineffable mysterious Emptiness which would then remain would be Mind in its pure primal and unmanifest state. If there is nothing that is relative in the Void this is not the same as nothingness. The Real is still there, transcending all relativity. We may not call it non-existence because it is the permanent ground in which all things are rooted, the foundational boundlessness in which all lives are contained.

Beyond the senses of all creatures, beyond the ideation of man, this alone forever *is*. This then is the only real existence, all else being but an intermittent appearance within it. Just as in actuality the body of man cannot be separated from his mind, so in actuality the All cannot be separated during cosmic manifestation from empty Mind. A matured understanding must see the World-Mind under these double aspects. The universe exists during its period of manifestation in this Void like a cloud in the sky, but before this period it is wholly merged in Mind. Hence we read in Genesis: "And the earth was without form and void." We can trace things back to thoughts and we can trace thoughts back to our mind and that again to the Supreme Mind. Therefore we may say that from the standpoint of common experience Mind is the cause of the universe.

"The mysterious quality of Mind-Essence is that though you may look at it, you cannot see it," said a Chinese sage. Psychologically, the Void means that purity of the Mind where it is devoid of all the colourings of creative imagination, that cessation of forms, feels, tastes, smells and sounds which means the cessation of earthly consciousness, that vanishment of the world of ephemeral appearances which leaves only the world of everlasting reality. Mind in its primal state has no attributes, no desires, no will and no shape; it has no visible perceptible or conceivable individuality, no possible magnitude and no adequate name; it is not a thing graspable by hand or thought. The reason why in the utter stillness of the Void there is no past, present or future, no time at all, no space-orders and no forms to fill them, no manifestation or dissolution of the universe either, is that such activity exists only for and within the imagination of the individuals within them, not for the Void-Mind. Just as a dream exists for and within the imagination of the dreamer and the birth or death of a dream-figure does not involve the dreaming mind itself, so there can be neither birth nor death, neither passion nor desire nor sorrow in the Void but only in the thoughts which individuals rooted in it impose upon themselves.

Because the mentalness of all things is seen to be a fact, this does not mean that they are non-existent and because the mind-essence is invisible, intangible and incomprehensible to the bodily senses, this does not mean it is to be regarded as nothing. Things are not to be denied but understood. They are the transient *forms* which the everlasting mind-essence takes. They are certainly there but they are appearances which are doomed as forms to pass away but as essence abide everlastingly. The world is *actual*, it is vividly present to our eyes, ears, fingers, and yet it is nothing less than an appearance. We achieve a measure of understanding only when we arrive at acceptance of this paradox. Mind is not mere emptiness but the very reality itself behind all our world-experience. The Void is only a blank nothingness from the materialist standpoint, whereas it is the fundamental reality, the basis of all manifested existence from the mentalist one. It is also the universal state before universal existence itself arises. Paradoxical of course but perfectly true, the Void, the No-thing which we never experience directly, is ultimate reality whereas the All, the Every-thing which we commonly experience, is an appearance within it. Everyone sees the world-appearance but few catch the truth of it. The world's reality is not a self-existent or self-supporting one for it depends on the original Void-Mind and indeed arises from and is merged back into it.

What the unenlightened regard as substance, that is the form of things, is really its negation, whereas true substance, that the essence out of which those forms emerge, is disregarded by them as non-existent. The hardest barricade for our Western understanding to break through is this simple acceptance of the Unmanifest as ultimate reality. We think in terms of measurable forms and solids so habitually that we have lost the power to think in terms of undimensioned formless Thought itself, which is the unseen reality of all those forms and solids, the hidden rock on which they all rest. He who hopes to find the Real where it is not, among transient shapes and fleeting conditions which are but appearances in the mind instead of looking where it is in the Mind-Essence itself, is like the ignorant monkey which tries to catch the moon's image upon the water's surface.

Mind does not lose its formless placeless intangible empty character when it intermittently assumes the universe-related nature of the World-Mind. It is void of all forms, personalities and ideas yet paradoxically it is the root of all forms, personalities and ideas. There is no movement, no activity in it. Yet it contains the endless possibility of all movement and all activity. From nothing comes everything, from silence all sounds, from unconsciousness emanates consciousness; from zero all numbers, from invisibility everything visible, and from intangibility all tangible things. This is what the Buddha meant when he made the momentous declaration of Nirvana: "There is, O disciples, a something that is not born, not produced, not created, not compounded. Were there not, O disciples, this something not born . . . there would be no possible exit for what is born."

How is it possible for the Unchanging to become the Changing, for the Immobile to pass into Motion, for the One Mind to manifest itself so abruptly as the multiformed universe? Nature has given us a glimpse of the answer in giving us sleep. For there we ourselves experience how mind in its unified and undivided state breaks suddenly into a multitude of thoughts and things, when it breaks into dream or wakefulness out of deep slumber. The One splits itself up into the Many. The individual mind loses nothing of its own integrity by this apparent self-division. The universal Mind spends itself in the evolutionary existence but yet remains unimpaired, undiminished and unexhausted. Mind can manifest itself in various ways but although none of them make it any the less Mind yet all of them appear to be different from each other. This is like the figure 10 which can be expressed arithmetically as 5 x 2, 6 + 4, 20/2, 10 × 1, 7 + 3, and so on. All these formulae are different representations but amid all their permutations all are equivalent to the same result—10.

Many intellectual wings will cease to flap in this rarefied atmosphere. This cannot be helped. Man must renounce his littleness and touch the universal if he is to honour truth. But experience confirms that those who fail to fly here at the first attempt often succeed at the fifth, the tenth or the hundredth attempt. If perseverance conquers in the end it is because they are dealing here with something which is not quite so remote as it seems but does indeed pertain to their own innermost nature. We have to study the Real by progressive phases. Thus this aspect of it as a great Emptiness is not to be taken as the final one. Yet its comprehension constitutes a necessary stage in such a study and has a twofold result. First, by depriving the whole universe of all its material substance, it breaks down our innate materialism. Second, by reducing all separate things to a seeming void, it removes our last excuse for attachment to them. Thus it is not only a metaphysical stage to instruct us but also a disciplinary one to liberate us.

This seeming nothingness is the secret basis of the whole universe's existence, the original source whence it emerges, the last refuge whither it retreats. It is the first and last of all things, the Nought and the All, the only enduring reality whose presence Nature is always hinting at but never disclosing. Its infinitude is unutterable, its existence immutable and, to earthly sense, its mystery impenetrable. When therefore materialist science and unillumined metaphysics lay Nature out on an analytical dissecting table like a corpse for cutting up and later announce the results in the name of knowledge they gain everything except the one truth worth gaining.

The World-Mind emerged from Mind and the universe emerged from the World-Mind. This preposition "from" must not be taken literally however; it is only used for want of a better term. The universe has never been outside the World-Mind nor has the latter been apart from Mind. Any preposition used about it which possesses spatial implications is deceptive. In its first aspect World-Mind is the Nought-conscious whereas in its second aspect it is the All-conscious. For in the first it gives itself entirely to itself whereas in the second it gives itself to thought about what appears as an "other" to itself. If we may regard the World-Mind as itself a thought of Mind-Essence and the universe as a thought of the World-Mind, the universe then becomes a thought within a thought! The primordial Void becomes World-Mind and does not create it. The World-Mind becomes both the world and man and does not create them. Man's mind becomes his thoughts and does not create them. Thus the hidden circular thread of continuity which runs through them all is completed. Just as it is one and the same element which is manifest as vapour, as water and yet again so differently as solid ice, so it is one and the same Mind which is as the World-Mind and manifest as the solid universe.

If it be asked why the universe is so incessantly restless, so constantly in motion, we may now answer that this very activity is striving in various ways to move towards the original state whence it emerged, a striving which is unconscious in almost all the individual centres but which rises into self-awareness in the human being at a certain stage of his development. Thus the ever-becoming character of the universe is simply a sign that behind and beyond it exists the ever-still essence of empty Mind. For here the Divine reveals its own indescribable nature, undimmed by mists and uncovered by illusions.

The Real World.

What is reality? It cannot be something which is here today and gone tomorrow. It must be something which over-passes the periphery of time. The first mark of reality is that it has always been in existence. Something of this universe, whether it be visible or invisible, whether it be so-called matter or so-called spirit, must have had an everlasting existence. For if the contrary were the case, if nothing whatsoever had even once been the condition of universal history, then the universe could never have arisen for out of nothing only nothing can emerge. Even the most primitive intelligence demands some reason to account for things. Therefore the original "something" must have always existed and must still exist. This we may call the ultimate reality. It is the never-ending origin of the All. It is Mind.

There is no thought of anything without a corresponding negation of that thought, without an opposing contrast. Hence no idea is ever along but a second one is always alongside it. It can never exist by itself. It may be said that the second mark of reality is that it should be able to exist by and in itself. It should be in no need of anything beyond itself upon which it must depend. Its strength should lie in its self-sufficiency. What it is in itself and not as it reacts differently on different observers, is the Real. This lifts it quite out of the space-time world of relativities. Neither the three transient states of consciousness nor the numerous transient ideas generated by mind can therefore be the Real. They are always dependent and never self-sustained. We must seek deeper for their unknown everlasting ground. Because we have found both the wakeful and dream worlds to be nothing but the movement of thought-forms and because the enduring unchanging element not only of those worlds but also of our own self, has been found to be the element of undifferentiated Mind, then this alone constitutes their reality.

The world being an appearance, there must be something which appears. This "something" is the inner reality—Mind. This use of terms like *inner* self and *external* person, *inner* reality and *outer* appearance, innermost essence and manifested form, is, it must never be forgotten, only a metaphorical and not a literal one. They are terms belonging to the concept of space. And space itself being only an idea, space-relations must also be ideas. The intellect possesses this power to spatialize reality and externalize experience. Nevertheless it would be misleading to believe that this happens otherwise than in appearance, for the reality necessarily always remains what it was and is.

Forms, things and existences in space—all these are themselves thoughts and as such necessarily changing appearances, necessarily constitute a "becoming". To find the reality behind them we must depart from the Many into the One. And that can only be undifferentiated Thought itself. Thought in its ultimate essence is reality, being oneness, so majestically self-described in the words of an old Sanskrit text, the *Atma Prabuddha Upanishad:* "I am not Thought itself stripped of all restlessness; I am alone and constant; I am without a body or birth; I only am the essence of being; I am the ultimate truth."

It is clear then that the ultimate existence is Thought-in-itself in its purity and integrity apart from its operations and productions, in all its boundless infinitude. Although mentalism converts things into thoughts it does not declare the latter to be the final reality. They are something which that reality constructs for itself. Nor does it declare consciousness, as *we* know it, to be this reality but something which that reality puts forth from itself. Beyond both thoughts and space-timed consciousness lies their mysterious essence, which dwells in a changeless Here, an everlasting Now. This essence of all things is one and the same Thought, which appears both in the ego which sees them and in the things themselves. Mind is the totality of all experience, the starting-point and terminus of all existence, that which knows and that which is known. Yet paradoxically it is withal for man the unconscious and the unknown. If ideas are transient, the stuff of ideas, Thought itself, is not transient' but is their reality itself, as Hegel saw, and also ever eludes our thinking, as Goethe grasped. But this elusiveness is due more to our ignorance of what to search for than to our inability to attain it. The metaphysics of truth fills this lack and the philosophic insight sees clearly where unillumined thinking fails to see at all.

When thought is driven inwards from the diversity of things to think upon itself, it undertakes its last and loftiest task. For here alone shall it find tnat mystic unity which underlies and contains all those things. Insight reveals and reason confirms that all the multitudinous objects in the world are manifestations of a single stuff—Mind, which is perpetually manifesting hints of its own substance. When this is grasped then the very unceasing existence of the Many is seen to prove the everlasting existence of the One. The movements of ideas are seèn to evidence the unmoving observing element in the background. They constitute a dwarfed revelation of that against which they are seen and by which they are known. Every finite mind is thus a hint, to the profoundly reflective person, of the everywhere-present infinite Mind itself.

We may win access to the emptiness of undifferentiated Mind, to the Void, either through mystical trance or through philosophic insight. If this is done through the former channel alone then only its edge is touched and our consciousness of the world will be temporarily annulled so long as the trance lasts. This is why Indian mystics, to whom the trance state represents man's ultimate achievement, declare the universe to be illusory, shadowy and unreal. For Mind at this level has no sense of being discriminated into separate "I's", and does not cherish any consciousness of being split up into countless forms. It transcends the consciousness of all other existence. It never breaks its own unity by descending to awareness of the manifold and multiple world. In this respect it is like man himself who has no awareness of the thousands of cell-lives which are born and die every few weeks within his own body, although they are so intimately a part of himself. It is true that the *forms* by which we experience the world are no longer possessed by the entranced mind but nevertheless the World-Mind which imaged forth those forms and which is their essence still exists in the Void and still knows them. This means that the mystical declaration of the world's unreality is one of those uncertain statements which must be linguistically analysed if it is not to lead us into error. If this is done, the net result will then be that our experience of the world's appearance is ephemeral but our experience of the world's existence is essentially real.

Some leading Oriental sages not mystics among the ancients also emphasized the illusory character of this world and put it forward as the most prominent part of their doctrine. But, as earlier explained, this was done only as a temporary measure, to help aspirants break their bondage to belief in materialism, and more particularly their bondage to the body-thought, for at a later stage the same teachers taught that this same illusory world was none other than a form taken by reality itself. The teaching of the world's unreality was given to beginners and intermediates on this quest so as to persuade them to shift the emphasis of attention to the unseen reality, that is to say it was given as much because of its disciplinary value as because it was true of the *forms* taken by experience. It was a tentative and not a final teaching. For at a later stage it was withdrawn in favour of the doctrine that all is of one substance, all is essentially real. Mentalism follows a similar course to that of these teachers and after converting matter into thoughts, it converts thoughts in Thought.

The metaphysical separation into Reality and Appearance, into Being and Becoming, as much as the mystical separation into Spirit and Matter, God and Illusion, must now be recognized for what it is—a tentative antagonism and not a final one. The student who can rise so high must now transcend even this distinction. He must see all things as not-different from the original Mind-Essence, must embrace them in a single realization with the essence itself. When we give up the traditional dualistic conception which has ever dominated mystical thought. The term "fallacy" is used only from the philosophic standpoint for every concept possesses a kind of truth on its own level. For the method of progressive revelation to suit a particular stage of understanding which was followed by wise men of all times, had a place for all views within its ample folds. The simplest mentality was provided with an explanation of the universe which was based on the existence of crude solid matter alone. The more matured mentality was provided with a more refined explanation which introduced the intangible element of Spirit as a force which interpenetrates and activates tangible matter. These were and are the two fundamental views of the universe upon which all kinds of variations and modifications have been made. But the third and philosophic view begins to present the universe in terms of consciousness, at first with the teaching that all we know are our own ideas but that these ideas are true copies or representations of material objects existing outside consciousness, with a unifying ground for everything in Spirit. But finally the advancing mentality is taught to get rid of all these materialist, semi-materialist and composite conceptions and advance boldly towards the ultimate

All the present-day human suffering on such a tremendous scale is due in the end to defective remembrance. Mankind have *forgotten* what they really are, whence they came and whither they are going. It is one purpose of writings like the present effort to help a little to restore such lost memory. For that which begins as recollection will end as recognition.

13

Initiation into Mystical Experience

WHEN a man attains the serious conviction that this ultimate ever-present and all-pervading principle behind and beyond the universe is sheer Mind, his very earnestness will naturally lead him one day to ask such questions as: Can I come into a personal relation with this transcendental reality? Can I transform the theoretical understanding which has so far been gained into a practical and conscious realization?

The answer of philosophy is clear and definite. It not only affirms that such a relation and such a transformation can undoubtedly be consummated but that they are the ever-shining goal of all philosophic endeavour. Therefore the primary duty of a thoughtful man is and shall forever be to seek this consummation. It is for this supreme self-fulfilment that he is here on earth at all, this is the glorious task which he has to accomplish above all other tasks, and this alone shall provide him with a genuine profit from his commerce with the tribulations and temptations of an all-too-brief existence.

How then can he come into first-hand knowledge of the Real? To find the answer we must first turn back to *The Hidden Teaching Beyond Yoga*, where the available sources of knowledge were progressively traced through authority, logic, pseudo-intuition, intuition and mystical experience. The work showed some of their chief merits and demerits and stressed the necessity of using reason as a check upon the others. The term "reason" was interpreted in its widest sense as the active functioning of human intelligence, stretching from the practical-scientific pole to the abstract-metaphysical one Care was particularly taken to point out that its use was not to be confused with the use of logic. The uncertainties of logic will for ever render its operation an unsatisfying one. He whose inspiration is derived from logic alone will never speak the language of complete assurance. Whoever looks for the ultimate truth rather than the mere preponderance of probabilities will become sick of syllogistic procedures in the end. In the words of an ancient document of this teaching, logic—as an instrument of ultimate truth-finding — leads only to "mere weariness of the tongue". Consequently the fact was emphasized that reason is superior to logic and that no man, whether he be a hard materialist or a soft mystic, can afford to dispense with it. His senses plainly tell him that sky and land meet at the horizon, but reason just as plainly tells him that this is a misapprehension of experience. Thus reason is one of the most important means whereby he may unfold his innate gift of intelligence, a gift which comes from the hands of God and not, as some believe, from the hands of Satan. Such an unfoldment will enable him to co-operate increasingly with the general evolutionary trend of cosmic life. The years when he comes to rational maturity are his best mental years as those when he comes to bodily maturity are his best physical ones. "The superiority of man rests on the jewel of reason," remarked the Emperor Akbar, one of India's most outstanding Muhammadan rulers. We concluded therefore that when purified from prejudice and egoism, when adequately based on a sufficiency of facts, and when appropriately used in combination with and in control of external authority, asserted intuition and mystical experience, reason is ordinarily man's most valuable guide to the adequate understanding and proper conduct of life.

But at the same time we hinted at the existence of *insight*, a faculty which although now merely latent in mankind will transcend all others when developed. It is needful to explain why reasoned knowledge has its own special limits and part of the business of metaphysics is to tell us what those limits are. When, for example, in the companion volume it was maintained that science must rise to the level of metaphysics and that metaphysics must take care to ascertain its starting facts with scientific accuracy and to collect them with scientific thoroughness, this did not mean that metaphysics is to be limited solely to a mere synthesis of the data collected up to the present day by all the various sciences, making it in fact nothing more than a generalization of existing scientific knowledge. It would be absurd to regard such a generalization as ultimate truth and its absurdity should be apparent to anyone who has absorbed the contentions explicit in the chapter dealing with relativity. For then metaphysics would share with science all the dangers which lurk in the latter's specialism, all the relativistic limitations implicit in space-time observation and experiment. Each of the five senses can only cut out certain definite details from the world which is given in experience; it cannot grasp the whole of experience at any particular point in time or space. Consequently it deals in the end only with such cuttings. Were metaphysics to be based only on science, it would then become a one-sided affair and fail to achieve that all-embracing comprehensiveness which should be its aim. It would become a glorified branch of science masquerading under a different garb. Again the scientific method cannot *alone* suffice for metaphysics because being analytic it deals with parts and thus overlooks properties which belong only to "wholes" and also because it treats with things only as sense-experienced facts and ignores their ultimate *meanings*. That music, for example, is more than a series of noises is something which only art and not science, only feeling and not reason, can appreciate. The intellect can calculate, measure and analyse quite effectively tangibles like salt and sugar, for that is its province, but it cannot effectively calculate, measure and analyse intangibles like unselfish love and musical charm, for here it is blind, deaf and dumb. It may, however, believe that it is able to do these things, but this is only a self-deception. For then it will be dealing only with its cold conception *of* them, its dead ideas *about* them. Still less can it deal in actuality with a transcendental principle like the Overself.

Finally the futility of making science the sole instead of a partial basis of metaphysics is evidenced by the impossibility of reaching any complete totality of scientific facts. These are always changing or increasing and consequently the knowledge based on them is altering too. Science as such can never get all the facts. The scientist who would attempt faithfully to find *all* the factors which go to the making of even a simple thing like a lump of rock crystal would probably find himself in a lunatic asylum. A final and fixed collection of all the *individual* facts about the universe is unattainable and hence sense-based knowledge must always remain partial and incomplete. The feat of compassing all the facts is an impossible one for science, which therefore is and must always remain imperfect. A perfect metaphysic cannot be based on science alone; it must embrace even what is yet unknown to science.

But if science, as the expression of concrete reason, cannot alone lead us into ultimate truth, neither can its higher octave, metaphysics, as the expression of abstract reason, do so. To explain this point we must revert again to the first volume. Those who deplored the space therein devoted to the analysis of word-meanings may have since begun to notice how useful such analysis is to the philosophical enquirer. If we went at greater length into it then the subject seemed to warrant, it was only to get readers to question their commonest experiences because they take such experiences far too readily for granted. In the foregoing metaphysical studies we have been forced to weigh certain words with scrupulous care. And the results have proved to be of much importance to fact-finding in our quest. For example, we have seen how the simple statement "I see a tree before me" will if properly analysed lead its utterer all the long way from materialism to mentalism. It is no simple process being simple! It is immeasurably easier to see a tree than to understand all that is involved in the act of seeing it. The whole wonder of world creation lies hidden in this little operation. The whole problem of the universe yields its final solution when this short three-letter word "see" is made to yield its own final meaning. Indeed the whole of *The Hidden Teaching Beyond Yoga* is nothing less than an extended application of semantics to the statement: "I see an external world." It is an attempt to get at the meaning of these disarmingly simple words. The value of this attempt will be vindicated by our final results. We have also seen how the glibly-vocalized word "God" will, if only the man who uses it can be got to attend to its meaning, lift him up from the concept of a humanized caricature of the Supreme Mind to the concept of the pure Mind itself. When we begin to get behind the masks of words to that which they really represent, when we begin to state a problem with an adequacy which conventional or careless language seldom attains, we begin to light up obscurities and remove difficulties.

There is a still higher reason why we must ask ourself to separate the meaning from the word. However useful such semantic analysis may be in clarifying metaphysical thought and correcting general error, this is not its final or most important use. But the higher use could not have been thought out until the present point in our studies was reached, Mind, the ultimate reality, transcends all individual thoughts because it is their pure undifferentiated source, because they are tied to relativity whereas it is absolute Consequently truth, as the knowledge which reveals the nature of reality, will not live up to its name if it merely offers us a collection of particular thoughts and not that which is the essence of all thoughts. All thinking of any kind whether scientific or metaphysical can in the end only provide us with a conclusion that is itself merely another idea, that is a thought. People talk of rising from higher to still higher truths, and of discovering more and more truth. What they really discover are higher *intellectual conceptions* of truth. But these are only ideas in their minds. This is not the same as truth itself. There is only one ultimate truth, not two. The intellect offers a reality which can never be a felt reality but only an indirectly reflected or verbally described one and then only in negative terms. When we ask intellect to seize, express or give conceptual form to ultimate reality, we ask it to perform a function which transcends it; consequently intellect must here break down and something higher take its place if we are to push on toward the successful completion of our quest. Reason, even of the most metaphysical kind, must at this point realize its own ineffectiveness to cope with the Real, which is the unthinkable, the untouchable, the unnamable. Ultimate truth being outside the relations and oppositions of space-time things escapes the grasp of thinking, which can deal only with such relations and pairs of opposites. It is these alone that constitute meanings for the mind. But when the mind has wholly returned its attention on itself, there is identity, not relation; unity, not duality. Consequently in this absoluteness no separate *particular* meaning can form itself. Mind can know that it *is*, but not that it is this or that. For any added significance would limit its infinitude. But thinking and meaning are expressed in words, nay, are interlocked with the use of words. Whatever is explicable by words is only a thought construction and as such subject to all its limitations. The Real, however, is also the unlimited. Therefore, all instruction and revelation given in verbal form, all learning dependent on verbal communication, all so-called union with God which needs verbal communion, must not be mistaken for the genuine knowledge of truth. We must beware not to deceive ourself into thinking that because we have intellectually laid hold of a meaning we have therefore laid hold of truth: we must not take the word for the thing. Hence we have the right, when anyone talks of God, divinity or reality, to probe semantically into his use of these words and ascertain whether he speaks out of inward understanding of what he is talking about, or merely makes a babbling noise in the air or simply runs after verbal shadows on paper.

It will be easier to ascertain this fact successfully with the keys now placed in our hands by these advanced studies. If the immediate purpose of such analysis is to shatter the materialism and illusion embedded by ancient habit in man through his use of language and so silence his unreflective utterance of such words as matter, time, sight, experience and Spirit, thus leading him eventually to change his views, the ultimate purpose is to show that what can be put into words is only the graven image of reality, never reality itself. That whatever we can formulate into phrases must be *a* thought, never pure illimitable Thought. That whatever we can speak of cannot be the indescribable element which makes all speech possible. For where is the room in thinking or speaking for such an unlimited and unlabellable principle? Where is the mould into which we can possibly press the infinite No-thing-ness? Whatever idea we form about it in consciousness will in the end be but a string of empty unfilled words, nothing more. The moment we think of Mind as being this or that by nature or as having this particular quality or that special attribute, we inevitably affix a limitation upon it. And this would falsify our understanding of what is utterly limitless. The truth is that so far as words can go, we can only correctly say that Mind is, not what it is.

Again, whether we describe the World-Mind as being ever-resting or ever-active, we are making only mental representations of what is really unrepresentable. Anything that can be written down cannot be a statement of ultimate truth; at best it can only be a statement of someone's idea of truth. Every word which is uttered about that Infinite Being is, if given as it must be given a relative meaning, a deception and not a description. Hence all writing by a pen and all utterance by the lips can only hint suggestively at it, never explicitly express or adequately explain it. For all that can be put between the hard walls of words are intellectual concepts alone. Let us be wary then. Thinking touches a profound mystery here. It cannot affirm that the Ultimate is like this or that but equally it dare not deny anything to the Absolute either. Here its antennae have stretched their farthest towards a shoreless sea. It may declare only that supreme Mind IS. And such a grave declaration is perhaps the most important it has ever been called on to make.

We have earlier seen how every word-meaning inevitably implies the existence and calls for the contrast of a second and opposite one, which is inseparable from it. Without this "other" it could not indeed explain itself. The word "white" for example assumes significance for us because it differentiates itself from "black". No meaning can exist unless its opposite also exists. But here, in nameless wordless silent Mind, we find the sole and only exception to this rule, the self-existing element which has no opposite at all because everything emerges or dissolves in it, the self-explanatory significance which is undifferentiated from any second thing, the unique Idea which not only shines by its own and not by a borrowed light but also illumines all other ideas because it is the unnoticed consciousness present in them, the unbounded Meaning in which all lesser meanings float as in an unbounded ocean. The Real cannot be discriminated as against a second thing: hence we cannot apply any names, i.e. words, to it. We cannot say that it possesses any particular property without implying that it does not possess the opposite property. But if it be really illimitable and absolute how can we rightly exclude anything from it? Consequently we are compelled not to stick any descriptive spoken label at all to it, but rather to let ourself fall into a significant silence on this matter.

Where both Jesus and Buddha kept their sublime silence whoever breaks it must pay the penalty. It is not hard to understand why they refused to enter into such discussions. They knew well that any possible statement affirming something about it would—such being the limitation of language—necessarily exclude something else. This would theoretically convert the unlimited into the limited and hence falsify the teaching about it. For here they were dealing with a region beyond the sphere of human sense-based thinking consciousness and the question naturally asked by all as to what happens within it to this particular consciousness is meaningless and inappropriate. And here they were dealing too with a region which cannot in any way be brought within the time-series, for there is nothing within it that can be chronologically placed as being before or after, just as there is no idea of time or succession within the deep sleep state. Mind can find perhaps some kind of expressive but still only symbolic utterance in silence or in action, but nobody will ever be able to utter the lost Word, the mysterious Name of God itself. Strive as we may it is impossible to form any clear and coherent idea of that which transcends all finite ideation. The Ultimate is unanalysable. We cannot make it into a positive conception. This Consciousness which transcends all space-time consciousness cannot be caught in an intellectual test-tube and passed round for every prying curiosity-seeker to handle.

The student should not forget however that the present explanations are not only intended to stimulate his own rational thinking upon the subject but also to awaken his own intuitions about the subject. Consequently it has been necessary to steer a way between that minimum of explanation without which he will remain in the dark and that maximum with which he may remain in a self-deceptive light. The metaphysical work of reason is to prove to us intellectually that something exists which the reason itself cannot grasp because of its super-intellectual character. This is indeed the loftiest service reason can render. Therefore it fulfils itself when it humbly points like a stretched-out finger beyond itself. And even if the conceptual figure of reality with which it provides us is only a figure and nothing more, the possession of a correct figure is immeasurably better than the possession of a wrong one or of nothing at all. And this indeed is what our efforts so far have really sought to achieve, which is not a useless undertaking.

If now we turn back to our studies in consciousness and to the relation between the hidden observer and its projected person-ality, we may further comprehend why it is that the latter is so completely unaware of the former and why it is that we never catch ourself in the very act of being truly self-conscious in this diviner way. The personality is continuously plunged in giving itself up to physical sensations or to the memories or anticipations of those sensations so that the experience of its own inward essence is continuously missed. It is always outward turned and never inward turned except in sleep. It is too absorbed in the ever-changing spectacle of the outside world to become a spectator of itself. For our whole being is absorbed in getting experience of the external world through the five senses, our whole attention is extroverted and turned away from the hidden innermost self, our whole life consists in a flight from the Mind within the mind. In such a condition the "I" cannot observe its surface life any more than a sword can cut itself. It always knows itself only as mixed up through the senses with the external world. It is consequently never genuinely and purely self-conscious. Completely to with-draw attention from the world, to turn round and bestow it upon its own self, the "I" would first need to shut down all those senses—an act which ordinarily causes it to yield to sleep or swoon. But such states are ordinarily useless for the purposes of conscious self-knowledge, however useful they may be for the purposes of bodily rest or thoughtful reflection about self-knowledge.

We are indeed like sleeping men when we compare our present field of awareness with the field of its possible extension. The hidden observer knows the person but the person does not know it. How can he get at it? For it is not like a stone pebble which we can pick up in our hand, not like any object which possesses the experienceable qualities of roundness, smoothness, hardness and so on. Compared with a pebble, Mind-in-itself is like a great nothing. For it can neither be seen or measured nor weighed; indeed it possesses no sense perceptible qualities at all. It is the most mysterious element in our mysterious existence. Our difficulty is that this pure awareness, this ever-present principle which enables us to know all experience, is not easily thinkable because it is not easily picturable. We can assign it neither dimension nor shape, neither beginning nor end. If therefore both science and metaphysics, both concrete and abstract reasoned thinking are revealed as unfit to provide a conscious return to such subtle reality, we must pick up the original questions and ask how this possibility is to be realized. For after the foregoing considerations reason will find itself wondering whether the Real is something which exists only to tantalize men from an unalterable distance, to mock them by offering itself only for fruitless speculation and not for first-hand experience, and whether thinking is to be left trembling on the verge of a bottomless chasm which it is forever unable to cross.

The answer which philosophy hopefully affirms leads us out of the impasse in which we find ourself. The absolute Mind is called unknowable only in the sense that neither the senses nor the intellect can directly know it. We may seek it through a quite different approach. The principle of awareness, being by itself unjoined to any particular idea or special form, must be known in a different way from that whereby we know the ideas and forms which are its objects. Where reason fails miserably to *think* the Overself because it cannot, it may however *become* the Overself by humbly merging into it. When this happens, luminous being supplies the answer which limited thinking cannot. We must ourself become absorbed, and with us all our baggage-train of thoughts, in that which is the hidden basis of both thinking and experience. The attempt to know the hidden observer must alter into an attempt to become it. That is to say, the distinction between the observer and the observed must disappear, the object of thought must dissolve into primal Thought itself, knowledge and being must unite with each other. The "I" and its transcendental father, the ego and its eternal witness, must somehow wed. Then only will there be an inward knowledge by self-identity of the lower with the higher. Then only can the "I" become aware of the sacred presence within its innermost shrine. Such is the path to which philosophy's extended hand beckons us.

The element of awareness must introspect into itself, the terrestrial personality must coalesce with the celestial source which it seeks to know. Now such a demand would ordinarily be regarded by Western psychology as an absurd one. Its science knows only of particular awarenesses. Consequently it refuses to admit that there is such a thing as the activity of bare awareness itself. It is perfectly right from the standpoint of its own thumb-and-fingers experience but perfectly wrong from the standpoint of sense-transcending mystical experience. Here there-fore the hidden teaching is forced to part company with science, which by the very nature of its activities is too shortsighted to discern the flies in its intellectual amber. For it knows from its own ancient tradition and modern experiment that such introspection *is* possible, that if the right conditions are first provided the power of making this element self-aware, independently of and aside from any particular object of awareness, may be unfolded. Such an exalted aim is set before itself by philosophy through a three-fold approach which yields insight into the Over-conscious as its result. That something exists whose intrinsic nature is so transcendental that it is not to be apprehended by human thinking need not now astonish us. That it may be apprehended by a profounder form of perception will not astonish us when our intellectual course is completed. This power of apprehension which is latent in all men although active in few, is such a form. The term "insight" is used for it primarily because he who possesses it can see what *is*, not merely what appears, can *see into* the inner reality behind the world-appearance which our image-making faculty has super-imposed upon it, can clearly feel the eternal life-essence within all the transient planetary forms. Sight is a function of the body, understanding is a function of the intelligence but insight is a function of the Overself. In the ancient hidden teaching the use of this faculty was originally called "opening the eye of transcenden-tal knowledge". The difference between an intellectually reached truth and a philosophically reached insight is like the difference between poring over a printed map of Rome and actually making a personal visit to Rome. Reason works by grasping one thought after another, whereas insight pierces at once like a sharp arrow through the thick hide of appearance. When man *reasons* about an object he arrives at knowledge only after the reasoning is finished, that is after a certain period of time has elapsed, whereas when he *sees* the same object the resultant knowledge of its existence is immediate and instantaneous. The supreme insight is like the stripping of a veil whereupon something not before presented to consciousness is seen, felt, understood and coalesced with at one and the same moment.

Where the intellect struggles in vain to grasp what is beyond both thinking and explanation, this insight with lynx-like keenness successfully perceives it in a single illuminative flash. With its final maturation there comes to an end all study in the realm of relative truths. For it yields a truth which is the unique all-embracing Whole in which all possible relative views can find a place and of which all the contending doctrines are really, if unconsciously, attempts at interpretation from different levels of thought. Where the intellect must go on endlessly collecting and comparing items of knowledge, insight disdains all particularity because it per-ceives that which affords the possibility of all knowledge and which is the ground of all things experienced—the secret Mind itself. This reality which ultimately rests behind yon dusty earth, that crimson flower, those toiling men; which makes them in proportion seem as mere shadows flung for a few moments on a screen, which scoffs at all the efforts of inquisitive scientists to detect it; which theologians have surrounded by impenetrable mystery and metaphysicians have gazed at in despair from a remote intellectual distance; which is the central tormenting enigma that turns thoughful men dizzy and weak men mad; which drove Herbert Spencer to declare finally, in his bewilderment, that it was and would forever remain "the unknowable"; which will yield neither to the bold advances of intellect alone nor to the frenzied call of emotion alone; this grand arcanum cannot nevertheless escape us in the end because it is the Mind within our own mind, the Self over-shadowing our own self.

The Three Stages of Meditation.

Thus we have reached a point where only some kind of trans-intellectual, that is some kind of mystical experience, can make sense of our declaration that this Mind is conscious and realizable in a positive sense. A reference to the dictionary gives the meaning of "realize" as: "to feel as vividly or strongly as if real; to bring home to one's own experience; to acquire as the result of labour or pains". Consequently we must now journey to the fresh waters of such a personal realization of Mind and leave behind the dry desert of merely thinking about it. Hence it will be necessary to speak now of ways and means of obtaining this kind of psychological experience. It is not enough to secure an intellectual conviction of the truth of mentalism. We have to secure also a practical experience of it. But the soul that seeks to soar up from our grubby earth to the pure empyrean must needs gain wings. No animal possesses this inner mystical eye which man possesses; hence no animal can ever behold the elusive reality of pure Mind which is the ignored essence of its own uncomprehended selfhood. In opening this new and transcendental faculty of insight lies the unique opportunity of human birth, which we may waste in the pursuit of ephemeral things or capitalize in the quest of divine ones.

Now manifestation means limitation. When the World-Mind manifested a universe, it had to manifest a bounded one. When the Overself projected the person it has to self-limit a fragment of its own consciousness. Hence the moment the person turns inward to aspire towards and contemplate upon its own origin and nature, that moment it has the glorious possibility of fulfilling the ultimate promise of its own limitation, evolution and involution. This necessarily involves detaching consciousness from the five senses which principally contribute to the materialist illusion. Without this there can be no personal realization of mentalism but only an intellectual echo of its truth.

We must learn the art of retreating from the sensuous and surface existence. This is best done through deliberate self-discipline. The broad threefold lines on which philosophy carries out this discipline will not only lead to the accomplishment of such an aim but also to the larger one of developing insight. They run parallel to and do not succeed one another. They are first, the re-direction of thinking, second, the re-direction of practical activity, and third, the re-direction of feeling. The first is achieved by metaphysical reflections of a mentalist character such as those recorded in the foregoing pages. The second is achieved through the abnegation of the personal will in a certain way which will be described in its proper place towards the end of this volume. The third is achieved by educating the attention through the employment of regular exercises in meditation or yoga, as it is called in India, and will be described now. Yoga is a twofold term, meaning both the process and the result to which that process leads. Yoga as a set of mental practices to be followed is one thing and yoga as the unified condition of mind which is the final fruit of those practices is another thing. Yoga as a process calls for constant efforts to achieve inwardly-turned mental concentration and as a result it yields its practiser a serene condition where thoughts subside and thus reveal the diviner background which their activity hides. When the mind is active we have thoughts; when it is still the thoughts vanish. Few have ever *consciously* attained this utter stillness of the mind's natural state and so few know what they really are. Yoga in its best sense is simply the deliberate attempt to accomplish this task and thus become conscious of the so-called "unconscious".

Who has not lost himself in some pleasant reverie or got wholly absorbed in completely pleasant intellectual work? Who has not then lost count of time, almost forgot his surroundings, over-looked his standing worries and perhaps even failed to notice something of his physical pain? This is an experience which has happened to most people. At such a time they are unconsciously practising meditation. Elsewhere we have pointed out that it is really the beginnings of a yogic experience only with the yogi it is deliberate and controlled whereas with others it is involuntary and uncontrolled. It indicates in its subtle way that when we are entirely wrapped in our inner self to the exclusion of the things, people and events around us with our mind concentrated upon some congenial idea, we tend to accept ideas as being the only realities. Definite and detailed instructions how to practise the art of meditation have already been given in three of the author's earlier books so it is unnecessary to recapitulate them here. But during the years since those books were written both a wider experience and a careful study of the efforts and results reported or observed among numerous students all over the world renders it most desirable to clarify certain rules, correct some misapprehensions and stress a few leading principles in a brief review of this art, which is still so unfamiliar and obscure to the average Westerner. The key to success in yoga is fashioned partly from the natural capacity for concentration which we bring to the task, partly from the energy with which we pursue it but more especially from repeated and regular self-training. Said so supreme an authority upon this subject as the Buddha: "Nothing know I that without exercise would be more inflexible than the mind. Nothing know I that by being exercised would become more flexible than the mind." Theorizing is useless; one must sit down and practise daily. If he does so and correctly even for only six months, good results will accrue. People have only to begin to make up their minds sufficiently that they would like the fruits of yoga to begin to put the rules of yoga into practice.

But meditation calls for a place and time in which to meditate; it must indeed be made into a habit as regular as the habit of taking meals, as attractive as taking dinner. The student cannot afford to leave its practice to chance moments or to occasional empty ones. This may call for a little re-arrangement of the day's programme; it may put him to a little inconvenience, but whatever it demands it will certainly give back much more. Habit rules human life. The man who has learnt the secret of creating new habits is able to control that which controls life. And among the best habits a man can make is that of meditation. We would not only emphasize but over-emphasize the value and urgent necessity of introducing this habit into modern life. Doubtless there will be difficulties in finding time. Most people have constructed a network of activities and pleasures around them from which escape is not easy. Some are certainly essential but others are often not. A sense of proportion is needed. The same man who complains that after a day's activity at unavoidable work or inescapable business he is too tired to take up meditation practices will reply if asked to do them in the morning instead, that he is then too busy dressing and breakfasting. In the end he cannot do them at all! Were anyone to promise him a substantial reward for each practice faithfully performed, however, it would be astonishing to watch how soon he would manage somehow to find time. He would curtail the inessential, rise a little earlier or do something else. For he would no longer give his time grudgingly to these practices but gladly. They are irksome only when he sees no swift or tangible reward in their train. A change of mental attitude towards them is therefore necessary. These exercises should in the beginning be practised daily at the same place and at the same hour but when enough progress has been made this rule may be ignored and the work may be done at any time and in any place. No monastery is needed for it. A room in which a half-hour can be spent alone morning or evening will be better than an ashram. For the progress made in such an artificial retreat will often be illusory and may even crumble to pieces at its first thorough testing in the outside world, whereas the progress made in the midst of ordinary duties and in spite of environmental opposition will be hard-forged.

There are certain physical hindrances to settling down to this practice and whilst they are present the attention will be diverted to them instead of to the proper theme. The first hindrance is noise. Each external sound becomes magnified during the internal quiet of meditation. Hence a silent convenient spot should be chosen. The meditator must have environmental seclusion if he is to fulfil his higher rather than his lower possibilities. The second is the active movement and sudden intrusion of other persons. He must be undisturbed during the practice period and this is best ensured by locking himself in a room. The advantage of choosing such a place for meditation is that no one can then enter to derange his thoughts or to detract from their central theme. This also is not a rule laid down for all time however but only as a preliminary and essential counsel concerning the aspirant's earlier efforts. It will become less important and less operative as he ascends into the advanced stage. The third hindrance is a fidgety swaying or fitfully turning body. This is most serious when it affects the head. Therefore it is better to keep the spine erect. If a stool or a chair is used, it should be as low as is convenient for one's legs. The student may rest his back against a wall if he is squatting or against the back of his chair if sitting. For, when the highest stage of meditation is reached, it is necessary to secure steadiness of the body because the consciousness enters a delicate and sensitive state where even a slight physical movement immediately disrupts the attainment. This is also one of the reasons why the cross-leg ankle-intertwined posture is used by the Himalayan (Indian yogis). It provides a firm stable seat when consciousness is partially withdrawn from the five senses, when bodily fluctuation would throw awareness back into the senses again. In their case the uprightness of spine is also sought because they seek through intensive breathing and will-power exercises to drive the vital force latent in the sex organs upwards along the spinal cord to the top of the head, thus sublimating and spiritualizing it.

A fourth hindrance is ill-health. The pains and unrest and malfunctioning of the body may become strong enough to distract attention to themselves so utterly as to render meditation an impossibility. Modern students who have to get rid of this hindrance of ill-health must avail themselves of all the knowledge and help, orthodox and unorthodox, which exists today, not forgetting that this is a region where personal karma is often particularly active. Paradoxically, however, there are not a few cases where the enforced leisure supplied by illness has successfully promoted meditation whilst the disgust for the body provoked by illness has actually made the mind meditative for the first time.

These physical hindrances to concentration are sometimes more easily remedied than the emotional ones, but sometimes not. Emotional upsets, moods of despair and depression, feelings of passion or bitterness, even a too flighty imagination—these will also interfere with the work. Therefore the student must at the beginning of his practice strive to drop all thought of his personal affairs, to exclude all memories whether pleasant or painful, to withdraw attention from the day's business or interests and to universalize his outlook during the period set aside for it.

A common hindrance among city workers as a reaction from the speed, clamour and bustle of the day is mental exhaustion. Although some persons find in their very fatigue an aid towards successful meditation because it provides them with the rest and relaxation they need, others find that a tired mentality leaves them too listless to derive any profit from meditation. In such a case it is better to abandon the exercise until they feel fully restored or if this is not easily brought about, to abandon it altogether for the day. A helpful means of restoration is to lie for a few minutes supine on a perfectly flat surface, with legs and arms totally relaxed and the giving-out and taking-in of the breath rhythmically equalized, slowed down and prolonged. No pillow or any other head support should be used.

Another psychic hindrance is impatience. The first few essays in meditation pass so slowly and so irksomely that most novices soon give up the practice. Such uneasiness arises naturally out of the conflict of being drawn in two opposite directions at once. Their thoughts are unaccustomed to being turned inwards towards something that seems vague, remote and unreal but, on the contrary, are well accustomed to being turned outwards towards the world of clear-cut definite things. It is easier to renounce such an unequal struggle than to continue it. Consequently the virtue of patience must become theirs if they are to eat the fruits of their sowing one day. Every aspirant must, from the beginnings of this practice, impress his mind with the sure hope that if it is unremitting and done with the deep interest, results will be sure to show themselves. Such a hope will not be an extravagant one. Most efforts made during a novitiate are irksome, self-conscious and often boring but time renders them pleasant, spontaneous and even interesting. When anyone learns the beginnings of a new art like cycling there is a certain history through which he passes which has its precise parallel when he learns the beginnings of a new art like meditation. Just as the bicycle runs hither and thither, to one side or another, despite his efforts to guide it and heedless of the will which he would impose on it, so the thoughts run hither and thither to one subject or another during meditation, despite his efforts and heedless of his will. The monotonous necessity of repeated practice, the unavoidable pain of mishaps and falls which mark the rudimentary attempts at bicycling have their mental counterparts which also mark the rudimentary attempts at meditating. But the happy day arrives when, as if by magic, the practiser of the one art finds he can ride steadily and straight ahead on his machine and the practiser of the other art finds he can keep his thoughts steady, concentrated and controlled. Thus with the passage of time from an irksome task the daily exercise in mental quiet becomes transformed into an easy and natural one.

The first and last steps of yoga are steps in concentration. The perfect concentration of attention is one of the essential keys to success. Every great achievement has been the result of intensified thought and single-minded effort. Unless thought and feeling are guided into well-defined channels, they are like steam hissing aimlessly into the air instead of driving a hundred-ton locomotive. The constructive engineer attempts to direct the power which his engine evolves into a few selected directions. In this way the power reaches a greater intensity and accomplishes more than if it had been scattered into many directions. This simple lesson in mechanics has an analogical truth for the student of mind. He must learn how to focus the power of his own thought along one line, thus heightening its intensity and increasing its influence. The burning-glass can focus the sun's rays on a single point of a paper sheet until the paper catches fire. This too is a good simile of what the student has to do in these exercises. The snake intently watching its hapless prey provides a final example of the kind of concentration he must adopt. If it is not easy to reach such a perfect point, it is because his heart lies elsewhere. Therefore unless the interest is engaged, his concentration exercise will be a failure. It is little use taking a particular exercise merely because somebody else likes it or has succeeded with it. Therefore the student is asked to select those exercises alone which make some appeal to his interest and imagination. If this is done he will not have to try deliberately or artificially to concentrate but will instead feel himself carried away spontaneously into a natural absorption in the subject.

He may begin by focusing his attention on any single point which may be either an external object, an internal idea, or simply within himself. His consciousness must be brought under control and kept upon one thought or thought series or one thing or detail of a thing to the exclusion of all others. His thoughts must be kept tied like a wild elephant by the cord of remembrance to the stake of a single object or subject selected and not allowed to run aimlessly hither and thither. It will inevitably be necessary to bring them back again and again from their attempted wanderings, which will require both skilful handling and hopeful perseverance. Just as fixing his sight on a single point ahead when bicycle-riding will eventually enable an inexperienced rider to retain his balance and become a successful cyclist, so the fixing of attention on a single thought-series in the mind whilst learning to concentrate will eventually enable the student to ward off all other thoughts and thus practice meditation successfully. But a physical object can only be a starting-point to enable his swarming thoughts to become collected and fixed. Sooner or later he must call attention from outside things and break it away altogether. With this he finishes the first stage (concentration) of yoga and enters its second one (meditation proper).

Metaphysically, yoga is really the retraction of awareness from the not-self to the self, the brushing away of all the disturbing thoughts and interfering ideas which obscure true self-consciousness. This is achieved through taking hold of a single thread of thought and firmly grasping it, through a supreme effort of concentration upon one idea, which may be anything at first but must be spiritual in the end. For meditation must always tend to gather itself up towards an increasing aspiration, towards something diviner than mere thinking, towards a final act of sacred communion with his better self.

The dictionary definition of meditation is "close or continued thought", but there is much more behind the term as it is used in mysticism. The student must now shut his senses against the outer world and his attention against intruding thoughts and wandering fancies. Although this cannot in any case be easy, it yields to patient striving. This stage is a process of undoing the work of the five senses, an operation leading eventually to loss of touch with the outside world, a wandering beyond it to an inner region of rapt reverie where no physical sensation will be heeded although thinking will still be active. Throughout the day a long and continuous siege of his mind by percepts from the senses takes place. Only in sleep or in the mystic mood is he released from this never-ending war. Hence the full power of one-pointed attention must be directed deep inside his being and the mood of rapt absorption cultivated. Only if he persists in doing so, only if he resists the backward pull of external environment and checks the sense-directed movement of wayward thoughts, only then shall he succeed in penetrating at length to the mystical core of consciousness which lies on the fringe of the true "I". The glorious climax of all these efforts will, by the grace of the Overself, come at last. On that memorable day the tension which is the inevitable consequence of his rigidly acquisitive attitude toward life suddenly falls away. The strain which accompanies his desire-filled existence relaxes altogether. With this a stillness of spirit comes over him and when meditation reaches its highest point, yoga passes into its third octave (contemplation). Then intellectual reasoning ceases and mental images no longer appear. Then the attention spontaneously empties itself of all its objectives save consciousness and centres itself in the heart, not head. Thus from willed concentrated thinking he passes gradually to passive reception, from mental activity he sinks inwards to relaxed quiescence. It is in this third stage particularly that great care must be taken to keep the body absolutely steady, for even a slight muscular disturbance or a slight change of its position will react quite disproportionately and may easily disturb and break up the contemplation.

A successful concentration takes about two and one-half minutes. This keeps the mind unbrokenly hitched to a single object, point, or thought. The time stated does not include the usual preliminary period required by beginners to settle the body, pacify the emotions, get rid of extraneous thoughts and get into the actual state itself, a period which may well take treble and quadruple the time taken by concentration. A successful contemplation takes about twenty-six minutes. This period yields the full quality; nothing more can be gained from a longer one. It is unnecessary and indeed difficult to extend contemplation beyond the stated time. Moreover on the philosophic path it is considered inadvisable to make a habit of such prolongations because social apathy and psychological negativity may then easily result. It is not possible to assign any particular length of time for a successful meditation, however, for this may extend from a few minutes to, in highly exceptional cases, a few hours. A fair average would be about a half-hour. Once the faculty of attention has been trained in this way it can be fixed at will upon anything, any object and any idea.

Art, its appreciation or creation, Nature, its love or companionship, likewise constitute ways of approach to the mystical state. Practical instruction in the use of both these mediums for mystical purposes has been given in *The Quest of the Overself*. For those who can enter into them naturally, they provide excellent paths which are nearly as important as the conventional yoga paths. Whenever they lose themselves for a few precious seconds through becoming absorbed in some beautiful landscape, some lovely masterpiece of art or even some refined personal affection, they touch the fringe of this state. The attraction which they feel for beautiful things is merely a foretaste of the attraction which they have yet to feel for Beauty itself, which is ethereal and not physical, formless Spirit and not a formed thing. Those who cannot understand what mystical theory seeks to express may more easily do so by remembering the indefinable charm of these fleeting moments. Contemplation seeks to recapture their soul, to prolong and stretch them into a mood and to make them a recurring part of the common daily life.

The artist is forever trying to bring his mental images before others, whether they are uttered in melodious sound, cut in shapely stone, brushed in coloured paint or written in poetic words. Consequently image-ing is the first part of his work. Whilst he is engaged in such activity these images assume complete and vivid reality for him. Hence every artist worth the name must be a mentalist, whether he knows the metaphysics of mentalism or not, else his creative impulse is meaningless. Now the artistic or inventive genius usually develops an absent-minded inwardly-absorbed mood when his ideas germinate or when his creative capacity becomes active. Such a mood is indeed the characteristic hall-mark of his temperament. But what the genius develops unconsciously and sporadically the mystic develops consciously and regularly. And whereas the genius makes the production of an external work the ultimate object of his contemplation, the mystic makes a complete withdrawal from all external experience into an internal one the ultimate object of his own practice. If artistic creation or aesthetic appreciation are forms of meditation, they are not ultimate forms. Nevertheless they are close enough to it to enable the inspired artist or the lover of Nature to enjoy as much as the mystic the blessedness of contemplation. This he can achieve only if at the supreme moment of aesthetic rapture and concentrated intensity of attention he will drop the very subject or theme which has induced his rapture and will rest suspended as it were in the pure feeling itself. All thoughts of the physical "thing" must be forsaken, only the super-physical "Idea" must remain. If he can succeed in doing this the emotional upheaval will subside in an immense and exquisite tranquillity. For in deserting the external object which awakened his rapt inward mood for the mood itself, he will desert in theological language Matter for Spirit. Thus a complete psychological experience will replace the mixed half-mental, half-physical one. Thus too art will become a means of evoking what is above art and every artistic creation will become a symbol of something more than the thing created.

An uncommon but unforgettable form of mystical experience may occur at a period of fated parting from a beloved person as a hearing of melancholy inner music. This happens when karma compels separation for the sake of the spiritual progress of one or the other. The inexpressibly sweet but poignant music will not be heard by the bodily ears but mysteriously and clearly felt within the heart. This does not mean it is merely a hallucination. The beautiful but sorrowful strains will echo throughout the whole of the inner being. The experience will last for a few minutes only and be followed by a great depression, but it will deeply imprint a certain spiritual instruction which time can never efface.

Even the bitterest critic of religion, the most mocking doubter of Deity, the hardest supporter of rationalism who has followed his generation and got caught in the serpentine coils of materialistic cynicism, will begin to unwind them in such a seraphic presence as he will feel during mystical contemplation. From the moment when he first experiences it he will date his life anew. But quite apart from its important place in this quest of the Overself, meditation has also a utilitarian value of its own in the common everyday existence of mankind. The peace and detachment which a man may develop from these moments deliberately set apart from his everyday existence for such a purpose are precious. It is therefore regrettable that its deliberate practice should have nowadays passed into the almost exclusive possession of monks and ascetics, and that it should be so little in vogue in the West as compared to the East. Part of our aim has always been to introduce this art to a wider circle. Everyone—and not merely a few cloistered hermits—should learn how to meditate. Too long has the modern Western world been a victim of the unbalanced view wherein life has spelt action alone; too long has it given itself solely to what concerns exteriorized day-to-day living and only if there has happened to be a minute to spare has it sometimes bestowed a few thoughts upon the eternal themes as a mere parenthesis. A nerve-racked mass-produced society which has lost its sense of proportion and thinks it sufficient for a man to listen only to the roar of machines and the clamour of close-built, close-packed cities, which turns with impatience from a leisurely listening to the quiet voice of its interior self or from the deeper music of life orchestrated by inspired artists or from the rich stillness of majestic forest-glades—such a society is a miserable pathological case. Its daily life is far too extroverted. This unbalanced and insensitive condition is deemed "natural". But the introverted state is not an unnatural one as so many foolish people and narrow scientists think. It is indeed a part of what should constitute the complete state of a normal man. Western society's healing can come only from a wise restoration of a lost integrality. Hence it must resort to the technique of meditation in order to restore the broken balance.

So far what the average mystic seeks to achieve is precisely what the philosophic mystic seeks to achieve. But at this point they must part company. The latter fully appreciates the significance of the other man's achievement but knows that if he has reached a marginal tract of existence over which blow strange winds from the Infinite, it is not the same as the Infinite itself. Indeed he not only sees a further yoga path opening out from here where the other man sees nothing at all, but he also perceives that meditation is only one of the phases through which he has to travel. Thus the ultimate path possesses a threefold character whose rounded integrality truly entitles it to the honour of being called philosophic.

Some of the reasons why higher forms of contemplation are necessary have been given in *The Hidden Teaching Beyond Yoga* but the more important ones will unfold themselves in the course of the following chapters. For the moment let it be enough to say that philosophy is not so foolish as to cast aside any of the worthwhile results of the lower strata of yoga. On the contrary it takes them up and absorbs them by relating their gains to its own higher processes. Only it asks the aspirant to push on with his work until he comes out on the other side of the hill where there is full enlightenment, not to stop halfway where there is only twilight.

The Unfoldment of Intuition.

Although the student who has come thus far will be well prepared to receive the higher forms of meditation which constitute part of the yoga of philosophic discernment, a world-wide experience shows that he will come still better prepared and will make an easier approach to them if he has previously unfolded some degree of intuitive sensitivity. Many creative artists and many layfold who appreciate their productions do possess such sensitivity but they do not understand the governing laws of its arisal nor the conditions under which it operates. Before disclosing those higher exercises therefore it may be helpful to consider what can be done practically to kindle or improve the intuitive faculty as a preliminary to kindling the superior faculty of insight itself. But still more important than this is the fact that most mystics depend upon what they call intuition as the principal source of their mystical knowledge. It is therefore also necessary to understand what intuition really is, what are the right and wrong ways of cultivating it and how to distinguish it from its counterfeits.

Remembering all the facts stated in the fifth chapter about the hidden source and true character of intuition the student may well ask whether it is possible to evolve a practical working method for the unfoldment of such an elusive, involuntary and subconscious activity. The answer is decidedly in the affirmative. Nevertheless it cannot strictly be said that intuition is a faculty which anyone can cultivate. For as our studies in deep sleep and the "unconscious mind" have shown us the source whence it arises is ever-present within him. All that he can really do is to cultivate giving attention to that source—which is a different act. The willingness with which he does so and the frequency with which he does so will measure the frequency with which intuitions will arise. It should be remembered also that although intuition can be brought to bear upon such widely different matters as intellectual difficulties concerning doctrine or practical conduct relative to worldly affairs or creating and developing an artistic theme, the underlying principle of its operation will always be the same. If anyone wants illumination upon a particular subject or guidance when confronted by an important problem and if he has exhausted all the ordinary means of getting it, the way to begin is to believe that the answer is already existent within him but that it is first needful to make it rise above the threshold of his mind's deeper levels and appear in his everyday consciousness. Such confidence will not be misplaced although the successful voicing of that answer cannot be altogether free from interference or assistance by the karmic factor. Quite naturally the next act should be to put his mind closely upon it, that is to *concentrate* his fullest attention and thinking power all round its various facets. This may call for some gathering together of the available facts concerning it. Such a concentration may have to be repeated several days, perhaps even for several weeks, according to the individual case, but on the other hand it may not.

The third point is highly important. After such an act of concentration he has to assist the transference of the answer from the hidden to the open level of consciousness. This is achieved by the paradoxical process of banishing altogether its theme or subject. The reason for such a strange device is that the intuition is *not* brought into manifestation by an act of his personal will. Its presentation is definitely an independent one. When therefore he reaches a position of complete bafflement in his reflections, the wisest course is to become passive instead of remaining positive. When he is tired of hunting for the solution of a problem in such a situation it is not seldom wise to abandon both altogether for a time. He should still the wakeful consciousness, as far as he is able, by letting go of the everlasting fussiness which insists on trying to solve problems or to secure direction through its own limited personal efforts alone. He should relax attention from the subject, close the shutters down upon it and turn his thoughts elsewhere. He must indeed take a little mental holiday. What the surface consciousness has failed to settle or solve must now be regulated to the deeper mind beneath it in the confidence that there lies the perfect answer which he seeks. Whether or not he can secure this answer is another question. It will always be strange however that after he has let the question sink away it is more likely to return unexpectedly of its own accord with the solution ready-made. Whilst he is searching for an intuitive answer it temperamentally eludes him. When he stops his search and sits down to take a cup of tea or gets up to take a walk, it temperamentally approaches him! Hence he who seeks the guidance of intuition or the touch of inspiration must, after concentration on a matter, drop it completely and not persist in forcing an issue earlier than the mind is willing to bring it about. If he does this, the answer which he seeks may arise spontaneously, may come unexpectedly in a sudden flash within a few seconds after he lies down to or gets up from a rest or it may not come until some other day. If he overdoes his tense pre-occupation with the subject he may unwittingly set up a barrier to receiving that which the deeper self may have ready to impress upon him. On the other hand, if he underdoes such pre-occupation he will not rightly deserve to receive the inner revelation about it. He must not rely too much upon the thinking self and yet also not too little! The proper balance in this procedure can only be found by sufficient practice.

The connection between deep sleep and the hidden mind has already been pointed out when accounting for the connection between intuition and sleep. It is now ripe to reveal that those subterranean activities which result in such manifestations as intuitions, artistic inspirations and problem-solutions do not really occur during the sleep itself but rather during the borderland region which lies between and vaguely overlaps both sleep and waking. It is during the momentary flash of such a twilight state of consciousness or during its parallel condition of waking reverie that the most authentic intuitions occur. This is why Oriental faqueers or Occidental clairvoyants enter into a half-trance when they want to gain intuitive knowledge, for it is a corresponding state. Consequently the fourth phase of this process is to pick up the subject again and ruminate it questioningly just prior to a short rest upon a couch during the day, or just prior to falling asleep at night. The result of doing so will be that something within will put forth antennae, as it were, which will grope beneath the so-called subconscious level of mind for the knowledge which eludes the conscious self. During such deep or half-sleep or reverie mind can solve the hardest problem, even though there is no consciousness of its activity at the time, and later present the solution entirely of its own accord. Such guidance will then appear either as a self-evident wakeful idea or as an experience during dream or as an imagination during moments of absent-mindedness. The proverb is well known in many different languages which bids worried people to "sleep on it!" It is a sensible one. Both Churchill and Roosevelt often took a short sleep in the late afternoon. How much, during the dark confused earlier days of the struggle against the Nazi gamble for world domination, did they owe to this habit? The Italian composer Puccini admitted that several of his best creative musical ideas had come to him during the course of his dreams. Rodin, the French sculptor of that celebrated figure *The Thinker*, told his friends that he had actually seen in advance during the dreams the pictures of his finest artistic creations. Nor is it only in the sphere of art and statesmanship that such things happen. There is indeed no sphere which is exempt from them. Niels Bohr, the scientist, discovered during a dream the fundamental principle of his remarkable atomic theory.

The fifth factor which must enter into the student's calculation is that an intuition when it comes is as swiftly evanescent and as delicately fragile as is the memory of most dreams after waking up from them. The intimations of its presence are so subtle and so brief that he may easily overlook them altogether and thus remain unaware that he has ignored a desired guest. A voice which is so soft and gentle is quickly smothered at the bidding of unbelief and over-sceptical reason, as also through the pressure of convention and affairs. And even if he does hear it the momentary character of its existence may easily cause him to ascribe a corresponding unimportance to it and thus dismiss it outright without understanding what he is doing. Only later may he become aware of his mistake and that through the severe instruction of painful events. Only then may he regretfully remember the still small voice whose leading he failed to follow. Therefore he must train his personality both to open itself to the faintest monitions which come from within as well as to cling on and follow them up until they develop into clearly formulated messages. Because the welcome whispers of intuition come on wings it is sound practice for those who want to hear them—whether laymen or artists—to keep a notebook at hand so that they may be instantly recorded before they can be forgotten.

An analogy will perhaps help to make this point clearer. Whoever owns a radio receiving-set which is only of medium power may be familiar with the following experience. As he idly twirls the station-finding knob in quest of an interesting speaking voice or some melodious music, he hears a faint sound coming as from afar off. If he is impatient he turns away from such a faint response and continues to twirl the knob until someone's voice clearly breaks forth or until the strains of harmonious sound stream out of the amplifier. If however he is not in a hurry or is well experienced in the moods of a radio set, he probably lingers for a while on the faint response which he first heard and keeps the station-finder concentrated upon it. Presently the sound grows in strength until it becomes sufficiently distinct to be recognized as a voice or melody of the kind which pleases him and therefore worth amplifying by the volume-knob. Now the beginning of intuition is just like that. A thought-emotion will first be lightly felt within. But it will leave almost as quickly as it came. Therefore it must be caught on the wing if the student would catch it at all. If it is not ignorantly brushed aside nor unconsciously suppressed, if the concentrated attention is fully engaged upon it, then it may gradually amplify itself until an idea whose truth seems perfectly self-evident will presently formulate itself in his consciousness. He may already be sensitive to atmospheres, places, people. If he will only extend this sensitiveness a stage further and grow more and more intelligently and discriminatingly conscious of his own mental processes, he will begin to possess intuition. It will however not be enough to recognize an intuition for what it is, nor even enough to comprehend clearly what it says to him. He must also learn to obey it. If he finds its bidding distasteful or if he delays such obedience for personal reasons, he may sometimes miss a valuable opportunity whose loss he may long regret afterwards. On the other hand, loyal obedience quickly brings a sense of smooth peaceful certitude about the matter which always increases as time progresses.

The sixth point is a corollary from all the previous ones. It is to learn how to wait patiently for the right answer. A strong hindrance to the manifestation of intuition is an impatient desire to gain the answer before the deeper mental processes have been able to lay hold and present it to the surface consciousness. If he is too premature in seizing what is thought to be an answer, he merely gets for his pains either a pseudo-intuition mistakenly regarded as the real thing or else a mixed answer which is an Irish stew of a genuine half-intuition interfused with an emotion or prejudice contributed by his own wishful thinking. Only by a profound patience which is willing to continue waiting until the correct answer comes can such pitfalls be avoided. Moreover, the consideration of all these practical points should not lead him into the wrong belief that intuition manifests itself only in a single form. The message he needs, the answer he seeks or the creative idea he gropes for may sometimes come to him from an external channel, such as a book opened at random, a sentence dropped by sheer chance during conversation or even a letter written just at the time by a friend. The truth of such an external response has of course still to be recognized by something within himself alone and hence it is still worthy of being called intuitive. All such strange happenings lose their strangeness when he thoroughly understands the mentalist basis of all existence, when he knows that one and the same deeper level of mind runs through and links together all men and all things.

The seventh outstanding rule in this art is to check every alleged intuition by the widest use of intelligence, of which reason is naturally the most important part, and where possible by experience and authority also. This does not mean that he should fall into the error of trying to make every intuition conform to the demands of these other three criterions, for then there would be no need to seek its help at all, but that they should be used as checks to guard him better against self-deception. Whoever accepts the attestations of what he believes to be intuition without trying to verify or test them has only himself to blame if later they lead him astray. Because he may be so carried away by the force of its undeniable immediacy and sacrosanct air, he may shrink from critically examining, revising, checking and testing the correctness of an intuitive response. It is however useless to submit the feeling of innate conviction as constituting sufficient proof of its validity. For in order to penetrate to the sphere of genuine intuition he has first to cross the treacherous region of pseudo-intuition. This is not an easy crossing if he has ignored or despised the metaphysical discipline. The response may come to him in an impure mixed form. For he must struggle against his own desires, wishes, hopes fears and selfishness—all of which are likely to masquerade as authentic intuition when they are nothing of the sort. One way to detect these smooth-tongued masqueraders is to note whether thay are clamant, overmastering and passion-filled; to observe whether they try to force and rush him into an act or course of action under great haste; if so it is most probable that their excited voices speak from the pressure of personal emotion. The authentic voice of intuition is usually received amid inner calmness. Even in the last case the emotional background may still be quite marked but it remains only a background and not a dominant factor. Both an alleged intuition and a genuine one may appear as self-evident. But the former is loaded with selfish desire or personal excitement whereas the latter is not. There are indeed among others three distinguishing marks of genuine intuition. It is calm, clear and certain.

The student must frankly recognize that although intuition will always function perfectly his receptivity to it will not, and that although it will always be faultless his understanding of it may not. Moreover, there is no guarantee that the appeal within will always be answered. The self-made karmic factor also and always has something to say. Do what he will there are times when no intuition will be forthcoming. It is wise then in such a case not to simulate one out of misleading rationalized feelings but frankly to fall back on his ordinary resources. Hence the errors which are ascribed to intuition do not justly belong to it. Hence too the need to introduce three checks as a corrective. Let him take warning of this need from a famous contemporary example. Hitler's intuition guided him to disregard the expert advice of his General Staff on some important strategical points in the early stages of the war, and guided him to astonishing success, yet the supposedly same faculty also guided him in later stages of the war to commit disastrous blunders of Himalayan magnitude. Just as willingness to listen to and follow the bidding of his trustworthy intuitions must be reckoned amongst a man's good fortune, so the willingness to listen to and follow the bidding of his pseudo-intuitions must be reckoned amongst his bad fortune. This obedience to a false light has wrought much misery in many lives and brought not a few to mental distress and material ruin.

There are two stages in the student's unfoldment and it is only in the earlier stage that such verification of claims is needful. For it is only then that the student's receptivity is faulty, uncertain and irregular. But this unfortunately is the stage in which most men still remain. Only when after long experience and careful watching of results a man becomes completely familiar with the way intuition really operates, detects its authentic signs at once and never resists its oncoming; only when in short the faculty becomes quite mature is there then no longer any need to apply a check to its correctness by reason or otherwise. It would indeed be foolish to do so because the perfected faculty is wider than reason and can reach where reason is only confounded. Such a development however is uncommon. Hence our warnings in the earlier volume about the need of discriminating between pseudo-intuition and that wonderful faculty for which it is so often mistaken. The mystic particularly has yet to comprehend that he often confuses belief with intuition just as the materialist has yet to comprehend that he always confuses existence with its essence. If he believes that an impulse is divinely inspired when in fact it is nothing of the kind, he is obviously putting himself in a risky situation. Anyone who seeks to find intuitive answers to the questions which arise on this quest of the Overself must set himself against the gross bias and idiosyncratic impulse which everywhere masquerade as the very voice of God.

The term "intuition" has, in unfortunate fact, been grossly abused. Its use has been dragged down by the stupid, the unbalanced, the cranky and the charlatanic to a low level where it is supposed to provide a hall-mark of divine authenticity for what are really errors, conjectures, exploitations, egoistic desires, wild hallucinations or even demonistic obsessions. The spontaneous arisal of mystical intuitive thoughts containing honest revelations, discoveries and predictions is an undoubted psychological fact, but this is a rarer occurrence than it is generaly exposed to be and the possibilities of error are so great that intelligence, experience and authority should always be applied to check their correctness.

Again, as has already been pointed out in the explanatory supplement* to *The Hidden Teaching Beyond Yoga*, the mystically-minded ought not to confuse intuition with the far superior faculty of insight. An adequate definition has therein been given of the difference between them, so here we shall merely stress the emphasis on the most essential of all these differences. It is incorrect to use the term "intuition" for the apprehension of what is beyond its own range. For it is a term whose ambiguity has made it just as much the play-thing of gamblers on a race-course who pick winners through their intuition as of mystics who receive ego-flattering messages direct from Deity through the same channel. There are primary and secondary levels of mind and consequently there are its primary and secondary products. The former are insights, the latter are intuitions. Sages speak from the highest level; mystics contemplate and geniuses speak, write, paint and compose from the secondary levels. Primary consciousness is exalted but calm; secondary consciousness is exalted but excited. The first does not change its settled mood, but the second falls intermittently into rapture, ecstasy or abstract reverie. Although both arise spontaneously and suddenly, intuition glimmers discontinuously now and then even at its best but when insight is fully and finally active it shines like an ever-burning Egyptian lamp. It is the business of intuition to offer correct guidance in earthly human and intellectual matters whereas it is the business of insight to transcend them. Intuition deals only with ephemeral ideas, whether they concern race-horses on the one hand or even metaphysics on the other, whereas insight deals with that eternal source whence all ideas ultimately arise. Insight, in

---

* First issued as a separate pamphlet but now bound in with the book itself.

short, is the faculty whereby man can penetrate through the terrestrial forms amid which he habitually dwells into the infinite and ineffable reality behind and beyond them. Nevertheless the unfoldment of intuition constitutes a valuable preliminary accomplishment which renders easier and quicker the unfoldment of insight.

14

The Yoga of the Discerning Mind

WHAT he has heretofore learnt may have seemed too remote in his metaphysical abstraction to be useful to him, but Nevertheless it is not without personal bearing for the seeker. He who has cared to go so far will possess in the foregoing pages a foundation for practical endeavours which, as part of the threefold qualification needed for success in developing insight, must take the shape of actively engaging himself in a series of mental exercises which will help to open the door of a higher consciousness for him. Once the truth of mentalism has soaked into his understanding it becomes very much easier for the student to follow this quest. Not only is his external life brought under control more quickly, not only are his emotions and passions subjugated with more awareness and hence with less difficulty, but the practice of meditation can be turned into new channels whence it emerges more usefully than in any other way. Such channels are these ultramystic exercises, most of which have been formulated on a mentalistic basis. They are the logical outcome of the metaphysical teaching. Indeed, they are hinged into it, supplement and complete it. He who has intellectually mastered its tenets will to that extent be able to enter understandingly and sympathetically into these exercises and thus follow them more easily and practise them more correctly than anyone who has not done so. It is now possible to grasp another one of the several reasons why such repeated stress has hitherto been laid on the doctrine of mentalism. The exercises cannot be properly done if mentalism is not correctly understood or fully accepted whereas if it is the student will have a clear knowledge of what he is doing when he practises them. All demand that the intelligence shall be brought into play—a demand which is not made by the ordinary yoga methods, with which they must not be confused as they differ in conception, purpose, spirit and technique. This is indeed why the system of ultramystic exercises is called "yoga of philosophic discernment" and also "ycga of the discerning mind"—names which may here be abbreviated to "philosophic yoga".

To keep the attention from flying inwardly to one thought after another, to transform its natural condition from one of restlessness to one of steadiness, should be the primary aim of all the junior yoga methods. Any other is a sidetrack to be avoided. But when this aim has been achieved the student is ripe to practise the senior methods here outlined. When the strain of meditation comes to an end, when the difficulty of keeping to a single line of thoughts is felt no more, the preliminary stage has been passed and the student is ready for philosophic yoga. Just as when the pull on a rope is sufficiently strong the resultant tension at last reaches a point where the rope snaps altogether, so the strain of concentration comes to a sudden end and vanishes altogether. From this memorable moment, meditation proceeds with ease and surety. It is no longer a necessary duty but a benign privilege. And it is to reach such a point that the yoga systems of concentration have really been devised.

Nevertheless it is not always necessary for everyone to pass through all these stages in sequence. There is no other objection to anyone practising these ultramystic exercises than (a) the probable inability to concentrate successfully and to withdraw his attention from externals if he has not practised ordinary yoga exercises, and (b) the probable inability through metaphysical ignorance to discriminate between the ultimate reality, Mind itself, and its mere products. This is not to say that the novice who attempts them will be wasting his time but that he may find them too difficult, too far beyond his reach. These are the only reasons why prior progress in ordinary meditation is usually required but in many cases they are all-powerful reasons. However, some are already if unconsciously advanced enough to start meditating directly on the ultramystic exercises, whilst others may unconsciously be prepared to utilize them successfully because of practices done in former incarnations but now forgotten. This is a matter to be determined by experiment. Moreover, in all such operations there is always a possibility that the mysterious x-factor of grace may come into spontaneous play direct from the Overself. Therefore even those who are still beginners may experiment with these exercises if they wish.

The exercises given in *The Secret Path* and *The Quest of the Overself* form excellent preparations for those given here. Indeed, there is an obvious line of progressive continuity from those earlier ones to the present ones, for the appeal to intelligence and understanding has been consistently maintained throughout, whilst their search for the source of the self-thought comes close to the present search for the source of all thoughts. Thus the present exercises absorb and then transcend the earlier ones. Because no single method of meditation will suit all people at all times nor even the same person all the time, the student should select the one which makes most appeal to him at present and feel himself free to change it for another if the moment comes when such a change seems advantageous. If at first sight it appears easy or attractive to a reader, this will probably be because he has practised it already in a former incarnation. Consequently it is preferable that he should take up this particular one before any other. In any case, all are *not* to be done simultaneously. A single exercise may be taken up for a few weeks or a few months at a time; then he may change over to a different one.

Because, in their present modernized form, they demand only a small fragment each day for their practice, small enough indeed to suit anybody who is something more than a mere dilettante, these exercises are fit even for use in this hurried twentieth century. Because they are intended for modern active people and not for medieval monkish ascetics who have fled the world, it will suffice to practise for a single sitting of about three-quarters of an hour daily or, if desired, for about one half-hour each at morning and evening sessions. Like all yoga practices they must be done as regularly as possible, for the rhythm of patient persistent repetition thus set up is a definite aid to success. What must also be impressed upon the student is that the beginning of philosophic meditation—unlike the monastic kind—may come of itself at unexpected moments, even when engaged in daily business. He will find that his active life is occasionally and momentarily interrupted by a spontaneous recall to the still rapt mood of these meditations. If this happens he should not neglect the precious opportunity but should yield at once to the mood. This can best be done by dropping whatever world business or pleasure he may be engaged in and turning his attention inward to savour the sweet stillness whilst reflecting intelligently upon it. Three or four minutes will usually suffice although it has been told of Socrates how he was caught and kept standing on his feet for the better part of a whole day by such an ultramystic reverie. It may start into sudden effortless activity through such obvious things as the hushed quietude of eventide, the colourful sky at dawn, the appealing strains of music or the profound lines of metaphysical prose. But it may also start quite inexplicably (to the surface consciousness) in the midst of mundane work, or in the midst of trivial duties as when lacing a shoe or even when lifting a soup-spoon to the mouth! Therefore he must not take a narrow pedantic and mechanical view of such meditation. He must not limit it only to set formal exercises practised at set times with the tick-tock regularity of a clock. For he should understand that although he is here dealing with what is most subtle and sensitive and mysterious in his inward existence, it is nevertheless not something which is really remote and apart from outward existence. He is dealing with Mind.

Everyone experiences Mind at every moment in its fractional and limited form as the flowing series of thoughts. It is always there with him and within him. Only, he has to open his eyes to its presence. Consequently it is not something too far off from him to be attained at all nor even too obscure to be attained without overcoming almost insuperable difficulties. If he sets about the task with intelligent understanding and in the right manner, and if the unpredictable influx of grace also occurs, anyone may attain this goal during his present lifetime. The first and foremost obstacle to the discovery of what is so intimately ever-present within him is his innate materialism. This need not necessarily be of the crude popular kind or of the polished scientific kind; it may also be of a subtler kind. It is indeed often disguised under religious, occult and mystical forms. The right cure for it is a grasp of mentalism.

1. *A Meditation on the Sun.* The course of higher practices is usually begun with a preparatory exercise which is at the same time of such a character that it may be continued alongside of the others and even after the most advanced stage has been attained. It is particularly valuable to beginners, whether in ordinary mysticism or on the ultimate path, because it helps on the one hand to purify their self-centred attitude and on the other hand to bring about a descent of grace from the Overself. The practice is extremely simple, even disarmingly so, but those who estimate its value by its simplicity will greatly err. It is really a humble invocation and worshipful salutation of that supreme power which has manifested as this universe. Theoretically, it is a recognition of man's fundamental oneness with Nature, his inescapable kinship with the cosmos, his sharing of a common life. Practically, it is a communion with Nature at her most significant symbolic and glorious point, the sun. Therefore this exercise is connected with the sun's appearance and disappearance from the sky. For light, when traced to its true source, is nothing else than the first energy emanated by God, the World-Mind, and consequently the first state of so-called matter.

The student may begin by resolving to rise from sleep before daybreak in time to watch the sky's transformation from the darkness of night. In ancient times those engaged on this quest of the Overself in non-European and Oriental countries were usually forbidden to remain asleep at this period. The regulations of the Mystery-schools of initiation required them to be found in the midst of performing this exercise when the sun was half-risen above the horizon. But it is more difficult to keep such a rule in our grey Northern climes and still more difficult in our high-pressure modern civilization. Therefore it will suffice for those unable to do so if they will practise this meditation at sunset instead, to watch the opposite process take place. One of the worst defects of modern civilization is that it tends to divorce man from Nature. Western man especially does not know what he is missing when he misses devoting a few minutes to catch the calm blessing of dawn or the beautiful peace of sunset. For he then possesses an opportunity to profit by Nature's secret operations because certain mystical forces are available to assist communion with her. These two periods are neutral points in the inner movement of our solar system, whose hidden activity then turns back and starts in a reverse direction. During them there is a profound pause on the part of Nature wherein the transcendental forces have the freest and fullest play. The precise times when he may come into contact with these sublime forces are (*a*) in the morning between the time when starlight begins to wane until the time when the sun has just risen; (*b*) in the evening between the time when sunlight begins to wane and the stars have just appeared. When the sun's first greeting arrives on earth or when the purple shadows of twilight surround the globe, or at both times, man may come into a closer harmony with Nature than is ordinarily possible, except at new moon, full moon and eclipse days, which are always very favourable to the successful consummation of yoga practice. But in any case whoever undertakes this exercise must repeat it daily until he completes the annual solar cycle if he wishes to become perfect in its practice and to obtain its full results. Not before 365 days have passed can this stage be reached.

The first practical essential exercise is to sit in an unobserved place either outdoors or indoors facing directly east in the morning or directly west in the evening. If the student is practising indoors then he must take up a position at a window which will enable him to see the sun. If, as often happens in Europe and America, the sun itself is obscured by clouds or mist, the exercise may be practised in just the same way and the eyes kept upon the growing or fading light in the sky in the same easterly or westerly direction where the sun would be found were it visible. The squatting posture which is permissible in ordinary yoga is to be avoided here. This is because such a limb-locked posture helps to kindle its practiser's own forces through his own will-power whereas here the object is to become the passive recipient of super-personal forces. The cross-legged hand-folded posture closes the magnetic circuit whereas the one required here keeps it open and receptive. He must sit in the style depicted in certain ancient Egyptian statues, that is resting on a seat, the legs crossed and slightly apart, the hands also unfolded and resting on the thighs just above the knees.

Thus he fixes his gaze upon the rising or setting sun or the coloured sky. All other thoughts should be put away at first and his whole attention concentrated upon the physical phenomenon which he is witnessing. The rays of light must enter his body through his eyes. In this way alone do they attain their utmost efficacy for the purpose of this exercise. Such rays when absorbed in this manner and when at their mildest as they are at these hours also possess the latent power to assist the healing of physical disease, to restore wasted strength, to pacify a troubled heart and to disinfect a noxious emotional nature, just as at noonday strength they possess the power to disinfect noxious places and polluted water in the tropics. His emotions will be uplifted and refined as he watches the gradual appearance and shifting play of the sky's colourings. Artists and poets with their superior intuition have often felt this truth that there is a profound inner significance in daybreak and dayfall, although they have not understood it. For they have observed that such a variegated movement of beautiful colours does not occur during the night, when the sky is dark or black, or during the day, when it is usually white or blue or grey.

In the second stage the student tries to partake of the profound inner pause wherein the entire solar system is so briefly plunged, to experience within himself what is actually occurring within the greater existence of which he is a part, to tranquillize all his thoughts so that personal matters are wholly absent. Just as the sun at dawn illuminates the physical world, so the Sun behind the sun, the mystical Light of the World-Mind illumines man's mental world at the same time, penetrates it through and through, provided he is present and passive in consciousness to receive its power. He must thoroughly steep himself in this wonderful mystical stillness wherein Nature is plunged for a few moments.

In the third and last stage of this exercise the student seeks to move with the outspreading or waning light until he embraces the whole planet along with it. For this purpose he has to picture himself as a purely mental disembodied being, as a formless consciousness mentally dissociated from the physical body, whilst at the same time he has to strive to identify himself sympathetically with the life of all beings, whether plant, animal or human. He should make the conception as alive as possible by permeating it with faith and conviction, and by holding the sense of countless creatures existing everywhere. Thus he exercises his belief that he is ultimately mind and not matter and also strengthens his perception of the true relation between himself and the cosmic life. In the first case, the same creative faculty of imagination which ties a man to the belief that he is only flesh and nothing more is used to help untie him from it, to help liberate his consciousness from the tyrannical rule of the body-thought. In the second case, the student makes use of the oft-neglected truth of his physical and vital oneness with the universe. He must reverentially hold the thought of being a part of the grand boundless Whole. He must try to realize that his own existence is inter-connected by a beginningless and endless web with all the other existences around him. There must be deep devotion and heartfelt feeling in his thoughts. Even the slightest understanding of the cosmic wonder should rouse the hope and instil the confidence that his little personal life is not without its sublimer significance.

He reaches the goal of this stage when the physical scene vanishes, when he is no longer conscious of it, when attention is turned inward wholly on the beautiful mood or spirit thus invoked, when all form is absent and he feels in complete rapport with the universal being, so complete that he knows he is an integral part of it. When he *feels* something of this relationship as a loving response—a feeling which may arise within ten to twenty minutes in the case of a moderately experienced meditator—he should cease trying to absorb support from the All, whose soul is the

World-Mind, and begin trying to pass it out compassionately and share its grace unselfishly with others. He sees them in his imagination suffused with its warm light and sublime peace. First he directs this effort with his love towards those who are near or dear to him and to any special individuals whom he would like to help in this way. Then he directs it towards mankind in the mass whom he must regard as unconsciously forming one great family. Third, he directs it towards individuals who are hostile to him, who hate, injure or criticize him. He must consider them as his teachers for it is their business to pick out and make him aware of his faults. Consequently, if indirectly, they are his benefactors. If in the process they exaggerate the facts unjustly or falsify them dishonestly, karma will come into appropriate and effective play and bring the needed suffering and purification. It is his business to desire their inner moral growth. He need not send them his love and indeed in the case of those who are obsessed or inspired by evil forces should definitely not do so, but he must send them his pity.

It is quite fitting for the student to close the exercise with a very short silent personal prayer to the Overself, if he wishes to do so. In that case it is best if the dawn exercise is used to ask for strength, light, truth, understanding, inspiration, and material help, whilst the eventide exercise is used to ask for peace, calm, freedom, unselfishness and opportunity to render service. For this meditation is particularly associated with the act of prayer and with the diffusion of grace. It is in effect a humble appeal from man to a higher power, a confession that he knows himself to be weak, erring, ignorant and that he needs its aid in overcoming his weakness, his sinfulness and his ignorance. It is also a cry to have made lighter the heavy karmic burden which he carries and for which he must frankly acknowledge he has no one but himself to blame. Divine forgiveness, guidance, grace and even regeneration are the fruits of this exercise. It is an abasement of the little self before the immensity of the cosmic one, a chastening confession of dependence on a higher being. It is a getting out of his blind littleness, his endless pre-occupation with his own narrow personality and a perception that he belongs to a larger order of being, that he is but a part of the magnificent Whole. It is finally recognition that the Sun, as the source of Light, as the supreme visible symbol of the World-Mind, is God's heart-centre in this world system as the heart in his body is the Overself's centre in his own little personal system.

This meditation occupies an unique place in the hidden teaching. Although traditionally regarded as either a companion exercise or a preliminary and purificatory one to whatever other practices may be followed, it is nevertheless one which the greatest sage will not disdain to follow even after his ultimate attainment, just as a mighty river which has joined the ocean still continues to pour its waters therein. In his case it will be both an expression of humility and an adoration of the Supreme. But in the case of the neophyte, its use is eventually to evoke within him a mysterious grace-giving force which shall by its own inherent intelligence lead him to the exquisite blessedness of the discovery that, despite all appearances to the contrary, he lives environed by a matterless world in which his own destiny is inescapably divine.

   2. *A Meditation on the Past.* In this exercise the student must set out on a strange journey. He must set out to visit the man he used to be and events he has earlier experienced. It is to be practised at night just before sleep. If, for any reason, it is inconvenient or impossible to do so, he may practise in the morning instead, immediately after waking up. But the power and the possibilities of this exercise will then be notably lessened. After getting into bed and settling himself down, with legs fully stretched out and not curled up, the student begins to direct his consciousness to the past. He reviews the chief events of the day starting from that very moment and works his way slowly backward from one experience or feeling or idea to another; first through the evening, then through the afternoon and the morning and finally he returns in memory to the moment of his first awakening. He must not however stop even here but must try to recall the dreams if any which he had during the previous night. He should indeed stop this review only when he reaches the mental picture of himself settled in bed and about to fall asleep the night before. If he is devoting the morning to this meditation then of course his thoughts will start instead with the night's dreams and end with the previous morning's awakening. The need for blacking-out all other images which will otherwise intrude themselves, thus defeating concentration, renders it desirable to meditate on images which are intensely vivid. Hence he must draw upon the mind's picture-making power to its utmost extent. He need not relive everything that has happened during the twenty-four hours which have gone by. It will suffice if he picks out a few major occurrences, activities, contacts and reflections which possess some importance both from a personal and from a philosophic standpoint.

   What is essential, however, is to see his own body with its actions as though it were someone else's. He has to behold it working, moving, talking, enjoying and suffering with the same easy sense of being separate from it that he feels when beholding the other figures which enter into the day's life. At the same time he should bring his own deeds and his own thoughts and feelings before the impartial tribunal of his better self for philosophical evaluation. He should adopt a detached attitude to enable him to expose unconscious complexes and hidden motives, to view critically and without favouritism his own dreams, acts and thoughts according to the higher ethical and intellectual demands of philosophy. He should stand spaciously aside from his personal life and view it as a thing apart; its excited joyous hours and its tragic unhappy days will then seem much less important as happenings and much more important as tutors to impart philosophical lessons. The exercise therefore requires the strong use of his creative imagination both to retrace his steps and to accomplish this bifurcation of consciousness.

As he calmly surveys the person, treats it theoretically and actually like a separate and different creature apart from himself, and then critically judges its thoughts, feelings and deeds quite impartially and quite sternly, he creates an effective means of self-betterment. This will purify his motivation, educate his emotions, strengthen his will-power and improve his mental capacity. Thus the mind's power to create its own pictures and recapitulate the past is utilized to modify his own character in an effective manner. Moreover, the repeated and faithful pursuit of this habit will eventually improve the powers of remembrance too. They will not only begin to yield up during the meditation little details of the past that would otherwise be permanently buried but will also yield its contents at any time of the day when he wants them—and that with a smoothness and readiness not before experienced.

But such benefits, excellent though they are, represent only a partial purpose of this exercise. For if the retrospective review is earnestly and intensely practised, in so far as it arrests and reverses the time-flow it lifts him out of the illusions which make the present alone seem real and the mental certainly seem material. Hence its philosophical purpose begins to achieve itself not during the actual meditation itself but only during the intervals between two meditations. Then the student begins to realize that the past day being now but a memory and hence but a thought-form everything he is now seeing—including himself, others, events and environments—is likewise but a series of thought-forms. He begins to see the results in exceptional experiences, in strange if brief interludes which unexpectedly enter his wakeful life and grip his thoughts without warning.

During these interludes the outside world will assume a new and amazing relation. The winding streets or lonely jungle which stretch all around will be felt as though they were like spider-webs directly spun out of the inmost point of his own being. The solid walls of a house will no longer be entirely separate from him, the very ground on which he stands will no longer be merely alien substance and the living person who stands at his side is no longer a wholly separate creature. The frontiers between self and not-self which make man a natural materialist somehow fade and fall away. Not that the particular objective forms of being vanish; they do not, but that their being itself becomes strangely intimate with his own at this mysterious central point within himself. He becomes luminously aware that the mind bestows reality upon its own constructions by bestowing concentrated attention upon them, and that they are projected by the mind outwards from within itself, as indeed is the whole world. He understands now that the mind makes *all* things for he sees within it all that he formerly believed to be outside of it. Whereas the popular and even scientific view is that sensations which produce the panoramic spectacle of the world are themselves produced within us by the physical objects which are outside us and are impressed upon our minds from without, he will experience the very contrary to be the truth.

These strange occurrences will be not merely a matter of reasoning but a matter of the most vivid experience which will be feelingly alive with actuality. Critics who think that this yogic initiation into mentalism is experienced only by befuddled dreamers or unbalanced mystics should consider that it has also happened to a famous scientist. Sir Humphry Davy, the brilliant English chemist and inventor of the miner's safety lamp, first discovered and experimented with nitrous oxide gas. He himself described how, after inhaling this gas, the old form of his familiar everyday world began to vanish: "I existed in a world of newly connected and newly modified ideas," he narrated. And this scientist whose life was devoted to the investigation of physical things was forced to confess: "Nothing exists but thoughts. The universe is composed of impressions, ideas!" Let nobody complain however that this view of the shifts and changes of our world-scene robs it of its reality and turns it almost into a mere dream. He is not robbed of reality but merely of a limited conception of reality. For the only thing that is continuous throughout the endless mutations of his world-experience is that which both makes and observes it—Mind.

The final philosophic purpose of this exercise is to awaken the student to the consciousness of the hidden observer. This is a more difficult achievement than the previous one and consequently comes at a later stage. It may manifest itself either during the meditation or when otherwise engaged. He will become intermittently aware that there is something in him which is other than the evanescent events themselves, which is indeed their unaffected imperturbable Witness. He discovers that in himself which notes the bare existence of the experience, which is pure consciousness dissociated from its personality and its forms. He will begin to watch the ever-changing stream of his own feelings, the pulsating waves of emotion and mood, with serene dispassion and calm evaluation as the screen between his everyday mentality and transcendental consciousness intermittently thins down. This will bring a great stillness to his heart and a great deliberateness to his active life. Again and again he will find his heart put under enchantment and his brain made mute, the while an indefinable peace and indescribable detachment proclaim that something unearthly dwells within and about him.

3. *A Meditation on the Future.* The moments just before falling asleep are important to every man. They contain latent power to transform his mental, moral and physical existence in an effective manner. If he utilizes them aright, he may gradually alter both his external environment and his internal character for the better. Such moments are even more important to the student on this quest of the Overself however, for they contain latent power to transform his consciousness also. When settled in bed at night he begins this exercise by suggesting some leading ideas and anticipating some leading activities of the following day. But he should not merely try to pre-determine something of its character; he should also pre-determine it in a particular way. It should portray him as the ideal philosophical man he seeks to be. It should reflect what his better self wants him to think and do. Hence he visualizes himself possessed of specific, desirable, moral and mental qualities and putting them in action. He imagines the way in which he should rightly react to any meetings with other persons likely to happen. He must visualize himself not only as he should wisely think and nobly act but also, as in the previous exercise, as though he were a detached spectator looking impartially upon the personality.

The focused clearness and uninterrupted intensity with which these images are imprinted on his consciousness together with the lulled quiescence of his physical senses will partly measure the results achieved. He must put vividly into his consciousness the precise images of the thoughts he ought to hold and the behaviour which he ought to manifest when confronted by the chief probable happenings, duties, moods and so on. The characters, scenes and events must be painted with photographic sharpness on his canvas. When it is alive, alert, concentrated, strong and disciplined, the imaginative power can greatly help a man to master himself. But on the other hand when it is vague, dreamy, wandering, feeble and diffused it becomes a hindrance and a drag, preventing progress and causing stagnation. Naturally the imagination which is going to succeed in such an enterprise must be a powerful one. The faith which must support and confirm it must be equally strong. Every idea which he impresses on himself in this way should be impressed calmly and feelingly and firmly but not violently; there should also be an easy confidence that success will salute his effort. He must perseveringly repeat these suggestions quite often not merely verbally but by the process of visualizing their fruition. Such repetition is important.

An ideative suggestion which he formulates and gives himself whilst in this rapt mood will tend to realize itself. His actions will spontaneously and involuntarily come into correspondence with the pictorial and reflective suggestions which were held in consciousness during this highly critical moment. Indeed they will have no option but to do so, for a profound psychological law is involved here. But the most essential point is to fall naturally asleep whilst in the very midst of practising the meditation itself. Therefore the least digression towards bodily consciousness may break the absorbed concentration and deprive the suggestion of its power. Whilst he is holding these beneficial thoughts which shall pre-determine his future thinking and conduct, if wakeful consciousness drops away the deeper level of mind will then take up the thoughts for him and work them out in its superior way. For next day he will find himself unconsciously carrying out the suggestion which he had deliberately given himself the preceding night. When the events or meetings actually happen he will feel a sudden inner impulse to act precisely in the way he had earlier pictured to himself. Hence the first important result of this exercise is the effective remoulding of character which it brings about, the steady wearing down of faults and vices and defects, the steady building up of merits, virtues and good qualities. By repeating it every night good habits can be created during the wakeful life and bad ones broken up. The power which is superior to thinking consciousness and emotional tendency is thus drawn upon to develop rightly and benefit permanently both together. It is perfectly possible for every student to call in the aid of such a higher force for his own satisfactory self-improvement. Here is a practical reasonable hope which can make him happier, strengthen his will and shape his life more closely to his higher ideas and finer ideals. The little successes which will sooner or later encourage him to continue this practice will be accompanied by a sense of growing power. To his amazement he will find that his visualized conduct will become spontaneously operative without any great strain on his limited strength of will and that his previous suggestions will actualize themselves without any inner struggle or opposition.

All this introduces a new factor into his karma which in turn brings about some modification of it and eventually some refashioning of environment. Indeed, all sustained and concentrated intense mental images affect his future circumstances because Mind is the real basis of all circumstances. Whatever is engraved on consciousness in vivid relief during the passivity of the senses in pre-sleep, especially tends to reproduce itself creatively and operatively in the external life, subject not only to adjustment by karma and evolution but also by the habitual trend of thought if it is in conflict with the images or ideas thus engraved.

This exercise is valuable to help him remain unaffected when unduly suggestive or unconsciously hypnotic influence is being exerted upon him by other persons or even by a deliberately impressive external environment. On the other hand, so far as he attempts to introduce other persons into his meditation, the student is earnestly asked to keep his mind and motives pure. Otherwise he may involve himself in karmic requitals of a painful character or, which is even worse than temporary physical pain, in the permanent degradation of his own character. The temptation to interfere for his own selfish benefit with the freewill of others may easily arise but its obedience leads in the end only to disaster. Indeed it would also defeat the very object of these exercises which seek to lift the practiser above the narrow agitated personality into the wide passionate atmosphere of truth, to make him feel that something which is over and above his ordinary self has taken hold of him and is lifting him upwards alike in consciousness as in ethics and understanding. To overcome the resistance of the person in moral issues is a primary task which has to be accomplished in the silence and secrecy of such meditation.

If however the student carries out his task faithfully he will, as in the previous exercise, arrive at a further important result. This practice will tend to shift his centre of spiritual gravitation and thus to overcome the emotional vacillations, the physical passions and the intellectual illusions of the person. He becomes increasingly conscious of an inner strength which paradoxically he recognizes to be great in proportion to his capacity to recognize that it is derived from something beyond himself, something which is universal and impersonal. It is indeed derived from the hidden observer. At unexpected moments of ordinary routine existence and amid his manifold duties he will suddenly become aware of its presence. He will rise from mere participation in events to calm witnessing of them as well, to see them as they should be seen. At such moments he feels that he is standing curiously still whilst the turbulent processional drama of the world moves all around him.

Thus he learns to separate the impersonal "soul" from the active self by metaphysical understanding of both these aspects of himself alongside the periodical mystical effort to bifurcate his consciousness. As his efforts are more and more successful he will more and more lose the egoistic sense of living and working merely for personal interests alone, a sense which really springs out of the materialistic self-identification with the body. It stands in the way of appreciating inspired truth as much as it stands in the way of appreciating inspired music. For to the degree that the thought that he is listening keeps on obtruding into his attention, to that same degree it causes a man to lose his emotional unity with the music and diminishes its pure enjoyment. Only when the consciousness displaces the *predominance* of the sense of being personally occupied with life does the hidden observer transform external existence from being the prosaic and materialist thing it ordinarily is into something veritably divine.

4. *A Meditation on the timeless Self.* Although this exercise is not done in the conventional way, that is in solitude and at the same set time every day, but is to be deliberately inserted into the external life of routine activity, it is from such an informal character that it derives its peculiar philosophic value. The student not only puts it into operation at odd moments or during waiting periods or when he finds himself free for a few minutes, but also deliberately breaks into whatever work he may be doing and stops. As a mere three or four minutes will suffice for the practice this need not disturb his exterior existence or interfere seriously with his exterior duties. Moreover it may be done almost anywhere, for the solitude which must needs be created is entirely an interior one. An important point is to train himself to start the practice suddenly and to let the thoughts of everything else subside at once, so that he can plunge himself instantaneously into the different outlook it demands. This is a knack which comes with experience.

He should abruptly reject the thoughts or desires which happen to engage him, calmly suppress all personal reference and put himself in the mental position of a man waking up from a dream and suddenly realizing that he was not only playing an active part in the dream but was also remaining quite immobile as the mere witness of that dream figure itself. In the same way, he must stand aside from what is happening around him and even from the personality which is fitting into the environment, becoming utterly aloof from its business or pleasure. He should remember the metaphysical tenet that behind all those thoughts which were changing continuously, the consciousness which observed them remained static throughout, unmoved and unaltered, that through all the flow of experienced events and things there was a steady element of awareness. He should try to identify himself with this consciousness and to disidentify himself from the accustomed one.

He will be chiefly helped in this endeavour by pondering again and again on the awakened dreamer's relation to the sleeping dreamer. He may also find some help in considering the cinema screen which remains stationary whilst pictures appear and pass over it. The first typifies the unchanging witness-self whilst the second typifies the person's ever-changing experiences. Just as the pictures do not really affect the screen so these experiences do not really affect the consciousness by virtue of which they alone exist. When this relation is immediately clear to him he completes the meditation by comprehending that whereas all these experiences assume form in space and follow successively in time, this witnessing element itself is formless and free from successiveness. This witness-self eludes the academic psychologist because he is naturally holding on to time and this is something which is mystically raised above time. Copernicus found that serious difficulties remained inexplicable on the conventional theory of supposing the earth to be fixed in space whilst the sun and other stars wheeled around it. He reversed the process and imagined that the earth wheeled around instead. This solved all the difficulties at a single stroke and revolutionized the scientific outlook of his era. During these moments of meditation the student must bring about a similar reversal of outlook in his own conscious life. He must temporarily drop the conventional belief and assume that space and time are travelling *in* him, in his higher individuality.

The utter intensity with which he abruptly lets himself slip out of the world of time is important. His ultimate aim is to arrive at the supreme acme of forgetfulness, to let his time-existence be swallowed up by the timeless one. The experience sounds like something to be feared. It is actually a delightful one. The townsman is comforted only when he thinks in modest short-term periods and profoundly frightened when the possibility of an endless existence extends before him. The desert dweller, on the contrary, who has watched Nature pursue her perennial unfailing course and assimilated something of the tranquillity which envelops such places, has a better appreciation of the beginningless and endless character of the cosmos and therefore of the "Soul".

That which never dies and was not born, which has existed from one eternity to another, can exist only in a timeless Now which is beyond human conception but not beyond human experience. He who can learn to live feelingly in this everlasting Now knows how artificial are all those oppressions of time to which humanity clings so slavishly and so short-sightedly. He knows that these divisions which it insists on making are mere conventions which help to make practical life possible but which are illusions in the greater absolute life of Infinite Duration. The passive submission to time keeps man enchained. The willed meditation on the infinite observer which is ever with him and within him is a revolt which weakens every link of his chains. If the unimaginably stretched-out time-life of World-Mind is beyond human reach the timelessness of pure Mind is within possible experience. As the Overself it is the stupendous ever-present fact of his life. If he ceases to ignore it and repeatedly strives to know it the hour will certainly arrive when he shall do so. For gently and gradually, a realization will come to the student that he is no longer imprisoned by the body, that an inexpressible spaciousness of being is now his. The planetary scene will seem like a shadow show. The people in it will seem like shadow actors playing allotted parts. He himself will feel fleshless and ethereal. A queer feeling that this is an experience he had been fated to meet since birth will creep into his heart. He will find in himself the wonderful confirmation of that which reason merely affirms and religion only hints at—the glorious fact of the timeless soul.

5.   *A Meditation on Dream.* When wakefulness slips down to zero a transformation of consciousness occurs; it either manifests as panoramic dream or is submerged in total unconsciousness. Usually a man falls asleep when occupied with a train of feebly-held thoughts or with a movement of erratic imagination, either of which may fitfully continue its interrupted existence through the merely mechanical activity of its related brain centre. The latter however being partially uncontrolled functions incorrectly and grotesquely. The memory of this distorted experience plus the suggestive memory of earlier wakeful experiences plus the association of ideas recently held during the wakeful state form the basis of the average confused dream. What he vividly remembers, however, is only the last few links of the chain. This is because they are still within the focus of concentrated attention whereas all the earlier links have faded out of focus altogether.

The condition which lies between sleeping and waking is not only extremely interesting, for it does not belong to either category and is indeed a borderland with characteristics which partake of both, but also extremely important, for it is very receptive to suggestion. This infinitesimal intermediate point on the verge of sleep offers a unique opportunity for the practice of concentration. It has already been explained that the final trend of thought held firmly and clearly in consciousness whilst one falls asleep is taken up by the deeper level of mind, which then works upon it in its own mysterious yet effective way. This strange mental power may be utilized to exercise control over dream life. The opportunity to develop it and to free it from foolish or even evil experiences exists within the ante-room of the nightly return to sleep, particularly for those who are more or less habitual dreamers. The others who rarely dream at all need not regret the fact, which is indeed to their advantage, for eventually the higher goal for aspirants is complete repose in an utterly thought-free and dream-free state.

The student settles himself at night for sleep and then directs his thoughts forward into the future, seeking first to imprint powerfully upon his consciousness the suggestion that his forthcoming dreams shall rationalize themselves and then to picture himself passing through certain definite experiences during them. He should pre-determine to introduce rational order and logical unity into them. He should aspire to see himself forcefully waking up in his sleep enough to be fully aware that he is still dreaming but not enough to be aware of the physical world which has been left behind. The mind must be utterly intent when giving the nightly self-suggestion and nothing else should be permitted to gain a mental foothold. He will assist this development if he takes particular note of the most vivid and most lucid dreams which leave a sharp impression on the mind and keeps a brief written record of them. If therefore he wishes to remember more of any dream he must take the utmost care not to get out of bed abruptly.

The transition to waking activity should be of the slowest, gentlest and most spontaneous kind. He should lie utterly still and inwardly attentive immediately on awakening, permitting no other thought to intrude and break his concentration than the thought of the last moment of dream.

Success will come more quickly if he is thoroughly convinced of the truth of mentalism. For if in the midst of his waking activities he can keep in the background of his mind the truth that all his experience is a mind-constructed one, he will inevitably carry the same attitude sooner or later into the midst of his dreaming activities. When this conviction becomes natural and habitual, it more easily extends itself to his dream experiences. It will help if at odd moments during the day he drops his accustomed standpoint and takes up that of a dispassionate witness. He should pull himself up to reflect that what he is doing will become *like* a dream a moment or two afterwards, for it will slip into the past and become ungraspable except as a memory-idea. Also, as he moves from place to place he should occasionally reflect that the place previously left has likewise become a content of memory and that what it is then it always was—a thought-form held by consciousness.

Again and again he will fail to proceed farther in this practice than the point of everyone's common experience, that is again and again he will pass into the incoherent and unsatisfying fitful dream condition or the full blank of unconsciousness which stamps the ordinary sleeping condition of mankind. Consequently much persistence is required to bring this exercise to its ripe fruition. But one day the strange event will occur which will assure him that he has opened a new door in his nightly life. True, it will open only a very little distance at first but after the initial success this distance will progressively increase with time and perseverance. He will pass into a paradoxical state during sleep when the dream life will no longer deceive him for he will clearly realize at the same time the fact that what he is experiencing is really nothing else than a vivid dream. He will possess the quaint sense of being awake in the very midst of his dream. Yet it will wear all the definite awareness, the clear shape and the luminous colour of wakeful actuality. Such a man does not dream in the ordinary sense, does not suspend the critical judgment and coherent imagery of his mental operations and does not waste his night in those vague, idle and fantastic constructions which pass with most of us for dreams. Nights spent in such coherent and connected dreaming will be in striking contrast to nights formerly spent in aimless and jumbled dreaming. It will be a rational existence wherein all his faculties of will, judgment, criticism, memory and so forth are just as effectively working as during wakefulness. His dream life will indeed eventually become in part a natural continuation of daytime activity, although within much wider limits. He is expected to utilize this exercise as an attempt to implement his highest ideals. Therefore his dream conduct should show a greater self-control and a loftier morality than his wakeful conduct shows. Any descent from this ethic will expose him to certain dangers. Vigilance is here needful.

The mind creates its own new time, space, matter and causality in dream. When this power is brought under conscious control, the student will attain almost magical powers of making dream events happen according to his will. Mentally he will not only be able to visit distant scenes and thus annihilate space or converse with distant persons and thus annihilate matter, but will also be able to create them at will, to imagine episodes and unfold incidents which spring into lifelike actuality the very moment he wills them. His movements will be delightfully free and his wishes instantly realized. The feeling of possessing both the freedom and the capacity to mould existence will naturally be an exhilarating one. Nevertheless he will be quite conscious that this is only an adventure into fantasy, a journey into Alice's exotic wonderland and that it will terminate all right by an awakening into the conventional daytime wakeful state.

A further development of this experience may arise in the course of time. He may find that should he engage in thinking about anything or anyone with sharply focused attention during the dream experience a kind of clairvoyance will manifest itself. Finally a peculiar power may attach itself eventually to his nightly existence, for he may even discover, to his initial amazement, that certain events, contacts and conversations of the following day will be foreshadowed by the previous night's clairvoyance.

A related exercise which one may attempt who has not yet developed to the point where he is able to get through this practice with surety and ease, if he ardently wishes to communicate safely with the "spirit" of a beloved departed person, is to concentrate just before sleep on the mental image of this person and to formulate the suggestion that a mental contact may be brought about during the coming night. Although the space-time levels are so different that Nature's veil ordinarily hangs thickly between them, the concentration may however evoke a certain kind of response. The mind of the meditator may reproduce this for the benefit of the dream consciousness. It is possible that the spirit will then enter his dream life in this half-indirect way although it is not possible for this to happen for more than a few minutes nor for more than a few times altogether. The practiser is strongly advised not to overdo this exercise, which will not contribute to his spiritual growth in any way and if repeated too often may even retard the growth of the other entity. It is mentioned here only for his personal comfort in case he is unable to get over his bereavement yet does not feel it right to resort to other methods. If however there is no demand for communication then he may rightly send his love and peace to such a spirit as often as he wishes at the close of any of his meditations throughout his lifetime.

Thus the control of dream life may lead to wide results. The practical value of this achievement lies in its transformation of the sleeping hours into conscious ones when useful mental work may be done for himself and useful spiritual work may be done for others. The metaphysical value of this achievement lies in its clear confirmation of the mentalist doctrine about the nature of the external world and of the person who experiences that world. The mystical value of this achievement lies in its power to divide consciousness into two parts, one being an impersonal observer who remains the same at all times and the other being the personality which experiences changes. For the ultimate goal of the principal meditation is not to live in a fanciful world nor even to know that he is dreaming but to introvert attention sufficiently to let go of the personal standpoint. If his motives have been pure and his aims exalted, the student will experience at occasional intervals during his ordinary wakeful life a condition like an absent-minded themeless reverie. Then the picture of his own face or body will continuously and vividly recur before the mind's eye. He will seem to be looking at himself from the outside. If this picture can be steadily held the next stage will soon supervene. It consists of a distinct sensation of being separated from the body and standing behind and above it like a fleshless spirit. We are not here speaking in a spatial metaphor but in literal descriptive terms. He should not be afraid of this experience. It will quickly pass off and cannot harm him. On the contrary, he will find in time that another presence has come to life within his mental orbit, a calm ethereal presence. He must try to hold himself, as it were, in this divine atmosphere from the first moment that he feels it around him.

The amazing mechanism of the dream mind which makes such things possible has then attained the fruition of its higher possibilities. This is of course a rare attainment. Hence *Tripura*, an ancient Sanskrit manuscript, says, "Unbroken supreme awareness even in dream is the mark of the highest order of sages." But nobody need be a sage to experience such a superior dream existence. Whoever has made some advance on the ultramystic path may (not necessarily) partake fragmentarily, fitfully and sporadically of it. So also may some who, like Descartes, through prolonged bouts of concentrated non-materialistic metaphysical reflection have unwittingly taken a number of steps on this path. The sceptic may stamp all these experiences as impossible. To anyone who has no faith in them, who believes that mind is brain and spirit is matter, they are certainly impossible. He may also stamp them as hallucinatory, as being the obvious result of suggestion or the natural activity of imagination. We answer; "You are not far from the truth. For if you knew how much suggestion and imagination entered into your waking life you would not find it so miraculous that they should also enter into your sleeping life. And if you knew that almost all your earthly experience is in a lofty sense hallucinatory, you would not deny man the power to control those private and broken hallucinations which you call dreams. When you shall understand what imagination truly is, when you shall break open the shell of comprehension which hides your greatest treasure, Mind, then and then only shall you dare to place bar and limit before the wonderful possibilities of man.''

6. *A Meditation on sleep.* When we wake up from a deep dreamless sleep and open our eyes we are at first aware only of what meets our gaze. The consciousness of external surroundings comes at that moment—and at that moment only—before anything else. It is only as a subsequent thought that we become aware of ourself as a particular person, as the bodily "I". This initial impersonality is psychologically something like that which belongs to the state of the witnessing self. Where are we during such a moment? We are not in our personal "I"—nevertheless it is there. We have merely disengaged ourself from its accustomed dictatorship. We have in fact forgotten ourself. Giving up the surface self therefore does not mean its annihilation. It is given up only to find it again in the higher individuality. It does not disappear but simply falls into its proper place within the latter's larger perimeter. It is still present, still alive throughout such an experience but it now knows that the tiny drop is within a boundless ocean and that the ocean supports the drop. From this we get a hint of what is the consciousness of the hidden observer not only during wakefulness and dream but even during deep sleep. The notion that such sleep is entirely devoid of all consciousness is another of those illusions which hold the human mind in powerful thrall merely because it relies on appearances rather than on enquiry. A round top whirling at high speed seems to an observer to stand absolutely still and motionless. In the same way the mind during sleep seems to the wakeful ego plunged in utter unconsciousness. Actually it is experiencing a kind of consciousness which is beyond the personality's power either to imagine or, ordinarily, to enter. Hence the reiterated request of philosophy that we give up the personal outlook, for its finite limitations block the way to the truest knowledge.

Both at the unexpected end of dream and when wakefulness has just run its course there is for the briefest instant a transitional condition of the mind when it is aware of nothing but itself. It is then quite free from ideas, all sensations have ceased and all imaginations have vanished. This intermediate moment when a man is beginning to pass in or out of sleep is a pivotal point. For although his thoughts have lapsed his consciousness has not. He is aware but he is not aware of any individual thing. Personality cannot function here and the change-over magically takes place above its head. This dark drowsy period between the end of wakeful consciousness and the beginning of its transformation is a wonderful one indeed. Being the line where waking consciousness meets sleeping unconsciousness, it is on a plane different from both.

Patanjali, author of the best-known classic Sanskrit manual on yoga, rightly lists sleep as one of the five hindrances which have to be overcome by the yogi. In its elementary technical significance this injunction applies to beginners, bidding them keep the mind awake and alert during meditation, for otherwise there can be no effective concentration of attention. In its advanced significance however it applies to those who are on the ultimate path and is an injunction to bring even their sleeping life as much under control as their waking life. It is impossible for anyone to fall asleep unless he withdraws attention from the sensations, images and thoughts which beat upon the door of consciousness. Sleep is simply the culmination of this process. The attention then falls into suspense, as it were. It is equally impossible to fall into the deepest yoga contemplation unless he likewise withdraws attention from these three. But here the attention is not submerged; rather it is more alert than ever. Those who have not been initiated into the ultimate path have often misinterpreted this paragraph of Patanjali. This misinterpretation led some Chinese yogis to drink tea copiously at midnight and some Indian yogis to spend the night standing on their feet or lying on beds of spikes in the hope of evading natural sleep. Philosophy disdains such misguided methods and explains that the wakefulness required is of an entirely different and superior kind.

This exercise, like the previous one, is to be practised at night just before sleep. It is a fact that man then first loses consciousness of the feet and then of the lower part of his body until at last he is aware only within his head. This is the crucial moment when the world which ordinarily filters through the five senses into consciousness disappears. Only after this does he suddenly lapse into sleep. It is the pause here for a fraction of a second which has to be detected by extreme vigilance. The attention must be kept from straying and held so acutely that the bed, the room and even the body become dulled to the point of obliteration. The student should try to overcome the all-round loss of consciousness, to conquer the overpowering swoon which comes with sleep. He cannot prevent sleep for Nature's habit must have her course, but he can prevent the fall into ignorance of what is happening to him during the passage into the new state. He must try to keep his awareness and to remain in it even whilst his body and thinking faculty are completely at rest. He must observe himself and be more than watchful against the tremulous coming of sleep in that delectable borderland through which he passes, in those fluttering fractions of a moment which time the passage from gross wakefulness to profound slumber. We may well ask whether anything could possibly exist between these two states. But experience offers the best answer. If this is the crucial moment when a man will lose even this tiny seed of awareness and fall asleep as almost all men do, it is also the critical moment when through advanced yoga practice he could enter into the Light itself. Those alone who have taken the trouble to practise these exercises are best entitled to say what practical possibilities they contain or whether they will "work" or not.

But this pause between the two states technically termed "the neutral point" is as brief as a flash of lightning. If he succeeds in seizing and keeping hold of it, he may pass from this stage into the pure Mind—the background of all his conscious thought-moments—and retain it as a mere glimmer of utter emptiness throughout the night. If by self-training and the force of his resolve he can fix and prolong this instant when he is still neither asleep nor yet awake, he will pass into a kind of complete self-absorption. The fourth state will come upon him unawares, that is he will not be conscious of his actual entry into it. One moment and he will be in the ordinary wakeful state and the next moment he will be in the transcendental one. The process of transition will take place in a sphere outside his own consciousness. He will then discover himself to be in a new world of being. The momentary conscious-ness has become a footprint which has led him to the hidden self whence it originated.

If the student is unable for any reason to practise this exercise at night, he may practise along the same lines in the morning. This does not offer the same full scope of attainment, however, but it is a valuable substitute. In this case he has to detect the pause which follows sleep itself just prior to wakeful awareness of the external world and to concentrate entirely upon it. He should close his eyes and immediately interiorize his attention and send his first waking thoughts back into the beatific silence, letting the world remain at a distance for a few minutes. He has to fill those minutes with a sharp search for the realization of the pure awareness. He should not let go too readily of that silencing of thought and that quiescence of personal activity which sleep has brought about. Each fresh morning that greets his newly-opened eyes should find him seizing this opportunity at once. The consequence will be that he will find himself experiencing intermittent flashes of this transcendence during all the coming day's activities.

The nature of the mind being awareness itself, whoever attains its transcendental state can never again fall into complete unconsciousness. Consequently he can never fall into deep slumber. He can fall asleep however, but his sleep will not be devoid of awareness. The loss of ordinary sleep will not affect him detrimentally for the body will have its natural recuperative rest, the brain will be free from the procession of vagrant thoughts and thus have its repose too and the emotions will be caught and held by an intense vivid illumined peace. Such a state is incomprehensible to mankind at its present state of evolution and can be verified only by personal experience. The average student will have to train himself for a long period before he is likely to reach this region wherein he will be neither quite awake nor quite asleep. Those who have thoroughly mastered the doctrine of mentalism and applied it habitually in their waking lives will have the least difficulty in entering this super-sleep state. In any case if anyone wishes to profit most from this ultramystic exercise he must both enter and leave in the same gradual unhurrying manner the mysterious corridor twixt sleep and waking to which it conducts him. More and more as he is able to remain in this condition will it spread from his sleeping hours to invade his waking ones. Whoever can succeed in this practice will find that the sublime beatitude of the transcendental consciousness will be intermittently present throughout the most feverish activities of the day and fully so throughout the slumber of the night. That which continues unbroken as the substratum of wakefulness and is never annihilated by sleep unconsciousness is the reality he has to find. It is a state which *is* but it is not this or that in particular. There is a mysterious inexpressible quietude and delightful stillness in this sensation-free thought-less state of wakeful sleep.

The curious thing about the hidden observer is that it is very much awake when we are very much asleep, as it is perfectly conscious when we are utterly unconscious. It is the "I" which is ever-aware and consequently our real self. The consciousness so gotten is a unified and universalized one and is not occupied with the self and not-self relation. Therefore and to this extent it keeps its similarity with the sleep of ordinary mankind. It hovers in a sort of watchful self-contemplation, never losing hold on itself and consequently never falling into the oblivion of ordinary sleep. With this entry into the consciousness of the hidden observer man will come at last to comprehend the proper significance of St. Paul's words; "Then shall I know even as also I am known." If we call it the fourth state of consciousness this is only to distinguish it intellectually from the waking, dreaming and sleeping states. It would be more metaphysically truthful to say that it is not a state but the very essence of all consciousness itself, and hence the very essence of all those three states. It is timeless, spaceless, matterless, causeless, impersonal and free. It is Thought clearly seeing its own pure universal blessed and absolute self, bereft of all divisions, free from all limitations and abstracted from all projections. Consequently it is not consciousness as we understand the term but rather its mysterious root. With its undifferentiated impersonal character it is almost incomprehensible and almost indefinable to the ordinary flesh-tied, sense-bound and thought-chopping consciousness, just as man's own activities of abstract ideation, unselfish idealism, religious aspiration, mystical adoration and aesthetic appreciation are unknown to the cat which sits smugly at his fireside. Thus the sleep state, which is so devoid of light and significance during the present psychological state of mankind, becomes full of both for the developed man.

7.   *A Meditation on the Serpent's Path.* A piece of music is not only composed of a series of sounds which follow each other but also of the series of silences which intervene between each note. Yet we are mostly conscious of the sounds alone, not of the gaps between them. Just as silence is the hidden background of all these sounds so mind is the hidden background of all our ideas. Thinking is normally an unobserved element in our common life. We pay no attention to the thought process but only to the objects which call that process into oscillatory activity. Our study of the nature of physical consciousness revealed its alternating and broken character. It was pointed out that the incredibly tremendous speed of its vibratory movement hid this character under the veil of an illusory unity and that actually there is an infinitesimal gap between each flash of the world-idea and the next. This gap is nothing else than the great stillness of Mind-in-Itself. Were there always an appreciable interval of time between two thoughts then we would find that interval filled with awareness of their root—Mind. Everyone would then be conscious of his divine nature. But unfortunately although the thoughts are themselves discontinuous the personal ''I''-thought dominates them all and behaves like a caterpillar which lets go of its foothold on one leaf only after it has firmly created a foothold on another leaf. Consequently the true gap between two thoughts is covered over by the personal thought which thus creates a continuous screen of sheer illusion that hides the reality of pure Mind out of which all these thoughts, including itself, emerge.

As this interval between the fall of one idea and the rise of the next does not exist for his ordinary consciousness the student has to set himself to create one by practising a formal exercise. It bears the peculiar traditional name of ''The Path of the Serpent'', because it seeks to make attention glide like a snake into reality by watching for and seizing the intervening state between ideas. His task is to make his thoughts examine themselves in an effort to trace back their own ancestry, a task which is like using one thorn to pick out another which has got in the flesh. The moment that thoughts try to know their source they start to travel on a path different from any that they have ever taken before and one which will bring them more and more into their own real hidden selfhood. As each sensuous image springs up in consciousness, as each movement of reason presents him with a new thought, he should dissolve it promptly again by a thrust of the will, as it were. He should seek to get his consciousness back to its primal pure state and to keep it there. The numerous individual ideas are to be displaced as they arise. He dis-identifies himself from them so that they find no foothold.

It would be a mistake however merely to suppress his thoughts and remain intellectually blank and bereft of all understanding as the ordinary yogi seeks to do. Rather must he recognize the relation between thinking as an act and himself as the thinker. The final consummation of philosophic yoga cannot come about unless the intelligence is brought to bear upon the relation between the world and thoughts, between thoughts and the thinking principle and lastly upon this principle itself. For two powerful thoughts stand in the way. The first is the world-thought. The second is the "I"-thought. And both are intimately inter-locked. They may be temporarily lulled by suppression but they will only be permanently overcome by comprehension. The ordinary yogi deals with the first by shutting his senses against what is outside them and thus evades its existence. The philosophic yogi must do it differently. He must do it by understanding that the space-time form of the World, *which includes those senses themselves,* is primarily the outcome of his image-making faculty, and that the whole world is really a great thought-form in which consciousness has become immersed. Hence he has to acknowledge and accept its existence as being but a mental one and then to disengage consciousness from the thought itself not by rejecting it but by absorbing it. Thus he takes the world-idea into himself and transcends it. The same kind of intelligent effort is demanded of him when dealing with the personal "I"-thought. It is the worst sinner and will naturally oppose him in his endeavour because its own illusion-creating rule would be threatened by his success.

He should dismiss each particular and separate thought continually as it comes into his field of awareness, as the ordinary yogi dismisses it, but he should affirm also the consciousness of which it is composed. He should not only comprehend the important mystical truth that thinking as an activity is only a habit but also that the Mind which makes it possible is ever present. The student's consciousness must insert itself through the gap between one thought and the next and if this elusive fleeting fraction of a moment is caught and extended longer and longer with every period of practice—and this requires an immensely sharp and dynamically alert attentiveness perseveringly cultivated to continue without fatigue—the time will come when the mind will sink deeper and deeper into itself. When he is so fortunate as to attain this glimpse of what undifferentiated Thought means he must exert himself energetically and unwaveringly not to let it slip away. This will certainly happen if he is not vigilant enough because he has upset the whole habitual tradition of personal existence. This sudden glimpse when the mind ultimately solves its own mystery and gains in the "lightning-flash" the solution of *its own significance,* must be caught, precisely as the flash of intuition must be caught, before it fades. The insight flashes so unexpectedly, so suddenly and so spontaneously that it must be treated like the unexpected visit of a great king to the house of a humble commoner, a king who, ignored, unattended or unwelcomed, may leave at once in abrupt offence at the discourtesy shown him. He will have to hold the citadel of consciousness strongly and steadily against the invasions which are sure to come, against the legions of memories, anticipations, reasonings, distractions and emotions which will try their utmost to enter the gates or climb the walls. If they cannot succeed straightforwardly they will try to enter in disguise. That is they will make pure Thought itself the subject of their activity and before he knows where he is he will be outside and they inside! The task demands a constant vigilance, a continual remembrance of what it is that he has set out to achieve. Eventually thought after thought—not about external objects, for he has long advanced beyond their tyranny, but this time about pure Thought itself—will insistently intrude itself in what is a masked and desperate effort to tear him away from increasing his intent concentration upon pure Thought itself, but he must vigorously thrust them aside.

The aim is self-reflectively to isolate Mind—that which enables him to think—from the images and thoughts which stream forth continuously from it, to achieve a state of *understanding* consciousness where there is no object of consciousness. And, owing to the inconceivable quickness with which the world-thought vibrates as successive sense-images, this cannot be accomplished in a merely intellectual way. It cannot be done without some kind of yoga, but when his thoughts are directed to search with determination and understanding for their own "stuff" they enter upon a form of yoga which is quicker in yielding results than almost all other forms. Consciousness is to be caught between two alternate ideas and thus cleared of all thoughts and kept attentively alert and wakefully alive to its own character at the same time. He must burrow beneath all thoughts to their deepest ground. He must reach inwards behind the endless series of disconnected thoughts to the pure element of undifferentiated Thought which exists behind them. The higher meditation begins when thought is no longer preoccupied with its offspring thoughts and is no longer directed to alien topics but seeks to get an insight into its own nature to succeed in recognizing itself and consequently be itself. Thought is that hidden ultimate element whose activity we know as consciousness, whose manifestation we experience as thoughts and whose existence contains the world-idea's own existence whereas *a* thought is something which the mind creates or has for itself and perceives in itself. The stages of deepening achievement in this meditation are: first, outward consciousness begins to dissolve until the world becomes a mere shadow and finally vanishes altogether; second, then the sense of personality becomes abbreviated and fainter and likewise vanishes; third, this is the profoundest stage when a formless, nameless, limitless, timeless existence alone remains.

Such an extreme state of lightness is experienced that he feels he has become as empty as space and as weightless as air. He has no consciousness of whether he is in or out of the body simply because he has no consciousness of the body at all. The extraordinary fact about it is that although there are no sensations of physical existence at all, the sense of bare existence itself is very strong and intense. The world-thought and its individual thinker have now blent and become one. So in that exalted state the duality between experiencing man and an experienced world suddenly vanishes. There is then only a single existence in consciousness. Thus in the end, in a grave calm and revelatory quietude of all his being, the contemplation becomes so intense that all thoughts will merge smoothly in their primary principle and no longer will effort be needful to restrain them. When his meditation uninterruptedly attains this profound depth the student will seem to be transformed into a veritable ocean of mind-stuff, a vast void wherein the personal self with its past history and present activity vanishes as though it never were and wherein the whole external universe is not even a memory. Mind—boundless, imperturbable and changeless—alone is. He passes out of his personal self and enters a condition of absolute inner emptiness. There is nothing here to be known as there is nothing to be named. It is not the annihilation, so expected by materialists, for consciousness of a new kind still exists. It is not the merger, so sought by absolutists, for individuality of a higher sort still exists. He has indeed come as close to God as mortal man on this planet may come. This is the ultimate being or be-ness. Yet there is nothing to see or hear, taste or touch or smell in this experience, which is entirely a supra-sensual one.

He has found the solution of his long long quest, not as a matter of mere speculation but of verifiable experience, yet at once finds himself without thoughts, his consciousness poised above the brain, his lips struck dumb at each attempt to communicate the uncommunicable. Here is a wisdom which trembles on the verge of speech and must forever remain unspoken. It is a state of beautiful quiescence, not of emotional rapture; no egoistic excitement may enter that holy shrine. No shadow of any external thing may fall across its illuminated threshold. No train of reasoning may be thought out in that sublime stillness. For the meditator then becomes what he sees; he alone is but he is not now what he was in the world outside. He has returned to the primal unity of being, to the sublime illimitable void.

Here, in this vast concept of thoughtless Thought itself, of pure Thought unbroken by any thoughts, is the true miracle of universal being, could mankind but appreciate it properly, something sacred indeed with a sacredness unknown to the petty and parochial views of religious materialists. Its blankness can terrify those alone who do not and cannot understand. Here, as thinking ceases and willing lapses, as imagination is no more active and personality becomes utterly passive, as the senses lie quiet like a sleeping bird, there opens a third eye in man. He sees not only that which he is but also that which always *is*. That which others ignore as non-existent, the immaterial "nothingness" of universal Mind, is precisely what offers itself now to his unveiled perception. It is not a state of non-existence. It is indeed a living actuality; otherwise it could never be inwardly realized. But it is not existence in the form which he can comprehend with the finite intellect. It is to be grasped only by each man for himself by a direct flash of insight whose content is not apart from the insight itself. It is not to be grasped by a conclusion reached by a succession of thoughts nor by a clairvoyant vision which is still within the limits of form. Thus Mind is to be worshipped silently, thought of negatively and realized in the Void. All other worship yields either an imagination in consciousness or a sensation in the body, that is it yields a symbol of the Real but does not touch the Real itself.

With these words we have reached the limit of what can be explained about this aspect of the ultimate reality. The truth about it is silent and scriptureless. Both reader and writer must now go into a strange wide ethereal silence if they would move a step further. Silence is the finest method of mystical perceptive worship. What the student has to grasp is that where there is seemingly nothing at all but a static Silence, the Real abides; where his individual perception fails to register either form or entity, there the Overself *IS*. When he can put the littleness of self aside for a moment and think of that Infinite Element within which he dwells, he will be overwhelmed with a sense of the wonder and mystery that surround the daily movements of mortal men. He can then neither sing its praises aloud with those who believe nor argue about its existence with those who disbelieve. He must remain as the thought finds him, with dumb lips and reverent heart, with quieted body and subdued emotion, silent indeed. This is his loftiest mood, this contented contemplation wherein the struggling *I* rests at last in the ever-peaceful I AM.

15

The Mystical Phenomena of Meditation

APART from any dreams which he may deliberately seek to induce, the student may or may not during his course of meditation perceive some of those clairvoyant visions or experience some of those mystical trances or occult phenomena with which all the historic annals of both Hindu-Buddhist yoga and Christian-Muslim mysticism are well filled. It is consequently needful to point out that such occurrences in the wakeful state are only the passing accompaniments of meditation for some students and not for all students, that those to whom they happen are not necessarily more mystically advanced or ethically superior to the others to whom they do not happen and that whether they happen or not is only of quite secondary or even of no importance upon the philosophic quest. They will manifest or fail to do so according to the individual karma and character of each student. He will be well advised to pursue his own inner course without trying to confuse it with another's. St. Bernard, one of the great Catholic mystics, spent much time in meditation yet confessed towards the end of his life that he had never seen any vision, never heard any inner voices and never experienced any supernatural revelation—this although he humbly disclosed that God had very often entered his soul during contemplation. And so great an authority as St. Juan de la Cruz, one of the front-rank Spanish mystics, openly stated: "many souls to whom visions have never come are incomparably more advanced in the way of perfection than others to whom many have been given."

If some part of this training may induce visions and dreams and ecstasies to develop, it does not like some ordinary yogas do so as ends in themselves but only as incidental means toward a single and higher end. This can become clearer if we consider certain questions which are often asked. Why do such pictorial visions vary so widely and conflict so sharply with each other? Why do so many mystical revelations merely confirm pre-existent historical beliefs but do not originate them? Why do they occur at all? What is the real significance of the trance state? These questions have perfectly rational psychological answers. But such answers may not satisfy either the ordinary scientist, with his initial materialist bias, or the ordinary mystic, with his initial emotionalist bias. They do however satisfy the philosophic student because he finds an honoured place for both science and meditation but ruthlessly discards their prejudices and errors.

We shall here disregard the fraudulent claims of imposters and the phantas-magoric hallucinations of the insane and deal only with authentic cases. When meditation is really what it ought to be, that is a fateful turning of man's spiritual face homewards, an actual endeavour to enter into communion with the everlasting source of his own being, a noble yearning of heart and reason for the realization of a super-sensuous life, then it calls forth eventually a response from the Overself. The reaction may be shown by ecstatic feelings which he may then enjoy for a time, or by mentally-impressed messages which he may receive in what seems to be an actual thought-conversation with an angel or a saint or by a conventional picture of the Supreme Being which forms itself in his consciousness. Whatever it is, it will be of such a character as precisely to suit his particular evolutionary degree, and also his temperament, predilections and expectations. God or the "soul", the World-Mind or the Overself will make an appearance to him in the way that he can best understand. This is because God is not apart from his own self, not an unrelated far-off Being. And such an appearance is made as a recognizable token that the Divine really exists, as a guarantee of the sacred character of the visitation.

The phenomenal visions of sacred personages or mythological events which embellish the experience of many mystics will be found on examination to vary in accordance with their previous beliefs, environment, expectancy, education and outlook. Nevertheless this does not invalidate such experience for the Overself has sought to speak to them in the language with which they are most familiar. If Jesus appears to Christians but not to Hindus, whilst Krishna or Shiva appears to the latter and not to the former, the impartial but sympathetic investigator need not be bewildered by these contradictions once he realizes that by spontaneously fitting its response to the aspirant's comprehension, the Overself manifests thereby what is really a channel of its grace. In this way the true self communicates with mankind in a multitude of different veiled forms during the long course of their history. What however they usually do not know is that alongside of the wonderful and genuine expansion of consciousness which they feel because of the Overself's touch, their own personal complexes and thoughts unconsciously interpret this expansion according to their own habitual trend. The interpreting activity starts so swiftly—sometimes simultaneously—that its secondary contribution actually seems to be an integral part of the primary experience itself. Thus the Overself lets them *unconsciously* fashion the phenomenal form for themselves whilst it pours its own formless essence into the mould which is thus proffered.

The ignorance which satisfies others cannot satisfy the philosophic student. He must bring to the surface of full awareness the processes by which mystical visions—whether his own or theirs—are manufactured. He must ascertain accurately how they actually arise, and not how he imagines they arise. He must stop working in the dark. And thus he finds that both experiences of the forgotten or remembered past may contribute their share no less than anticipations of the unborn future; that both the immediate physical environment and an imagined distant one may have their say; that both the beliefs absorbed in early childhood and the beliefs acquired in later manhood may be partly responsible; that both statements read in books and the mind's own imaginative power may be active and, finally, that both the naturally expectant desire to experience a vision no less than the vanity-born wish to impress others may be at work. Usually there are seven personal factors which tend to construct or at least to affect and colour such mystical phenomena. These are: (1) the pre-conceived religious or mystical notions of the meditator, (2) the character of the original focus of his concentration, that is the line of thought, the physical object or the particular personage that he is meditating upon, (3) general tendencies and habit-energies brought over from past births, (4) innate complexes and acquired prejudices, (5) emotional temperament, (6) physical circumstances and environment including bodily condition and historical-geographical situation, (7) mental capacity. Hence the mystic subconsciously builds his vision not only out of the inspiration supplied by his Overself but also out of these materials taken from his own personality. He sees what he has unconsciously projected.

If we refer to the earlier studies in dream analysis and note the several different factors which may singly or in combination mould the form which a dream takes, we have ready at hand most—not all—of the factors which may mould the form which a mystical vision takes too. Just as there is no one universal cause which will correctly account for all dreams, so there is no one universal cause which will correctly account for all visions. The same study has also taught us that physical, mental or emotional experience may symbolically represent itself in the form of dream. Just as the dreamer may witness the dramatic self-realization of his own unconsciously projected ideas and desires, so the mystic may witness a parallel operation too. For the rapt body-free reverie of the one is not too dissimilar from the rapt body-free reverie of the other. Mentalism has incontestably demonstrated that it is the depth and intensity with which we hold our thoughts of things that makes them real to us. The seeing of visions may be at one and the same time both a species of spontaneous self-hypnotization and a sacred inspiration. When thought is even momentarily suppressed and the mind left empty, the meditator who is not proceeding on philosophic lines himself fills this void with a vision, either by his present unconscious expectancy of a particular form or by his previous conscious concentration upon it. His visions may be in part his own thoughts returned to him but they do not return alone.

Something has been added. There is in them, as the reward of his aspiration and meditation, the unearthly inspiration of the Overself, the compelling certitude of the Overself, the exalted serenity of the Overself. Unfortunately if he does not understand what has happened to him, if he does not discriminate between the one and the other but super-imposes the accidental upon the essential, then he may get his spiritual revelation but may also get back his own intellectual beliefs and emotional attributions magnified a hundredfold with it, because they now come supported by the certitude which the authentic glimpse always brings with it—but a certitude which he has partially misplaced.

Dozens of biographical illustrations of this psychological process could be given but it is rarely that its verification from a mystic's own confession could be given. One of the most outstanding of well-known Indian modern yogis was Ram Teertha, who suddenly renounced a brilliant academic career as a Professor of Mathematics to live alone and remote from civilization in the inner recesses of the snow-topped Himalayas. He meditated constantly and quickly attained a superlatively joyous realization of the presence of divinity, as was evidenced later during his brief return to ordinary society in the plains and in lectures which he then delivered to amazed audiences. We lived for a while in the mountains overlooking the deep narrow valley wherein his hut had been built and in whose bed flowed a stream in which his body was eventually found drowned. As an admirer of this renowned yogi we sought out two or three mountain folk who had attended on his wants and later, on returning to city life, we were fortunate to meet a well-educated devotee of his who related some interesting and instructive anecdotes about him. The yogi had been a devotee of the Hindu Saviour, Krishna, and during the nights he would often see in vision the blue-bodied figure of Krishna dancing on a cobra's head and playing a flute. This is the figure which has been made familiar to all India by pictures to be found in millions of homes. Ram Teertha said the Krishna-figure appeared to him quite outside his own body, when his own eyes were wide open and when all his five senses were fully awake. It was completely external and completely objective. What interested us most however was the frank statement made to this disciple years after these experiences by the yogi himself. He said, "This marked a particular stage of the mind-concentration and it was really the materialization of my own imagination, the precipitation of my own mind."

Vivid and real and external enough though they may seem to be to the person "seeing" them, nevertheless clairvoyant phenomena "emanate from the mind and into the mind they sink" as the Tibetan adepts say about them. The discerning critic sees that the form is man-made and naturally rejects it altogether as an illusion. But unfortunately he does not feel the inspiring mystical realization which is expressing itself through that form. Hence the psychological fact must be carefully separated from the metaphysical interpretation of the fact if we want to get at the truth about a mystical revelation. And because the two are almost inextricably intertwined the mystic who does not care to do so but accepts them as if they were a single thing merely misapprehends his own experience.

The key to this problem is therefore that the form of response is provided by the man himself; the power which animates or fills that form is provided by the Overself. As a witness that his faith in something beyond himself and beyond matter is really justified, it is not an illusion. Hence the sceptics need not congratulate themselves. They are easily deluded by their own scepticism. For over and above the possible causes which the scientist may detect there still remains a substantial residue of another possible cause which he is unable to detect because it can fairly be described as being entirely outside any personal origination in the seer himself. That which it brings to birth in a mystical vision is not a respinning of old material but a veritable creation of new life. This truly divine element in a vision which is felt rather than seen makes it authentic and, in the numinous sense, a veritable revelation.

Allied to these manifestations of the Overself's power there is a whole group of manifestations of the mind's wonderful power. They are based on the fact of telepathy. If any sensitive person has only once met a highly developed practitioner of meditation, visions of the latter may recur spontaneously merely when and if either thinks of the other. Moreover it is also possible to establish some kind of mental rapport with such a person, especially if he has undertaken to give spiritual help. Experience will gradually reveal that certain definite thoughts have been immediately impressed on the mind by the advanced yogi without being embodied in vocal or written speech. A successful relationship between the two requires however a syntonic connection between them—sensitivity or devotion on the one side and powerful concentration on the other. In all thought-transference however the first impression is a subliminal one and can only be converted into a conscious one if the recipient does not hinder the process by brusque initial rejection or by immediate utter scepticism.

The communication of two minds independently of material means, the projection of thought from one individual to another, the penetration of space and the transfer of personal atmosphere regardless of the distance intervening between two bodies, the strange interaction of being wherein the stronger one is the sender and the weaker one is the recipient need not surprise us. Something of it manifests itself even in ordinary experience as between an orator upon a platform and his audience seated in chairs, between lovers separated in different lands and between a hypnotist and his entranced subject. Science, which learnt to recognize space as a medium for the transmission of light, must learn also to recognize it as a medium for the transmission of thought. Thought-transference becomes possible when the thoughts of one man can set up sympathetic vibrations in the consciousness of another. The principle involved is similar to the one involved in wireless telegraphy and radio broadcasting, where the receiver must be adjusted to the same period of vibration as the transmitter. Again, just as broadcasting becomes possible because there exists a single universal medium connecting both, namely electricity, so there is a universal connecting medium between both brains, namely Mind. An understanding of mentalism provides the proper key to understanding the basis of such telepathic phenomena. This is also the hidden basis of many so-called miracles, the secret foundation of many so-called supernatural feats and yogic magic. He who can realize for himself and *in* himself the truth of mentalism will find wonders occurring to him in his presence, not seldom without his own seeking. Indeed various other occult phenomena may or may not occur but they are not to be looked upon as being anything more than incidental to the quest, never as essential to it. The student should not commit the common mistakes of misunderstanding their psychological character, of over-estimating their worth and of over-concentrating his efforts upon them. They should provide but a subordinate interest. He must understand that they are only the possible accompaniments of meditation and are far less important than people suppose they are. Even the mere fact that these experiences are usually fugitive and fragmentary indicates this. Sometimes there is quite a spate of supernormal experience for a brief while and then it fades away and vanishes altogether for several years.

It is here needful to utter some further words of warning. Whether in the East or the West much pernicious nonsense, riddled by charlatanry, poisoned by commercialism and rendered futile by superstition, is being passed off as mysticism or occultism. Whoever plunges into mysticism and occultism without at some stage or other pausing to pass through some of the philosophic discipline, to acquire the rudiments of its protective metaphysical and moral qualifications, exposes himself to possible errors and deceptions. A number of strange, silly or sinister movements illustrate the freak forms which mysticism has taken when wrongly understood by its votaries and unscrupulously abused by its champions. At their best they are tainted with the fact that they promise but can never give man his highest happiness; at their worst they are tainted with serious psychic danger. The philosophically disciplined student's reason must remorselessly cut through their false or insane suggestions like a sharp-edged sickle. Again, whether at the beginning, the middle or even towards the end of this quest, the aspirant must beware of glib exploiting teachers or even insane self-styled "New Messiahs'' who, with exaggerated claims to supernatural powers and with extravagant promises of speedily advancing him toward their attainment, can only cause him to deviate dangerously from his true course and lead him away from his principal aim of realizing the Overself. It is much safer to walk alone than to walk in such company. The inner promptings of the Overself—if only he will take the trouble to separate them from the promptings of his own ego—will lead the student more honestly and less tortuously than the outer beckonings of any such man. The evolutionary changes in mental life and the karmic changes in external life have also rendered unnecessary much—not all of course—of the ancient dependence on a human teacher. Moreover it is a Himalayan task to find an authentic sage in the modern world, although it is easy enough to find reputed ones. The situation today being what it is, as predicted by the Buddha, the average student, if unable to get truly inspired personal guidance, should not waste his aspiration on the search, for thoroughly competent and genuinely altruistic teachers are like needles in haystacks, but should cultivate his own power, reason, intuition, meditativeness and understanding of experience. The loving devotion to the ideal which has already been felt or glimpsed must be cherished unremittingly in the heart. It is such a love whose significant reaction acts as a force to uplift the seeker beyond his present level. Thus in very truth he becomes his own teacher.

Let it never be forgotten what earlier studies have iterated and re-iterated. The Overself is the real teacher in the heart, the one initiator of all struggling aspirants. It is the final bestower of insight. It is the benign mediator of grace to the imploring ego. It is not a theoretical presence but a living one with whom the aspirant can remotely or intimately commune. It can liberate him from his ignorance, instruct him in super-intellectual truth and guide him to philosophic enlightenment. All his efforts in yoga should be interfused with warm devotion to the inner reality for unless he really loves it he will never unite with it. He should therefore comprehend that a leading principle of all these ultramystic meditation exercises is that success ultimately depends not on the conscious efforts he puts forth but on the mysterious reaction to those efforts. This does not of course mean that the efforts are valueless in themselves for without them there would be no reaction. It means that the over-conscious gets to work independently upon him at a certain stage. When this actually manifests itself it will not be during any of his struggles to obtain it but during the periods of cessation from those struggles, not during positive concentration but during the absence of concentration. It becomes articulate not during the thinking about it but during the intervals of not thinking about it. Henceforth, whatever has to be done will not be done by himself. Instead, it will be done to him. He will be taken by the hand, as it were, and led into the profound stillness which guards the threshold of the Overself. Across that threshold he will receive the reply to the question: What Am I? Like a loving mother the Overself will take its progeny up into itself at this wonderful moment of initiation and thus the inner rebirth will occur. It will come as the culmination of long striving but it is not itself an act of striving. For only the divine grace can bring it about.

From Sight to Insight.

The pictorial visions which may attend ordinary meditation, however beautiful or impressive they may be, are not the true vision which comes ultimately with philosophic meditation. This is because anything which can be perceived in space-time dimensions must needs belong to the world of finite relativity. They are, as St. Juan de la Cruz wisely said: "only graces to prepare them for this greater grace. . . . Those who have the less clear vision do not perceive so distinctly as the others how greatly He transcends their vision." What is this greater grace? It is the awakening to what is outside space-time existence, the enlightenment of consciousness by a transcendental formless knowledge. To apprehend pure thought it must be apprehended as empty of any forms. The ultimate has no shape, size, colour or voice whatever. Consequently whatever is seen standing before one's inner clairvoyant vision cannot be ultimate but rather something inferior to it. The mystic who has not purified his space-bound outlook by metaphysical knowledge, who clings stubbornly to concepts suited only to a lower grade, may quite easily expect to perceive the Divine in the same way as he perceives a house or to see God in a particular figure as he sees a man standing on the other side of the street in a particular body. In such a vision he merely sees his *idea* of God. The moment his thoughts are made perfectly still he has prepared one of the two pre-requisite conditions whereby he may become aware of pure Thought. But such a desirable consummation will not arrive with the appearance of further thoughts, however exalted they may be, or with the appearance of any vision, however wonderful it may be. If he wants to *see* and *hear* God with the mind's eyes and ears, however subtle they may be, he is still in a semi-materialist stage. He has to advance to the higher philosophic position which rejects all the senses in its approach to divinity and wants only to *know* God through the pure faculty of being attuned to God. Every picture of the Real which the mind forms during its onward progress may delude the mystic into the belief that it is the Real itself. He must guard himself against such easy self-deception. For only when he ceases to externalize God in alterable pictures, only when he attains the unalterable insight into the formless realm where there are no pictures doomed to vanish at all, can he trust the sense of reality which has hitherto flitted from one timebound mental experience to another.

Thus one far-reaching value of our metaphysical study emerges.

If, in the end, reality is spaceless, formless and timeless, then no transient phenomena unrolling before the inner view a series of spaced, timed and formed images can ever be a direct manifestation of reality *as it is in itself.* Those who have embarked on the ultimate path and seek the very root of reality are warned not to get carried emotionally away by them but to minimize their importance. Nothing that has shape or size or colour, nothing visible or tangible, whether physically or psychically so, is to be accepted for the final reality as such. When their vision of God is no longer obscured by visions, when their thought of God is exempt from thoughts about God, they will be quite close to the goal. The philosophic mystic is less interested in forms seen subjectively and more interested in the power which pervades those forms; therefore he gains a greater enlightenment. The philosophic yoga consummates itself when it directs attention away from every kind of externalized thought whatsoever, however subtle it be, towards the formless reality. It makes consciousness introspect *itself.* In other words, consciousness must ultimately become its own object, its all in all. The ancient texts called the threefold philosophic approach "the path of the bird", whilst they called the lower yoga "the path of the ant". Both lead to the attainment of the Overself, they said, but whereas the first confers quick salvation the other confers it indirectly and gradually. Persistent reflection and earnest effort to understand those ideas is as needful for the mystic as for the materialist. For he may come close to reality but through sheer ignorance of what constitutes it may pass it heedlessly by. Practising mystics need not therefore be disheartened by our warnings, which are intended only to encourage them not to stop halfway on the quest but to search and strive for entry into the higher degree, not to come to a standstill with their immediate objective but to remember that there is also an ultimate one.

Why do so many mystics experience ecstasies during the course of their meditations? The answer is that when in the earlier stages the grace touches them their emotions are so powerfully aroused as a natural consequence that they suddenly burst out in passionate transports of ecstasy. This is the consequence of the impact of a higher power, an impact to which novices are so unaccustomed as to be temporarily thrown off their balance. The ecstasy usually appears either at the beginning or at the end of an individual meditation, according to the kind of path followed. If the first is the case, then it will die down as the meditation proceeds and yield to the calm serenity of a higher plane. If the second is the case then its arrival will destroy the peace previously touched during meditation, which was on this same higher plane. In both cases its presence is due to the uprising of personal emotion whereas the serenity will be due to experience on a more impersonal level. Rapturous visions and emotional ecstasies usually come at an early stage in the career of the would-be mystic because they come to encourage him to continue with an unorthodox aspiration or a practice which unfortunately the world at large will discourage. They are satisfying phenomena which may or may not mark the preliminary stages of devotional yoga and they always wear off and disappear when a well-advanced stage is reached. When a man gets completely intoxicated with the raptures arising out of meditation he has fallen into an extreme as dangerous to mental balance and inner growth as when he gets intoxicated with metaphysics. Mystical ecstasies must be fleeting by their very nature and cannot be otherwise. It is utterly impossible for any human being to enjoy them permanently. It is better to attain a state of constant balance than an alternating state of glowing ecstasy and brooding depression. Ecstatic joy implies emotional activity, and activity implies transiency, change; thus there is no final rest in such a state. That this is so is evidenced by the history of both Eastern and Western mysticism, which is punctuated with references to the melancholy descent at a more advanced stage into what is called "the dark night of the soul", when all ecstasies totally disappear and are replaced by shadowed moods of melancholy spiritual dryness. Most mystics tell of this recoil from rapturous heights of emotional sweetness to dreary valleys which are filled with tantalizing memories. But this is simply the effort of Nature to bring about proper readjustment, to restore the balance of forces on a higher level. And out of the tragic experience of the dark night of the soul there will come, if the mystic lets it, the growing realization that mystic ecstasy alone is no longer a sufficient goal for him and that an unbroken serene assurance of the divine ever-presence is immeasurably better.

The mystic is chiefly concerned with his personal feelings about God. The philosopher is chiefly concerned with God. This is one of the several differences between them. It is a tremendous difference. Devotion guided by knowledge can achieve what simple devotion can never achieve. Knowledge inspired by devotion can likewise achieve what simple knowledge can never achieve. This is a secret which neither the undergraduate mystic nor the unillumined metaphysician comprehends. This is why when the mystic reaches his deepest point in meditation he should not allow himself to be carried away by his personal feelings to the extent of forgetting his higher aim. That is, he may enjoy them quietly but should not luxuriate in them. At this point he should instead have the presence of mind to turn his attention to the Mind-in-itself, turning it still deeper inward to try to understand itself and seek its own reality. Such criticism does not mean that emotions are to be extinguished. They are and must remain the great driving force in active life for every man at every stage all the way to the very end. But whereas they often run amok in a man at a lower stage, they become purified and controlled through right culture at a higher one.

Veneration is even more essential to the aspirant than erudition. Nobody need be ashamed to weep, for example, even despite his metaphysical training, if he weeps for exalted things or in compassion for others or for the sacred presence. So long as he has not reached the last goal so long is he an aspirant. And so long as he is an aspirant he must be ready to weep for God, to yearn for divinity and to shed tears over its absence from his consciousness; in short, to *feel*. Indeed the acutest intensest feelings must be possessed and not killed off. Without them a man will never realize the goal. For God is to be felt in the profoundest possible manner, not as a cold intellectual concept. Nevertheless he has to use such a concept and play it off against his feelings in order to check and to purify them if he is to find the *true* God. He has to play feeling against reason. For out of this interaction will emerge a deeper, a more chastened attitude towards God.

Why do so many aspirants get brief glimpses of the supersenuous state and then fall away from them? Why are these glimpses so rare and spread out at such long intervals, if indeed they do recur at all? Why are they unable to fix them? Why, when they seek to hold them, do they find only the cold dead ash of a mere remembrance in their hands? Why can they not recapture those wonderful moments which elude them even whilst their fingers are closing around them? The answer is in part that these are refreshing foretastes of an attainment which still lies far beyond and are sent by the Overself to encourage hopes, to act as incentives to pursue the quest and to tell the neophytes—however stammeringly—what its culmination is like. Then Nature thrusts them back for a while from meditation in order to get them to readjust themselves on their two other sides, inspired action and metaphysical reflection, for it is only out of the integral fusion of all these three that insight can be born and retained.

In the opening chapters of the companion volume to this work there was stated, somewhat briefly, barely and incompletely, certain problems connected with what yogis usually regard as the culmination of all their efforts—the trance state. They concerned its temporary character, its failure to stabilize its own exceptional but fugitive insights, its results in unfitting a man for further social existence, its creation of an attitude of complacent indifference toward the welfare of others, its persuasion of the yogi to withdraw permanently from society and its inability to show ethical improvement at all proportionate to the effort involved. These problems must now be provided for. But this term "trance" has some unmystical associations in the spiritualistic-seance sense, some unfortunate ones in the Western consciousness and some ugly ones in the medical consciousness. Indeed, it carries with it offensive pathological suggestions of danger and is freely used in connection with the unpleasant phenomena of insanity. But the peak state of right meditation is not a morbid or unhealthy or dangerous one, as a trance is usually thought to be, but rather one of special exaltation and emotional happiness. It is a fruit of mental discipline, not of mental aberration. The average Western reader is likely to form a wrong notion of what is meant here by such a term. He is more likely to catch the correct meaning if the term "reverie" is used instead but here again there is the implication that reasoning processes are still actively working, albeit in a vague dreamlike way. "Samadhi", the Sanskrit word under discussion, has also been translated by Orientalists as "ecstasy". This too may be misleading when we remember that its highest stage is entirely thought-free. Therefore it may be less likely to lead to misunderstanding if we here use "self-absorption" as an equivalent and refrain henceforth from using the term "trance" altogether. What is meant is a rapt absorption of the thoughts in the essence of oneself and a profound immersion of the feelings in indescribable felicity. If used at all for yogic experiences the word "trance" ought to be reserved for those cataleptic states which consummate the efforts of practicants in the final phases of the yoga of body control, with which we are not here concerned, for such a path can never directly lead to that realization of the Overself which is the proper goal set out in these writings. The unconscious state attained by this system is not regarded as desirable or necessary on the path which is unfolded here. It would indeed be useless. The trances of the hatha yogis, of the fakirs who permit themselves to be buried alive for a few hours or days, render the man unconscious just as the "I"-thought falls back into its source within the heart. When it returns, he has had no more spiritual benefit than he has had from ordinary sleep, whereas in the higher self-absorption of mystical meditation the ego merges back into the heart while fully conscious. Nobody need be frightened away from the practice of meditation therefore by the belief that it is beyond the reach of all but a select few or that it will be necessary for them to fall into a trance in the sense of a fainting away into unconsciousness. On the contrary, the practice itself is not only within the capacity of all but seeks a state of fuller consciousness, a psychological condition of expanded awareness.

The first problem of self-absorption is its fleeting character. Whether in its lightest phase of soothed nerves, its intermediate phase of suffused sense-free reverie, or its final phase of full absorption, world-remoteness and self-mergence, it is always labelled with impermanence. The mystic may climb all the foothills and summits of a divine existence during this experience but he has always to descend them again. His way yields magnificent glimpses of growing breadth and luminosity but it does not yield a permanent foothold. He cannot hibernate forever in self-absorption even if he wants to. Or as the Chinese mystic, Lao Tsu, put the problem: "One cannot remain forever standing on tiptoe." Consciousness cannot be kept on the stretch of formal contemplation all the time; it can only enter this condition at intervals. The interior immobilization is not an enduring one and their trances are transient—this is the constant complaint of the few mystics who have cared to analyse their own experience.

Many Western mystics, like St. Gregory and St. Augustine, and not a few Eastern yogis like Vivekananda, have mourned this fact that they could not maintain what they believed to be the highest stage in mysticism, the stage of complete withdrawal from sensations and thoughts, for more than a few minutes or a few hours but always had to fall back again to their prosaic everyday condition. St. Bernard too has well described this recoil in his own melancholy words: "All these spiritual powers and faculties began to droop and languish as if the fire had been withdrawn from a bubbling pot. Then my soul was necessarily sad and depressed until He should return." The discontinuance of the experience is always something which the mystic cannot control or prevent. Consequently he is faced by the difficulty of bringing it into smooth adjustment with the necessities of his bodily existence, a difficulty which he never really overcomes. Philosophy, perceiving this, remarks that his particular method of approach has reached a point where it has exhausted its servicableness to him and that Nature has consequently hoisted a warning signal. But philosophy alone can interpret this signal for him. The mystical experience must be brought to completion by the unfoldment of a profounder insight and not left with its ultimate end unattained. Thus its very transiency becomes useful eventually to make the mystic aware that this cannot be the final goal itself and to make clear to him that he has yet to advance in a different direction. The hidden teaching most emphatically affirms that the state of self-absorption is not the supreme objective for mankind, however much the common run of yogis may assert the contrary. It is only when waking that the person is fully projected by the Overself whereas when dreaming it is only partially projected whilst when sleeping it is not projected at all. Therefore it is only in the fully awakened state and not in an entranced one—which corresponds to dream or sleep—that the higher purpose of its limitations can be recognized and the widest consciousness of reality attained. Hence although he may or may not have to pass through trance on his upward way the aspirant certainly does not have to pass through it when he reaches the crest. The fourth state of consciousness is something which, in its finality and fullness, persists at all times and does not depend on transient trances for its continuance.

The second problem by which the mystic self-absorption is beset—its failure to stabilize its own exceptional but fugitive insight, its inability to provide an ever-active awareness of reality—is also solved only by philosophy. To understand this we must first understand that out of the repulsion and compulsion of a strongly-held world-view, the meditator of necessity deliberately turns his back on his external environment, forsakes and spurns his earthly existence during the inward progression towards his spiritual self. He first discovers or grasps the existence of the intangible invisible imageless Mind during a rapt contemplation, where he becomes intensely absorbed within himself in utter forgetfulness of the external world. So intense is his concentration that eventually all sensations and thoughts vanish, all mental images pass away and he abides in a great void, where no-thing is and where he is, in theological language, merged in pure Spirit. But the mind can no more rest permanently in this void than the breathing lungs can rest permanently in a complete vacuum. The individual thought-waves soon swing inexorably back into the ocean of universal mind, his absorption breaks and the world is precipitated once again into his consciousness. He can abide there only for a while for he is then driven out of the mystical Garden of Eden by the symbolic Angel with a flaming sword. Hence this cannot constitute its ultimate goal. The yogi who attains this point may strive hard to retain it by plunging himself anew in prolonged absorption but he can recover it again only by disregarding the world and retreating into himself once more. Yet all-wise Nature will have none of it and hurls him back as often as he tries. Misunderstanding her intent, he strives all the more, ascribing his inability to wrong causes and failing to learn its hard lesson that Nature has built the flesh for instructive experience, not for stultifying desertion. The finite world is insistently there. He cannot annul it permanently although he can do so intermittently. He may and usually does console himself however by arriving finally at the belief that whilst in the flesh this is as far as man can go and that perfect liberation will come after death.

Mere mental quiet is an excellent thing as a step on the upward way but it is not the true transcendence. The mental blank which is so often the absorption state of ordinary yogis is not the same as the self-understood awareness which is the absorption state of the philosophic yogi. The peace of the first may easily lead to world-fleeing weakness and lethargy whereas the peace of the second can only lead to world-helping strength and inspiration. To look at this state from the outside only and to believe that both enter into a similar condition is to be guilty of a grave misapprehension. The diffuse drifting negativity of the first is inferior to and different from the discriminative intelligent alertness of the second. The one merely refrains from thinking. The other actively engages the thought-free consciousness in understanding its own nature. The one is all flowers but no fruit. The other is all flowers and all fruit. Hence in *The Supreme Path,* a text of rules for aspirants compiled eight hundred years ago in Tibet and still highly cherished there, the warning is plainly given that: "The stillness of inactive thought-processes (in the individual mind) may be misunderstood to be the true goal, which is the stillness of the infinite Mind.'' The key to this extremely subtle situation is therefore twofold. First, the possession or absence of metaphysical knowledge. Second, the mental attitude with which the contemplative enters the state of self-absorption. These factors are firmly intertwined and cannot be separated from each other for the second depends naturally on the first.

The moment when wakefulness turns into dream or sleep is, we now know, a highly critical one. The general direction of the consciousness at this moment can determine the character of the dreams or the sleep which will follow it, can indeed transform either the one or the other into something entirely superior. The moment when thinking activity merges into complete self-absorption is likewise highly critical. The general direction of consciousness can then also determine the character of the state which follows it. The mental attitude at such a time is truly creative. The mystic passes through this moment intent only on his *personal* reactions to the experience, carried away by his *personal* feelings of its great delight. He is made very happy by it and can never afterwards forget it. But he has left his task only half-done, a melancholy fact which is attested by his return sooner or later to the ordinary prosaic state to stay there. Owing partly to this personal reference and partly to his metaphysical ignorance and consequent unpreparedness, he enters into the state of contemplative self-absorption like a man walking backward through an open door into a room, keeping his eyes stubbornly fixed on the familiar place he has started from and refusing to look where he is going. Just as this man will only half-know where he is even when he is inside the room, so will the mystic be only half-aware of the nature of pure Mind even when he is immersed in self-absorption. Moreover this personal reference causes his preconceived views and dogmatic beliefs merely to be left temporarily at the threshold of Mind, as it were, and not to be held in its purifying flame; hence they are picked up again when he emerges once more from the experience. If however meditation is practised jointly with the philosophic training, that is, if it no longer remains a merely mystical exercise only but is informed by rational reflective knowledge, then the erroneous view of reality can never revive again because the pure being will be experienced *as it is*. Bliss is present in both cases but in the one its satisfying character becomes a hindrance whereas in the other it does not. Both have touched reality, but one has touched its quivering surface whereas the other has penetrated to its immutable depth.

The Yoga of the Uncontradictable.

Thus there is a large difference between the states arrived at by the two methods, whose surfaces are so deceptively the same but whose results are so strikingly apart. The yogi empties out the contents of his consciousness blindly and ignorantly and then passively accepts the vacuum. The illumination by pure Thought overwhelms him with its dissimilarity from all previous experience and dazzles him with its lustrous mystery. He has opened the mystical eye within himself but has not fully understood what it is that is fitfully presented to it at set times and during formal meditations. It has yielded total forgetfulness of space-time limitations but his body is still within them and his consciousness must still return to his body. When he has to return and pick up his thoughts of the world again the descent fills him by its contrast with a sense of abysmal difference. Hence he regards the world as being the very negation of reality and the chasm which separates them as being uncrossable. So he lets the great prize slip from his hands, through a despairing sense of being utterly unable to hold both within consciousness at the same time. Henceforth he is a dualist, an upholder of the belief that reality can be attained only in trance and that the world is Matter standing at the opposite pole to Spirit and so a snare or an illusion to be despised. The harsh ascetic who scorns it or the dreamy mystic who ignores it is always puzzled at the end of his own path how to relate his spiritual triumph with the universal life which surrounds him. He does not know how to do so and consequently disposes of the problem by pretending it does not exist. All this arises because his method of approach does not attempt to deal with the problem of the world but ignores it. He banishes reason and shuts his eyes to the supposedly material outside world. Hence he has no means of relating it to the undoubtedly immaterial inside world which he so blissfully experiences.

The philosophic student, however, studies the nature of matter and discovers it to be a manifestation of Mind. Through such mentalistic reflection he comes to perceive that all the different evolutionary explanations of the universal existence are true only from the relative point of view; that all the elements, principles, energies, substances and processes out of which, it is taught, the universe has grown are themselves mental manifestations; and that just as water cannot be different in *reality* from the oxygen and hydrogen of which it is composed, no matter how different it is from them in *appearance,* so these images of earth, water, air and fire cannot be essentially different from the Mind out of which they came. In this way he establishes himself thoroughly in the comprehension of the ultimate mentalness and hence the ultimate oneness of all things and permits no appearance to dislodge him from this intellectual position. He is imbued with the fact that with every breath and every thought he is co-constructing this universe with the World-Mind and that therefore, in the *New Testament* phrase, "in Him we live and move and have our being".

The mystical exercise in which he engages himself is not a blind one. He overcomes the world-idea by absorbing it. He utilizes the reason to go beyond reason but he does not dismiss it prematurely.

He not only discovers pure Thought but also meditates reflectively upon his own discovery. When he empties out the contents of consciousness he does so with open eyes, holding steadily to the understanding that they are the froth and foam thrown up by reality and not essentially different from it. After the vacuum is filled by the presence of pure thought, he returns to them with less and less sense of having to cross an abyss of difference, with the consequence that he has less and less difficulty in bringing them into relation, continuity and harmony with his previous meditation experience. He trains himself to bring this reflective attention directly into his everyday active existence and to insert it continuously into whatever thoughts may engage his awareness and whatever deeds may engage his body. He disciplines his consciousness to hold the body-thought without identifying itself with it, to function through the five senses without ceasing to function in the infinite Mind.

As he continues to unite metaphysical reflection with mystical contemplation there suddenly arises within him out of their fusion a new faculty which has neither the limitations of reasoning intellect nor the one-sidedness of mystical emotion but is actually superior to both. This mysterious state of consciousness is called in Sanskrit "that which is all-full", a reference to its completeness and finality. It yields an enlightenment beyond that of ordinary yoga.

Its actual realization takes place in the twinkling of an eye, as it were. For the long preliminary course, the ardent preparations, finally reach a crisis when an upheaval in the aspirant's whole nature suddenly occurs. It is as though a hard shell, which encases his inner being, breaks asunder and frees it. But despite the sudden arisal of this insight like a flash of lightning it has not yet achieved its own fullness and needs time in which to mature. Unless it is effortless and natural and continuous, it is not the final and most revelatory degree. The moment there is the slightest strain towards being or knowing, that moment there is a descent from the true insight, a degradation of the true existence. Such a state of effortlessness can of course arise only after a long novitiate. The enduring transcendental awareness can come only through unremitting mental toil throughout the day to keep the Real ever in focus. It is the long-ripened, slowly-grown fruit of vigilant watching over the attention as an unbroken process of harmonizing the Unmanifest Mind with its ever-appearing ideas. Thus the proficient is not only able to get a true glimpse of reality but, because he gets it with intelligent understanding, he is also able to stretch out these glimpses more and more into his ordinary worldly life. Finally they are stretched at full length into all the twenty-four hours of the day and night. Thus they are stabilized and made permanent and henceforth he dwells in unfettered unity. With this attainment the ultramystical training of the philosophic path completes itself. The thinking activity which still continues is not quite the same as it was formerly. For it is now an illumined activity. Thus the ultimate aim is not to suppress thinking and sit in prolonged solitary trances. It is not even to keep the mind free from thoughts but from their tyranny, to bring it to understand the true significance of their characteristic manifestations as "I" and the world, and to make the man effortlessly over-conscious of his own innermost essence alongside of his personal existence. Once he thoroughly enters into the fourth state the sage is never able to escape from it again. Whether awake or asleep, in repose or at labour, he is *held* abidingly by its enigmatic transcendence. The fourth state if fully attained is continuous throughout the other three. It does not vanish with the oncoming of either bodily sleep or bodily wakefulness. It is effortlessly retained in the sense that a man in the wakeful state effortlessly retains his personal identity.

There is no desire here to underrate the great worth of even the mystic's achievement but it may be said that whereas he attains a partially true insight the philosopher attains a perfectly true one. Nature wants the mystic to rise from a merely emotional understanding to a calmly intelligent one which will never be *contradicted* by its own lapse or recoil into a lower condition. Both the imperceptibly changing thoughts of outside objects and the incessantly changing thoughts of the thoughts of objects, that is both things and imaginations, take their original birth and find their eventual death in this essence of Mind, which itself persists formless, changeless and *uncontradicted* by anything else which has ever arisen or could ever arise. In spite of the innumerable forms under which it manifests itself Mind-essence never gives up its own eternal identity. An illusion may be contradicted by subsequent experience; an appearance may be denied by enquiry: *but the Reality can never be negated in any way nor the Truth contradicted.* Therefore the method of cultivating the higher faculty of the mind which blooms into such deeper unshakable insight bears the traditional name of the "Yoga of the Uncontradictable". At the bottom of all the stream of thoughts the philosopher perceives always the divine Thought. Without falling into trance, without closing his eyes, without shutting his ears and without folding his legs like the ordinary yogis, he successfully keeps his awareness of the immaterial formless matterless reality. When he can transcend the need of trance he arrives at the perception that the differences between Thought and thoughts, the distinctions between Mind and its manifestations exist only from the standpoint of human beings and not in these things themselves; that everything is gathered up in a sublime unity in God; that everything is a *manifestation* or *representation* of reality, and that in very truth the whole world is a showing-forth by God. Thus the ultimate state to which evolution tends and man attains is one of conscious rest in Mind but not one of conscious idleness, one where sense-activity survives but not its tyranny, one where being continues but not domination by personal being and one where the wheels of thinking whirr on but do not run away with the thinker himself.

It is only such an abiding insight which can thoroughly penetrate the sensuous world-appearance and permanently realize that it is not radically different from the Void itself. This explains why two inspired little treatises intended for *advanced* theosophical aspirants contain certain paradoxical statements, The one, *Light on the Path*, based on an old Egyptian source, first gives the admonition: "Seek the way by retreating within," and then, only after this has been done, gives the further admonition: "Seek the way by advancing boldly without." The other, *Voice of the Silence*, based on an old Tibetan source, tells the developed aspirant: "Thou hast to study the voidness of the seeming full, the fullness of the seeming Void."

With this the student arrives at the grand climax of all his ultramystical endeavours and must bow in awed homage not only before the sacred emptiness from which all things flow, not only before the holy darkness which is the source of all light, but also only before the visible world which is so secretly and ineffably rooted in God, before the incessant activities and living processes which make up the beginningless and endless history of this marvellous universe itself. Men marvel at this or that new thing which science discovers *in* the world but they do not realize that the greatest marvel is that the world itself should exist at all. Whoever sees that every atom of this earth scintillates mystically within the all-containing universal life, whoever comprehends that there is no spot from which the One existence is absent, realizes that the human adventure is as sacred as anything else. He understands too that man's everyday existence is itself as mysterious, as momentous and as miraculous as the unseen and ineffable existence of any archangel could be. The concept of this transcendental insight for those who have comprehended its significance must necessarily be the most stupendous one ever gestated in the human mind. And yet such supreme sagacity, such a mature and complete penetration into the fundamental character of all existence is really nothing more than the natural *intelligence* of man brought to its best pitch.

16

Some Fruits of Philosophy

IF the universe had not been formed out of the divine essence none of the creatures within it could ever truly hope to come into a diviner state. But because the universe is the World-Mind manifesting itself, because they too are inwardly of the same sacred stuff, all living creatures within it have the ineluctable certitude of eventual self-enlightenment. Here then is their brightest hope, their best assurance that they can find the Overself as its intimate relation to them is sufficient guarantee that they can get its help.

Again, a transparent glass prism does not change its own essential character with the changing blue, red and yellow colours which it may reflect. Mind too never changes its own original character with the different thoughts and sensations which it may activate. The Real has always been there even when remembrance has not been felt. It is not something which can ebb and flow like personal emotions *about* it. For it is self-existent and therefore ever-existent. If man were really and completely bereft of God at any moment during his earthly career, even for a fleeting fraction of an instant, he would never be able to ascend from his present consciousness to a higher one. All the vocal injunctions of religion, all the silent monitions of mysticism and all the rational persuasions of metaphysics would be in vain. But the Overself is with him *here* and *now*. It has never left him at any time. It sits everlastingly in the heart. It is indeed his innermost being, his truest self. Were it something different and apart from him, were it a thing to be gained and added to what he already is or has, he would stand the risk of losing it again. For whatever may be added to him may also be subtracted from him. Therefore the real task of this quest is less to seek anxiously to possess it than to become aware that it already and always possesses him. If he says that he cannot follow this quest because he cannot find a master or because he cannot go to Asia or because he cannot practise a particular mystical technique, he is merely deceiving himself. By such pessimistic thoughts he sets up unnecessary handicaps which have then to be overcome.

All methods and techniques—and of course all human beings who propound them—are merely instruments to help the student attain a methodless technique-free teacherless state. Let him not get enslaved by the thought of their necessity. Let him not confuse the attitudes towards life which they provide, with life itself. Let him not turn the way into the goal nor the means into the end. All techniques were originated for the purpose of opening a door to the inner essence. But undiscriminating people cling stubbornly to the door and do not permit it to open! The wise student will keep his attitude subtle, elastic and dogma-free. He must not, for example, forge iron attachments to his favourite form of mystical meditation. He should not worship a technique or a doctrine for its own sake; he must worship the new illumination, the new understanding, the new consciousness that is to arise from it or he will simply tie another psychological knot which will have eventually to be untied. He should not become paralysed by a particular metaphysical formula. It should exist to serve, not to enslave him, to make him more alive, not to entomb him. He should rise not only above the reverence for things but also above the reverence for thoughts—above even, at the very end, the thought of seeking salvation too. The significant lightning-flash of insight may shoot across his sky at any moment, perhaps at the most unexpected moment, nay even at the most incongruous moment, and he ought not unconsciously resist it by his egoistic anchorage in some pet practice or with some worshipped teacher. He should, in short, learn to relax from his own yogic efforts to relax.

There is always a tendency in those who become totally engrossed in a single aspect of life to lose their sense of humour. Such people become cranks. But because philosophy deals with the grand whole of life and therefore insists on seeing mutually contradictory aspects this is not likely to happen to its faithful votaries. Life is universal being which is to be experienced, not a particular system to be followed. The task before us is much more to feel our oneness with this boundless formless principle of life, to understand its own innate freedom as against the confinement of its formal expressions, than to become entrapped in any of those expressions. We attain such freedom only when we cease to cling slavishly not only to our possessions but also to our conceptions and beliefs.

Those who do not feel drawn to formal exercises in meditation and those who do not feel drawn to formal study in metaphysics may perhaps, in the last resort, find consolation or aid in another way. They may avail themselves of all these facts to practise a simple exercise that can either take the place of all study and all meditation or, if others wish and as is recommended, that can also accompany them. It is so simple that it is called an exercise only for name's sake and after it has been set in habitual motion it becomes quite easy and effortless. Just as a mother anxious for the safety of her only son who is fighting as a soldier in a great battle will not forget him whatever conversations, movements and activities may engage her surface attention, so the aspirant should not forget the Divine whatever he may be doing with his surface consciousness. Just as a girl who is deeply in love with a young man will be able to keep his mental image before her mind's eye all the time even though she may appear to be properly attentive to external matters, so the aspirant should train himself until he is able to keep the thought of the Overself as a kind of setting for all his other thoughts. Thus the practice is based on the profound significance of memory and utilizes it for unworldly purposes. It consists in the constant loving recall to mind of his inner identity with, and the existence of, the Overself, in the repeated and devoted recollection at all times all places and under all bodily conditions that there is this other and greater self overshadowing him. If, however, he has ever had a glimpse, a feeling or an intuition—however momentary it may have been and however long ago it may have happened—of a super-sensuous higher existence which profoundly impressed him and perhaps led him to take to the quest, then it is most important that he should also insert the remembrance of this experience into his exercise. That is he should try to bring as vividly as possible to his mind the sense of exaltation and peace which he then felt.

The fundamental aim is to keep the exercise always or as often as possible in the mind's background whilst paying attention to duties with the foreground, and to let attention fly eagerly and more fully back to it every time there is a relaxation from them. It must become the unannounced and impersonal centre of his personal gravity, the unmoved pivot upon which the pendulum of external activity swings perpetually to and fro. Thus though the foreground of his consciousness is busy attending to the affairs of daily living, its background abides in a kind of sacred emptiness wherein no other thought may intrude than this thought of the Overself. This inward concentration behind and despite outward activities should be made habitual. What benefit will its practice bring the aspirant? Although so different from a formal meditation exercise which is usually practised for a limited time, in a sitting posture and in an undisturbed place, it has a peculiar potency of its own. Such continuous remembrance of the Overself will bring him, when its practice has become firmly and successfully established as ceaseless flow, a remarkable fruitage of grace. For the power that is here at work is not the ego's but the universal power. When the grace starts working this is likely to turn to remove a number of the internal and external obstacles in his path, sometimes in a seemingly miraculous manner, and eventually bring him to a truer self-awareness. The unexpected effectiveness of this method is therefore not to be measured by its obvious simplicity.

If anyone is not prepared to follow this practice, let alone to study metaphysically or meditate mystically, he may make use of a related one which will make still less demands upon him. Whenever he is suddenly faced by unexpected misfortune or unpleasant environments, when clamorous problems raise their ugly heads or when grave danger menaces his very life, he should take whatever practical measures are ordinarily called for on the external plane and yet alongside of them should abruptly drop his habitual ego-centric attitude and hand the problem over, as it were, to a higher power. This will paradoxically and eventually bring about a sense of inner detachment even whilst he takes outer action to deal with it. A whole-hearted faith in the existence of this super-material power is of course the first essential to make this practice successful. A resigned trust in the outcome of its hidden operations is the second one. He should cease to worry about the matter, cease to cling in alarm or depression to its present details and possible developments but rather yield them all up and forget them. Indeed if he permits anxious thoughts to continue to harass him they may break the inner remembrance and obliterate the effectiveness of the technique. Moreover it will become effective only if maintained for a sufficient time and with sufficient concentration. That is, through all his personal efforts at making the necessary readjustments he should firmly switch a part of his consciousness constantly inward, carrying (not denying) the hostile problem with it and then letting the thoughts which constitute the problem dissolve in remembrance of the impersonal ever-calm Overself. He must try to conceive this power as supreme, formless and abiding in an imageless Void.

This abrupt appeal from a narrow personal outlook to the refuge of a wide impersonal one will effectively help to control not only his emotional reaction to what has happened but may also help to introduce the higher factor of grace and thus control the exterior condition itself. He may not only draw from this act of self-surrender the strength to face his problems undismayed but may also draw a protective power beyond his own capacity. We know now from our analytical studies of mystical experience that this grace may not only take an imaginative or intellectual form but may also manifest itself in many other ways. It may, for example, give such inner support to a man in a time of grave danger that the fears which his situation would quite naturally arouse will be effectually quelled. The same war which arouses panic in some men arouses heroism in others, making them listen and march to a braver music than that to which they were hitherto able to march. Thousands of unknown and obscure soldiers, sailors, aviators, air-raid wardens and civilians have experienced this unexpected reaction during the terrible dangers of the past few years. Why? Because they unconsciously opened the long-locked doors of the Overself and experienced its grace. Confronted by the appalling horrors of destructive scientific ingenuity which surrounded them, they became suddenly and acutely aware that at any moment a mere turn of the wheel of chance or of fate of God's will might bring the bitter end of all for them. Therefore they deliberately and utterly resigned themselves entirely to the inevitable, to chance, fate or God—which are merely three different ways of saying the same thing. By this act of supreme faith they unconsciously invoked the deeper principle of their own being and without knowing it lifted the heavy bar which fastens the door of the Overself. The lack of clear metaphysical understanding of what they were doing could not and did not prevent the practical results accruing to them all the same. Amid the menacing roar of shells and bombs they unaccountably felt that whatever the issue of their external experience might be, whether the latter were to end in sudden death or eventuate in continued life, all would be well with them. They felt, in fact, inexplicably lifted high above the agony and terror of the tragic events in which they were plunged. Such fateful moments havè left a profound memory in the soul. They cannot be forgotten. The silent instruction which they conveyed will sooner or later affect the spiritual outlook of those who experienced them.

'This is your bondage, that you practice meditation.' In the second chapter of *The Hidden Teaching Beyond Yoga* we quoted this sentence from Ashtavakra, an Indian sage who lived some thousands of years ago. This quotation—and indeed most of the chapter in which it was set—hurt the feelings and alarmed the anticipations of many readers, who feared that it would lead eventually to the teaching that meditation should be dropped and that metaphysics should replace it. How unnecessary was that emotion and how false was that anticipation those who have had the patience to suspend judgment until the whole course was run and finished may now see. It was a ninth-century Tibetan sage, Tilopa, who similarly said: 'Don't meditate. Keep your mind in its natural state.' Such negative counsel does not represent unexpected revolt but rather natural advance. It is not given to unfledged neophytes because it would be inappropriate and indeed harmful to them, but it is given to experienced proficients. It is simply an attempt to set meditation in its rightful place among all the other elements which compose the complex pattern of life, to recall its enthusiasts to the fact that the quest does not end with it alone and to remind them that what they seek is already here and now deep within them.

For insight is something which flashes down to a man and is not fabricated by him. His toil in meditation is not to manufacture it but to manufacture the requisite conditions which will attract it. If he mistakes the means for the end and insists on immuring himself in the former alone, he will never reach the end. He is not on earth for yoga's sake. Yoga is here for his sake. He is here to *live.*

Yes, action also is an essential part of this quest of the Overself. For Nature will not let anyone enter her holiest sanctuary until he has fulfilled her threefold demand, although she will gladly let him peer inside at her treasures for fleeting moments so as to encourage him to make a better valuation of them. And this demand is simply that he pursue and finish the three parallel lines of evolution along which she is so patiently shepherding all mankind: activity, intelligence and contemplation. But if he accede to this demand then he will no longer be a mystic or a metaphysician but will become transformed into a philosopher. Because man is a threefold being, a working trinity of thinking, feeling and doing, it is inevitable that the quest should involve an effort corresponding to his own nature. Consequently the three lines which he must pursue in harmony with the threefold division of his own character are: metaphysics as an exercise of reasoned thinking, mysticism as an exercise of intuitive feeling and altruistic activity as an exercise of bodily doing. Knowledge, meditation and self-abnegating work constitute the holy trinity which can lead him to enlightenment. These three conceptions of right human endeavour—the intellectual, the mystical and the practical—are not to be kept in fratricidal and dangerous tension but are to be brought into a conscious harmony; all are to work together at the same time and for the same goal. They must come into loving concord, must put forth their arms and embrace each other and find the integral unity of a philosophic life. Thus wisdom is generated out of the totality of life-experience, not out of a mere part of it. All these qualities do not merely mix; they fuse and produce a new and positive quality—insight—which has its own special meaning and special nature. If the aspirant starts his quest of salvation with reverent mystical love of the Overself alone he will be led to add sharpened intelligence to it in the end, and if he starts with intelligence alone he will be led to add love later. For they are two horses who must be made to run together. If he begins his quest by following the integral threefold path he will achieve a smooth, even, untroubled and balanced movement, but if he follows only a single one of these phases then, towards the end of that phase, he will be forced back by Nature through an abrupt troubled overturning of both his inner and outer life. This is because the harmonious integration of all three phases is something which cannot be escaped in any case. He has indeed to make the quest into a practical way of everyday living. But such activism is not to be a blind one. 'I am all for action,' said Mussolini. 'Immobility is to me like the torment of damnation.' So he boasted. But he forgot that action is useful only in so far as it is allied with wisdom. His forgetfulness led him to promise a great empire to his people. But in the result he brought them a great disaster.

Wise action in the case of a would-be philosopher consists of energetic striving for the triumph of Good. He must seek its triumph not only within his own inner character and outer life but also in the character and life of others. As such a double aim cannot be achieved by idly sitting wrapped up in reveries or by being self-centredly pre-occupied with his own development alone, it necessarily implies the need of altruistic activity. Instead of letting contemplation die with itself he must let it fertilize his deeds. This makes the quest intensely practical, something which indeed must inspire his moment-to-moment everyday existence. It does indeed end in inspired action. And such is the unified nature of philosophic truth that, when adequately comprehended, it cannot help but express itself through its student's own contribution toward his external experience.

One of the most important implications of mentalism is the power of concentrated thinking to affect such external experience. The builder gets his plans from an architect but the architect gets his ideas spontaneously from his own imagination. Our studies in the birth of the universe told how the first characteristic activity of the World-Mind is image-ing. Its creative forms are indeed nothing else than vibrations within its own mental substance. In our own limited and finite way we, as the World-Mind's own progeny, likewise carry on a parallel activity. When we make a mental picture and when we hold an abstract idea, both picture and idea are ultimately born out of the same ungraspable unseeable energy-substance. When we understand that the world-drama is played out in the mind we can also understand that karma gives us back in the end our own fructified image-ing no less than the pleasurable or painful compensation which it calls for. If our present environment is, in part, but our ancient thoughts returned to roost, then we cannot disclaim some of the responsibility for its quality and form. We must learn to think aright. It is not the idle thoughts which pass lightly through consciousness now and then that matter but the habitual trend of thought, the constantly recurring ideas which are most powerfully dynamized by faith and will. Intense imagination thus becomes a matrix in which, under the adjustments of karma and evolution, both environments and events are fashioned. The mental pictures and rational ideas which are most often and most strongly and most lengthily held in consciousness can help lift us up to spiritual nobility and worldly harmony or drag us down, as they have already dragged the Nazis down, to spiritual degradation and worldly disharmony.

When man becomes aware of his creative possibilities, when he knows that by identifying himself with what is best within his thought and feeling he will eventually manifest by reaction what is best within his earthly environment, when he discovers that sooner or later the ideas upon which he habitually dwells and the images he most frequently holds influence both character and circumstance, then indeed he will become more vigilant about his mental life as he is already vigilant about the use of poisons. Just as the same arsenic may kill a healthy man or cure a diseased one, so may proper concentration and right use of mental power lift every man on to a loftier pinnacle as its ignorant dissipation and abuse will degrade him. And this power is naturally and inalienably his own. He will assist the process of improving himself and his fortunes if he holds firmly amid all circumstances to the comprehension that everything seen is seen in his own mind as a thought, that the person who sees it is a thought-made self too and that the reality behind both is pure Thought. Finally there must be repeated the warning already given in connection with the Third Meditation exercise. The moral restrictions upon the use of such methods must be remembered and no attempt to coerce the free will of other persons against their own interests should be made. Motives must be kept clean or the boomerang of karmic retribution will come down painfully on the wrong-doer.

The Surrendered Life.

There can indeed be no plucking of life's best fruits without abnegating the personal will at some time or other. This is because each man is called to battle with his own animal instincts and egotistic human weaknesses. But philosophy demands no ascetic vows from its follower in such a battle. It demands only that he discipline himself and that he try to keep on trying, however many times he fails and falls. For it believes in the benign Overself and in the eventual descent of grace. He can arrive less painfully and more pleasantly at such self-abnegation by accepting inspired promptings, by not brushing them aside when they conflict with fleshly desire or selfish interest. If he has not deluded himself about the path he is following and the goal he is seeking, such promptings are sure to arise. They will necessarily include and stretch beyond what is ordinarily called moral living or ethical conduct. The more he pursues the quest the more there will inevitably and spontaneously arise an effort to abandon mean, animalistic and materialistic motives and to replace them by generous, noble and idealistic ones. The thought will penetrate him increasingly that he must purify his character and purge his heart and that he must seek out ruthlessly and throw aside resolutely the baser tendencies which darkly shadow his inner disposition.

A new factor has entered his life. For he has to think of the inescapable effect of his deeds upon others as well as upon himself. Thus he enlarges his sense of personal responsibility and widens his ethical perspective. It is true that he should bury his blunders with the dust of the mouldy past and not stir them up again and again merely for melancholy brooding. But unfortunately it is also true that before he can let them go he must earn the right through contrition and expiation to do so. Neither the remembrance of the Overself nor the practice of meditation absolve him of the need to comprehend the causes and results of both his ethical and practical errors, nor of the need to make belated amendment in himself or to others. If the student has done an injury to someone in the past and now regrets the deed or if he fears the nemesis of karma for some unpunished sin or if he wishes to counteract some already existant bad karma which he can clearly trace to wrong-doing in the present earth-life, what is the proper course for him to take? There are four progressive steps open to him. First, *confession*. He must not only straightforwardly acknowledge his sin but also frankly comprehend what motives and bluntly recognize what forces led him to commit it. No human confessor is needed for this purpose? his Overself is better. Second, *repentance*. He must not only repudiate those motives and forces as belonging to his baser self but also desire to transcend them. Therefore his self-censure must be strong and his remorse sincere or his whole effort will be useless. This calls for a clear resolve never to repeat the sin. Third, *amendment*. He must make such just reparation to the person he has wronged as may now be possible. Fourth, *resignation*. Having done all that is humanly possible about it he should free himself from the sorrow of this unpleasantness of the past and loosen himself from the bondage of its memory. He can then, and then only, hand over his sin and its karmic consequences to the Overself and thus find peace. But he should not make the mistake of expecting that a single effort will necessarily suffice to bring this about. The first and second steps may need to be repeated again and again, the lesson of the whole affair may need to be printed and reprinted on his mind before the problem can be dismissed as no longer his own. But when that happens the Overself will take better care of it than ever he can. That it has heard his plea and made a response which inwardly absolves him whether or not it outwardly mitigates his karma will first be evidenced by a welcome feeling of relief and by freedom from further anxiety in the matter.

The supremely crucial ethical stage on this quest is crossing over from life in the underself to life in the Overself. It begins within the hushed depths of the heart as an arisal of a subtle certitude, which no man and no book can break, that the right way has been found. It ends as an entire uprooting of old habits of thought. It works a gradual revolution of attitude towards all other living creatures. Despite himself, the student must thenceforth begin to alter all his patterns of thought, feeling and conduct. From this mysterious moment his life in the Overself—however feeble its beginnings may be—grows ever more important and more glorious than his life in the personality. Naturally he finds that to will what shall be done only out of the Overself's light and bidding is not easy. It is indeed an art, and like all arts has to be learnt through the painful trials and elated triumphs, the bitter errors and miserable failures and joyous successes of constant endeavour. Nevertheless against this soft and subtle command growing from within, he feels increasingly that it is sacrilegious to pit his own personal will, he obeys more and more because he begins to comprehend that it is verily for such sublime obedience that he was born at all and because he now knows that those who have never found anything higher to obey than the personal ego have failed in life, however much they may have succeeded in the surface society of their fellows.

But because the crossing-over is so crucial, so momentous in its broad consequences, this stage is necessarily one which can be passed and completed only after the utmost struggle. For it demands everything from a man. It claims all that he has hitherto looked upon as his personal existence. The Bible picturesquely describes how Abraham was asked by the Lord Jehovah to offer up the life of his beloved Isaac as a proof of obedience and loyalty. Abraham was about to slay his child when Jehovah's voice stopped the sacrifical knife in the very act of its descent. Something like this happens eventually to the sincere aspirant too. If he has the courage to obey the command which comes forth from the divine silence within himself and to cast out his egotistic will and egotistic seeking, then his attempt at self-immolation will be brought to an abrupt end. The ego will be restored to him but never again can it hold the same primary place in his life. For henceforth he can act only under the permission of this impersonal being which is his diviner self. Henceforth he is 'the servant of the Lord'. Henceforth he adopts an ever-attentive ever-listening attitude and, with that other Biblical child Samuel, says: 'Speak, Lord, for thy servant heareth.' In short, he surrenders himself to a numinous presence which he vividly feels as active within his own heart. Surrender is therefore the chief note to be struck on the keyboard of his being during this crucial stage.

It is said that the sage's character will always be selfless and serene, detached and disciplined, passionless and impersonal. But it will lead only to illusion if the student thinks—as so many usually do think—that he can enter such a state solely by his own striving or will. He cannot. It is indeed beyond mortal strength. He can enter it fully only by the mysterious grace of his Overself. When this happens he feels some power other than his own take hold of his consciousness and lift it into this exalted state and keep it there. Hence he feels his humble dependence upon its bounty as an inexperienced child feels its dependence upon its mother. Hence too the apt words of Jesus: 'Except ye become as little children ye shall in no wise enter the kingdom of heaven.' These words do not at all mean that a spiritually illumined man will renounce his adult intellectual acquisitions and revert atavistically to a primitive condition of understanding as so many mystics and ascetics believe. Nor do they mean that he should confront with infantile helplessness the world which is a stage for continuous conflict between good and evil forces. On the contrary, he will use all his keen intelligence, all his practical shrewdness and all his secret power in this inescapable conflict.

He who has once passed through the transforming experience of inward surrender can never again be the same man. His centre of selfhood shifts, his circumference of outlook expands. The more the Overself works through him the less does he feel the heavy strain and burden of contemporary living. When its presence becomes a settled thing in his heart; when he feels the Overself within him as a consecrated living force at every moment of his existence; when he lets himself become a submissive and sacrifical instrument for this inner rule of his personality, then he may confidently go ahead into whatever activity his will decides upon for he finds at last the secret of inspired action. It is nothing occult, nothing magical, but seems as natural as the joyous humming of bees around thyme. Thus he is able to take part from a calm unbroken centre within himself in the world's life without being deviated from his higher purpose by that tumultuous life.

Whoever believes that the awakening of insight is something which affects the intelligence only, believes wrongly. For with it there is a simultaneous awakening of the finest qualities of the heart. Indeed, in this transcendent sphere to which the philosopher penetrates, thought and feeling are inseparable. Compassion is released automatically *along with* the mental insight itself. One and the same Mind is the inner nature of all men. This is why he who realizes it for himself throws down the hard barrier which isolates the 'I' from the 'you'. This is why he understands the puzzling and paradoxical description of the Overself, that it is distinct from but not separate from the Overself of another man. For he will be able to feel completely with and for others and yet retain his own personality to the full. This is why he can no longer be a passive onlooker at the struggles of mankind as, in his mystical days, he may have been; and why too he can no longer remain enchained by merely personal interests alone as, in his materialistic days, he certainly was enchained. He will then serve for the pure love of service rather than for the love of personal profit. In the words of St. Teresa: 'Yours are the eyes through which is to look out Christ's compassion to the world, yours are the feet with which He is to go about doing good, and yours are the hands with which He is to bless us now.' Nevertheless let it not be thought that his compassion will waste itself in a merely effervescent sentimentality or misplace itself and do actual harm in a crime-condoning flabbiness. Its successful application will be guaranteed by the fact that it will be guided by rational intelligence.

One curious consequence of his altruism is that the philosopher, who does not primarily seek his own happiness, finds it, whereas the intense egotist, who is always seeking it, never finds it. So long as a man tries to wrest only his own personal benefit from the closed fists of life, be assured that in the end he will not find it whatever he may find for the moment. How could he when his own welfare is inseparable from the common welfare? Let him generously seek *that* alongside of his own and then he will miss neither. This, the practical wisdom of the Overself's insight, is firmly endorsed by the reasoned theories of enlightened metaphysics, by the first-hand observations of wide experience and by the lengthy records of collective history.

It is true that a great calm settles in the heart as a natural consequence of progress in this quest, that the restless passions, the anxious agitations and the inner conflicts which turn so many lives into troubled heaving waters are first lessened and later pass away altogether, but does this mean that the philosophic student lives less zestfully than other people? No—he need not deny a disciplined happiness of the senses, transient though it be, even when he seeks a loftier happiness which is beyond their reach. If he sees through the pitiful illusions and errors which holds so many people in pawn, he also sees the glorious realities and truths to which evolution is slowly leading their reluctant feet. Again, does this teaching stultify its votaries with a sense of the barren fruitlessness of human ambitions and the sad ephemerality of human desires? Does it reduce the world to a dream and man to a shadow? No! It is a clarion call to a natural and rational life, to an inspired and inspiring outlook and to a pursuit of truth, peace and beauty in the face of blind, harsh and ugly convention. Only now, only at the end of this course can we see that it offers, when understood aright, practical hope, authentic guidance and good cheer. If the reality to which it seeks to lead us were nothing more than a bloodless intellectual concept or an effervescent emotional movement it might be interesting to mankind but it would never permanently help mankind. It could never convincingly make life worth living, for instance. But because mind is the secret and vital basis of all existence, its proper understanding will bring us the greatest help in living. And because philosophy offers a supremely wonderful and enduring experience to all, it necessarily offers our best and brightest hope. All language is hopelessly inadequate, shabbily poverty-stricken, when confronted with this grand experience which one day awaits the whole human race and even now awaits every individual who truly and perseveringly seeks it.

It is a mistake therefore to believe that the external life, the personal existence and the social relations of the philosophic student will be come impoverished, mutilated or narrowed. On the contrary, they will become enriched, animated and expanded. For he has to bring down here into this space-time world something of that felicitous grandeur and evergreen wonder which he has glimpsed in the world which transcends it. Although the Real in its indescribable absoluteness and stainless purity lies forever as a Void beyond its manifested and relative world-form, nevertheless it is the paradoxical source and infinite inspiration of the highest values within that finite form. Consequently he finds in philosophy, according to his inward bent and outward circumstances, what he fails to find in mystical asceticism—an intense incentive to create dynamic new values in art and literature, in culture and work, in education and politics, in economics and industry, indeed in all that pertains to human living.

It is specifically our twentieth-century problem to learn how to combine rapt contemplation with energetic activity, sharp reason with subtle intuition, altruistic service of the common welfare with personal self-interest, the following of Christ with the demands of Caesar in a way that men of earlier times never had to trouble their heads about. This was clearly seen by two great Orientals, the late Maharaja of Mysore and the present (1942) Maharaja of Pithapuram, who had absorbed the best ancient wisdom of their own hemisphere and yet respected the best modern achievements of the Occident. They repeatedly affirmed it during our private discussions and helped us to see it clearly too. Brain and body, heart and soul must all become close co-operators. And not only are they needful to us but their right balance is needful to themselves. Too much doing without enough understanding of what they were doing, for instance, has brought the moderns perilously close to the edge of an abyss.

It is not an accidental fact that almost from the very beginning Jesus told his hearers to repent. To repent means to change an erroneous outlook and to give up an erroneous way of living. But deeds spring forth from ideas. It is fundamentally a change of thinking for which Jesus asked. During these momentous days, when an apocalyptic combat envelops our planet, the worth of such counsel becomes painfully plain. The conventional world, judging by appearances instead of judging appearances, has been jolted into achieving a most rudimentary and fragmentary awareness of what is happening beneath the surface of things. It is learning that those who look on this as a war in the same series as all previous wars, only on a larger scale, are mistaken. It is something much more than that. We must attach special and even unique significance to it. For it is fundamentally the sign of the closing hours of a dying world of thought, the end of a long epoch of ideas now outdated. Out of the death pangs of an old order we are merely starting to struggle for new values. They must obviously be the fruit of a nobler conception of life than that which served the old order.

Meanwhile we shall not be able to endure this terrible experience with untorn soul unless we possess the profound inward assurance that the world conflict manifesting itself in both violent war and so-called peace has only one outcome—the ultimate triumph of the forces of Good. There is a Master Idea behind the universe. We may fit our little lives smoothly into it and find worthwhile happiness, if we wish, or we may oppose them to it and suffer the inexorable consequences. This is true for single individuals and for whole peoples. But the redemptive spirit of the plan itself can never be defeated. Therefore we may rightly hope on. We may rightly look upward. The sun's beams break though the night's heavy darkness and the sun itself, amid waves of orange and mauve gloriously outspread over the arched vault of the sky, gives us its benign greetings. How far from the world's folly and stupidity, from mankind's hatred and passion, are those waxing rays which glow with friendly warmth! How grand is this colourful solar message!

For man will assuredly pursue the supreme value, the Good, not only because there is no other way to free himself from his endless troubles but because he *must*. All that is evil and bestial in him will slowly be burnt out whereas all that is benign and angelic will slowly be developed. He will not have to live forever after death with what is foolish and sinful in his being but with what is wisest and noblest. Only the worst in his nature shall die, as it ought to die. Only the best shall live, as it ought to live. This is the true immortality and this is the only one which awaits him.

PEACE TO ALL WHO READ THESE LINES!

INDEX

General note—† Denotes Quotation